Five Mountains

HARVARD EAST ASIAN MONOGRAPHS
85

FIVE MOUNTAINS
The Rinzai Zen Monastic Institution in Medieval Japan

MARTIN COLLCUTT

Published by COUNCIL ON EAST ASIAN STUDIES, HARVARD UNIVERSITY, and distributed by HARVARD UNIVERSITY PRESS, Cambridge (Massachusetts) and London   1981

The Council on East Asian Studies at Harvard University publishes a mono-graph series and, through the Fairbank Center for East Asian Research, administers research projects designed to further scholarly understanding of China, Japan, Korea, Vietnam, Inner Asia, and adjacent areas.

Library of Congress Cataloging in Publication Data

Collcutt, Martin, 1939–
Five Mountains.
(Harvard East Asian monographs ; 85)
Bibliography: p.
Includes index.
1. Monasticism and religious orders, Zen—Japan.
2. Monastic and religous life (Zen Buddhism)—Japan.
I. Title. II. Series.
BQ9294.4.J3C64   294.3′657′0952   80-23316
ISBN 0-674-30498-5

To My Parents

Foreword

In the past two decades, young scholars writing in English on Japan have increasingly left the well-traveled highroads of traditional historical and cultural studies to explore the byroads and the large tracts of still unstudied terrain in Japan's past. In doing this they have often been following in the pioneering footsteps of new generations of Japanese scholars, but often enough they have led the way themselves. Through these explorations, they have opened up whole new vistas on Japan's past and greatly expanded our understanding of its complexities and diversities. Martin Collcutt, who teaches in the Department of East Asian Studies at Princeton University, leads us in such an adventure into new terrain in his *FIVE MOUNTAINS: THE RINZAI ZEN MONASTIC INSTITUTION IN MEDIEVAL JAPAN*. It explores the history and organization of the *gozan* organization within the Rinzai branch of Zen, which reached its apogee from the late thirteenth to the early fifteenth centuries and played a prominent role in medieval Japanese Buddhism and an even more dominant role in the culture of the time. This volume is an important addition to the Harvard East Asian Monograph Series, which is published by the Council on East Asian Studies at Harvard and is designed to present contributions of lasting scholarly value based on original research.

While Buddhism has been Japan's leading religion for most of the nation's history, playing a part in its culture only slightly less important than Christianity in European civilization, we know little about Buddhist institutional development in Japan. There has been a great deal written on its sects and their philosophies and the whole theological, philosophical, and even artistic development of Japanese Buddhism, but little on its internal organization and development or its economic and political role in society. We would find strangely distorted an account of European civilization which, while discussing the development of Christian theology, told us almost nothing about the Christian church. But we have been satisfied with such one-sided portrayals of Buddhism in Japan.

It is ironic that Zen philosophy, which is commonly characterized as being beyond words, has inspired millions of words in English print, whereas Zen institutions, though vastly important in many aspects of medieval Japanese civilization and in no way beyond description in words, have drawn so few. Professor Collcutt goes a long way toward redressing the balance by describing *gozan* history and organization fully and with meticulous care for accurate detail. Most readers will have much to learn from this book: the gradual introduction of Zen in the late twelfth and early thirteenth centuries and its easy eclecticism during its early years; the close patterning of Zen institutions on Chinese Sung and Yuan models; the huge role played by a large number of Chinese immigrant monks, many of them refugees from Mongol rule, and by semi-Sinicized Japanese monks who had studied for long years in China; the size and novelty of the Chinese cultural impact that accompanied Zen and made that period in some ways comparable to the time of the first great wave of Chinese influence in the seventh to ninth centuries; the determining role of the patronage of the late Hōjō *shikken* of Kamakura, the ill-fated Emperor Go-Daigo, and the early Ashikaga, particularly Takauji's brother Tadayoshi; the huge size, the elaborate structure, and the complexity of organization of the whole *gozan* system; and the deep penetration of this system into the economic and social fabric of medieval Japan. Professor Collcutt takes his reader over fascinating new terrain. The thoroughness of his work and his eye for careful detail make one feel that the trail he has blazed will need little later correction or even widening by others.

Edwin O. Reischauer

Contents

Illustrations

Preface

The Buddhist institution was as powerful a force in medieval Japan as the Christian church in medieval Europe; and Buddhist monks, nuns, and shavelings as ubiquitous in medieval Japanese society as nobles, warriors, peasants, or merchants. We know woefully little, however, about the organization of Japanese Buddhist monasteries, the ways in which they acquired, extended, and managed their lands, the kinds of economic activities they engaged in, or the political and military influence they exerted. Nor have we a very much firmer grasp of the individual character and interaction of the various schools of Buddhism, of the daily religious lives of monks and nuns, or of their social, cultural, and intellectual interests. Without a more detailed understanding of the Buddhist church and its pervasive presence in society, our intellectual map of medieval Japan must remain vague and misleading. Recent Western scholarship on medieval Japan has tended to focus on emerging warriors, declining nobles, militant peasants, and nascent townspeople. Important as these groups undoubtedly were in the shaping of medieval society, a rounded view must also take into account the still potent religious institutions.[1]

Comprehensive treatment of the many streams of "old" and "new," or popular, Buddhism in medieval Japan would go well beyond the scope of a single book. Even an adequate discussion of the history of the various schools of medieval Zen Buddhism, just one segment of the whole Buddhist institution, would call for several volumes. This book describes the institutional development and organization of one important branch of medieval Japanese Zen, that embracing the three hundred or so officially sponsored monasteries—and their several thousand sub-temples and branch temples—of the Five Mountains (*gozan*) schools of Zen during the period from the introduction of Zen teachings from China by Eisai (or Yōsai)[2] and other monks in the late twelfth century, through the zenith of the *gozan* system under the patronage of the Ashikaga shoguns in the fourteenth and early fifteenth centuries, to its enervation and eclipse by rival schools of Zen in the late fifteenth and sixteenth centuries. Some mention is made of non-*gozan* Rinzai Zen, of Sōtō Zen, and of Ōbaku Zen introduced to Japan in the mid-seventeenth century. The primary concern of the book, however, is with the medieval *gozan* network.[3]

Many early Chinese Zen (Ch'an) communities were established in remote mountain fastnesses, and most later Zen monasteries, whether built in mountain valleys or on level ground, continued to imply this ideal of a detached and lofty spiritual retreat by adopting the name of a mountain as part of their official title. Thus the full title of the Kyoto Zen monastery of Nanzenji is Zuiryūzan Taihei Kōkoku Nanzen Zenji or "Auspicious Dragon Mountain Southern Zen Temple for the Promotion of Great Peace and the Prosperity of the Realm." During the Southern Sung Dynasty some fifty leading Chinese Zen monasteries are thought to have been ranked in a three-tier, officially regulated hierarchy headed by Five Mountains: the Ching-shan wan shou ch'an ssu, Pei-shan ch'ing te ling-yin ch'an ssu, and Nan-shan ch'eng t'zu pao en kuang hsiao ch'an ssu of Hangchow and the Tai-pai-shan t'ien t'ung ching te ch'an ssu and A-yü-wang-shan kuang li ch'an ssu of Ming-chou.[4] This Five Mountains system was imitated and enlarged in medieval Japan and came to include most, though not all, of the medieval Rinzai Zen lineages and one branch of the Sōtō school.

Here, a note of caution should be sounded. Throughout this book, I refer frequently to Five Mountains "systems" in China and Japan. In Japan, as the ensuing chapters will demonstrate, there certainly developed a carefully regulated, centralized system of officially sponsored Rinzai Zen monasteries. In Sung and Yuan dynasty China, however, the character of the Ch'an monastery and the extent of a Five Mountains system are somewhat more problematic. Some doubt may be expressed as to whether so-called Chinese Ch'an Buddhist monasteries ever assumed the exclusive sectarian character that was typical of the great Zen monasteries of medieval Japan. Even if the teaching, practice, and ceremonial in individual Chinese monasteries was dominated by Ch'an monks, it is possible that the same monasteries also sheltered monks whose primary commitment was to Pure Land or Lü (Vinaya) teachings. Moreover, although Japanese scholars of the history of Zen all point to the creation of a system of officially regulated Ch'an monasteries in late Sung China, they say little or nothing about the actual operation of that system. The Chinese documentary evidence commonly cited in support of the Five Mountains system is a reference by the early Ming scholar-official Sung Lien (1310–1381) to the existence of "Five Mountains and Ten Temples." Sung Lien provides neither a detailed description nor a history of the network.

On the other hand, in spite of the dearth of descriptive evidence, it would be rash to deny the existence of distinctively Ch'an monastic centers or of a cluster of government-sponsored Ch'an monasteries in late Sung China. Many monasteries used the characters "Ch'an monastery" as part of their formal title; codes such as the *Ch'an-yuan ch'ing-kuei* were written specifically for Ch'an monasteries; and diagrams made of their distinctive features. Further, in setting up the Five Mountains system in Japan, Japanese Rinzai monks and their secular patrons were convinced that they were faithfully reproducing a type of monastery and monastic organization that existed in contemporary China. Japanese monks, many of whom had been to China, had the guidance of Chinese émigré monks. Thus, even if the Chinese Five Mountains system was less sharply defined than its Japanese offshoot, it was unlikely to have been a figment of their imaginations.

It is with the above proviso in mind that I refer to the Chinese

Five Mountains. For a clearer picture of Ch'an Buddhism in the Sung and Yuan dynasties, we must await further research by scholars of Chinese history and religion into the Buddhist institution as a whole and into the religious environment of such Ch'an centers as A-yü-wang-shan or Ching-shan.

Although most modern Japanese Rinzai Zen traces its spiritual ancestry to the Chinese Zen patriarchs, not via the old *gozan* schools but through Hakuin (1686-1769), the extra-*gozan* lineages of Daitokuji and Myōshinji, and their founders Shūhō Myōchō (1282-1337), and Kanzan Egen (1277-1360), the *gozan* schools and monasteries are worthy of more careful scrutiny than they have hitherto received in Western scholarship on Japan. The *gozan* was certainly the most socially influential, economically powerful sector of medieval Zen. Moreover, the fully articulated *gozan* network spread from Kyoto and Kamakura throughout all the provinces of Japan, and *gozan* monasteries served as centers for the introduction and diffusion not only of Zen Buddhism but also of Chinese learning and culture, contributing inestimably to the enrichment of medieval intellectual and cultural life. Although eclipsed by other branches of Rinzai Zen in the late medieval period, *gozan* monasteries—Shōkokuji, Nanzenji, Tenryūji, Kenchōji, Engakuji—continued to play a significant role in Tokugawa society, and some of the former *gozan* are among the most visited present-day Japanese Zen centers.

The *gozan* group comprised several distinct Zen lineages, of which those deriving from Musō Soseki (1275-1351) and Enni Ben'en (1202-1280) were the most numerous. Nevertheless, the *gozan* network lends itself to study as a single unit. All the monasteries were regulated by similar monastic codes and shared a common pattern of layout and organization. All were linked to the center, eventually regulated from within Shōkokuji in Kyoto, and treated as a single group by warrior governments. Famous Zen masters from Kyoto or Kamakura *gozan* were invited to head provincial monasteries, while able or well-connected young monks from the provinces could rise to the headship of one of the Kamakura or Kyoto *gozan*. And, in their style of Zen

and their Chinese cultural predilections, the *gozan* shared common
traits which distinguished them subtly, but decisively, from
non-*gozan* Rinzai and Sōtō Zen monasteries.

Surviving documentary source materials for the history of the
gozan are plentiful, but hitherto only partially explored in the
Western literature. Zen monastic codes, ground plans of Chinese
and Japanese Zen monasteries, the records and diaries of leading
gozan prelates, volumes of poetry in Chinese, as well as religious
paintings, portraits, and ink paintings all shed light on the daily
monastic life and cultural activities of the *gozan*. While documentation for provincial *gozan* monasteries is sparse, documents
detailing the organization and economic life of some of the major
Kamakura and Kyoto *gozan*—Engakuji, Kenchōji, Nanzenji,
Tōfukuji—have survived and been printed, and the copious documentary record of Daitokuji also throws light on the *gozan*
economy. *Gozan* monasteries were also frequently mentioned in
secular legal codes and diaries of the day. With this wealth of
documentation, the *gozan* system is one medieval Japanese institution that invites the writing of a detailed history. A number of
fine studies by Japanese scholars have been written. There are
excellent studies of Nanzenji and Engakuji by Sakurai Kageo and
Tamamura Takeji.[5] Imaeda Aishin's *Chūsei Zenshū-shi no kenkyū*
looks in great detail at the articulation of the *gozan* system.
Haga Kōshirō's *Chūsei Zenrin no gakumon oyobi bungaku ni
kansuru kenkyū* is still the finest introduction to the intellectual
life of the *gozan*.[6] Three excellent essays on aspects of the *gozan*
organization and culture have recently appeared in English,[7]
some *gozan* poetry has been translated,[8] and catalogues prepared
for exhibitions of Chinese and Japanese ink paintings at the
Boston Museum of Fine Arts and the Art Museum, Princeton, in
1972 and 1975, have also enlarged our understanding of the cultural pursuits and talents of Zen monks.[9] Most of the work in
English to date, however, has tended to focus on the cultural
aspects of the *gozan*.[10] This book seeks to describe the monastic
environment within which *gozan* Zen culture emerged; to relate
the medieval *gozan* monasteries to the political and economic

life of the age; and to present the *gozan* as a working Buddhist monastic system in a warrior-dominated society.

To this end, Part One provides a historical survey of the introduction and development of Sung dynasty Zen in medieval Japan viewed, as far as possible, from the standpoint of the Japanese secular patrons of Zen monasteries. Part Two examines the structure of the medieval Zen monastery, its characteristic buildings, community organization, monastic rule, and economic life. Throughout the book, the emphasis is on the institutional development and organization of Zen monasteries, rather than on the spiritual content of *gozan* Zen or the intellectual, literary, and cultural activities of Zen monks. Readers seeking an understanding of Zen enlightenment or of the essence of Zen-related aesthetics are unlikely to find it here.[11] They should, however, gain some insight into the importance that Zen monks have always attached to the disciplined organization of monastic life and the careful management of resources in sustaining an environment conducive to the monk's striving for enlightenment. They should also, it is hoped, attain a fuller understanding of the place of *gozan* Zen monasteries in the social, political, and economic life of medieval Japan.

In the course of writing this book, I have become indebted to many friends, fellow research workers, librarians, and foundations. Professor John M. Rosenfield first stimulated my interest in Musō and his regulations for the Rinsenji community.[12] To understand the *Rinsenji Code* I quickly found I had to learn more about the tradition of Zen monastic codes, the organization and economic life of Zen monasteries, and the development of the *gozan* system. Professors Donald H. Shively, Albert M. Craig, Masatoshi Nagatomi, and Edwin O. Reischauer have always provided generous guidance and encouragement. Professors Kenneth Grossberg, James Kanda, Marius B. Jansen, Frederick W. Mote, James H. Sanford, Carl Steenstrup, Patricia Tsurumi, Denis C. Twitchett, Holmes Welch, and Philip B. Yampolsky have provided invaluable criticism of all or parts of the manuscript. The staffs of the Harvard-Yenching Library and the Gest Oriental Library, Princeton, have been unfailingly helpful. Peter Bol and Anders Hansson kindly reviewed the glossary.

A Harvard Traveling Fellowship allowed me to spend 1972–1973 in Japan, where a grant from the Nomura Foundation permitted me to visit many more Zen monasteries than I would otherwise have been able to see. Completion of the book has been facilitated by a National Endowment for the Humanities Research Fellowship for 1977–1978. In Kyoto I was given generous assistance by Professors Hayashiya Tatsusaburō, Yoshida Mitsukuni, Kumakura Isao, and other members of the Kyoto University Jinbun Kagaku Kenkyūjo, and by Professors Yanagida Seizan and Kimura Shizuo of Hanazono University. In Tokyo, Professors Fujiki Hisashi, Haga Koshirō, Hirose Ryōkō, Imaeda Aishin, Nagahara Keiji, Sasaki Ginya, Tamamura Takeji, and Tamamuro Fumio answered many questions and directed me to new materials. The temples, universities, and publishers who kindly gave me permission to use illustrations are acknowledged on the appropriate pages. I wish to express a personal word of thanks to Professor Hirose Ryōkō, Komazawa University, Tokyo; Professor Isao Kumakura, Tsukuba University, and Professor Kikuchi Yujirō of the Historiographical Research Institute (Shiryōhensan-jo), Tokyo University. The Reverend Morinaga Sōkō, Dashu'in in Kyoto, kindly provided the calligraphy for the binding. In Florence Trefethen of the Council on East Asian Studies, Harvard, I found the ideal editor: patient, meticulous, and always ready with suggestions for improvements in the clarity of presentation. Her colleague, Mary Ann Flood, generously undertook the task of providing an index. To Teruko Craig I owe thanks for her calligraphy in the bibliography and the glossary. I owe a special debt of gratitude to my wife, Akiko, who, in addition to typing drafts, prepared maps and diagrams, and checked translations. If errors of fact or judgment remain in the book, they are the responsibility of the author.

Princeton, New Jersey
January, 1981

Introduction

Zen monastic life is still carried on in Japan today substantially as it was practiced in medieval Japan or Sung dynasty China. More then 21,000 Zen temples are active. Of these, 15,000 belong to the 7 branches of the Sōtō school, some 6,000 to the 15 Rinzai lineages, and a small number to the Ōbaku school.[1] The majority are small, run by a Zen priest, with his wife and family if he is married—celibacy has been optional since the Meiji period—and perhaps two or three novices. There are also a number of training centers, known as *sōdō* (literally, "monks' halls") or *senmon dōjō* (specialized training places), within such historically renowned monasteries as Engakuji in Kamakura; Daitokuji, Myōshin-ji, Nanzenji, Shōkokuji and Tōfukuji in Kyoto; Eiheiji in Fukui prefecture; Sōjiji in Yokohama; Manpukuji at Uji; and many more. Although their meditation halls do not contain as many monks today as formerly, most *sōdō* probably have between fifteen and thirty monks enrolled at any one time. It is the *sōdō* that most faithfully preserves the spirit and forms of the Zen monastic tradition.[2]

Those young Japanese who choose the spiritual and physical rigors of Zen monastic life are sent, after several years of preparatory training in meditation, sutra chanting, and basic Zen monastic regulation at a small temple, to one of the large *sōdō* for four, five, six, or more years of intensive Zen monastic practice.

While in the *sōdō*, the young monk lives a communal life in an open hall, rises daily at three or four A.M., sits in meditation for six or seven hours; or for fifteen or sixteen during the monthly week-long retreats known as *sesshin*. He visits his master frequently for guidance in meditation or to offer his interpretation of a *kōan* (case). With his fellow monks he regularly chants the sutras, engages in manual labor (*samu*), or goes out seeking alms (*takuhatsu*). His life is silent, lived within the framework of a detailed rule and under the strictest discipline.

Few Zen monks today spend their whole lives in a *sōdō*. For a typical monk, this rigorous phase ends in his late twenties when he is appointed as an officer or assistant head of a smaller temple. There, administrative duties, the training of novices, discussion with local people and temple patrons, and, perhaps, the demands of family life will impose their own pattern on the daily life of the Zen priest and inevitably temper the severity and regularity to which he was accustomed in the *sōdō*.

There are critics who say that Japanese Zen monastic life is now little more than a hollow shell, the unthinking repetition of past forms, and that, like many other branches of Japanese Buddhism, it has lost its spiritual energy and been infected by secular values. Zen monks are themselves among the first to admit that young men whose fathers are monks and who will in time themselves inherit a family temple may enter the Zen monastic life from a sense of family responsibility as much as from any deeply felt spiritual need. They will also agree that it is possible for monks to treat their *sōdō* experience as a spartan initiation, severe while it lasts but, thankfully, not a lifetime commitment, and that monks who have "graduated" may sometimes seem to show, by the standards of Theravada or Western monastic and religious life, a too-ready compromise with secular values. But they will go on to assert that the practice of Zen is a personal experience, depending less on forms than on the sincerity of each individual in meditation, self-examination, and debate with his Zen master; that a perceptive Zen master, or *rōshi*, will quickly expose hypocrisy; that some young men may enter a monastery out of a sense of duty, but that that alone will hardly be sufficient to sustain them through the long and searching years of *sōdō* life. Most important, they urge, is the simple fact that Zen itself has not changed, that it is today what it has always been—the most direct path for the determined seeker to the intuitive enlightenment experience of the Buddha himself. This book is less concerned with the allegedly unchanging reality of Zen than with the mutable institutional framework, the Zen monastery, in which the teaching and practice have been borne through time. Although we cannot say with any certainty that Zen today is purer or less pure than it was in medieval Japan or T'ang or Sung dynasty China, there can be no question that the Zen institution in Japan today, notwithstanding the impressive number of surviving monasteries, is very much less prominent than in medieval society.

Knowledge of Zen teachings and meditation techniques seems to have first been introduced to Japan from T'ang dynasty China by the Japanese monk Dōshō (629–700), who founded the Hossō school in Japan and is said to have built a number of meditation halls, and by the Chinese monks Tao-hsuan (Dōsen, 702–760) and I-k'ung (Gikū), who expounded Zen to Emperor Saga (786–842).[3] The Japanese monks Saichō (767–822), the founder of the Japanese Tendai school, and Ennin (793–864) were also familiar with Zen as a result of their travels on the continent. Ennin, for instance, records several encounters with Chinese Zen monks:

> After the forenoon meal thirteen Zen and other monks came to see us. [They were] Hui-yün of the Tendai Sect from the Ch'ien-fu-ssu of Ch'ang-an and the Zen Scholar Monks: Hung-chien, Fa-tuan, Shih-shih, Hsing-chüan, Ch'ang-mi, Fa-chi, Fa-chen, Hui-shen, Ch'üan-ku, Ts'ung-shih, Chung-ch'üan, and T'an-yu. They wrote by brush:
>
> Together, quite idly and without attachments, like clouds floating about the landscape, we descended from Wu-feng and wandered to Ch'u and Ssu. Now, having reached this region, we are particularly happy to pay you our respects. It is most extraordinary, and great is our rejoicing. We now intend to go to [Mt.] T'ien-t'ai, and so we take leave of you and depart.
>
> Our great esteem.
>
> Writing by brush, we then replied:

> We Japanese monks now meet with you monks because in the past
> we had important affinities with you. We know for certain that one
> must dwell in the emptiness which is the nature of the Law. [Our meet-
> ing] is most fortunate. If we reach [Mt.] T'ien-t'ai, we shall certainly
> see you.
> Our great esteem.[4]

Later in his travels he met another group of Zen devotees:

> After we had eaten, we drank tea, and then, heading due north, we
> went twenty-five *li* to Hsing-t'ang hsien in the territory of Chen-chou
> and went to the Hsi-ch'an-yüan inside the walled town and spent the
> night. There were over twenty Zen monks who were extremely unruly
> men at heart.[5]

Zen did not immediately take root in Japan as an independent
school of Buddhism, however. For centuries it was incorporated
within the Tendai tradition as one element in the fourfold Tendai
practice of sutra study, esoteric rituals, the Vinaya, and contemplation. It remained in this subordinate position until the thirteenth century. The failure of Zen to establish its independence on
initial contact can be attributed to the overpowering vitality and
popularity of contemporary Tendai and Shingon Buddhism among
the Japanese court nobility, to the extreme novelty and paradoxi-
cal character of the Zen teachings, to the relative sectarian imma-
turity of Ch'an in T'ang dynasty China, and to the interruption of
official relations between Japan and China from the close of the
ninth century.

Contact with China was reopened in the late Heian period (794–
1185), and from the closing years of the twelfth century Ch'an
teachings again began to flow into Japan. The religious situation
in China had changed in the intervening period. While Pure Land
Buddhism was spreading widely among the people, Ch'an had assumed more clear-cut sectarian form and outstripped T'ien-t'ai,
Hua-yen, and the other older Chinese Buddhist schools in religious
and social influence to become the dominant branch of monastic
Buddhism in China.[6] It was only natural, therefore, that the growing number of Japanese monks visiting Southern Sung China and

staying in monasteries in the Hangchow region that were filled with Ch'an monks and headed by Ch'an masters should have been impressed by Ch'an monastic life and teachings and should have wished to introduce them to Japan. For the first half-century or so, growth was slow. Although with monks like Nōnin, Eisai (Yōsai), Dōgen, and Enni Ben'en it was beginning to make its presence felt, in the year 1250 Zen was still a relatively obscure and alien teaching in Japanese Buddhist circles. While many young monks, discouraged by spiritual decline within the established Buddhist sects in Japan, were being drawn to Zen as a more vital form of reformed Buddhist practice and monastic life, there were still, in the mid-thirteenth century, very few monasteries in Japan where even a diluted form of syncretic Tendai-Zen was practiced. By the mid-fourteenth century, however, both the Rinzai and Sōtō traditions were firmly rooted as independent schools in Japan. Many hundreds of "pure" Zen monasteries and temples were scattered throughout the country, with the metropolitan monasteries under shogunal or imperial patronage, and lesser temples supported by provincial warriors.

Aśvaghoṣa in the *Buddhacarita* (Deeds of the Buddha) relates that Prince Gautama suffered a spiritual crisis at the age of twenty-nine when, venturing for the first time outside the security of his palace, he saw the evidence of individual human suffering, old age, and death. Shaken by the knowledge that human life was not the round of pleasures to which he was accustomed, the prince set out on a personal search for liberation and passionless understanding. Failing to find an answer in intellectual speculation or in mortification of the body, Śākyamuni eventually attained his enlightenment and entry to Nirvana through meditation, the Middle Path.[7]

According to the Buddhist tradition, therefore, the Buddha was not an enlightened being from birth. He had to seek his own enlightenment and found it in meditation. The Zen schools teach that each individual, through the practice of meditation (*zazen*), can, in his own lifetime, relive the spiritual enlightenment attained by the Buddha; can "see into his own nature and become the

FIGURE 1: East Asia in the Year 1200

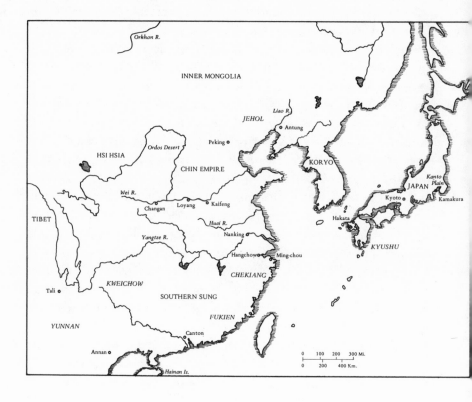

Buddha." According to subsequent Zen tradition, the essence of Śākyamuni's enlightenment experience, a teaching pointing directly at the heart of man, was passed not in sutras or texts but in secret mind-to-mind "transmission outside the scriptures" to his disciple Mahākāśyapa and thence, via twenty-six Indian patriarchs, in uninterrupted succession, to Bodhidharma, who brought the meditative teaching to China in the early sixth century to become the first patriarch of Ch'an in China.[8]

Although the historicity of Bodhidharma is in question, and the origins of the Ch'an sect obscured by the accretions and deletions of centuries of selective tradition-making, there can be little doubt that Indian yogic and meditation techniques, or *dhyāna* (Ch'an in Chinese), were carried to China with the early waves of Buddhism. While the Chinese do not seem to have been attracted by extremes of yogic asceticism, there appeared, from a fairly early period, Chinese Buddhist monks like Tao-an (314–385), who practiced meditation or who combined meditation with the study of Buddhist texts and Vinaya regulations and the conduct of Buddhist ritual. Chih-i (538–597), for instance, a founder of the T'ien-t'ai school and a leading protagonist in the Buddhist circles of his day, regularly engaged in contemplation and produced some of the earliest Chinese guides for meditation.[9] The Buddhist contemplative practice struck a responsive chord in Chinese society in part, at least, because of its resonance with the older Taoist philosophical mystical tradition and the Taoist ideal of attaining an intuitive awareness of the underlying Way of the natural universe. At first, contemplative monks lived within the monasteries of the older schools of Buddhism. But as *dhyāna* meditation gained in popularity and was elevated by its adherents from being merely one of several types of Buddhist practice to being the most direct approach to enlightenment, it was natural that some contemplative monks should establish their own small communities. These had begun to appear by the fifth century. In the seventh century, the monk Hung-jen (601–674), who was later designated the Fifth Ch'an Patriarch, is said to have attracted more than five hundred monks to his community at the East Mountain in Hupei.[10]

During the T'ang dynasty (618–906), the meditative stream of Buddhism attracted the attention of an increasing number of Chinese monks and laymen, came under occasional imperial and aristocratic patronage—Empress Wu Tse-t'ien, for instance, patronized the venerable Ch'an master Shen-hsiu (d. 706)—and was, as we have already seen, introduced to Japan. In the eighth century, there was a polarization within Ch'an circles. The crux of the problem was doctrinal, but the conflict was exacerbated by personal rivalries. The monk Shen-hui (d. 762), rejecting the established quietistic or gradualist approach to enlightenment based on the study of the scriptures accepted by such leading Ch'an masters as Shen-hsiu and his disciple P'u-chi (d. 739), urged a "sudden enlightenment" interpretation that rejected the written word. He claimed that his own master, Hui-neng (638–716), not Shen-hsiu, was the Sixth Patriarch and heir to the true Ch'an tradition. In time the dynamic subitist interpretation gained the ascendancy and flourished within the Southern school and its offshoots, while Shen-hsiu's interpretation and the Northern school which advocated it slowly atrophied.[11] Lin-chi I-hsuan (Rinzai Gigen, d. 867) and other spirited masters of the Southern school introduced the use of shouts, slaps, and mind-breaking "cases" (*kung-an*, or *kōan*) to shock their followers out of everyday patterns of thought and into spontaneous enlightenment.[12]

While Ch'an was developing doctrinally and shaping its particular methods of encouraging enlightenment, it was also taking a more clearly defined monastic form with the compilation of distinctive Ch'an "pure regulations" or "regulations for the pure community" (*ch'ing-kuei*). Pai-chang (749–814) is generally thought of as the first Ch'an codifier and as the architect of Ch'an independence from the Lü (Vinaya) school. It seems likely, however, that some Ch'an regulations had been drawn up before Pai-chang's time.[13] He probably did little more than lend his name to a developing corpus. Nor is it certain that the groups of meditating Ch'an monks were all confined to Lü school monasteries prior to Pai-chang. There is plenty of evidence to suggest that they had already begun to establish their own independent communities, like that at the East Mountain, with characteristic buildings and patterns of monastic organization and daily life.[14]

The communal type of meditation and daily life practiced by Ch'an monks produced the characteristic Ch'an monks' hall (*sōdō*). Ch'an stress on the direct transmission from master to disciple and rejection of excessive reliance on textual study also contributed to the development of the Dharma, or preaching, hall, another distinctive Ch'an building. It is not clear when these buildings first began to appear, but their prototypes may well have been in use in Hung-jen's day. By the T'ang dynasty, large, predominantly Ch'an complexes were being built in the major cities as well as in remote mountain areas.

Other features of early Ch'an monastic life were its stress on frugality and the sustenance of the community by the joint labor of all its members. Pai-chang is accepted as the author of the Ch'an work ethic with his famous phrase "No work, no food." Again, it is probable that he did no more than advertise a practice already well established.[15] The positive value of manual labor in Ch'an monastic life was strengthened by the acceptance of the concept of sudden enlightenment. If meditation were actively and constantly practiced, enlightenment, it was argued, could be achieved while in the midst of such everyday activity as cutting firewood, heating bath water, tilling the fields, or sweeping the monastery floors. Taken to an extreme, this could have meant the rejection of seated meditation (*zazen*). In practice, Ch'an masters did not go this far; *zazen* maintained its central place in Ch'an practice. It was the still malleable character of Ch'an, its strong rural roots, emphasis on simplicity, frugality, and discipline, together with the directness of the doctrine, that allowed it to weather the storms in which more powerful schools in the capital lost their lands, their tax privileges, and their wealth in the persecutions culminating in that witnessed by Ennin in 845.

By the Sung dynasty, Ch'an was firmly established as the dominant Buddhist monastic school in China. It was, however, not quite what it had been in the early T'ang dynasty. The simple communities had coalesced into an organized church. Like the monasteries of other Buddhist schools, Ch'an monasteries now included Buddha halls, with Buddhist images, where monks engaged in elaborate ceremonies and chanting of sutras in addition to meditation, debate with the master, and manual labor. Doctrinally, Ch'an teachings interacted with the ideas of the T'ien-t'ai, Pure Land, and Hua-yen (Kegon) schools. Ch'an monasteries were in intimate contact with society, especially elite society, and Ch'an monks performed religious functions for the intentions of secular patrons. In this way, while imparting Zen Buddhist ideas on the one hand, on the other Ch'an monks absorbed the cultural values and intellectual concerns of the Chinese social elite, while their monasteries shifted from a self-sufficient economic base to reliance upon patronage and incorporation within the general economy.[16]

That the Ch'an school was still vital and disciplined is clear from examination of the *Ch'an-yuan Code* (1103).[17] But even in this code, although meditation and labor are still emphasized, there are indications of an elaborate formalization of monastic life and ceremonial. Evidence for this tendency becomes more marked in subsequent codes. The height of Ch'an social prestige and influence was probably reached in the late twelfth century when a group of 5 central Ch'an "mountains" and some 35 lesser provincial monasteries were honored with official status. It was this imposing Sung dynasty Ch'an monastic establishment that the Japanese monk-visitors encountered when contact with China was reopened in the twelfth century.[18]

In the following pages, we shall be looking at the development and organization of the *gozan* Zen monasteries in medieval Japanese society. First, however, we should perhaps, as a frame of reference, have some impression of the scale and influence of the whole Buddhist institution of which the Zen schools were to form an increasingly significant part.

There are, unfortunately, no reliable statistics for the total number of monasteries or of monks and nuns in medieval Japan. One estimate, and it is no more than an extrapolation from later figures, suggests that there may have been as many as 90,000

Buddhist monasteries and temples.[19] In more recent research, Professor Tamamuro Fumio cites figures of 465,049 temples throughout the whole country registered by 10 Buddhist schools in 1872 and 2,377 temples belonging to 11 Buddhist schools registered in a single *han* (Mito) in 1663. Of the Mito temples, 1,357 were Shingon temples, 206 Tendai, 38 Rinzai Zen, and 136 Sōtō Zen. According to his researches, only 38 of the 2,377 temples surviving in 1663 had been founded before 1200. A further 419 dated from between 1200 and 1500. An explosion in temple foundation occurred between 1500 and 1650 when 1,219 temples were established. In the small district of Mito, then, there were some 450 Buddhist foundations in existence by 1500.[20] The total for the whole country, whatever it may have been, included the great monasteries of Nara, Kyoto, and Kamakura, the sprawling, mountain-top complexes of Kōyasan, Hieizan, Negorosan, and Hakusan, as well as many thousands of smaller provincial temples, meeting halls, and hermitages. The medieval period saw not only the survival or recovery of the older schools of Nara and Heian Buddhism and the rapid development of Zen but also the startling growth of the Nichiren, Pure Land, New Pure Land, and Timely schools.[21]

The largest monasteries had scores of buildings and housed several thousand monks and monastery servants. In the year 1211, for instance, more that 13,000 monks participated in a Buddhist ceremony sponsored by Emperor Go-Toba (1180–1239). Four thousand of these monks came from the single monastery of Kōfukuji in Nara.[22] Kōfukuji was then undoubtedly one of the largest and most powerful monastic centers in medieval Japan, having been revived and rebuilt by the Kamakura shogunate, but there were many other monasteries with populations of well over 1,000 monks and as many, or more, novices, monastery servants, artisans, and field laborers. Even the larger metropolitan Zen monasteries, which came late onto the scene and thus had less opportunity to build up the landed base needed to support a large monastic population, had, by the mid-fourteenth century, monk enrollments of between 500 and 1,000.[23] The older centers may

FIGURE 2: The Provinces of Medieval Japan

have declined slightly in numbers as Zen and other new schools of Buddhism gained ground, but the fact that they remained populous and powerful until the late sixteenth century is clear from the numbers slaughtered by Oda Nobunaga and Toyotomi Hideyoshi in their efforts to break the back of the Buddhist institutions as a political and economic force. Estimates of the numbers killed at Enryakuji range upward from 1,000 to 3,000 or 4,000. Kōyasan is said to have lost between 600 and 1,300 monk-soldiers (*sōhei*) repelling an attack by Nobunaga in 1581–1582.[24]

The Buddhist church was a pervasive economic presence in medieval society. Temples and shrines controlled or held rights in many of the estates (*shōen*) scattered throughout Japan. To take one example, the Shingon sect monastery of Tōji in Kyoto was founded in 796. According to Professor Takeuchi Rizō, until the late Heian period, its landed base was fairly small, comprising about 500 *chō* in six different localities. However, in contrast to the Nara monasteries of Tōdaiji and Kōfukuji which did not acquire many new *shōen* proprietorships in the medieval period, Tōji domains grew rapidly between the late twelfth and early fourteenth centuries. During this period, the number of *shōen* proprietorships and steward rights more than tripled to 30. Most of these were gifts from the imperial princess Sen'yōmon'in (1181–1252), Cloistered-Emperor Go-Uda (1267–1324) and, later, by Emperor Go-Daigo (1288–1339) and the warrior leaders Ashikaga Takauji (1305–1358) and his younger brother Tadayoshi (1306–1352).[25]

According to an *Ōtabumi* (register of landholdings) for the year 1197, of the 8,064 *chō* (about 20,000 acres) of registered land in Hyūga province, southern Kyūshū, 2,106 *chō* (26 percent) were shrine domain (*sharyō*) and 238 *chō* (3 percent) temple land (*jiryō*), These are modest amounts. In Buzen, northern Kyūshū, at about the same time, out of a total of 13,300 *chō*, 5,141 *chō* (39 percent) were classified as shrine domain and 3,809 *chō* (29 percent) as temple domain. Shrines and temples thus laid claim to well over half the registered rice-producing land in the province. In Bungo, northern Kyūshū, a century later (1285), out of a total of 6,873 *chō*, shrine domain included 1861 *chō* (27 percent) and temple domain 2,663 *chō* (39 percent), together more than 65 percent of the land included in the registers. Since many Shintō shrines in the medieval period were adjuncts of Buddhist temples, the weight of temple influence was even greater than these figures suggest. The above *Ōtabumi* entries all relate to Kyūshū. That a similar situation prevailed in other parts of Japan is suggested by *Ōtabumi* for Awaji (1223), where 633 *chō* (51 percent) of the registered total of 1,354 *chō* were nominally held by Buddhist temples, and Wakasa province (1265), where, out of a total of 2,217 *chō*, 136 were held by the Enryakuji (Hieizan) branch of the Tendai school, 83 *chō* by the rival Onjōji (Miidera) line of Tendai and 17 *chō* by the Shingon temple of Jingoji. Nearly 10 percent of the land was thus registered in the names of these temples alone.[26]

Some provinces were particularly heavily affected by temple rights. Most of the *shōen* in Yamato, for instance, had the Tōdaiji or Kōfukuji as proprietor. The province of Kii was dominated by Kongōbuji (Kōyasan), which claimed an ancient domain of 10,000 *chō* around the mountain,[27] and by Daidenhō'in (Negoroji). *Shōen* in the province of Ōmi near Kyoto were nearly all under the control of one or other of the many sub-temples of Enryakuji, which loomed over the province, or Onjōji.[28] Although the landed interests of Buddhist temples were most extensive and deeply rooted in the Kinai and western Japan they were by no means negligible in northern and eastern provinces, as a glance at any list of medieval *shōen* will immediately demonstrate.[29]

The older Buddhist monasteries suffered a relative decline in their political and military influence with the establishment and extension of warrior government after the late twelfth century. Moreover, like such other absentee central proprietors as nobles and members of the imperial court, they lost many of their rights in distant *shōen* holdings to local warriors (*jitō* or *kokujin*) or provincial military governors (*shugo*) during the disturbances of the fourteenth and fifteenth centuries. However, although this period is frequently described as the age of the dissolution of the *shōen* system,[30] it would be a mistake to think that all Buddhist monasteries had lost all access to their *shōen* income by the mid-fifteenth century or even by the early sixteenth century. The erosion of the *shōen* was erratic and protracted and only completed by the land reforms of Hideyoshi in the late sixteenth century. Some provincial *shōen* were still providing tax income for Buddhist temples in the sixteenth century. Partly because of their sacrosanct character, but also because of the ability of large Buddhist monasteries to organize a stout military defense and to mount and sustain effective political pressures, many monastic holdings, though eroded, were more resistant to warrior intrusions than less capably defended civil *shōen*. Dr. Peter Arnesen, who has investigated the Ōuchi provincial governor (*shugo*) family during the medieval period, finds that the Tōdaiji, although increasingly subject to Ōuchi juridical and fiscal authority, maintained some proprietary interests in Suō province until well into the sixteenth century.[31]

In a more recent study of Tōji holdings than that cited by Professor Takeuchi Rizō above, Professor Nagahara Keiji identifies 71 *shōen* proprietorships held by Tōji at different times prior to 1600. Of these, he found that 32 had been lost as sources of income by the Kamakura period, a further 25 were reduced or alienated during the wars of the fourteenth and fifteenth centuries, and 14 remained sources of income until the sixteenth century.[32] Tachibana Kōsen has found that Buddhist temples were major landholders in late sixteenth century Tosa,[33] while Miyazaka Yūshō states that Kōyasan in the 1590s still controlled 2,613 villages aggregating an estimated annual yield equivalent to 173,137 *koku* (about 865,000 bushels) of hulled rice.[34] Enryakuji, Kōfukuji, and many other Buddhist monasteries also maintained extensive landed interests until they were stripped of most of them by Toyotomi Hideyoshi or Tokugawa Ieyasu.

The wealth and economic influence of Buddhist monasteries was not due solely to their enjoyment of tax income from holdings in distant *shōen*. Monasteries and temples received donations and bequests from patrons, for whom they provided memorial services. They were exempted from many of the provincial tax levies imposed by warrior-rulers. They also engaged in *sake* brewing, medicine making, the sale of lumber and produce from monastic domains, and other commercial activities. The wandering monk-peddlars from Kōyasan, the Kōya-hijiri, who traveled the length and breadth of the country selling small items, produced a substantial income for the monastery.[35] Profits were also derived from moneylending. Enryakuji had interests in the Kyoto pawnshops (*dosō*), and many temples, following the example of Zen monasteries, made loans from "mortuary funds" (*shidōsen*) at relatively low rates of interest to the general public or made high-interest private loans to nobles, high-ranking warriors, and merchants.

Guild sponsorship and market licensing were other important sources of income for some monasteries. Privileged merchant guilds (*za*) in the Kinai region were major agents of commercial activity throughout the medieval period. Many of these guilds were under the protection of temples and shrines to which they paid regular dues in return for their monopoly privileges. In Yamato province, for instance, the salt, roofing-reed, bamboo-screen, cypress wood, and metal-casting guilds were all under the sponsorship of Kōfukuji, while the carpenters' guild was attached to the Tōdaiji and the Kasuga shrine. In Ōmi province, the salt and paper guilds enjoyed the protection of the Hie shrine which was associated with Enryakuji.[36] By the late medieval period, extensive market networks had developed in and beyond the Kinai region, and markets were being held regularly six times a month at transportation nodes or outside the gates of temples. Traders using such a market paid dues to the temple, but the markets must also have attracted many casual visitors and donors.[37]

As centers of pilgrimage and nodes in the commercial and market network of the medieval economy, some Buddhist temples stimulated the development of quite substantial townships at their gates (*monzenmachi*) or within their compounds (*jinaimachi*). While the deserted capital of Heijō-kyō fell into ruins, the medieval town of Nara developed nearby as the *monzenmachi* of Tōdaiji, Kōfukuji, and the Kasuga Shintō shrine. Sakamoto, on Lake Biwa in Ōmi province, developed rapidly from the mid-Heian period as the supply center for Enryakuji. Annual rice taxes and other produce were brought from distant *shōen* to the warehouses of Sakamoto for storage and redistribution. *Sake* breweries sprang up, and the town became a center for local packhorse traders.[38] Ōtsu, also on Lake Biwa, began as the *monzenmachi* of Onjōji. By the sixteenth century, being on a main road to Kyoto, it had become an important rice market in its own right. Kanazawa and Ōsaka owed much of their early development to the proximity of growing Honganji communities.

That the Kinai region around Kyoto and Sakai remained the most economically advanced area in Japan throughout the medieval period was due, in part at least, to the stimulus provided by the presence of many monasteries, monastery-sponsored markets and guilds, and *monzenmachi*. But monasteries could also impede trade to their own advantage. Many shared in the profits derived from toll barriers (*sekisho*). From 1196, for instance, Tōdaiji reaped profits from the use by rice-bearing vessels belonging to other temples or merchants of the strategically placed Hyōgo barrier. Kōfukuji was later given a part share in the proceeds from this same barrier. Tōdaiji, in the mid-Muromachi period, anticipated an income of 1,700 *kan* from the Hyōgo barrier. In 1463 Kōfukuji collected 2,000 *kan* from the southern section of the barrier, and in 1484 the same monastery is recorded as taking 1,100 *kan* from the Kusaba barrier and 500 *kan* from the Udono barrier. Kōyasan is recorded as having an income of 1,500 *kan* from the Yodo barrier in 1308.[39] (One *kan*, or *kanmon*, equaled 1,000 copper cash [*mon*] and was approximately equivalent in value to 1 *koku*, or 5 bushels of rice.)

It should be evident that the larger Buddhist monasteries, especially those in the Kinai, were able, in a variety of ways, to exploit the growing, increasingly monetized and urban commercial economy of the Kamakura and Muromachi periods. Professor Kuroda Toshio argues that, as their distant *shōen* rights were alienated, temples and shrines actively sought new sources of landed and commercial income, including the acquisition of nearby small-scale supplementary rental rights (*kajishi myōshu shiki*) and the sponsorship of guilds and markets.[40] By these means, Buddhist temples maintained considerable economic influence throughout the medieval period. From the mid-sixteenth century, *sengoku daimyō*, in their efforts to gain full control over the commercial activities within their domains, sought to abolish toll barriers within domains, to free local markets and guilds from the control of Kyoto- and Nara-based guilds, and the nobles and religious institutions sponsoring them, and to both encourage the activities of domain-based merchant groups and the centralization of commercial activity within the *daimyō's* garrison town.[41] Although these policies met with varying degress of success in outlying domains, they were difficult to enforce in the Kinai where *sengoku daimyō* domains were mostly small and where the power of nobles, religious institutions, and established merchant groups was interlocking and deeply entrenched.

As well-organized, enduring institutions, Buddhist monasteries were able to marshall considerable political pressure in defense of their landholdings, tax exemptions, and commercial interests. Monasteries, temples, and hermitages of whatever school had devoted, politically active secular patrons. Many of the leading prelates in the central monasteries of the older schools had come from Kyoto noble families and naturally made use of these social connections in the interests of their monasteries. Through a system of imperial designation, certain monasteries and nunneries provided havens for imperial princes and princesses who wished to withdraw from the secular world, or for whom it was necessary to provide an office and income. These were known as *monzeki* temples. The Ashikaga shoguns also made use of such arrangements to provide for some of their offspring. As Zen monasteries developed in the thirteenth and fourteenth centuries, they quickly established close ties with politically influential nobles and warriors. It has been suggested that, in elite circles, of those who were to enter the religious life, the children of high-ranking consorts were usually placed in Kyoto and Nara temples belonging to the older schools of Buddhism, while those of lower-ranking consorts were sent as novices to Zen monasteries.[42] At lower levels of warrior society, too, Zen monasteries and nunneries provided a new and expanding "career" alternative for the younger sons and daughters of warrior houses.[43] As such, Zen monasteries rapidly meshed into the fabric of the political society of medieval Japan. Other new schools of Buddhism, the Nichiren school and the Jōdo Shin (New Pure Land or Ikkō) school, who drew their adherents principally from among peasants, lower-level warriors, and small merchants, also had powerful, high-ranking secular sponsors and, with their devoted, well-organized followings, were able to exert considerable local and national political influence.[44]

Where family connection, legal complaint, and political pressure failed, some of the larger monastic centers would not hesitate to have recourse to arms. The monk-soldiers (*sōhei*) from Enryakuji on Mt. Hiei, who periodically terrorized Kyoto throughout the middle ages, are notorious. Enryakuji, however, was not the only monastery to have at hand large numbers of men trained to fight with a halberd. Tōdaiji, Kōfukuji, Kōyasan, Onjōji, Negorosan, Kaga Hakusan, and other older monasteries had their own powerful companies of *sōhei*. *Sōhei* were most threatening in central politics during the eleventh and twelfth centuries, and their military influence was greatly reduced with the establishment of the warrior government of the Kamakura *bakufu*. Monasteries, however, continued to maintain *sōhei* throughout the medieval period. When the complex at Negoro was burned out by Hideyoshi in 1585, there are said to have been nearly three thousand monks and armed men on the mountain.[45] Moreover, from the late fifteenth century, newer branches of Buddhism began to emerge as military forces. Armed followers of the Honganji New Pure Land school toppled the local provincial warrior governor (*shugo*) and controlled the province of Kaga from 1488 until their defeat by Nobunaga in 1580. Similar Jōdo Shinshū-affiliated leagues (Ikkō *ikki*) based on Ishiyama, Nagashima, and Mikawa fiercely resisted the efforts of Nobunaga, Hideyoshi, and Tokugawa Ieyasu to impose their authority over these areas.[46] Within the city of Kyoto, Nichiren (Lotus) school adherents took up arms and assumed the government of the city in the Hokke (or Lotus) uprising from

1532, until crushed by Enryakuji *sōhei*.[47] Thus, until their eventual disarming by Hideyoshi at the close of the sixteenth century, *sōhei* and adherents of the New Pure Land and Lotus schools contributed to the instability of medieval society by fighting among themselves, pressing their demands on the court and warrior governments, taking sides in political disputes, and struggling with the emerging hegemons (*sengoku daimyō*) of the Age of Wars.

The spiritual authority and surviving military might of the Buddhist monastic institution in the late twelfth century is well illustrated in an incident involving Enryakuji monks and Minamoto Yoritomo (1147–1199), the founder of the Kamakura *bakufu*. Yoritomo was one of the most determined and astute military leaders in Japanese history, certainly not a man to be challenged lightly. By 1185, he had destroyed the Taira family, secured effective control of western as well as eastern Japan, and instituted the Kamakura *bakufu*. In 1191, Sasaki Sadashige and his father, Sadatsuna, Yoritomo's housemen, military governors of Ōmi province, and the local proprietors of the Sasaki-no-*shō* (Ōmi), of which Enryakuji was the central proprietor, became involved with Enryakuji in a violent dispute over tax-rent payments in which officials visiting the *shōen* were killed. At first, Yoritomo supported his vassals but, as Enryakuji raised *sōhei* and applied political pressure in Kyoto and Kamakura, he capitulated and allowed the exile of Sadatsuna and the execution of Sadashige. Possibly Yoritomo acted out of ultimate respect for a powerful religious sanction. It is at least as likely, however, that he feared continued disorder in Kyoto and perhaps the united opposition of all armed temples if he pressed the case against Enryakuji.[48] Another four centuries were to elapse before warriors emerged who were sufficiently powerful to challenge directly and finally curb the military might of the powerful religious institutions. That achievement was one of the marks of the transition from medieval to what is frequently called "early modern" society in Japan.[49]

It was into this turbulent political and religious environment that Zen teachings and monastic practices were introduced in the late twelfth century. Monks of the established schools, especially

Enryakuji and the Nara monasteries, were generally unsympathetic, and used their connections with the court and *bakufu* to try to impede the activities of the advocates of Zen. At the same time, Zen had to compete for influence at the popular level among local warriors and peasants with the vigorous Amidist and Lotus schools, deriving from Shinran, Ippen, and Nichiren, which gave to medieval Japan much of its vital religious character. Had the Chinese Zen teachings and their advocates not attracted the attention of some leading members of the Japanese ruling warrior-elite, the chances for the survival and independent development of the Zen schools in Japan would have been slight.

PART ONE

The Development of the Institution

ONE

Japanese Zen Pioneers and their Patrons

It is widely accepted that the Zen introduced to medieval Japan from Sung China by Eisai (Yōsai), Dōgen, and their successors took root and flourished as an independent branch of Japanese Buddhism because of its intrinsic appeal to the newly dominant class of warriors. Faced daily with the forbidding realities of war, disfigurement, and death, such men, it is believed, were immediately receptive to the stoic, non-scholastic religious philosophy of Zen, which encouraged self-reliance and directness of action derived from relentless introspection, calmness of mind, and discipline of body.[1] This general statement obscures some very important features of the transmission and acculturation process.

During the first century of Zen development, the mass of Japanese fighting men and many of their leaders were totally ignorant of, or indifferent to, this new form of Chinese Buddhism.[2] They remained wedded to longstanding beliefs in the promise of the Pure Land, the terrors of the Buddhist hells, or the efficacy of esoteric incantations in time of sickness or adversity. If they had a symbolic patron deity, it was still the fierce-visaged, sword-brandishing Fudō Myōō rather than the calmly meditating Śākyamuni.[3]

Zen developed—and took the form it did—in medieval Japan not simply because of a spontaneous spark of affinity between the Zen spirit and Japanese warrior mentality (this affinity was found only on closer acquaintance), but principally because, at critical moments in its early development, the monks who advocated the new religion found powerful secular patrons. Without these patrons, it is inconceivable that Sung Zen could have established its independence in the medieval Japanese religious world. In all likelihood, it would have been absorbed as a subordinate doctrine of one of the powerful established Japanese schools, just as the Ch'an teachings introduced earlier from T'ang China had for centuries survived passively as one facet of a fourfold Tendai practice.

The early patrons of Zen included Kyoto nobles and members of the imperial family, as well as the warrior-rulers in Kamakura and some of their leading retainers, the military governors (*shugo*). Impulses to patronage were complex. They included attraction of the forthright personalities, mental alertness, wide learning, and physical vigor of Zen monks; admiration for the strict discipline of the Zen monastic life and rule; curiosity about the intellectual horizons reopened through Zen to continental secular culture; the occasional temptation to use Zen as a counterbalance to the overweening claims of the established Buddhist sects and, in the case of the warrior-rulers in Kamakura, an awareness of a need to provide themselves with cultural credentials appropriate to their newfound military and political power. Although it would be an exaggeration to suggest that these early patrons were completely indifferent to the spiritual potential of Zen, there is very little indication, during the first five or six decades of its development, that they engaged strenuously in meditation, that they attained much insight into Zen teaching, or displayed any great interest in acquiring such knowledge. Their religious commitment to Zen was hesitant, and long subordinate to their ingrained devotion to established modes of religious expression.

The basic teaching of Zen is starkly simple: each person can, by his own efforts, relive the spiritual awakening attained through meditation by Śākyamuni himself. The Zen introduced to Japan from China in the thirteenth century, however, involved much more than this call to direct personal enlightenment. The central core of Sung Zen teaching was embedded in a complex intellectual and cultural exegetical corpus. This corpus was formed from the accretions of centuries of development of Ch'an thought and monastic practice. It was blended with elements derived from other branches of Chinese Buddhism, and had been influenced by Taoist and Neo-Confucian thought and by the intellectual and cultural assumption of the Chinese literati who were the principal patrons of Sung dynasty Ch'an.[4]

Those Japanese and Chinese monks who introduced Sung Zen to Japan brought the core teaching. They brought it, however, as part of the religious, intellectual, and cultural framework in which they found it in the great Buddhist monasteries of the Hangchow region of twelfth and thirteenth century China. Japan had only recently reestablished formal contact with China after a lapse of several centuries. Official Japanese embassies to T'ang China ceased from 894. During the early eleventh century, there were some informal cultural and commercial contacts between Japan and Sung China. Active official relations, however, were only reestablished from the mid-twelfth century by Taira Kiyomori (1118–1181). During this hiatus, Japan had moved away from its earlier dependence on Chinese civilization to establish a distinctive culture of its own. On the continent, meanwhile, there had been major developments in Chinese thought and in Ch'an itself. In these circumstances, the complex of Sung dynasty Ch'an teachings was not immediately assimilable by even the most educated and sympathetic Japanese warriors or courtiers, and was still less accessible and attractive to barely literate fighting men.

The introduction of Sung Zen was made even more difficult by sectarian rivalry. On the one hand, exponents of the new Zen teachings encountered the determined opposition of the established Buddhist schools in Japan, especially the Enryakuji branch of Tendai, which vociferously pressed their claims for exclusive aristocratic and warrior attention. On the other, they were met by competition from the very vital contemporary devotional religious movements based on faith in the efficacy of the *Lotus Sutra* or in the prospect of salvation in the Pure Land of Amida that were winning many thousands of enthusiastic adherents at lower levels of Japanese society.[5]

The full acceptance of Sung Zen in medieval Japan and its emergence as an independent school was, therefore, a slow and sometimes halting process which extended over the century and a half from the late twelfth to the early fourteenth century. Within this time span, three basic developmental stages can be discerned.[6]

STAGES OF ACCULTURATION

The first active and largely syncretic stage, lasting for approximately fifty years, centered mainly on Hakata and Kyoto. Japanese Tendai monks who had journeyed to China were the principal agents. This stage was one of uneasy coexistence of Sung Zen teachings within the perimeter of the scholastic and esoteric framework of Japanese Tendai Buddhism. The only major exceptions to this initial syncretic pattern were the Kyoto monk Dainichibō Nōnin, a contemporary of Eisai, and Dōgen Kigen, who introduced Sōtō Zen teachings to Japan. Both these monks rejected accommodation with the established sects.

The syncretic phase was followed, during the second half of the thirteenth and early fourteenth centuries, by a period of consolidation involving the vigorous introduction of what is frequently referred to as "pure" Chinese Zen to Kamakura monasteries by Chinese émigré monks. These monks were patronized by elite groups in Japanese society, especially the Hōjō regents. This stage saw the building of large-scale Zen monasteries on the Sung model, the imposition of characteristic Zen monastic regulations, and some diffusion of Zen-related Chinese culture. By the end of this phase, Japanese Zen was free of Tendai domination, and monastic practice was qualitatively equivalent to that in contemporary Chinese monasteries. Quantitatively, however, Zen was still insecurely and narrowly rooted in Japanese society and understood by very few outside the walls of the new monasteries.

The beginning of the third stage of metropolitan Zen development can be dated from the opening decades of the fourteenth century, when Japanese disciples of émigré Chinese monks and Japanese monks who had studied in Chinese monasteries began to assume the headships of proliferating Japanese Zen monasteries. One of the most striking developments during this phase was the nationwide articulation of a system of official monasteries (*kanji*) known as the "Five Mountains" or *gozan* system. The mature Japanese *gozan* network eventually comprised some 300 official monasteries ranked in 3 tiers: *gozan, jissatsu* (Ten Temples), and *shozan* (Many Mountains). The network was dominated by the Musō and Shōichi (Enni Ben'en) lineages of Rinzai Zen and developed rapidly under the patronage of the Ashikaga shoguns and their principal provincial retainers. The Japanese *gozan* network was an elaboration of the Five Mountains system of official Ch'an monasteries established in Sung dynasty China, which in turn is said to have derived from an early Indian Buddhist system of 5 monasteries and 10 pagodas. In the Chinese and Japanese officially sponsored Zen monasteries, the appointment of abbots and promotions of monks and officers, as well as monastic discipline, were under the supervision of the secular authorities.

The powerful, officially sponsored medieval *gozan* Zen monasteries are sometimes collectively referred to by modern historians of Zen as the *sōrin* (thicket, grove). Zen schools not included in the *sōrin* grouping are known as the *rinka* or *ringe* (below the grove). The precise historical origins of these terms are unknown. It is unclear, at least to this writer, whether these terms were in common use in Sung dynasty Chinese or medieval Japanese Zen monasteries. Whatever its origin, the distinction between *sōrin* and *rinka* is used to emphasize fairly obvious differences of style between "insiders" and "outsiders," between "metropolitans" and "provincials." The *rinka*, for their part, self-consciously declared that they preserved the true tradition of the early Ch'an masters, a tradition that had been muddied and obscured in secularized official *sōrin* monasteries. Japanese *rinka* included the Rinzai schools centered on the Kyoto monasteries of Daitokuji and Myōshinji as well as most branches of the Sōtō school. During the fifteenth and sixteenth centuries, the *rinka* expanded rapidly, while the *gozan* experienced a relative decline.

By the time the third phase was under way in the mid-fourteenth century, although it probably still did not appeal to the mass of Japanese warriors, Zen was firmly rooted as an independent branch of Japanese Buddhism. It was exerting an active influence on Japanese religion and culture, and had become a significant element in Japanese social and political life.

It should be noted that the developmental phases outlined above were neither uniform nor static. During the early phase, degrees of syncretism varied. Eisai, for instance, was more accommodating towards the established Buddhist sects than Enni (Shōichi). During the second phase, while most Chinese monks sought to impose the standards prevailing in Sung and Yuan monasteries, some, like Ch'ing-cho Cheng-ch'eng (1274–1339), attempted to modify Chinese monastic regulations to suit Japanese conditions.

The neat three-stage model is also complicated by vertical fissures. The pattern of Sōtō school development in medieval Japan was very different from that of the metropolitan schools.[7] Within the metropolitan schools, there was a major cleavage between the *gozan* lineages patronized by the Ashikaga shoguns, and the Daitokuji and Myōshinji *rinka* lineages, which were patronized initially by the imperial court and later, from the mid-fifteenth century, by wealthy townsmen from Sakai, by Warring States barons (*sengoku daimyō*), and by lower-ranking provincial warriors.[8] With a closer look at the *gozan* lineages it is possible to detect differences and rivalries among them. In Kamakura, for instance, an ongoing feud developed between monks from Engakuji and those from Kenchōji.[9] These vertical fissures, however, significant as they are for understanding Zen sectarian development, do not invalidate the three-stage acculturation model. We now examine the early syncretic phase in greater detail.

MOTIVES OF JAPANESE ZEN PIONEERS

Those Japanese pilgrim-monks, including Chōgen (1121–1206), Eisai (1141–1215), Kakua (active late twelfth century), Shunjō (1166–1227), Dōgen (1200–1253), and Enni Ben'en (1202–1280), who made the hazardous journey to China during the second half of the twelfth and early thirteenth centuries, were moved by a strong reforming impulse. Most were monks from the great Tendai complex of Enryakuji on Mt. Hiei, high above Kyoto. Oppressed by the prevailing mood of decline of the Buddhist Law (*mappō*) and discouraged by the worldliness and laxity of late Heian Buddhist monastic life, they journeyed to China in the hope that there they would find new texts, practices, and regulations that would help them put new life into Japanese Buddhism. Although some returned to Japan as advocates of Zen, few set out with that intention.[10]

Other Tendai monks, among them Hōnen (1133–1212), Shinran (1173–1262), Nichiren (1222–1282), and Ippen (1239–1289), who were equally dissatisfied with the aristocratic, secular tone and formalized ritualism of their sect, responded by rejecting the monastic life with its rules of seclusion, abstinence, and celibacy. They quit their mountain retreats and moved among the common people, advocating salvation for all through self-denying faith and constant invocation of the name of Amida, the *nenbutsu*, or of the *Lotus Sutra*.

Out of the one seemingly exhausted Tendai scholastic tradition thus emerged two powerful currents of medieval Buddhism. One stream was radical and popular. It appealed to absolute faith in some exterior saving grace during the latter age of the law (*mappō*) when man was powerless to save himself or to accumulate merit by his own efforts; it welcomed all men and women, rejected the exclusivity of the monastic life away from the world, and questioned the relevance, in an age of *mappō*, of formal religious rules and regulations. The other current was more conservative and exclusive. It reaffirmed the monastic life and rule, stressed that each individual must search for enlightenment by his own spiritual efforts, and turned for inspiration and energy not to the common people of Japan but back to the Buddhist traditions and culture of China.

The Japanese Tendai monk Ennin (793–864) was on pilgrimage in China during the suppression of Buddhism in 845. He found T'ien-t'ai Buddhism still at the height of its glory, one of the dominant forms of T'ang dynasty Chinese Buddhism. Ch'an does not figure very prominently in his diary. He makes no mention of visiting any Ch'an communities. Those Ch'an monks he encountered on his travels—some of them, "extremely unruly men at heart"—were, like himself, on pilgrimage to famous T'ien-t'ai centers.[11]

Japanese Tendai monks who visited China three centuries later found a very changed religious situation. The Southern Sung empire, although smaller than the T'ang and beset by Mongol pressure from the north and west, must still have seemed, to the eyes of Japanese visitors, a great center of civilization. Its capital, Hangchow, was an elegant city of canals, palaces, and Buddhist monasteries, and there were still many thriving Buddhist communities throughout the empire, although, of course, older centers of Buddhism in the north like Wu-t'ai-shan were inaccessible.[12] Of the Buddhist schools in the south, however, T'ien-t'ai and the older monastic schools were now moribund. Ch'an had survived persecution better, adapting itself to Chinese intellectual and social values to become the most vital school of Chinese monastic Buddhism. By the Northern Sung dynasty (960–1127), Ch'an had established its own history and traditions, compiled distinctive monastic codes, introduced new religious practices, and developed new monastic and architectural forms. Ch'an monasteries—some of them taken over from other Buddhist sects and including monks of very diverse doctrinal interests—were integrated into the Chinese local economy, acted as centers of culture and learning, and enjoyed the patronage of the Chinese gentry class.[13] In the Southern Sung and Yuan dynasties, a network of major Ch'an monasteries throughout the empire, headed by the Five Mountains (*wu-shan*) of Hangchow and Ming-chou, were eventually designated official monasteries—

or at least given the titles of *wu-shan*, *shih-ch'a* (Ten Temples) or *chia-ch'a* (Principal Temples)—and established close ties with the civil government bureaucracy.[14]

Japanese monk visitors to Sung China were not completely unfamiliar with Ch'an. T'ang dynasty Ch'an teachings and the meditation posture and breathing techniques used by Ch'an monks had formed one part of Japanese Tendai training in the sutras, esoteric practices, Vinaya precepts, and meditation. Moreover, in Sung Ch'an monasteries, basic T'ien-t'ai texts, especially the *Lotus Sutra*, were held in high regard, and some Ch'an masters accepted varying degrees of accommodation with scholastic and esoteric Buddhism.

In many other respects, however, Sung dynasty Ch'an displayed very novel features. The primary emphasis was on the regular communal meditation carried on in the monks' hall. The use of the *kōan* as an instructional device was widespread. This, in turn, emphasized the individual encounter between the monk and his master rather than the lectures, general debates, or sutra expositions which seem to have been more important in pre-Sung Ch'an.[15]

Ch'an had been challenged and deeply affected by the Neo-Confucian revival of the eleventh and twelfth centuries. Under attack from Confucian and Taoist critics, some Buddhist apologists had fallen back on the doctrine of the Unity of the Three Creeds. They argued that Confucianism, Taoism, and Ch'an Buddhism were simply three facets of a single truth, three different roads to the same end. The elaboration of this synthesis helped bring Ch'an into conformity with Chinese values. It also opened the way for the influx of Chinese secular culture into Ch'an monastic life and thought.[16] Much of this Sung culture and learning—whether in the Chinese classics, Neo-Confucian and Taoist thought, poetry, painting, calligraphy, or etiquette—was completely outside the experience of the Japanese monks. Even on the more material level, they found much that was new in the architecture, layout, furnishing, lifestyle, and regulation of Ch'an monasteries.

It must have been with feelings of great excitement, therefore,

FIGURE 3 The Monastery of T'ien-t'ung-shan

Taken from Supplement to the Gazeteer for T'ien-t'ung-shan *(1921 edition). Photograph supplied by permission of Komazawa University Library, Tokyo.*

This photograph shows a major Chinese Ch'an center much visited by Japanese Zen pioneers during the late Sung and Yuan dynasties. The walled monastery was set in a mountain valley. The central hall line of ceremonial buildings, including the Buddha hall and Dharma hall, was flanked by the meditation halls, dormitories, and other residential buildings. The complex containing the abbot's hall was to the north of the compound.

that the Japanese pilgrim-monks enrolled in the great Southern Sung monasteries and set themselves to pursue their quest for enlightenment under Chinese Ch'an masters. Even if T'ien-t'ai had lost its vigor, in Ch'an they found an impressive, vigorous, and viable substitute. With Ch'an meditation and discipline, they could indeed, they believed, revitalize Japanese Buddhism.[17]

EISAI AND THE KAMAKURA SHOGUNATE

Myōan Eisai (1141–1215) is revered as the founder of the Japanese Rinzai school. Eisai, however, performed this role almost by accident. He did not originally go to China in search of Zen, nor did he ever break finally with Tendai, the school in which he received his early training.[18] During a first short pilgrimage to China in the summer of 1168, Eisai, in company, it is generally believed, with the Japanese Shingon school monk Chōgen, visited such famous Buddhist sites as the stone bridge at T'ien-t'ai-shan and the Buddha reliquary at A-yü-wang-shan. Like Ennin before him, he also collected T'ien-t'ai texts and studied esoteric practices. Although he was aware of the dominance of Ch'an and his interest in that teaching was aroused—he put questions about Ch'an teachings to the guest-master of a Ming-chou Ch'an monastery—Eisai did not actively pursue the study of Ch'an under a Chinese master on his first visit. And after his return to Japan, for the next twenty years, it was esoteric Buddhism, not Zen, that Eisai practiced and taught.

In 1187, Eisai set out on a second voyage to China. His motive was not to study Ch'an but to make a pilgrimage through China to Buddhist sites in India. Only when his request for a travel permit was refused by the Chinese authorities did he make his way to Wannien-ssu on Mt. T'ien-t'ai, where he enrolled under the Ch'an master Hsu-an Huai-ch'ang. Eisai spent more than three years as a disciple of the elderly Chinese monk. When, in 1189, Hsu-an was appointed abbot at T'ien-t'ung-shan, Eisai accompanied him to his new post. Before Eisai returned to Japan in 1191, Hsu-an recognized the Japanese monk's enlightenment and gave him the seal of direct transmission, authorizing him to spread Ch'an teachings in

Japan. In spite of his long apprenticeship in Ch'an, Eisai did not relinquish his esoteric interests. He had found a compatible mentor in Hsu-an, who was interested in esoteric Buddhism and advocated the unity of Ch'an and esoteric teachings. Hsu-an also stressed the importance of the Vinaya and insisted that Eisai, before proceeding with his studies in Ch'an, should formally profess both the Mahayana *bodhisattva* precepts and the Hinayana precepts. Eisai's Ch'an practice, thus, did not involve any great wrench with his early Tendai training. He was able to learn something of the new doctrines and monastic practices of Sung Ch'an while deepening his understanding of esoteric Buddhism. The emphasis on discipline and the strict observance of the precepts in Sung Ch'an monasteries provided him with an invaluable means of reforming Japanese monastic practice. The threefold experience of Ch'an meditation, esoteric rites, and the Vinaya gained by Eisai during his second visit to China shaped his subsequent thinking and determined the character of the Zen he taught upon his return to Japan.

After his return to Japan in 1191, Eisai proceeded to build temples and introduce Zen teachings, ceremonies, and regulations, first in Kyūshū, then in Kyoto and Kamakura. However, attempts to spread the new Chinese Zen doctrines and meditation practices in the capital by Eisai and others quickly aroused the opposition of Enryakuji supporters who, in 1194, petitioned the imperial court to have the "Daruma school," as Zen was then known, proscribed. The court bowed under pressure and a temporary ban was placed on the propagation of Zen in Kyoto. Eisai attempted to defend himself and his teaching. He pleaded that Saichō (767–822), the founder of Japanese Tendai, had recognized Zen as a genuine teaching of the Buddha introduced by Bodhidharma from India to China and that Zen had since been accepted as an integral part of Tendai. For Enryakuji followers to reject Zen at this stage, Eisai argued, would be to deny the intentions of their founder and the traditions of their sect.

As part of his defense, Eisai also compiled the *Kōzen goko-kuron* (Promulgation of Zen as a defense of the nation). In this long apologia, Eisai argued, in a characteristic Tendai fashion, that it was to the advantage of the "Secular Law" to protect the "Religious Law," since Buddhist deities would, in return, protect the state and Buddhist monks serve as a spiritual leaven in society. He then asserted that the essence of Buddhism was to be found in Zen, and that the life of Zen was itself maintained in the regulations and precepts of the monastic life. Since Zen was the purest and most vital expression of Buddhism, it clearly merited the most active patronage of the secular authorities. Eisai's arguments won him some sympathy in court circles but did nothing to deflect the opposition of Enryakuji. In 1199, he decided to make his way to Kamakura, the center of warrior rule, where Enryakuji influence was less oppressive.

In his youth, prior to his entry to Enryakuji, Eisai had studied at the monastery of Onjōji or Miidera. Onjōji had close ties with the Minamoto family, and this connection may have helped Eisai to gain a favorable audience in Kamakura.[19] Hōjō Masako (1157–1225), the widow of Minamoto Yoritomo, founder of the Kamakura shogunate, appointed Eisai founder (*kaisan*) of the monastery of Jufukuji, the first Zen center in Kamakura. Minamoto Yoriie (1182–1204), the second shogun, later provided lands and funds for the building of Kenninji in Kyoto (completed 1205) and appointed Eisai founder. It was for Yoriie's ailing younger brother, Sanetomo (1192–1219), the third Minamoto shogun, that Eisai wrote his treatise on tea, the *Kissa yōjōki* (1214). With the backing of the shogunate, by making himself useful to the imperial court as a rebuilder of temples, and by adopting a deferential attitude towards the Buddhist establishment in the capital, Eisai was able to establish a small but active Zen community at Kenninji.

Eisai was not the only monk who attempted to introduce Sung Zen teaching to Kyoto in the last decades of the twelfth century, and the anti-Zen polemics of Tendai supporters were not aimed exclusively at him. Kakua, who was probably the first Japanese monk to go to China deliberately in search of Zen, introduced Rinzai Zen to Kyoto before Eisai.[20] According to the *Genkō shakusho*, Kakua, when invited by Emperor Takakura (1161–1181) to explain the tenets of the Chinese Zen schools, answered with a melody on the flute.[21] If this was the first expression of Sung Zen in Japanese court circles, it must have mystified the young monarch and disturbed his scholarly Buddhist advisors. Kakua, however, seems to have established no temples and trained few disciples.

The monk Dainichibō Nōnin was also active in Kyoto in the late twelfth century.[22] Nōnin never visited China. In his place he sent two disciples with a copy of a verse he had composed to demonstrate his enlightenment. They had this authenticated by a Chinese master. Thereafter, Nōnin devoted his energies to spreading his brand of Sung Zen, the teaching of the Daruma (Bodhidharma) school, in Japan. He was an uncompromising opponent of any accommodation between Zen and Japanese Tendai scholasticism. His defiance was an invitation to hostilities which Enryakuji supporters could not allow to go unchallenged.

Eisai seems to have been embarrassed by the aggressive purism of Kakua and Nōnin and sought to disassociate his Zen from their Daruma sectarianism. Eisai never finally rejected Tendai. He was syncretic in outlook. His aim was to reform and strengthen Japanese monastic Buddhism both by substituting the newer Sung Zen teachings for the T'ang Zen hitherto accepted within Tendai and by reemphasizing the importance of taking and keeping the Vinaya precepts. Moreover, in addition to his interest in Zen and the Vinaya, Eisai maintained a lifelong interest in esoteric Buddhism.[23] He taught esoteric rites as well as Zen to his followers and built halls of worship within Kenninji dedicated to the Shingon and Tendai patriarchs. It is sometimes suggested that Eisai's accommodation with established Buddhism was carefully contrived to allow him to practice Zen secretly. His writing and actions, however, suggest that his eclecticism derived from conviction rather than convenience. Even the practice of tea drinking, which he had probably learned in Ch'an monasteries in China, was advocated not as a stimulant during meditation but as an esoteric ritual conducive to the harmonious functioning of the bodily organs.[24]

The eclectic Zen espoused by Eisai was continued by his principal disciples, Gyōyū (d. 1241), Eichō (d. 1247), and their followers who were active in the Kantō region. Gyōyū, besides teaching Zen, opened a temple in the Shingon stronghold on Mt. Kōya. He also acted as the officient at the esoteric Buddhist temple attached to the Tsurugaoka Hachiman Shintō shrine in Kamakura and, like Eisai before him, held the office of intendant of the Tōdaiji in Nara. Eichō, likewise, combined esoteric Buddhism with Zen.[25] It was only in the third generation, with Daikatsu Ryōshin (fl. mid-thirteenth century), who studied Zen in China and converted Jufukuji into a pure Zen monastery, that esoteric and scholastic elements were filtered out and Eisai's line began to advocate Zen exclusively.

Although Eisai eventually established amicable relations with the imperial court in Kyoto and was granted honorary titles by ex-Emperor Go-Toba in return for his temple restoration activities, his principal patrons remained the warrior-rulers in Kamakura. Eisai's disciples were also patronized by the shogunate and by such leading Kantō warrior families as the Nitta, Shiba, Uesugi, and Ashikaga. To judge from the *Azuma kagami* and other contemporary sources, however, Eisai and his immediate disciples were not engaged by the shoguns and their retainers as teachers of Zen meditation or philosophy. Their principal function was to conduct invocations and prayers for the memory of the deceased or the intention of the living, and to make appropriate incantation in time of warfare, drought, or natural disaster. Their religious function, therefore, hardly differed from that of Tendai or Shingon priests who had previously performed these very same activities.[26] The shoguns and warriors who patronized Eisai and his disciples were neither very knowledgeable in, nor exclusively devoted to, Zen, nor did they make any great effort to distinguish it clearly from existing forms of Buddhism. They may have admired Eisai's practical character and been curious about the new knowledge he had gained in China, but they treated him and his followers as a local, more amenable branch of Tendai than the unruly, militant enclave at Enryakuji which was so closely linked to the imperial court and the Kyoto aristocracy.

ENNI AND KUJŌ MICHIIE

Like Eisai, Enni Ben'en (Shōichi Kokushi, 1202–1280) began his monastic training in the Miidera (Onjōji) branch of Tendai.[27] He then studied syncretic Zen with Eisai's followers Eichō, Gyōyū, and Daikatsu Ryōshin. In 1235, conscious that there was nothing more to be learned from Ryōshin, Enni made his way to China. His passage was paid for by a wealthy Chinese merchant from Hakata. After visiting a number of Ch'an monasteries in the Hang-chow region, Enni enrolled at Ching-shan, the foremost of the Five Mountains, under Ch'an master Wu-chun Shih-fan (1177–1249). Wu-chun was a central figure in the Yang-ch'i school which dominated Ch'an circles in the thirteenth century. By accident or design, Enni had thus introduced himself into the mainstream of Sung dynasty Ch'an Buddhism.

In nearly seven years spent in China, Enni gained a deep under-standing of contemporary Ch'an-related Chinese culture. Before his return to Japan in 1241, he was accepted as a direct disciple by Wu-chun. In addition to the many Buddhist and Neo-Confucian texts, monastic regulations, and medical manuals Enni carried back to Japan, he also took a portrait (*chinsō*) of Wu-chun and samples of his master's calligraphy. Enni and Wu-chun corre-sponded regularly until the latter's death. After Enni, a steady stream of Japanese monks made their way to Ching-shan to study under Wu-chun and his disciples. The Chinese master, for his part, took an active interest in the propagation of orthodox Sung Zen in Japan and played a decisive role in shaping its development.

Upon his return to Japan, Enni established, with the financial backing of the Chinese merchant who had helped him make the journey to China, a number of temples in Hakata. With these as his base, he sought to spread Zen in northern Kyūshū, but his activities stirred the resentment of local Tendai supporters who, in

FIGURE 4 Ch'an Master Wu-chun Shih-fan

*Portrait (chinsō) of Wu-
chun Shih-fan (1177–1249)*

*Hanging scroll, colors on
silk Dated 1238*

*Registered National Trea-
sure, Tōfukuji, Kyoto*

*As the abbot of Ching-
shan, Wu-chun was instru-
mental in training many of
the monks, including Enni
Ben'en, Lan-ch'i Tao-lung,
and Wu-hsueh Tsu-yuan,
who brought Sung-style
Rinzai Zen teachings and
practices to Japan.*

*Photograph courtesy of
Shōgakkan Publishing Com-
pany, Tokyo*

1243, petitioned the court to have the new Zen temples closed down. This move was blocked at court, possibly because Enni had by this time come to the attention of a very powerful figure in contemporary Kyoto court (*kuge*) society, the regent Kujō Michiie (1193–1252).

Michiie had already conceived the ambition of building in Kyoto a temple to rival the great Nara monasteries of Tōdaiji and Kōfukuji. The new monastery was to be known as Tōfukuji. Work began in 1235. Built at the very considerable cost of 138,500 *kanmon,* Tōfukuji took more than ten years to complete and remained for centuries one of the most impressive monastic compounds in Kyoto. Although Michiie was not averse to the incorporation of the latest continental Ch'an monastic elements, there is nothing to suggest that he deliberately set out to build Tōfukuji as a pure Sung-style Ch'an monastery. What he seems to have had in mind as an expression of his devotion and as a symbol of Buddhist guardianship of and association with the Japanese state and its capital was a grandiose complex, incorporating the very latest and finest of the Indian, Chinese, and Japanese Buddhist traditions. Thus, although the original Tōfukuji had a Sung-style Ch'an ground plan and such characteristic Zen buildings as a Dharma hall and monks' hall, like Kenninji it also included halls for Shingon and Tendai observances.[28]

In Enni, who had been trained in the Indian metaphysical niceties of the Nara Buddhist schools as well as the esoteric and scholastic doctrines of Japanese Tendai and who was accepted as a full-fledged member of the leading school of contemporary Chinese Buddhism, Kujō Michiie had found an ideal religious advisor and founder-abbot for Tōfukuji. Enni's religious posture was eclectic. He accepted the Unity of the Three Creeds synthesis and lectured frequently on such texts as the *Dainichikyō,* one of the three principal esoteric sutras of the Japanese Tantric schools, and on the syncretic *Tsung-ching-lu (Sugyōroku)* and *Fo-fa ta-ming-lu (Buppō daimeiroku),* texts he had brought back from China, both of which argued the basic identity of Zen thought with scholastic and esoteric Buddhist teaching.[29] Enni was also deferred to on doctrinal matters by leading prelates of other

FIGURE 5 The Monastery of Tōfukuji

Painting attributed to Sesshū Tōyō (1420–1506)
Description above by the Zen monk Ryōan Keigo, dated 1505
Hanging scroll, ink on paper
Registered Important Cultural Property, Tōfukuji, Kyoto
Photograph courtesy of Shūeisha Publishing Company, Tokyo

Buddhist sects. Many of the monks who enrolled in the monks' hall of Tōfukuji had a Tendai or Shingon background and combined their textual or esoteric studies with the practice of Zen. Thus, the Shōichi school, centering on Tōfukuji and its many subtemples, preserved a strong eclectic bent throughout the middle ages.

In spite of his eclecticism, however, there is no doubt that Enni thought of Tōfukuji as a Zen monastery and of himself as a Zen monk who had inherited, and would establish in Japan, the Ch'an teachings of Wu-chun Shih-fan: "With the practice of seated meditation (*zazen*) as the core . . . [we] should be faithful to the teachings of the Master of Ching-shan."[30] In his *Jūshū yōdōki* (Essentials of the Way of the ten sects), Enni adds to the eight traditional Japanese Buddhist sects two new ones—Pure Land and Zen. Although he outlines the essentials of all ten sects, his exposition of Zen takes up one third of the whole and is clearly the centerpiece of the work.[31] Moreover, although Tendai and Shingon buildings were in regular use at Tōfukuji for the first half-century of its history, and Enni himself taught esoteric rites and practices to his disciples, the monastery was organized as a Zen monastery under Zen regulations, with Zen ceremonial, Zen bureaucratic structure, and the four daily sessions of *zazen* mandatory in Sung Ch'an monasteries.

Whereas Eisai had hardly been more than a tolerated intruder in Kyoto, and Nōnin and Dōgen were both forced to withdraw from the city, Enni, from the first, was welcomed into the Buddhist elite in the capital. This easy acceptance was due in part to his formidable learning, to his long experience in China and direct association with the major school of contemporary Chinese Buddhism, and to his tolerant attitude towards other Japanese sects. The most important reason for Enni's success, however, was his good fortune in finding a secular patron who exercised unrivaled influence, not only with the Kyoto court and aristocracy, but also over the Buddhist establishments in Kyoto and Nara. Among Kujō Michiie's progeny were abbots of such powerful non-Zen monasteries as Enryakuji, Onjōji, Tōji, Ninnaji, Shōgo'in, Tōdaiji, and Kōfukuji.[32] With Michiie's patronage, Enni was thus guaranteed

FIGURE 6 Gozan Woodblock Printed Book

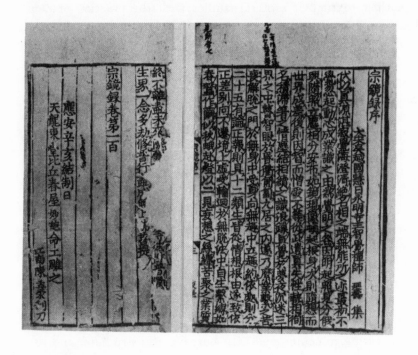

Preface and conclusion to the Sugyōroku.
Printed on the orders of Shun'oku Myōha of Tenryūji in 1371.
The name of the Chinese block carver, Ch'en Meng-jung, is given in the extreme left column.
Photograph courtesy of Heibonsha Publishing Company, Tokyo, taken from Sho no Nihonshi, *3, 276.*

Many of the larger gozan monasteries in the late Kamakura and Muromachi periods produced woodblock printed books. These included writings of Zen masters, sutras, and collections of poetry and essays. The syncretic Sugyōroku was a popular text in gozan circles and would have been frequently reprinted. In this edition, the Chinese text is "marked" to allow it to be read as Japanese.

entrance to the most exclusive Buddhist circles in the capital. Michiie himself, his son Nijō Yoshizane (1216–1270), and other Fujiwara noblemen studied Zen and took the Zen Buddhist precepts under Enni. He was also called upon to lecture on Zen and such texts as the *Sugyōroku* before the Emperors and ex-Emperors Go-Saga, Go-Fukakusa, and Kameyama. An imperial prince, one of the sons of Go-Saga, eventually entered Tōfukuji to train as a Zen monk. This monk, Kōhō Kennichi (Bukkoku Zenji, 1241–1316), studied under the Chinese masters Wu-an P'u-ning and Wu-hsueh Tsu-yuan, founded the Unganji at Nasu, was patronized by Hōjō Sadatoki and Takatoki, acted as abbot of most of the major Kamakura monasteries, and had as his leading disciple the influential prelate Musō Soseki.[33]

In his dealings with the *kuge* and the imperial court, Enni did his best to instill a correct understanding of Zen. He saw no inconsistency, however, in also elucidating, as pointers to Zen, forms of Buddhism more familiar to his audience. In response to imperial requests, he also employed his knowledge of Chinese monastic architecture in the restoration and rebuilding of the temples of other Buddhist schools and, like Eisai, was appointed to honorary office in non-Zen temples in recognition of these services.

In keeping with its eclectic tone, the Shōichi school maintained close ties with the court and Kyoto aristocracy throughout the middle ages. Enni's disciple Mukan Gengo, or Fumon (1212–1291), was invited by retired Emperor Kameyama to convert a former imperial palace into a Zen monastery. Named Nanzenji, this monastery became one of the most eminent Zen foundations in Japan and was set at the apex of the *gozan* hierarchy of official monasteries.

Although Enni was well known to the Kamakura warrior-rulers and made three visits to Kamakura to serve as abbot of Jufukuji and mentor to Hōjō Tokiyori, the roots of his school and of its patronage remained in Kyoto, close to the court. The Shōichi lineage flourished as one of the two most numerous and powerful of the *gozan* schools. Mujū Ichien (1226–1312), the compiler of the collection of Buddhist moral tales, the *Shasekishū*, was a disciple of Enni's, and Tōfukuji monks like the painter Kichizan Minchō (1352–1421) contributed much to the *gozan* cultural movement. Its intimacy with Kyoto *kuge* society, however, tended to hold it at a distance from the Ashikaga shoguns, the principal patrons of the *gozan*. They preferred to lavish their attentions on Musō Soseki and his disciples.

SHINCHI AND THE IDEAL OF THE RECLUSE

Another significant figure in the early, eclectic phase of Zen development in Japan was the monk Muhon or Shinchi Kakushin (Hottō Kokushi, 1207–1298).[34] After early training in Shingon tantrism on Mt. Kōya, he studied Zen under Eichō, Gyōyū, Dōgen, and Enni. In 1249, with Enni's encouragement, and financial support from the monk Ganshō of Kōyasan, Shinchi made his way to China in the hope of deepening his understanding of Zen under Wu-chun Shih-fan. Unfortunately, Wu-chun died before Shinchi reached Ching-shan. The Japanese monk eventually enrolled under Wu-men Hui-k'ai (Mumon Ekai), the compiler of the classic collection of *kōan* known in Japanese as the *Mumonkan*.

Shinchi returned to Japan in 1254 after five years' study in China. Like many monks and laymen of the day, he was strongly drawn to the life of the recluse. Instead of engaging in active proselytism in Kyoto or Kamakura, he sought obscurity in the mountains of Kii province where, under the patronage of the warrior Katsurayama Kagetomo, the military steward (*jitō*) of the Yura domain (Yura-no-*shō*), he founded the small temple of Kōkokuji. In spite of his hunger for obscurity, Shinchi's name became known at court, perhaps noised abroad by Enni. On several occasions, Shinchi was summoned to Kyoto to instruct the ex-Emperors Kameyama and Go-Fukakusa and Emperor Go-Uda. Each time, however, he found some pretext to return quickly to Kōkokuji. On one of these visits, he was urged to accept the first abbacy of the monastery that was to become Nanzenji but declined the honor and fled Kyoto.

Shinchi's writings suggest that, throughout his life, he never rejected his early esoteric interests and devotion to such Shingon-related deities as Fudō Myōō, Aizen Myōō, and the Thousand-Armed Kannon. Regulations he compiled for the daily monastic life of monks were based on Chinese Ch'an codes and stress such things as the four daily sessions of *zazen*, but they also allowed for the conduct of traditional Shingon observances. As with Eisai and Enni, however, there is no doubt that the primary component in Shinchi's eclecticism was Zen. His *Hottō kokushi zazengi* (Principles of meditation) echoes Dōgen's writings in its stress on the primacy of *zazen* as the most effective form of religious practice. Shinchi helped popularize the use of *kōan*, especially those in the *Mumonkan* collection, in Japanese Zen circles. His school, however, did not spread widely. This was partly due to his obvious disinclination to proselytize actively in the capital. It is also partly attributable to the fact that his followers were loyal to the Southern court and therefore failed to find favor with the Ashikaga shoguns and their warrior retainers.

DŌGEN AND HIS PATRONS

Dōgen, under whom Shinchi had studied briefly, was also something of a recluse, who rejected Kyoto and Kamakura in favor of the mountains of Echizen.[35] In Dōgen's case, however, there is some question as to whether he followed this course by natural inclination, as Shinchi obviously did, or by pressure of circumstances which made it impossible for him to spread his teaching or establish a community in proximity to the strongholds of the established sects.

Dōgen was a determined opponent of syncretism. In the *Bendōwa* (Distinguishing the Way), for instance, he says:

> When I was in China I asked the masters there for their true principle. They answered that they had never heard of any of the patriarchs, who have transmitted rightly the Buddha-seal from the past through the present in India and China, engaging in such combined practice. Indeed, unless you concentrate on one practice you cannot attain the one wisdom.[36]

Dōgen's anti-syncretic posture was assumed after his return from a five-year pilgrimage to China (1223–1227), during which he attained his enlightenment under the Ch'an master T'ien-t'ung Ju-ching (Tendō Nyojō, 1163–1228), a Ts'ao-tung (Sōtō) master renowned for the purity and severity of his Zen practice. Dōgen's confidence that the practice of silent sitting (*shikan taza*) he had inherited from Ju-ching was the authentic Buddhist Dharma was strengthened by the hostile reception he received after his return to Japan.

Dōgen was rare among Japanese Zen monks in daring to question the standards of monastic life he found in Chinese monasteries. Although he had great respect for individual masters and monks, he was critical of contemporary Chinese Rinzai monastic practice, especially that of the powerful Ta-hui school of Lin-chi (Rinzai) Zen, as lax, formalized, and secularized. His censure derived both from personal observation and from Ju-ching, who was himself extremely critical of abuses in contemporary Ch'an and argued in favor of a return to a simpler, less ceremonial, monastic life rooted in meditation:[37]

> Commitment to Zen is casting off body and mind. You have no need for incense offerings, homage praying, *nenbutsu*, penance disciplines, or silent sutra readings; just sit single-mindedly.[38]

Dōgen's first assertion of the unique importance of *zazen* as the "right entrance to the Dharma" and rejection of Zen-Tendai syncretism was contained in a tract on meditation, the *Fukan zazengi* (Principles for the universal promotion of *zazen*), written immediately upon his return from China in 1227:

> Although the Buddha was endowed with great wisdom, he sat in meditation (*zazen*) for six years. Bodhidharma transmitted to us the legacy of the Buddha-mind, but he too sat facing a wall for nine years. Such were the ancient sages. Why cannot our practice be like theirs? Do not, therefore, study words and letters [of the sutras] intellectually but rather reflect upon your self-nature inwardly. Thus, your body and mind will be cast off naturally and your original nature (*honrai no menboku*) will be revealed. If you wish to realize this, be diligent in *zazen*.[39]

From Dōgen's point of view, this was a declaration of independence. It was taken as a declaration of war by Enryakuji supporters, who demanded his expulsion from the city. The monks of Kenninji, where Dōgen was staying, were embarrassed. Eisai was dead, and Zen practice there, if Dōgen can be believed, had grown lax. Kenninji was, moreover, nominally a branch temple of Enryakuji and subject to pressure. Dōgen must have been something of a thorn in the flesh for Zen syncretists as well as Tendai supporters. He was forced to leave Kenninji and moved to Fukakusa, to the south of city, where he established the monastery of Kōshōji, began to build up a community under orthodox Chinese monastic regulations, and started to produce the writings that were eventually to comprise his masterwork, the *Shōbō genzō* (An eye-treasury of the true Dharma).

At Kōshōji, Dōgen was patronized by the nobleman Kujō Noriie, a distant cousin, and by the aristocratic nun Shōgaku, who may also have been a relative of Dōgen's. Although religious conviction doubtless inspired his patrons, Dōgen clearly benefited from family connections. With the backing of these two well-placed patrons, he was able to remain undisturbed at Kōshōji for ten years and to build the basic constituents of a Sung-style Zen monastery.

Dōgen suddenly quit Kōshōji in 1243 and with his followers moved to a remote mountainous part of Echizen in northern Japan. A number of interrelated factors had made life so close to Kyoto increasingly difficult. As the Kōshōji community grew and "poached" monks from Tendai and other sects, it came under heavier ideological attack from the Buddhist establishment in the capital. In an attempt to justify his teaching and defend his community, Dōgen, like Eisai before him, presented to Emperor Go-Saga (1220–1272) a tract entitled *Gokoku shōbōgi* (Principles of the true Buddhist law in defense of the country),[40] in which he argued that, far from being a threat, his teachings were positively beneficial to the nation. Dōgen may have been emboldened to make such a direct appeal because of a change in the political balance at court. With the accession of Go-Saga, the grip of

Kujō Michiie and his branch of the Fujiwara on the imperial office was broken. Koga Michimune, Go-Saga's maternal uncle and
political advisor, was Dōgen's brother.

The appeal did not go unchallenged. Enryakuji quickly marshal-
ed arguments and supporters and sent in its own counter-plea. In
response to pressure from Enryakuji and other powerful Kyoto
and Nara monasteries, the court was forced to put the dispute
before a committee of eminent clerics. The judgment went against
Dōgen. He was sharply rebuked. His teaching on the unique efficacy of *zazen* was described as a dangerously personal interpretation of Buddhism. Continued teaching, it was claimed, would not
only undermine the basic foundations of Mahayana Buddhism in
Japan but threaten the security of the state. This judgment was
naturally a severe setback for Dōgen and lent authority to his
critics. This repudiation was, in all probability, the primary reason
for the move. Dōgen's decision may also have been influenced by
the building of Tōfukuji not far from Kōshōji. Although Dōgen
did not directly criticize Enni's interpretation of Zen, he was critical of the syncretic doctrine of the Unity of the Three Creeds
(*sankyō itchi*) prevalent in Rinzai circles:

> Of late, shallow-minded monks in the land of Sung . . . study the doc-
> trines of Lao-tzu and Chuang-tzu, arguing that these are the same as the
> Way of the Buddhas and patriarchs. Some stress the unity of Confu-
> cianism, Taoism, and Buddhism. They argue that the three are like the
> legs of a tripod vessel which cannot stand upright if it lacks even one
> leg. The folly of such views is beyond belief.[41]

It is also unlikely that Dōgen looked very favorably either on
Tōfukuji's lavish patronage by the Kujō or its friendly relations
with Enryakuji. Such feelings of distaste may also have contributed to his abrupt departure.

Dōgen's opposition to Enryakuji and its version of Tendai
esotericism (*taimitsu*) was now absolute. That his differences with
the Kyoto Tendai establishment were as much personal as religious, however, is suggested both by his lifelong devotion to the
Lotus Sutra, the principal text of Tendai Buddhism, and by his

cordiality towards the other great stream of Japanese Tendai, the Onjōji (Miidera) line. Although Dōgen stressed the undivided practice of *shikan taza*, he retained great personal devotion to the *Lotus Sutra*, lecturing on it frequently and describing it as the "King of Sutras." Moreover, his relations with Onjōji, especially its branch at Hakusan in Echizen, were always friendly. For centuries there had been bad blood between the Miidera and Hieizan branches of Tendai. Their longstanding differences were also reflected in their different attitudes to the new Sung Zen teachings. Enryakuji remained intransigently hostile. Miidera was more receptive. Some monks of the Hakusan Miidera school had studied with Dōgen at Kōshōji and may have encouraged him to move to Echizen. When he did move, he made use of Hakusan Tendai monasteries until his own new monastery was built. By secluding himself in Echizen, Dōgen knowingly cut himself off from court and *bakufu* patronage of the kind extended to Eisai and Enni. The move to Echizen also marked a shift in Dōgen's thought from emphasis on the possibility of easy enlightenment for all, including women, as espoused in the *Fukan zazengi*, to emphasis on the exclusive monastic life and rule as the proper environment for the realization of the *bodhisattva* ideal and for the true transmission of the Dharma:

> Wherever the Dharma of the Buddhas and Patriarchs is transmitted . . . there is always the rite of receiving the precepts as the means of initiation into the Dharma. Without receiving the precepts you are not yet true disciples of the Buddhas and Patriarchs.[42]

Dōgen's principal patron in Echizen was the warrior Hatano Yoshishige, a retainer of the Kamakura *bakufu*, member of the *bakufu* representative council in Rokuhara, Kyoto, and military steward (*jitō*) of the Shihi domain, of which the proprietor (*ryōshu*) was the Kyoto Miidera line temple of Saishōkō'in. Dōgen had known Hatano for many years. The warrior had close ties both with Kenninji and with Hakusan Tendai circles. While at Kenninji, Dōgen had lectured to Hatano on Buddhism. One further factor in his choice of Echizen was this bond of personal

friendship. Hatano urged Dōgen to come, and began the construction of a new temple. As the *jitō* of only one of more than twenty
shōen in Echizen, Hatano's means were not extensive. This limited
the assistance he could provide in the way of buildings and sustenance for the new community. He did, however, bring Dōgen
to the attention of his warrior overlord, Hōjō Tokiyori, who, in
1247, summoned Dōgen to Kamakura, discussed Zen with him,
and offered him the abbacy of a new monastery he was building.
Dōgen declined the offer and returned to Echizen. He was prompted, no doubt, by a longing for his own community and the feeling
that, with the exception of Tokiyori, Kamakura warrior society
was too addicted to the teachings of the devotional sects or to
the eclectic Zen of the Eisai line to offer much immediate hope
for the effective diffusion of the unadulterated meditative Zen of
shikan taza.

At Dōgen's death, the community he had established in Echizen
was still fairly small. Those who came to join him in the mountains and could endure the severe discipline and bitter winters
were welcome to stay. He showed great concern for the training of
his community but made no great efforts to proselytize. This
attitude was preserved by his immediate successors. From the
third generation, however, the community was divided over the
question of whether to spread the doctrine actively or to continue
the austere practice instituted by Dōgen. The proselytizers gained
ground under the leadership of Keizan Jōkin (1268–1325) and
Gazan Jōseki (1275–1365) in the fourth and fifth generations, and
Sōtō Zen began to spread rapidly along the Japan Sea coast and
into Kyūshū.[43] This expansion was achieved, however, at the expense of many of Dōgen's ideals. Making Zen acceptable to
provincial warriors and peasants inescapably involved the adultura-
tion of *zazen* and strict monastic practice with prayer meetings,
esoteric rites, and simplified Buddhist funeral services. Although
this movement can be described as a genuine "development" of
Zen at the popular level, the resulting religious synthesis was far
from the strictness of Dōgen's original teaching. It was not until
the Zen revival of the seventeenth and eighteenth centuries that,

under the stimulus of the newly introduced Ōbaku sect, the Sōtō school made a determined effort to recapture the spirit of the monastic Zen taught by the founder.

To take stock of the Japanese religious scene in the year of Dōgen's death, 1253, some half-century after Eisai's second visit to China, it is apparent that Sung Zen had, as yet, made only a very limited impression on Japanese society, principally in the areas of Hakata, Kyoto, and Kamakura. Dōgen had asserted his independent determination to introduce unadulterated Chinese Zen practice in the spirit of Pai-chang and Ju-ching. He had attracted to his community monks from other sects and come to the attention of Hōjō Yasutoki and Hōjō Tokiyori and members of the imperial court as an original thinker and admirable personality, but his community in Echizen remained small and isolated. The Rinzai Zen transmission made by Kakua and Dainichibō Nōnin did not long survive their deaths. Eisai, Enni, and Shinchi Kakushin, the principal Rinzai pioneers, had established monasteries, attracted devoted followers, and founded schools. They taught and practiced Sung Zen, but their Zen was, in varying degrees, diluted by traditional Japanese religious elements. At this juncture, therefore, it was still unclear whether Rinzai Zen would shake itself free of the established Japanese religious framework to establish an independent sectarian identity or whether it would be slowly reabsorbed by Shingon and Tendai. Although some young Japanese monks were studying in Sung monasteries with disciples of Wu-chun and deepening the Japanese understanding of Zen, their influence would not be felt for some years.

Members of the established Buddhist schools, Enryakuji monks in particular, conscious of the dominant place of Ch'an in the contemporary Chinese religious world, had organized determined opposition to proponents of the new Sung doctrines and monastic practices. Wherever possible, they had driven Zen monks from Kyoto. When this was impossible, they did their best to ensure that Zen was safely neutralized. From their point of view, in the year 1253, there was room for complacency. Certainly there was little indication that, within the next half-century, Zen would have broken these restraints and be on its way to becoming a powerful, independent, rival school.

Although the Japanese Rinzai pioneers numbered among their patrons shoguns and their retainers, as well as emperors and courtiers, much of the interest shown by these patrons in the first decades was cursory and implied no deep religious commitment to Zen. Hōjō Masako, Minamoto Yoriie, Minamoto Sanetomo, Kujō Michiie, and Emperors Takakura, Go-Saga, and Kameyama displayed no more than a passive interest in Zen practice. Hōjō Tokiyori was one of the first influential laymen to take a genuine active interest in Zen as a meditative spiritual experience. He was, however, an exception in his day, and his devotion to Zen was by no means exclusive. In the case of Sōtō Zen, Hatano Yoshishige was one of very few loyal and devout warrior patrons of Dōgen. At lower levels of warrior society, the new religious current from China had certainly not swept the mass of Japanese warriors off their feet or carried them away from their traditional religious allegiances.

Metropolitan Zen might have remained indefinitely in this tentative eclectic state but for the fortuitous coincidence of the development of a positive interest in Zen by the Hōjō regents and the willingness of a number of eminent Chinese Ch'an monks, uprooted in the Mongol conquest of China, to come to Japan and inculcate Sung Zen as it was practiced in continental monasteries. The first ripples of this second vital surge were already evident a few years before Dōgen's death.

TWO

Chinese Émigré Monks and Japanese Warrior-Rulers

Zen was established as an independent school of Buddhism in Japan during the second half of the thirteenth century and early years of the fourteenth under the patronage of the leaders of the Hōjō warrior band who, as regents (*shikken*) to the shogun, were the de facto rulers of Japan. The Hōjō invited Chinese Zen masters to Kamakura, built and endowed Zen monasteries, enforced regulations for monastic behavior, and initiated the *gozan* system of officially patronized Zen monasteries. They also encouraged their leading vassals to patronize Zen monks and stimulated some members of the imperial family to take a greater interest in Zen.

HŌJŌ PATRONAGE

The pattern of Hōjō patronage was set by Tokiyori (1227–1263), the fifth regent, an astute and energetic warrior-ruler. Immediately upon gaining office in 1246, Tokiyori isolated and crushed the Miura, his principal rivals, thus helping to guarantee for the Hōjō a position of unchallenged supremacy within the *bakufu*. He then continued to work tirelessly to tighten the Hōjō grip on power and to strengthen the control of the *bakufu* over its retainers and the country at large.[1]

Prior to Tokiyori, neither the Minamoto shoguns nor the Hōjō regents had displayed any profound interest in Zen. Minamoto

Yoritomo (1147–1199), the founder of the Kamakura *bakufu*, had a deep personal devotion to the *Lotus Sutra* and patronized Tendai, Shingon, and the temples of other Buddhist schools as well as the Tsurugaoka Hachiman Shintō shrine in Kamakura.[2] His widow, Masako, and immediate Minamoto successors, the shoguns Yoriie and Sanetomo, patronized Eisai and his followers, but as esotericists rather than as Zen monks.[3] Early members of the Hōjō line, including Yoshitoki (1163–1224) and Yasutoki (1183–1242), showed a similar ceremonial interest in esotericized Zen, coupled with a deathbed attraction for the promise of the Pure Land.[4]

Tokiyori was the first member of the Hōjō family, and one of the first Japanese laymen, to explore fully the religious and philosophical assumptions of Zen, to devote himself seriously to the practice of Zen meditation (*zazen*) and confrontation with a Zen master (*mondō*), and to finance the building of monasteries in which Sung Zen monastic discipline and practice were enforced. Tokiyori was a generous patron of Shintō shrines and Buddhist temples. That his commitment to Zen was not merely the result of ephemeral curiosity, however, but derived from a sincere desire for Buddhist enlightenment is evident in the steady progression from his early interest in the syncretic Tendai-Zen of Eisai and his school, through the "purer" Zen of Enni, to the undiluted Sung Zen of Dōgen and émigré Chinese masters.[5] Of Tokiyori's successors in the office of *shikken*, Tokimune (1251–1284), Sadatoki (1271–1311), and Takatoki (1303–1333) extended his interest.

Tokiyori's devotion to Zen was primarily personal and spiritual. His successors, however, soon detected qualities other than the strictly religious which added to their enthusiasm for the new sect with its intrinsically alien character and difficult teachings. They drew on Zen not only as a source of spiritual enlightenment but also as a medium of intellectual and cultural improvement. Zen monks also provided valuable information about political conditions in China.

In spite of considerable construction work by Hōjō Yasutoki, Kamakura in the late thirteenth century was still very much a provincial garrison town. Although it was the center of *bakufu* authority, the town lacked the cultural refinement and intellectual traditions of Kyoto, the imperial capital.[6] As effective rulers of the country, the Hōjō were well aware of their real power but also increasingly conscious of a need for cultural credentials appropriate to themselves as warriors, which would rival, or even surpass, those of the Kyoto nobility and add luster to Kamakura. Zen provided these credentials.

The established Buddhist monastic schools had their roots in Nara or Kyoto and were dominated by prelates who were themselves aristocrats or princes of the imperial blood. Warriors were invited to patronize these great monasteries but could hardly escape feelings of cultural inferiority in dealing with their aristocratic abbots. Moreover, the more powerful of the older monasteries, like Enryakuji or Kōfukuji, with their bands of warrior-monks (*sōhei*), were rival and still potentially dangerous military powers. The newer devotional sects, deriving from Hōnen, Shinran, Nichiren, and Ippen, included many lower-ranking and some high-ranking *bushi* among their devotees, but patronage of the ragged mendicants who wandered the country chanting the *nenbutsu* conferred no cultural prestige on the Hōjō. Moreover, these popular religious movements were, from the point of view of the *bakufu*, a continual menace to the public order.[7] Shintō, too, had a strong emotional appeal to warriors—Hachiman, the Shintō deity worshipped at the Tsurugaoka shrine in Kamakura and at many smaller shrines was revered as the spiritual protector of the Minamoto warriors—but its blend of animistic beliefs and fragments of Buddhist cosmology hardly constituted a coherent intellectual or cultural system; nor was Shintō the exclusive spiritual preserve of the warrior.[8] Existing forms of devotion were capable of satisfying the basic religious needs of most warriors, but it became clear with time that Zen offered a more appropriate religious experience, with the added advantage, to the warrior-rulers, of access to the cultural and intellectual achievements of Sung China and the Chinese gentry and aristocracy. Patronage of Zen, moreover, raised few of the political problems

FIGURE 7 Hōjō Tokiyori in the Robes of a Zen Abbot

The fifth Hōjō Regent, Tokiyori (1227–1263), was an active and able administrator who did much to consolidate Hōjō control over the Kamakura bakufu. He became a devoted student and patron of Zen, sponsored the building of Kenchōji in Kamakura, and had his enlightenment recognized by the Chinese Ch'an master Wu-an P'u-ning.

Photograph courtesy of Kenchōji, Kamakura.

posed by association with the established Japanese Buddhist sects.

The Zen stress on active meditation, man-to-man debate, physical self-discipline, and practical, rather than bookish, experience, appealed naturally to the warrior spirit.[9] But the Chinese monks who came to teach Zen in the new Zen monasteries in Kamakura brought not only the primary message of Zen—the impermanence of life and death and the possibility of individual enlightenment through meditation—they also introduced the cultural and intellectual values of the Chinese gentry and scholar-officials with whom many of them had consorted. Japanese *gozan* Zen monasteries rapidly became centers for the study of the Chinese classics, poetry, painting, and thought, in addition to Buddhist and Zen texts. This cultural influx was completely new to Japan and as exciting to the aristocrats in the Kyoto court as it was to warriors in Kamakura. Furthermore, as a predominantly monastic form of Buddhism, Zen was socially stable, politically non-volatile, and as amenable to secular supervision and control in Japan as it had been in China. Finally, as a new arrival on the Japanese religious scene, the Zen sect, unlike Enryakuji and other branches of the Buddhist establishment, was neither a power unto itself nor yet the pawn of any rival power in Japanese society.

These cultural, intellectual, and political factors, though they may not have been consciously defined at the time, must be taken into account in explaining the growing attraction of Sung Zen to the warrior leadership in Kamakura, to their powerful retainers, and to some members of the imperial court in Kyoto. The same cultural and intellectual accretions made the new doctrine difficult of access to less-educated, lower-ranking *bushi*, most of whom continued to find a less demanding, but equally satisfying, religious experience in the simpler teachings of Shinran, Nichiren, or Ippen. Sōtō Zen did spread fairly widely among rural warriors, but only after its dilution with Shingon and other indigenous Buddhist elements. It should perhaps be noted, too, that, although the Hōjō became devoted adherents of Zen, they were compelled for political reasons to continue to patronize other Buddhist and Shintō foundations. During the Mongol invasions, the *bakufu* enlisted the spiritual energies of all temples and shrines in Japan in a campaign of prayer for national deliverance. As a result, until well into the fourteenth century, the *bakufu* had to respond to claims from temples and shrines for national recompense for services rendered in calling forth the "divine winds" (*kamikaze*), alleged to have been the chief cause of Mongol defeat.[10]

In spite of its natural resonances with the requirements of the Japanese warrior-leadership, it is unlikely that Sung Zen would have taken roots as strongly in Japan as it did had it not been for an unstable political situation in China which sent to Japan experienced Ch'an monks who would otherwise have lived out their lives in Chinese monasteries. Individual Chinese monks and scholars, like the monk Ganjin in the mid-eighth century, had occasionally found their way to Japan. The arrival of a score of Chinese Zen monks around the time of the Mongol invasions was unprecedented and of major significance in the history of Sino-Japanese cultural relations. During the thirteenth century, the Southern Sung empire came under increasingly heavy pressure from Mongol invaders, who first conquered northern China and then worked to outflank the empire from the west. The closing years of Tokiyori's lifetime coincided with the final decisive onslaughts of Khubilai (1225–1294), which brought the collapse of the Sung empire and Mongol rule over the whole of China in 1275–1279. The Mongols also turned their attention to Japan, and Hōjō Tokimune was obliged to organize warrior resistance to repel large-scale invasion attempts in 1274 and 1281.

In China, the repercussions of Mongol pressure and conquest were felt as strongly in Buddhist monasteries as in other areas of society. The Buddhist monastic institution was too closely enmeshed in Chinese local society and too well regulated by the Chinese state bureaucracy to remain unaffected while the Sung government struggled to organize the defense of the empire against the inroads of nomads. During the invasions, monastic economies were disrupted, monastic life disturbed, and the spiritual energies of monks directed away from meditation into prayers and ceremonies for the safety of the nation. Monasteries had no physical means of resisting the new regime, however, and, once the Mongols had seized control, the leaders of the Ch'an and other Buddhist schools were forced to acquiesce in the change or risk a decimation of monks and a destruction of monastic property.[11] Acquiescing, they survived. Confronted with the problem of ruling a country as vast and politically complex as China, the Mongol answer was to enlist the aid of non-Chinese, mainly Central Asian, collaborators and to rule through established organs of government. Although this was to prove a shallowly rooted system, it did allow a small ruling elite to impose its authority rapidly over an empire without losing its own identity in the process.

The principal losers were the Confucian scholars who had manned the Chinese civil bureaucracy. With the examination system in abeyance and the top posts in government held by aliens, most Chinese scholars found themselves restricted to the roles of minor functionaries at lower levels of the bureaucracy. As partial compensation for the political exclusion of Confucianists, and in the hope of blunting the edge of Chinese bitterness and contempt, the Mongols sponsored the state cult of Confucianism. They had, however, little interest in the orderly rationalism of Confucian teaching. Confucian ceremonial lent dignity to the new court, but Khubilai and his successors found their emotional satisfaction in the mysteries of Shamanism and Lamaism.[12]

Far from being a scourge of Chinese Buddhism, the Mongols became its enthusiastic patrons. Buddhist and Taoist, as well as Confucian, Nestorian, and Islamic temples were exempted from taxation. Derelict buildings were restored and new temples established.[13] Under such generous patronage, Buddhist cloisters filled as they had not been filled for centuries. Ch'an shared in the material well-being. By the late thirteenth century, after a brief hiatus during the Mongol invasions, large numbers of Japanese monks were again making their way to China to enroll in the monks' halls of the great Ch'an monasteries. Although the transition was relatively painless, it was not achieved entirely without cost. To judge from the tone of the *Ch'ih-hsiu Pai-chang Code* (1336), Ch'an monasteries in the Yuan dynasty were very much more subservient to the state than even Southern Sung monasteries had been. This code gives greater prominence than any earlier Ch'an code to monastic ceremonies for state occasions and imperial intentions. Chapters stressing loyalty and reverence to the imperial court and service to the state are not found in the earlier *Ch'an-yuan ch'ing-kuei,* which opens with a chapter stressing the importance of precepts and the proper practice of the monastic life.[14]

In spite of widespread Chinese detestation of the Mongols as rank-smelling, uncouth barbarians, some leaders of the Buddhist community in China, who saw the possibility of advancement for themselves and their school or even of a national revival of Buddhism after several centuries of Neo-Confucian intellectual domination, were prepared to laud Khubilai as a latter-day Aśoka.[15] Others, however, found it more difficult to come to terms with the new regime or feared for the quality of monastic life. Ch'an monks who felt that Chinese monasteries were no longer conducive to the rigorous practice of Ch'an, and who had heard that Zen was evoking a growing interest in Japan, were naturally predisposed to accept invitations from Japanese monks or warrior leaders where previously they would have hesitated before leaving China.

Apprehension at conditions in China was not the only motive for departure. In the century of upheavals and adjustment in China, some branches of Ch'an were more successful than others in maintaining or extending their social influence. Since the T'ang dynasty, the relative balance of power within the growing Ch'an sect had shifted periodically among its different branches. By the Southern Sung dynasty, according to Dōgen, the Rinzai schools held almost unchallenged sway in China.[16] Among Rinzai lineages some were very much more numerous, influential, or socially well-connected than others. Eisai brought back to Japan the teachings of the Huang-lung lineage (Ōryū-ha), but already when he went to China the Yang-ch'i lineage (Yōgi-ha), centering on Ta-hui and his disciples, with its aristocratic connection and literary interest, was the dominant branch of Ch'an. During the thirteenth century, primacy shifted to the P'o-an line (Hoan-ha) of Wu-chun and his disciples.[17] The literary, aristocratic Zen derived from Wu-chun via Enni, Lan-ch'i, and Wu-hsueh was the dominant influence on medieval Japanese Rinzai Zen.

Ch'an emphasis on the vertical transmission of the doctrine from master to disciple could generate factional rivalry between different lines and within individual monasteries. Such internal differences within Rinzai circles in China during the unstable period of transition to Mongol rule may have contributed to a willingness on the part of some Ch'an monks who felt that the prospects for the development of their particular line were circumscribed in China, to consider Japan as a possible sphere of activity, especially when they had met young Japanese monks in Chinese monasteries who were ardent in their pursuit of Zen, and who spoke in glowing terms of their hopes for the new doctrine in Japan. Thus, while political and social instability helps to explain the willingness of some eminent Ch'an masters to forsake Chinese monasteries and make the hazardous journey to Japan, the fact that most of these émigres, and all but two or three who came of their own initiative and spent the remainder of their lives in Japan, came from the less influential Sung-yuan line (Shōgen-ha) may have been related to factional pressures within Chinese monasteries.[18]

HŌJŌ TOKIYORI AND LAN-CH'I TAO-LUNG

The first émigré Sung master to make the journey to Japan was a member of the Sung-yuan line, Lan-ch'i Tao-lung (Rankei Dōryū, 1213–1278), who arrived in Hakata in 1246. Lan-ch'i was then thirty-four years old. He was to spend the remainder of his life in Japan and to play a major role in introducing undiluted Sung monastic practice and setting the pattern for the development of metropolitan Zen. Born in Szechwan, Lan-ch'i had entered the monastic life at the age of thirteen. In his study of Ch'an, he had visited many leading Chinese monasteries and debated with some of the most renowned contemporary masters, including Wu-chun, before accepting the teaching of Wu-ming Hui-hsing. Thus, although Lan-ch'i had not held high office in a major Chinese monastery, he was a fully trained and experienced monk whose spiritual attainments had been recognized by a leading Chinese master.[19]

While enrolled in one of the official Ch'an monasteries near Hangchow, Lan-ch'i had met the Japanese Ritsu school monk, Getsuō Chikyō. From Chikyō, Lan-ch'i learned much about the religious situation in Japan and determined to make the journey. There is no indication that he received a formal invitation from the Japanese authorities. After a short stay in Hakata, he made his way to Kyoto to visit Chikyō in Sennyūji. Chikyō, who was well aware of the hostility to Zen in Kyoto Buddhist circles, probably advised him to go to Kamakura. In Kamakura, Lan-ch'i stayed at Jufukuji with the monk Daikatsu Ryōshin, a member of the Eisai line, who had been to China and was eager to exorcise Tendai elements from the Zen teachings he had learned from Eisai's followers. Daikatsu was friendly with Tokiyori and introduced Lan-ch'i to the regent, who became an enthusiastic patron of the young Chinese monk. Tokiyori installed Lan-ch'i as abbot of Jōrakuji, which was converted into a Zen monastery for him. The warrior visited the Ch'an monk frequently and questioned him, through an interpreter or in writing, about Zen. Lan-ch'i introduced at Jōrakuji the monastic regimen he had learned in the great Ch'an monasteries of Sung China and built the first Sung-style Zen hall (*sōdō*) in eastern Japan.[20]

In 1249, the year in which he first met Lan-ch'i, Tokiyori decided to build in Kamakura a full-scale Zen monastery in the Sung style of layout and architecture. Lan-ch'i was consulted, the site of a former execution ground chosen as the location, and the work of clearing and construction pushed ahead. Named Kenchōji after the year period, the new monastery was modeled on Ching-shan. At its completion in 1253, Lan-ch'i was installed as founder-abbot (*kaisan*).[21] Kenchōji was dedicated to "the longevity of the emperor, the welfare of the shogunal line and its ministers, peace under heaven, the repose of the souls of three generations of the Minamoto, of Masako, and other deceased members of the Hōjō family."[22] Lan-ch'i attracted numerous disciples, and Kenchōji soon had an enrollment of several hundred monks.[23]

Kenchōji was one of the first Zen monasteries in Japan to include among its buildings a communal meditation center or monks' hall (*sōdō*), a characteristic Ch'an building but one that was new to Japanese monastic experience. Lan-ch'i stressed the importance of the *sōdō* and composed strict regulations for the mandatory four daily meditation sessions held there. His Zen emphasized meditation and discussion of *kōan* within the context of a monastic life based upon strict observance of Ch'an regulations (*shingi*).[24] "The practice of Zen and the pursuit of the Way is nothing other than grappling with the great problem of birth and death. Even on bath days or holidays do not allow your practice of Zen to relax for an instant" (*Kenchōji kisshiki*). Unlike some of the Chinese monks who followed him to Japan, Lan-ch'i did not encourage his disciples to indulge in scholarship or literary activity: "The practice of Zen (*sanzen bendō*) does not lie in the study of four and six character parallel prose . . ." (*Ikai gojō*, article 4). He did, however, share with other Sung dynasty Ch'an masters a willingness to accept, at a secondary level, the validity of the existing social order and the man-made law. After centuries of accommodation to Chinese society and interaction with Confucian thought, Ch'an teaching, while stressing the primary aim of individual enlightenment, sometimes couched this teaching in Confucian terms. Thus, Lan-ch'i could say in one of his sermons that "faithful observance of the laws of the [secular] world does not differ from faithful observance of the laws of the religious world."[25] Acceptance of the present world by Chinese Zen monks dovetailed with the contemporary teachings of Nichiren.[26] Nichiren's appeal to "attain Buddhahood with this body!" (*sokushin jōbutsu*), for instance, was an assertion that salvation could be found in daily life, even in the pursuit of profit, if accompanied by genuine devotion to the *Lotus Sutra*. Approval of the political order and its laws by Zen monks naturally gave to the sect an added attraction in the eyes of practical-minded warrior-leaders whose chief concerns were keeping the peace and holding, if possible increasing, the loyalties of their vassals.

The completion of Kenchōji at mid-century marks an important stage in the development of the Zen schools in Japan. Unlike Kenninji and Tōfukuji in Kyoto, Kenchōji had no Tendai or Shingon building within its compound, nor was it a branch temple of any other established monastery. A plaque, said to have been written by Emperor Go-Fukakusa (1243–1304), placed above the main gate, publicly proclaimed its independence: *Kenchō kōkoku Zenji* (the Kenchō [era] Zen monastery for the prosperity of the country).[27] This would have been one of the first recorded public uses of the characters *Zenji* (Zen monastery) in Japan and an implicit formal recognition of Zen as an independent branch of the Buddhist church. Kenchōji remained throughout the middle ages the leading Kamakura monastery. It served as a model for many subsequent Zen foundations in Japan, including a rebuilt Tōfukuji and a new Tenryūji, and provided the base for the expansion of the Lan-ch'i school and of Sung Zen in the Kantō region.

HŌJŌ TOKIYORI AND WU-AN P'U-NING

Tokiyori did not confine his patronage of Chinese monks to Lan-ch'i. In 1260, Wu-an P'u-ning (Gottan Funei, 1197–1276) arrived in Japan. Like Lan-chi, Wu-an seems not to have received an official invitation. He probably made the journey because of unrest in China and the glowing picture of Japan painted by his friend Enni, a fellow disciple of Wu-chun. Unlike Lan-ch'i, however, Wu-an, who was already in his sixties, was renowned in Chinese Ch'an circles as one of the foremost disciples of Wu-chun, and had held the offices of "chief seat" and abbot in a number of Sung monasteries. It is an indication both of the degree of dislocation in China and of the growing reputation of Japan as a suitable ground for Zen that a monk of Wu-an's caliber should have come to Japan.

Upon arrival, Wu-an stayed first in Kyoto with Enni, who introduced him to Hōjō Tokiyori. Delighted that such a dignitary should have come to Japan, Tokiyori promptly invited him to Kamakura and installed him as second abbot of Kenchōji.[28] Lan'ch'i moved to Kyoto, where he encouraged the revival of Kenninji and Tōfukuji as pure Sung-style monasteries and lectured on Zen at the imperial court.

Under Lan-ch'i, Tokiyori had made considerable progress in his understanding of Zen. He continued to practice meditation and engage in debate (*mondō*) with Wu-an, who eventually acknowledged the warrior's enlightenment and, as a mark of transmission of the Zen Dharma, gave Tokiyori a documentary seal of succession (*inka*) and one of his own robes. This was the first instance of the recognition, by a Chinese master, of the enlightenment of a Japanese warrior. There may have been a touch of flattery and political expediency in Wu-an's granting of *inka* to the powerful warrior, but Wu-an did not grant such recognition lightly. Apart from Tokiyori and a few monk-disciples, Wu-an found no one in Kamakura to understand his teaching, and, after Tokiyori's death in 1263, he requested to be allowed to return to China and left Japan a year or so later. His departure suggests that, in spite of growing interest in Zen in Kamakura, undiluted Sung Zen teachings were still not widely understood.

Wu-an is said to have shocked the religious sensibilities of many warriors and monks when, in what has been interpreted as a deliberate attempt to sever the connection between Zen and prayer in Japanese minds, he publicly refused to worship before a statue of Jizō in the Buddha hall of Kenchōji on the grounds that, whereas Jizō was merely a Bodhisattva, he, Wu-an, was a Buddha.[29] Hōjō Tokimune (1251–1284), Tokiyori's son, was hardly more than a child when he was appointed to the office of regent in 1268. He was too young to have any interest in Wu-an's Zen teachings and made no attempt to persuade the elderly Chinese monk to stay when he expressed the desire to leave.[30] Rumors were spread that Wu-an was a Mongol spy. These also contributed to his departure.

After Wu-an's departure, Lan-ch'i was again installed in Ken-chōji. Enryakuji monks, however, began to spread the rumor that he, too, was an agent of the Mongols, and he was forced into inter-mittent exile in the provinces of Kai and Mutsu. He took this opportunity to open Zen temples and to spread Sung Zen teach-ings in these areas. In 1278 he regained the confidence of Toki-mune and was again installed as abbot of Kenchōji, where the warrior visited him "to enter the chamber and study Zen" (*nisshit-su sanzen*). Tokimune broached with Lan-ch'i the idea of building another large Zen monastery. Lan-ch'i helped to choose the site in one of the narrow mountain valleys ringing Kamakura but died before work could be started. Awarded the title of Zen Master Daikaku (Daikaku Zenji), he left behind him at Kenchōji the nucleus of a powerful school, known as the Daikaku-ha, which contributed to the solid establishment of Sung Zen in eastern Japan.[31]

In 1269, the Chinese monk Ta-hsiu Cheng-nien (Daikyū Shōnen, 1214–1288) arrived belatedly in Japan. He had been invited by Tokiyori, but the warrior had died before Ta-hsiu arrived. Since Ta-hsiu was younger than Lan-ch'i and belonged to the same line of Zen, the older monk welcomed him and introduced him into Kamakura Zen and warrior circles. Ta-hsiu was appointed abbot of Zenkōji and other Kamakura monasteries, including Kenchōji. He remained in Japan until his death nearly twenty years later and, although his following was less numerous than that of Lan-ch'i, did much to introduce Sung Zen teachings to Japanese monks and warriors.[32]

HŌJŌ TOKIMUNE'S PATRONAGE OF ZEN

Hōjō Tokimune was a generous patron of the Japanese Ritsu sect monks Eison (1201–1290) and Ninshō (1217–1303). As he grew older, he also became, like his father, a student of Zen and enthu-siastic patron of Chinese Zen monks. It is difficult to plumb the sources of his interest in Zen. Filiality may have played a part. But it is also possible that his interest in Zen sprang from an acute sense of personal crisis. Throughout his youth and early manhood, Tokimune had to confront dangers at home and abroad. Before he was twenty, he had destroyed several rivals for the office of *shikken*, (regent) narrowly escaped assassination himself, and been confronted with the first of the Mongol onslaughts.

Tokimune's precise contribution to the organization of resistance to the invaders is unclear. He did not lead the fighting and may have been little more than a rubber stamp for decisions made by leading vassals within the *bakufu*, at least at the outset of the first invasion.[33] He is said to have found strength in Zen meditation. This may well have been so but it is certainly an exaggeration to attribute the defeat of the invader to the regent's practice of Zen as some propagandists have done. No doubt Tokimune received sympathy and support from Chinese and Japanese Zen monks who were in Kamakura. Although most Zen monks were politically undemonstrative, there were exceptions. Wu-hsueh Tsu-yuan, for instance, was an ardent Sung nationalist and may have helped stiffen Tokimune's resolve in the face of Mongol threats. Tōgan Ean (1225–1277), a Japanese Zen monk who had been a disciple of Wu-an P'u-ning, maintained a vigil, from the winter of 1268 until the spring of 1270, before the Iwashimizu Hachiman shrine, at which he offered constant invocations for the protection of the nation. Among his prayers was the verse, *Sue no yo no sue no sue made waga kuni wa yorozu no kuni ni suguretaru kuni*. (Until the end of the end of the world our country will be superior to all other countries).[34] As the crisis mounted, Zen monasteries and temples in Kamakura, Kyoto, and throughout the country joined in the clamor of prayers and ceremonies for national survival. At Kenchōji, Lan-ch'i was requested to offer prayers for the safety of the country. Musō Soseki later attributed a reduction in time spent in meditation and an excessive indulgence in prayers and invocations (*kitō*) in some Zen monasteries to habits acquired during the Mongol crisis.[35]

HŌJŌ TOKIMUNE AND WU-HSUEH TSU-YUAN

Lan-ch'i Tao-lung died in 1274. Tokimune immediately dispatched two monks from Kenchōji to China to seek a suitable successor. Their choice fell on Wu-hsueh Tsu-yuan (Mugaku Sogen, 1226–1286), a disciple of Wu-chun, who was serving as "chief seat" at the important monastery of T'ien-tung-shan. Initially reluctant, Wu-hsueh was persuaded to make the journey by his abbot. He was no doubt also encouraged by the reports of Tokiyori's enlightenment and death in the meditation posture, as well as of Tokimune's devotion to Zen and determination to build a new Zen monastery. Wu-hsueh, accompanied by his Chinese disciple, the monk Ching-t'ang Chueh-yuan, reached Kamakura in the eighth month of 1279. Tokimune appointed him abbot of Kenchōji and resumed his practice of Zen. In their encounters, the Chinese monk, Zen master though he was, did not forget that he was dealing with the most powerful warrior in Japan. Discussions on Zen (sanzen) were conducted through an interpreter. When the master wished to strike his disciple for incomprehension or to encourage greater efforts, the blows fell on the interpreter.[36]

Only two years after Wu-hsueh's arrival in Kamakura, the Mongols launched a second and greater invasion attempt. Fighting lasted for a month before the invaders were repulsed from the beaches of Hakata, their fleet again broken by storms. After the victory, Tokimune had little in the way of material spoils to award to the warriors who had beaten off the attack. He did, however, begin building the Zen monastery in Kamakura which he had discussed with Lan-ch'i. It was to be dedicated to the memory of those warriors who had lost their lives on the Kyūshū beaches or in the waters of Hakata bay.

The Buddha hall of the new monastery, named Engakuji, was completed by the winter of 1282, and Wu-hsueh formally installed (juen) as founder-abbot.[37] Engakuji, like Kenchōji, was built in the Sung Ch'an style. Within a few years, two monks' halls had been built to house the many monks who wished to enroll. For the economic support of the monastery, Tokimune commended to it in 1283 the steward rights (*jitō shiki*) to Tomita-no-*shō* in Owari province. To formalize this grant and to give the monastery official status, Tokimune, in the same year, requested that the shogun bestow on Engakuji the official rank of shogunal Invocatory Temple and confirm the title to Tomita-no-*shō* and the Kameyama district (*gō*) in the adjoining province of Kazusa. With a formal document of consent from the shogun, the core of the Engakuji domain was thus established.[38]

On the fourth day of the fourth month of 1284, Tokimune was suddenly taken ill. He at once asked Wu-hsueh to give him the tonsure and took the robes of a Zen monk and the Buddhist name Dōkō. That same day, aged thirty-four, he died. One means by which Zen monks extended their influence in society was by the conduct of funeral services for important patrons. Wu-hsueh and Ta-hsiu presided at the Zen-style obsequies for Tokimune. At the cremation ceremony, Wu-hsueh lamented the passing of the warrior who had been such a devoted student and patron of Zen: "Since I cannot be much longer in this world, I shall soon follow Tokimune because he is solitary [by nature] and has no one to help him."[39] After Tokimune's death, his consort became a Zen nun and foundress of the Rinzai nunnery of Tōkeiji in Kamakura. Many of Tokimune's vassals also "left the world" with the passing of their lord. Wu-hsueh, who had wished to return to China but stayed at Tokimune's urgent entreaty, died two years later in the knowledge that Sung Zen was firmly rooted in Kamakura. Like Kenchōji, Engakuji has remained an important monastery up until the present day. The Engakuji school included Japanese monks of the stature of Kōhō Kennichi (1241–1316), who served as abbot of most of the major Kamakura monasteries and Kian Soen (1261–1318), who was among the founder-abbots of Nanzenji in Kyoto.

HŌJŌ SADATOKI AND I-SHAN I-NING

Hōjō Sadatoki continued the policy of inviting Chinese Zen masters to Kamakura and of building or rebuilding Zen monastery buildings. During his term in office, several new developments can be detected: the Chinese literary and cultural tone of the Kamakura monasteries became very much more pronounced; and Zen monasteries were subjected to greater formal *bakufu* regulation and control.

Sadatoki's principal Zen mentor was the learned Chinese monk I-shan I-ning, (Issan Ichinei, 1247–1317), who came to Japan as a Mongol emissary in 1299. Suspected of being a Mongol spy by the *bakufu*, he was initially confined to the Shuzenji in Izu. Sadatoki later recognized I-shan's qualities and installed him as abbot of Kenchōji and later of Engakuji and Nanzenji in Kyoto. Where Lan-ch'i and Wu-hsueh had largely confined their activities to Zen training, I-shan, who was well-read in Neo-Confucian philosophy, Chinese literature, and classics, besides being a talented calligrapher and connoisseur of Chinese painting, introduced these more scholarly and literary interests to the monks who studied with him and to his secular patrons in Kamakura and Kyoto. He was therefore instrumental in first giving to the metropolitan Zen monasteries that aesthetic tone that was to find expression in the Literature of the Five Mountains (*gozan bungaku*), in ink painting, and in the other arts associated with medieval *gozan* Zen.[40] I-shan's reputation was such that more monks flocked to Engakuji than could be accommodated by the monastery. To select the most suitable candidates for instruction, he instituted an examination in the composition of Zen-style verse in Chinese. Among the monks who passed this test was the young Musō Soseki, who was later to play a critical role in the development of Japanese Zen.[41]

Sadatoki also invited Tung-ming Hui-jih (Tōmyō Enichi, 1272–1340) to Japan. Tung-ming arrived in Japan in 1309 and was appointed successively abbot of most of the major Kamakura monasteries. At Emperor Go-Daigo's invitation, he also served as abbot of Kenninji in Kyoto. Tung-ming, like Dōgen, advocated the teaching of the Sōtō tradition of Zen but, unlike Dōgen's Zen, that of the Tung-ming school belonged to the lineage of Hung-chih Cheng-chueh (Wanshi Shōgaku), shared the literary propensities of metropolitan Rinzai Zen, and remained within the *gozan* network. Many monks of this Wanshi school went to study Zen in Yuan China and, upon their return to Japan, contributed to the *gozan* literature movement. The school was patronized initially by Sadatoki and the Hōjō and exerted great influence on Kantō warriors. Later, Wanshi monks came under the protection of the Shiba and Asakura warrior bands in Echizen and the Nijō and Asakai *kuge* in Kyoto.[42]

Sadatoki's familiarity with Zen was broader than that of his immediate predecessors. He regarded it not only as a compelling religious experience but as a source of intellectual and cultural illumination. Under the influence of I-shan, Sadatoki furthered his own interest in Chinese culture and encouraged Japanese monks and warriors to study the Chinese "outer classics" (*geten*) as well as Buddhist or Zen subjects. He also showed his determination to keep the new sect under close *bakufu* supervision. In 1294, Sadatoki published a list of regulations for Zen monasteries. These prohibitions provide an insight into the kinds of social problems— seen from the point of view of the secular authorities—generated by the development of Zen.

All Zen monks were obliged to have correctly validated monk certificates. They were not to leave their monastery at night or to spend the night away from the monastery without the permission of their abbot. Nuns and lay-women were forbidden to enter Zen monasteries except on specified Buddhist festivals or on memorial days of the Hōjō regents to visit particular mausolea. Ceremonial feasts were not to be too lavish. Monks were not to wander off in search of flowers, nor to go outside the monastery without making their destination known. Monks convalescing in the infirmary were not to go outside the monastery. Members of the community were not to visit nunneries; nor were they to take expensive seasonal gifts to other monasteries or give farewell gifts to monks leaving the community. Zen monks were to wear Chinese-style robes. Infringement of these regulations was to be punished with expulsion from the monastery.[43]

In 1303, Sadatoki supplemented these general regulations with additional regulations for Engakuji. According to these, the total enrollment of monks was not to exceed 200. Novices and postulants were not to be accepted by the monastery without the consent of the principal patron of the monastery. Frugality was to be observed, with meals taken only at the regular hours. Cakes served at tea ceremonies were to be limited to one variety. Visiting patrons were to be entertained simply. Monks and members of the community were forbidden to wander outside the monastery gates and women to enter. Monastery assistants (*anja*) and laborers (*ninku*) were strictly forbidden to bear arms.[44]

New concerns are apparent here. Sadatoki was obviously anxious to ensure that Zen monasteries would not become armed camps of the kind that existed on Mt. Hiei and within many other Japanese Buddhist compounds. Restriction of numbers of monks was aimed at preventing the monastery from taking in more monks than it could readily feed, clothe, and discipline. The presence of large numbers of postulants (boys in their teens) within monasteries could also be a source of distraction and of deterioration of monastic morale. The fact that articles relating to these problems are repeated in many subsequent codes suggests that they were not very carefully observed.

It is from Sadatoki's time, too, that the development of an officially patronized system of Zen monasteries, based upon the Sung Five Mountains and Ten Temples hierarchy of officially designated monasteries becomes noticeable in Japan. The system saw its full development under the Ashikaga, but already, by the early decades of the fourteenth-century, monasteries like Kenchōji, Engakuji, and Nanzenji had been given *gozan* status. While the grant of such a title conferred prestige on a monastery, it also brought it even more firmly under official regulation and control.[45]

HŌJŌ TAKATOKI'S PATRONAGE OF ZEN

Hōjō Takatoki was still a child when he was appointed *shikken* in 1316. Actual power was held by warrior-advisors, and his regency was plagued by the political upheavals attending Emperor Go-

Daigo's attempts to overthrow the *bakufu* and restore direct imperial rule.[46] In these troubled circumstances, with dwindling resources, Takatoki's patronage of Zen was necessarily more modest than that of his predecessors. He did, however, try to continue the two-pronged Hōjō policy of patronage and strict regulation.

Although he did not himself invite Zen masters from China, Takatoki extended a welcome to those who came to Japan at the invitation of powerful warrior-leaders in northern Kyūshū and around the Inland Sea. The Chinese monks Ch'ing-cho Cheng-ch'eng (Seisetsu Shōchō, 1274–1339), Ming-chi Ch'u-chün (Minki Soshun, 1262–1336), and Chu-hsien Fan-hsien (Jikusen Bonsen, 1292–1348) were invited to Kamakura by Takatoki and appointed to the headships of major Zen monasteries.[47] All three shared the cultural and literary avocations of I-shan. Besides encouraging the practice of meditation, they did much to strengthen the cultural tone of metropolitan Zen and helped spread Sung and Yuan Zen teachings in provincial centers as well as in Kamakura and Kyoto. Ch'ing-cho reemphasized the importance of the Ch'an monastic rule by encouraging in Japan the veneration of Pai-chang Huai-hai, the accepted author of the first Ch'an monastic rule, and by compiling a monastic code, based on prevailing Chinese codes, appropriate to Japanese monasteries with their smaller scale and different social circumstances.[48]

External regulation of Zen monasteries was enforced by Takatoki in an 18-article list of prohibitions for Engakuji issued in 1327.[49] This code makes it clear that, by this time, a *bakufu* office had been established to supervise the burgeoning Zen monastic institution. The first article states that "in accord with the wishes of Tokimune, the abbot (*jūji*) is responsible for the spiritual conduct of monastic life (*buppō shugyō*), but in matters relating to the secular (*seji*), the temple superintendent (*jika gyōji*) must be consulted." The precise character of the *gyōji* office is unclear, but its holder evidently had considerable influence over the running of the monastery. Article 2 indicates that, while the lower monastery officers in the two ranks were to be appointed on the basis of consultation between the abbot, the members of the community, and the *gyōji*, the heads of the two ranks and the *inō* were to be appointed only after the *gyōji* had consulted the regent himself. Other articles require that the *gyōji* be consulted on the enrollment of monks in the monks' hall (article 3) and that matters of dispute relating to monastic domain be settled by the bursar (*tsūbun*) and the *gyōji* (article 10). The *gyōji* was also to be consulted before any recalcitrant monk was expelled (article 11).

Between the arrival of Lan-ch'i and the demise of the Kamakura *bakufu*, the Rinzai Zen school, under Hōjō patronage, had thus put down deep roots in Kamakura. New, purely Zen monasteries had been built and many Japanese monks given an intensive training in Zen and Zen-related Chinese culture by Chinese masters. The importance of Zen in Kamakura society in the early fourteenth century and its intimate ties with the Hōjō are perhaps best exemplified in the elaborate Zen-style ceremonies held at Engakuji in 1323 on the thirteenth anniversary of the death of Hōjō Sadatoki. The ceremonies themselves lasted for ten days and were attended by more than 2,000 monks and nuns from 38 Zen monasteries and nunneries in the Kantō region.[50]

THE ZEN CONTRIBUTION TO WARRIOR CULTURE

While Zen meditation and private interviews with a master (*sanzen*) enriched the spiritual lives of individual regents, patronage of Zen monks completely transformed the cultural style of the Hōjō and their court. In the early years of the Kamakura regime, few Kamakura warriors displayed any pretensions to literary accomplishment. By the late thirteenth century, however, poetry (*waka*) by members of the Hōjō family and other leading warriors was being included in imperial anthologies, warrior lords were holding literary gatherings, and it would have been a rare, and rude, member of the warrior-elite who could not quote tellingly from *The Tale of Genji*, or produce a moving verse at the onset of autumn or the departure of a friend.[51]

The Hōjō were not totally uncultured, therefore, when Chinese

Zen monks began to visit Kamakura in the mid-thirteenth century. Moreover, during their deepening involvement with Zen, the Kamakura warrior-rulers contined to cultivate Japanese literary arts. Proficient as they became in these, however, they remained neophytes in comparison with those Kyoto courtiers and aristocrats who had nurtured and continued to command the Japanese literary tradition. Zen monks helped free the Hōjō from this cultural subordination by offering them access to the intellectual and cultural interests of the Chinese gentry and literati. Under the guidance of Chinese monks, the Hōjō regents and their circle acquired a rudimentary knowledge of Neo-Confucian metaphysics, statecraft, and theories of social hierarchy (*taigi meibun*). They were also introduced to the whole range of Chinese classical literature, thought, and art.

As mentioned earlier, the syncretic current of thought known as the Unity of the Three Creeds (*sankyō itchi*) was in vogue in the Ch'an monasteries of the Sung and Yuan dynasties. In the hope of nullifying the anti-Buddhist polemics of Neo-Confucianists and Taoists, some Ch'an monks asserted that Confucianism, Taoism, and Buddhism were merely three different paths to the same truth.[52] Literary-minded Ch'an masters like I-shan I-ning, Tung-ming Hui-jih, and Ch'ing-cho Cheng-ch'eng, who were active in Japan in the early fourteenth century, found it perfectly natural, while instructing their patrons in Zen, to make use of the *Analects, Lao-tzu,* or *Chuang-tzu* and to encourage the study of Chinese poetry, painting, and calligraphy.

Before the close of the thirteenth century, the collecting of Chinese art objects (*karamono*) had become a consuming passion in Kamakura society. The vessels bringing these treasures from China were eagerly awaited, and the objects disgorged from their holds were admired at tea meetings (*cha yoriai*). The vigor of this Zen-related surge of Chinese cultural influence can be guessed at from the *Butsunichi'an kōmotsu mokuroku*, a catalogue, first compiled in 1320, of treasures in the Butsunichi'an, a sub-temple of Engakuji. This one sub-temple held several hundred Chinese treasures, including not only portraits of Ch'an masters (*chinsō*) and samples of their calligraphy but also paintings attributed to Mu Ch'i, the Emperor Hui-tsung, and other Sung masters.[53]

Familiarity with Sung learning and culture lent to the Hōjō a cultural self-assurance befitting their military power—in time it may also have worked to sap their martial vigor—and gave to Kamakura a livelier, more cosmopolitan atmosphere. Although Kamakura probably still did not equal Kyoto in urban sophistication, some of its more spartan features were softened. In this broader Chinese cultural context, the Hōjō were no longer quite such neophytes. They could claim to be heirs to the traditions of the Sung social and intellectual elite and have the satisfaction of seeing at least some members of the imperial court follow their lead in the study of Zen and Chinese culture. Emperor Go-Daigo and the Ashikaga shoguns, in their turn, continued to build on the twofold cultural base established by the Hōjō, blending, in varying degrees, Japanese and Chinese ideas, institutions and cultural idioms.[54]

PROVINCIAL DIFFUSION OF ZEN

Only when Sung Rinzai Zen was firmly established in Kamakura under Hōjō patronage did it begin to percolate downward through provincial warrior society. This diffusion began in the closing decades of the thirteenth century. It gathered momentum steadily but did not become a spate until the middle decades of the fourteenth century. Even at the height of its influence in the late fourteenth century, Zen—including the more widely diffused Sōtō Zen— probably had still not replaced devotion to Kannon, Jizō, the *Lotus Sutra*, or the Pure Land of Amida in the hearts of most ordinary, and many high-ranking, Japanese samurai. Zen in the Kamakura and Muromachi periods can be called "the religion of the samurai" only in the sense that most patrons of Zen were samurai, not in the sense that it was practiced assiduously or exclusively by all, or even perhaps the majority, of those who would be described as warriors.

Nichiren (1222–1282) was active until the final quarter of the thirteenth century. His teachings, based upon fervent devotion to the *Lotus Sutra*, spread widely in the Kantō district, the heartland of Hōjō power. Their appeal was not confined to peasants or townsmen. There were followers of Nichiren among the samurai and officials in the Hōjō and Ashikaga entourages.[55] The teachings of the Ji sect founder, Ippen (1239–1289), who wandered the country urging total reliance on the saving mercy of Amida, also appealed to many warriors. We get a vivid impression of the intimacy of the ties between the Ji sect and warrior society from the *Taiheiki*, which includes a number of descriptions of Ji-sect monks accompanying warriors to the battles between the Northern and Southern court factions. On the battlefield, they performed the *nenbutsu*, gathered the bodies of the slain, and conducted last rites and burials.[56] The affection of ordinary warriors for the direct simplicity of the Lotus and Pure Land teachings was too strong to be easily replaced by the new Chinese Zen teachings.

Provincial patrons of metropolitan Zen in the Kamakura period were mainly warriors of the military governor (*shugo*) class. The Ashikaga, who were identified with patronage of Zen, served the Hōjō as *shugo* of the provinces of Kazusa and Mikawa. Although the Ashikage patronized the syncretic Tendai-Zen of Eisai's successors, their association with "pure" Sung Zen did not begin until the fourteenth century, when Ashikaga Sadauji (c. 1274–1333) converted Jōmyōji in Kamakura into a Zen monastery. Other powerful warrior families who were known as patrons of Rinzai Zen—among them the Akamatsu, Hosokawa, Kikuchi, Kira, Ogasawara, Ōtomo, Ōuchi, Sano, Shōni, Takeda, Uesugi—only began to display this interest from the closing decades of the Kamakura period.[57] Like the Hōjō, their interest in Zen was not always simply, or even primarily, religious. Religious, political, and cultural factors were all involved in the spread of Zen within the upper levels of provincial warrior society.

Religious interest cannot be discounted entirely, however. The experience of intensive meditation, *kōan* study, and face-to-face encounter with a Zen master offered to warrior-leaders a new and profound spiritual experience, and one that perhaps helped some face the prospect of painful and untimely death with equanimity. There were certainly a number of *shugo* who practiced Zen meditation eagerly. Ōtomo Sadamune, Ōtomo Ujiyasu, and Ogasawara Sadamune, for instance, all took the Zen precepts under Ch'ingcho, and Ōtomo Ujiyasu became a Zen monk.[58] The spiritual benefits of Zen, however, were not immediately self-evident. They could only be known after serious practice. Making the initial commitment normally involved the rejection of a more familiar form of Buddhist devotion. It also meant, in practice, the conversion of the local clan temple (*ujidera*) into a Zen monastery. The wide-scale provincial diffusion of Zen during the fourteenth century was based upon the conversion of *ujidera*, most of which in the late thirteenth century were still Pure Land temples affiliated with the Ji sect, into Zen temples.[59] The acceptance of Zen was, therefore, a serious step, not only for the individual leader himself, but also for his warrior band.

It is clear from the case of the Ōtomo, the *shugo* of Bungo province, that conversion to Zen was sometimes made reluctantly, and only upon the insistence of the Hōjō regents. The Ōtomo had established a reputation as enthusiastic patrons of Zen before the destruction of the Hōjō regime in 1333. Ōtomo Sadamune (fl. early fourteenth century) is mentioned with great affection in the writings of contemporary Chinese and Japanese Zen masters for his hospitality to Zen monks journeying between China and Japan. The Ōtomo, however, gave their formal allegiance to Zen only in 1306. Sadamune's grandfather had been a patron of the mendicant Ippen, and the Ōtomo would probably have continued this tradition had not Hōjō Sadatoki intervened. In 1305, before an assembly of vassals in Kamakura, Sadatoki is said to have asked Sadamune's father, Sadachika, whether the Ōtomo had built a Zen monastery and how many monks were being supported. There was at the time no Zen monastery in Bungo, but Sadachika felt it would be impolitic to acknowledge this publicly. He declared that a monastery for 100 monks was being built—then hurried home to build it. By the following year, a disciple of Enni of Tōfukuji had been installed as the founder-abbot of the new Zen *ujidera*.[60]

There were, no doubt, other lords present at that assembly who concluded that it would be expedient to patronize Zen, if they had not already begun.

Hōjō encouragement of the acceptance of Zen by its leading vassals and allies was all the more effective because the Hōjō house (*tokusō*) was, in the late thirteenth century, at the zenith of its power and influence. Throughout the thirteenth century, the Hōjō had steadily extended their private control over the official organs of the *bakufu*. The crisis of the Mongol invasions and the long period of national mobilization hastened this growing autocracy. During this period, Hōjō Tokimune and Sadatoki formulated policy not in the official Council of State (Hyōjōshū) but in their private chambers. While the Hōjō house was increasing its control over the machinery of central government, it was also extending its landed base, tightening its grip over temples and shrines, and making its own vassals, and those of the principal branch families, into *shugo*.

The Hōjō landed base was enlarged considerably by Tokiyori, who took over Miura domains when that powerful rival family was crushed, and by Tokimune, who acquired land in Kyūshū during the Mongol disturbances. The *Jōei shikimoku* (1232), the basic legal code of the Kamakura government, restricted *bakufu* authority over temples and shrines to those within its own domains. By the end of the century, this regulation had lapsed, and many hitherto state-supported shrines and temples had been brought under *bakufu* control.[61] On the death of Yoritomo in 1199, the Hōjō house had direct control over only 2 of the 36 *shugo* appointments. By 1286, it controlled 26 out of 52, and, by 1332, 30 out of 57.[62] The diffusion of metropolitan Zen was naturally facilitated by this aggrandizement of Hōjō authority.

Powerful provincial warrior families, like the Hōjō, were also attracted by the cultural potential of Zen. Ogasawara Sadamune, for instance, is said to have studied Zen monastic practice with Ch'ing-cho and incorporated this into the rules of etiquette of the Ogasawara school (Ogasawara-ryū), which regulated the social behavior of warriors in the Muromachi period, and were later adopted by the Tokugawa shoguns, *daimyō*, and wealthy townsmen.[63] Other warrior-lords studied calligraphy and painting with Chinese Zen masters. In the case of those families like the Ōtomo and Ōuchi, who were engaged in the China trade, cultural enthusiasms were reinforced by commercial interests in the continent.

Japanese warlord interest in Zen and Chinese culture, however, was neither exclusive nor universal. Ashikaga Takauji, who is regarded as a major patron of Zen, reflects what may have been a fairly common ambivalent attitude. Although he patronized Musō Soseki and provided financial support for the building of Tenryūji and other Zen monasteries, his deepest religious sympathies were expressed in devotion to the *bodhisattva* Jizō, and he seems to have been more comfortable with Japanese culture than Chinese.[64] His younger brother, Tadayoshi, on the other hand, had a profound grasp of Zen, of Chinese culture, and of Chinese bureaucratic practice.[65] Since these two warriors were central to the development of metropolitan *gozan* Zen in the Muromachi period, more will be said about them in the next chapter. Here it is sufficient to note that understanding of, and interest in, Zen varied considerably, even among the small group of warrior-leaders who were its major patrons.

IMPERIAL PATRONAGE OF ZEN

Although the Hōjō and their allies and vassals were the principal patrons of Zen in the late Kamakura period, the new Chinese teachings were not ignored by the imperial house in Kyoto. We have already seen that Enni Ben'en of Tōfukuji was instrumental in introducing some knowledge of Sung Zen teachings to Kujō Michiie and the imperial court. Enni Ben'en was patronized by Emperor Go-Saga (1220–1272), who also invited the Chinese monk Lan-ch'i Tao-lung to instruct him in Zen.

At Go-Saga's death, the imperial house was split by a succession dispute into the rival factions later known as the Jimyō'in and Daikakuji lines. The first three emperors of the Daikakuji line, Kameyama (1249–1305), Go-Uda (1267–1324), and Go-Daigo

(1288–1339), all patronized and studied Zen.[66] Kameyama began the construction of Nanzenji, which was to become a major link between metropolitan Zen and the imperial court. Go-Uda installed the Chinese master I-shan I-ning as third abbot of Nanzenji and practiced Zen under his guidance. This was the first close contact between continental Zen and the Japanese imperial family. No doubt I-shan's talents as a calligrapher also impressed Go-Uda. On I-shan's death, Go-Uda arranged for the Chinese monk to be buried near the tomb of Kameyama. He continued his study of Zen with I-shan's disciples. Go-Daigo was a devoted patron of the Chinese monk Ming-chi Ch'u-chün and of Musō Soseki, whom he persuaded to serve three times as abbot of Nanzenji. The ties between the Daikakuji line and the Musō school remained close, and a number of imperial princes, sons of Emperors Go-Daigo and Go-Murakami (1328–1368), subsequently entered Musō-school monasteries to train as monks.

The commitment of Kameyama, Go-Uda, and Go-Daigo to Zen, though deep, was only partial. They were attracted by the aristocratic quality of Rinzai Zen, by its novel emphasis on self-reliance, and by the vistas it offered into Chinese culture. Zen did not supplant esoteric Buddhism in their lives, however. Go-Uda, for instance, while supporting Nanzenji, embarked upon the rebuilding of the ancient Shingon temple of Daikakuji. Go-Daigo, who needed all the support he could muster in his struggle for power, was careful to maintain amicable relations with the monasteries of the established Buddhist sects which had powerful monk armies. He installed his sons and relatives as abbots of leading Tendai and Shingon monasteries.[67] Even his patronage of Musō can be seen as a politically motivated compromise with Zen, since Musō's Zen was didactic and esoteric in tone, and Zen was a factor to be reckoned with in the contemporary political arena.[68] Moreover, although these emperors practiced meditation, that too was conceived of as a source of magical power and a means of exorcising baneful spirits.[69]

One of the first emperors of the rival Jimyō'in, or Northern line, to show a positive interest in Zen was Hanazono (1297–

1348).[70] A classical scholar and fine *waka* poet, Hanazono also gave himself wholeheartedly to the practice of pure Sung Zen under the stern master Shūhō Myōchō (Daitō Kokushi, 1282–1337) for whom the emperor helped establish the monastery of Daitokuji. After Shūhō's death, Hanazono continued his Zen practice under the guidance of Shūhō's disciple Kanzan Egen (1277–1360), the founder (*kaisan*) of Myōshinji. Though eclipsed by monasteries affiliated to the Musō school in the fourteenth century, Daitokuji, Myōshinji, and their branches came into their own after the mid-fifteenth century, and it is from these two monasteries that modern Japanese Rinzai Zen derives.

Hanazono was among those who criticized Musō's Zen as bookish. His imperial successors in the Jimyō'in line, Kōgon (1313–1364), Kōmyō (1321–1380), and Sukō (1334–1398), however, had close ties with Ashikaga Takauji and his successors, and through them with the Musō line. They studied Zen with Musō or his disciples, took the vows and tonsure, and lived Zen-style monastic lives in private hermitages. Kōgon was the first emperor to be given a formal Zen funeral. Many of their offspring, too, entered Zen monasteries. This infusion of imperial blood into Zen cloisters naturally affected the character of medieval Japanese metropolitan monasteries, especially those of the Musō line, accentuating the aristocratic tone and also the stress on literary and artistic pursuits of that school.[71]

By 1333, when the Hōjō regime was overthrown, it was evident that Sung and Yuan Rinzai Zen, introduced by Chinese masters, had taken firm root in Japan. This transmission had involved not only Zen meditation techniques, *kōan* study, and Zen metaphysics but the continental style of Zen monastic life, under Chinese monastic regulations, within monasteries carefully modeled on Chinese prototypes. Besides establishing new schools of Zen, Chinese masters had also reformed and revitalized the syncretic Rinzai schools deriving from Eisai and Enni. The activities of scholarly Chinese monks had also imparted to Japanese Zen monasteries in Kamakura, Kyoto, and the provinces a strong Chinese literary and cultural imprint.

This continental Zen monastic system was patronized by the Hōjō regents, their immediate families and housemen (*gokenin*), by leading warriors of the *shugo* class, and by some members of the imperial court. However, Rinzai Zen had as yet made little impact at middle and lower levels of warrior society where Tendai, Shingon, the Lotus teaching of Nichiren, and Pure Land Buddhism maintained a dominant influence. Even among the small number of high-ranking patrons of Zen, there were many who combined their patronage with active support of other Buddhist sects. On the whole, there were very few laymen, warrior or noble, who practiced Zen meditation actively or who can be said to have fully understood the religious teachings of the Chinese Zen masters.

Why, then, had Zen taken root, large monasteries been built, and lands granted to the new sect? Hōjō patronage of Zen was crucial. Without it, it is doubtful that the Rinzai teachings would have made much headway in Japan. The Hōjō combined religious interest in Zen with cultural and political opportunism. They saw the Chinese religion as an alternative to entanglement with the established, Kyoto-oriented Buddhist sects. Zen also bequeathed to the Hōjō the cultural legacy of the Sung empire which could be set against the Japanese cultural tradition of the imperial court and Kyoto *kuge*. Most provincial warriors and members of the imperial court who patronized Zen also seem to have been drawn to it as an avenue to Chinese culture rather than as a purely meditative or religious experience. Some warrior patrons were also persuaded by the example or command of the Hōjō to convert their family temples into Zen monasteries. Finally, in explaining the surge of Zen development in the late Kamakura period, we should take into account the proselytizing activities of Chinese monks. Largely as a result of the Mongol conquest of China, many high-caliber Chinese monks came to view Japan both as a refuge and as a promising mission field. Most of those who made the journey to Japan spent the remainder of their lives there, devoting their energies to spreading Zen. They were sufficiently flexible and talented to offer whatever their Japanese patrons seemed most interested in—whether this was Confucian political theory, Taoist thought, calligraphy or secular poetry and painting—in the hope of arousing enthusiasm for Zen practice.

In comparison with established Japanese Buddhist schools, the new metropolitan Rinzai Zen school was economically and politically powerless and therefore heavily dependent upon powerful secular patrons for its development and diffusion. Parenthetically, we should perhaps point out that Dōgen's Sōtō Zen was, by this time, also expanding rapidly in northern Japan and Kyūshū, but on the basis of patronage by farmers and warriors of *jitō* (military steward) rank and below, and at the cost of diluting Dōgen's strict Chinese Zen with infusions of Japanese esoteric Buddhism. The other branch of Sōtō Zen in Japan, the Wanshi line, took root in Kamakura and displayed many of the cultural interests of metropolitan Rinzai Zen.

The Hōjō, who were wary of the military and political influence of older monasteries like Enryakuji, Onjōji, Negoroji, Kongōbuji (Kōyasan), used metropolitan Zen to counteract this influence while, at the same time, making every effort to ensure that the new sect did not grow out of control and that Zen monasteries did not become armed camps. Patronage was therefore combined with detailed supervision and regulation. *Bakufu* regulations for Zen monasteries dealt not only with those areas where monastic life impinged on secular social and political activities; they also enforced secular control over the appointment of abbots and senior monastery officers and other domestic affairs of monasteries. The establishment of the *gozan* system was another means of according prestige to selected monasteries while bringing them under secular control.

Although metropolitan Zen was still poorly understood as a meditative practice, small in scale as an institution, heavily dependent on elite patrons, and subject to close regulation, it was still expanding in 1333.[72] Chinese masters had attracted many Japanese monks to the new Zen monasteries in Kamakura, Kyoto, and the provinces. This was due, no doubt, to the considerable reputations and genuine spiritual insight of Chinese monks. It can also be attributed, in part at least, to the fact that they had been singled out for patronage by some of the most influential figures in contemporary Japanese society. By this time, there was a growing awareness in Japan that Zen was in the ascendant. This, combined with the novelty of the teaching, was no doubt sufficient attraction for many monks. Unfortunately, Chinese monks do not seem to have been overly impressed by the motivation and dedication of some of their Japanese monk and lay devotees. Both Wu-an and Wu-hsueh, for instance, were critical of the attainments in Zen of the majority of their Japanese disciples. [73]

Many of the most enthusiastic and able of the young Japanese monks were sent to China for further study. Enrollment of Japanese monks in Chinese Zen monasteries reached a peak in the first two decades of the fourteenth century; so much so that, in some Chinese monks' halls, Chinese monks were said to have been outnumbered by Japanese and Koreans. Many of the visitors spent five, ten, or even fifteen years in Chinese monasteries before returning to Japan. Thoroughly steeped in Chinese Zen teaching, monastic practice, and secular culture, they served as the instruments for further provincial diffusion of metropolitan *gozan* Zen during the third stage of rapid expansion and consolidation under the Ashikaga shoguns.

THREE

The Articulation of the Gozan System

The destruction of the Hōjō, who had been the most powerful and generous patrons of Zen, and the ensuing shift of political life to Kyoto had little adverse effect on the fortunes of metropolitan Zen.[1] Its roots were already sufficiently deep in court and warrior society to allow it to survive the disruption in Kamakura and to make a relatively painless transition through the short-lived imperial restoration of Go-Daigo to the warrior regime of the Ashikaga, under whose patronage the Rinzai Zen of the *gozan* lineages was to reach its zenith.

By the end of the fourteenth century *gozan* Zen had become one of the most vital and influential branches of the Buddhist institution in Japan. The great metropolitan monasteries in Kyoto and Kamakura comprised the central nodes of a carefully articulated and highly centralized nationwide network of several thousand monasteries, sub-temples, and branch temples. Until the Ōnin War (1467–1477), *gozan* Zen monasteries played a major role in the political and economic as well as in the religious and cultural life of medieval Japan. The Ōnin War weakened the Ashikaga regime and brought destruction and depredation to the *gozan*. From the later fifteenth century, the *gozan* schools were steadily eclipsed by those deriving from Daitokuji and Myōshinji, who found eager patrons among newly emerging *sengoku daimyō* and townsmen of Kyoto and Sakai.

GO-DAIGO AND MUSŌ

Emperor Go-Daigo, like his immediate predecessors in the Daika-kuji line, was an enthusiastic patron of Zen. He appointed the Chinese Zen masters Ch'ing-cho Cheng-ch'eng and Ming-chi Ch'u-chün to the headship of Nanzenji and had them lecture to him on Zen and Chinese culture. He also patronized the newly built monastery of Daitokuji and its founder, the Japanese monk Shūhō Myōchō (Daitō Kokushi, 1282–1337). But it was with Musō Soseki (Musō Kokushi, 1275–1351) that Go-Daigo established the closest rapport. In 1325, the emperor invited Musō to Kyoto and installed him as abbot of Nanzenji. This precipitated a tug of war, with Go-Daigo seeking to keep the influential monk in Kyoto, the Hōjō trying to entice him back to Kamakura, and Musō himself striving to maintain neutrality, although sensing, perhaps, that the Hōjō were losing their grip.[2] Go-Daigo's attempt to detach Musō from his erstwhile warrior patrons may be seen as one small but significant part of the emperor's anti-*bakufu* maneuvering.

One of Go-Daigo's first actions on coming to power in 1333 was to recall Musō to Kyoto. The emperor then offered himself to the monk as a disciple and bestowed on him the monastery of Rinsenji, newly converted from an imperial palace. Under Go-Daigo's patronage, Musō quickly became one of the most influential monks in Kyoto. He had much to recommend him to Go-Daigo and the Kyoto nobility. Reputedly of aristocratic birth, Musō had begun his Zen training under the Chinese master I-shan I-ning. He had completed it as a disciple of the Japanese monk Kōhō Ken-nichi (Bukkoku Zenji, 1241–1316), under whose guidance he had attained his enlightenment. Kōhō Kennichi was an imperial prince by birth, the son of Emperor Go-Saga. He had studied Zen under Enni at Tōfukuji, then under the Chinese masters Wu-an P'u-ning and Wu-hsueh Tsu-yuan in Kamakura. Patronized by the Hōjō, he had served as abbot of many of the major Kamakura monasteries. In the eyes of Go-Daigo and the Kyoto *kuge*, Musō's association with I-shan established his credentials as a student of Chinese Zen. His contact with Kōhō Kennichi added an aristocratic, Japanese tone. Moreover, Musō's Zen, with its esoteric strain and tolerance towards the teachings of other Buddhist sects, made it easily accessible to Japanese *kuge*.[3] By 1336, Musō had also become a protégé of the Ashikaga. Takauji, in particular, liked the eclectic, Japanese quality of Musō's Zen.

REORGANIZATION OF THE GOZAN

In addition to patronizing Musō, Daitō, and other Zen monks, Go-Daigo also instituted a major reorganization of the *gozan*, swinging its center of gravity from Kamakura to Kyoto (see Chart 2, p. 110). When, in 1307, Emperor Go-Uda had wished to have Nanzenji ranked as an "associate *gozan*" (*jun-gozan*), he had had to secure the consent of Hōjō Sadatoki. It is an indication that the developing Chinese-style *gozan* system was then recognized as a Hōjō monopoly and effectively restricted to Kamakura monasteries. Nanzenji was accorded the requested distinction and, in the following year, the imperial court, with some nudging from the *bakufu*, bestowed on Kenchōji and Engakuji the title of *jōgakuji* (imperially sponsored monastery). Taken together, these two events suggest that, by the opening of the fourteenth century, Kyoto *kuge*, like Kamakura *bushi*, conceived of Zen monasteries in traditional terms—as adjuncts of state, to be awarded honors and ranks on the one hand, subjected to regulation and control on the other.

It was natural, therefore, when Go-Daigo came to power, that he should shift the balance of power in the *gozan* to Kyoto Zen monasteries, especially those with close ties to the imperial family or Kyoto nobility. Nanzenji and Daitokuji replaced Kenchōji and Engakuji at the head of the *gozan* rankings. Tōfukuji was promoted, in spite of the fact that it was closed to monks of any but the Shōichi school, a type of monastery known as *tsuchien*, and thus in violation of the principle of open monasteries (*jippō satsu*) whereby abbots were chosen from any lineage on the basis of merit, advocated in Chinese Ch'an monasteries. Kenninji, another Kyoto monastery, was raised to *gozan* status for the first time. Kamakura

Zen monasteries, with their strong associations with the Hōjō, might have been excluded altogether had it not been for the influence on Go-Daigo of Musō, who had close ties with Engakuji and other Zen monasteries in the Kantō.[4]

GO-DAIGO'S MOTIVES

Go-Daigo's patronage of Zen monks, reorganization of the *gozan*, and promotion of Kyoto monasteries was not motivated solely by devotion to Zen or admiration for Musō and Daitō. Political calculations were involved. The political overtones of Go-Daigo's interest in Zen become apparent when we set his treatment of Zen in the larger context of his religious eclecticism, his policy towards other branches of Buddhism, and his conception of imperial sovereignty.

Go-Daigo did not confine his patronage or religious interest to Zen. The *Jinnō shōtōki* (1339), for instance, stresses the emperor's devotion to esoteric Shingon Buddhism. He was a generous patron of the monks Kenshun (1299–1357) of the Sanpō'in, and of Keichin (fl. early fourteenth century) and Monkan (1278–1357) of Enryakuji, all of whom were esotericists and played active political roles in the Kenmu Restoration and the defense of the Southern court. A well-known portrait of Go-Daigo shows him not in Zen robes but dressed as a Chinese emperor holding esoteric Buddhist ceremonial objects. Go-Daigo is also said to have indulged in the practices of the debased Tachikawa school of esoteric Buddhism.[5] The emperor combined his eclectic Buddhist interests with patronage of Shintō shrines and regular performance of Shintō ceremonies. In sum, Go-Daigo's deepest personal spiritual convictions are difficult to fathom. As a practical problem, however, he lacked substantial military power of his own and was obliged to seek the support of all segments of the Buddhist and Shintō institutions as well as disaffected warriors in his efforts to overthrow the warrior government in Kamakura. To this end, the active military support of the great Tendai and Shingon monastic centers with their thousands of *sōhei* (soldier-monks) was vital.

Kansai temples and shrines suspected the centralizing efforts of the Hōjō and resented the pressures the Kamakura warrior government had used to curb their power. Go-Daigo sought to capitalize on these long-standing enmities. In 1329 he appointed his son, Prince Morinaga, abbot (*zasu*) of Enryakuji. Morinaga immediately set to work to organize Enryakuji military support in the struggle to overthrow the *bakufu*. Other imperial princes were strategically placed to perform similar functions in other monasteries. At the same time, Go-Daigo set to work to restore the fortunes of Shingon Buddhism. He granted money and lands to Tōji and Daijoji in Kyoto, ensuring that monks loyal to him held high monastic office. Early in 1330, the emperor visited Nara to pay his respects at the Kasuga shrine, and the powerful monasteries of Kōfukuji and Tōdaiji. Later in the same year, he visited Enryakuji and Hie shrine. It was many years since these religious establishments had been honored with an imperial visit. Go-Daigo's show of favor sprang less from religious compulsion than from a desire to drum up support for his political cause.

Although Kōyasan, in spite of repeated appeals for support, remained aloof in the fighting that brought down the *bakufu*, Enryakuji, Kokawadera, and other Buddhist temples and Shintō shrines sent troops into the field in support of the emperor.[6] The victorious Go-Daigo quickly confirmed their holdings and rewarded them for their aid. When, in 1336, Ashikaga Takauji and other dissatisfied warriors turned against him, it was to Enryakuji that the emperor turned for assistance. Enryakuji could throw 3,000 warrior-monks into battle. It also had an economic stranglehold over Kyoto. Commodities entering Kyoto from Ōmi and Echizen were brought by packhorse traders from Sakamoto who were under Enryakuji control. Moreover, Enryakuji monks operated most of the pawnshop and moneylending businesses (*dosō*) in the capital. Enryakuji's power and wealth and its active support of Go-Daigo naturally earned it the hostility of Ashikaga Takauji and Tadayoshi in their efforts to conquer and control Kyoto. Enryakuji's actions reinforced Ashikaga determination, on the one hand, to curb the military power of the monastery and to break its economic control over the capital and, on the other, to use Zen as a counterweight to the influence of the established Buddhist sects.

Compared with Enryakuji, Kōfukuji, or Kōyasan, even the greatest of the new Zen monasteries were militarily insignificant, although repeated prohibitions against weapons in Zen monasteries suggest that they were not totally defenseless. The major Zen monasteries, however, and the growing Zen institution of which they formed a part, with their thousands of able-bodied men and their close links with powerful warrior-rulers, were not something to be neglected. Patronage and monopoly control of the Kamakura *gozan* monasteries had added luster to the Hōjō regime. Go-Daigo's assertions of control over the *gozan*, and his setting of imperially connected monasteries at their apex, was an expression of imperial authority and a denial of control to warrior rivals. The Kenmu Restoration demonstrated that the Zen institution had become a powerful factor in the complex interplay of forces shaping medieval society.

Go-Daigo's interest in Zen assumes still clearer definition when it is seen in the context of his interest in Sung dynasty political thought and bureaucratic institutions. Assessments of the significance of the Kenmu Restoration are mixed. The prevailing postwar orthodoxy, expressed by Matsumoto Shinhachirō,[7] Satō Shin'ichi,[8] and Nagahara Keiji,[9] and reflected in English by John Hall[10] and Paul Varley,[11] has tended to dismiss Go-Daigo's short-lived Imperial Restoration as a futile attempt to swim against the tide of warrior expansion, an anachronistic effort to return to the age of Emperors Daigo (885–930) and Murakami (926–967) when, it was believed, emperors not only reigned but ruled.

This negative assessment of the Kenmu Restoration has been questioned by Kuroda Toshio and Akamatsu Toshihide. Kuroda, in particular, has argued that the Restoration, notwithstanding its seemingly anachronistic slogan, was a positive and realistic attempt by Go-Daigo to establish a species of feudal monarchy.[12]

The brevity of the Restoration, barely two years, inevitably makes any judgment of the character and direction of Go-Daigo's reform policies speculative. It is possible to suggest, however, that

Go-Daigo was trying to develop the trend toward autocratic centralization pursued by the more powerful of the Hōjō and that his intention was more fully realized by the third Ashikaga shogun, Yoshimitsu, who did succeed in establishing something that could be described as a feudal monarchy.[13] Nor does it seem unreasonable to suggest that Go-Daigo looked not only to the ancient Japanese past but to the more recent Sung empire for inspiration.

Satō Shin'ichi, who emphasizes the autocratic, reactionary character of the Kenmu Restoration, has pointed out the importance to Go-Daigo of Sung political theories and institutions.[14] From an early age, Go-Daigo was interested in the Chinese Confucian and historical classics, especially the Sung dynasty interpretations of the classics by the Ch'en brothers and Chu Hsi. From his study of Sung political theory, he undoubtedly knew of the heightened authority given to the Chinese emperor as the linchpin of a centralized empire.

It was a small step from an interest in Sung theories of imperial authority to the study of the actual operation of the government of the Sung empire. When the policies initiated in the Kenmu Restoration government are examined closely, a number of them seem to reflect Sung practice. The regulation that monks should wear yellow robes instead of black, and the institution of a revised coinage using copper cash and paper notes have been pointed to as Sung-inspired reforms. Satō Shin'ichi has also suggested that Go-Daigo, in order to strengthen his autocratic control, used high-ranking aristocrats to perform bureaucratic functions as heads of eight government ministries. Although it is not clear whether this was based on the Sung bureaucratic model, Go-Daigo's use of provincial intendants (*kokushi*) alongside the *bakufu*-appointed military governors (*shugo*) closely resembled the Sung system of local administration employing magistrates and prefects.

While the precise character and significance of the Kenmu Restoration and the degree of Chinese influence on it are still matters for debate, there is no doubt that there was a strong tide of Sung influence in late thirteenth and early fourteenth century Japan, that Zen monks played an important role in transmitting knowledge of Sung loyalism and of the theory and practice of Sung imperial rule to Japan, and that the *gozan* system, in which Go-Daigo took such an interest, was conceived of as a Sung bureaucratic institution.

ASHIKAGA PATRONAGE OF ZEN

Metropolitan Zen reached its peak of influence and prestige under Ashikaga patronage during the second half of the fourteenth century, when the mature institution came to play an increasingly significant role in the social, political, and economic life of the country. Ashikaga Takauji (1305–1358) and his brother Tadayoshi (1306–1352), as Kantō *bushi*, were well acquainted with Zen. After ousting Go-Daigo from Kyoto in 1336, they proceeded to further the policies of patronage and regulation of Zen which had been initiated by the Hōjō and carried forward by Go-Daigo. They were assisted by Musō Soseki, who remained in Kyoto when Go-Daigo fled to Yoshino.

If one looks at Ashikaga patronage in general terms, a number of characteristics are immediately apparent:

(1) The shoguns lavished most attention on monks belonging to the *gozan* schools, especially to the Musō school. Musō served Takauji as spiritual mentor, social conscience, and political intermediary in his negotiations with the Southern court. This bond between the founder of the shogunate and Musō was respected by later Ashikaga shoguns, who used the leading disciples of Musō and monks of the Musō lineage as their closest confidants.

(2) Few Ashikaga shoguns actually practiced Zen. They discussed Zen, attended elaborate and exotic Zen ceremonies, sponsored vegetarian feasts, and organized literary gatherings at Zen monasteries and sub-temples. None, however, sat consistently in meditation or engaged very seriously in *mondō* or *kōan* practice. The third, fourth, and eighth shoguns, Yoshimitsu (1358–1408), Yoshimochi (1386–1428), and Yoshimasa (1436–1490), were among the most enthusiastic in their patronage of Zen; yet not

one of them can be described as a determined seeker after Zen enlightenment.

Yoshimitsu did practice Zen for some years under the guidance of Gidō Shūshin (1325-1388). After Gidō's death, however, although he affected the name and lifestyle of a Zen monk, Yoshimitsu gave up meditation practice and turned instead to ceremonies and invocations as the expression of his religious feelings.

Yoshimochi commissioned the painter Josetsu to illustrate in allegory the Zen aphorism "The heart cannot be grasped" (*kokoro ubekarazu*). The result was the well-known Catfish and Gourd ink painting. Yoshimochi then had Daikaku and other Zen monks add interpretive verses. Painting and verses were mounted as a screen which the shogun kept by him and used as an aid in *zazen*. Of all the Ashikaga shoguns, Yoshimochi probably had the deepest interest in Zen. Yet he too seems to have enjoyed Zen ceremonies and sermons more than the rigors of meditation.[15]

Yoshimasa also took the tonsure and name of a Zen monk and frequented *gozan* monasteries. His consorting with Zen monks, however, was almost entirely restricted to satisfying his enthusiasm for literature and the arts. The core of his religious life was not Zen but Pure Land salvationism. The Tōgudō, a religious retreat he built for himself in his Higashiyama villa, was an Amida hall; and Shinshō Shōnin, the monk who attended him on his deathbed, was a Tendai-sect *nenbutsu* practitioner.[16] On the whole, the interest of the Ashikaga shoguns in Zen, like that of most of the later Hōjō, was cultural rather than religious. To their political and economic power the patronage of Zen monks and monasteries added a cultural distinction, vital in the rarified aristocratic atmosphere of Kyoto.

In the long run, Ashikaga patronage was a mixed blessing for the *gozan* Zen schools. The backing of the shoguns gave unprecedented prestige, wealth, and influence to *gozan* monasteries. Shogunal interest also fostered the development in Japan of ink-painting, calligraphy, poetry, architecture and garden design, the tea ceremony, domestic etiquette, printing, and other Zen-influenced arts and crafts which made the Muromachi period one of the most brilliant and fertile cultural epochs in Japanese history. Eventually, however, the cultural avocations and secular interests of leading monks weakened the religious spirit of *gozan* monasteries.

This spiritual enervation can be traced in the diaries of *gozan* monks of the period. Gidō's diary, the *Kūge nichiyō kufū ryakushū* (late fourteenth century), stresses the ideal of the stern, frugal, meditation-centered Zen monastic life.[17] His vigorous advocacy of *zazen* and repeated strictures against literary activities and pomp and luxury, however, suggest that the ideal, if it had ever existed, was already eroding in practice. By the mid-fifteenth century, secularization and formalization had taken deeper hold. That the semi-official diaries of the *gozan* institution, the *Inryōken nichiroku* (from 1435) and the *Rokuon nichiroku* (from 1487 to 1651), should have little to say about the actual practice of Zen is perhaps understandable. It is surprising, however, that private diaries of *gozan* monks, such as the *Ga'un nikkenroku* (1446–1473) of Zuikei Shūhō (1392–1473), or the *Hekizan nichiroku* (1459–1468) of Unsen Taikyoku (1421–?), should be silent on the spiritual aspects of Zen monastic life. Both these diaries are replete with details of Buddhist ceremonies, feasts, appointments of abbots, gifts from patrons, temple domains, literary gatherings, political happenings, social events, and climatic changes. They have little to say, however, about *zazen* or *mondō*, and nothing at all about manual labor (*samu*), a vital ingredient of early Ch'an monastic life.[18]

(3) The Ashikaga conceived of the *gozan* Zen institution as a quasi-political adjunct. Go-Daigo had made only a qualified commitment to the Zen institution and had relied for political and military support on the older Buddhist sects. The Ashikaga, following the example of the later Hōjō, gave almost exclusive attention to Zen, deliberately trying to build a nationwide institution under their direct control which they could use as a counterweight to the influence of the *kuge*-oriented established sects.

The building of Ankokuji and Rishōtō, the establishment of Tenryūji, Tōjiji, and Shōkokuji, the extension and centralization of the *gozan* system were all part of this policy. Moreover, since the provincial Zen monasteries included in the *gozan* were, in many cases, patronized as family temples by *shugo* or *jitō*, manipulation of the *gozan* network gave the shogunate a measure of leverage over the leaders of the warrior class upon whom it depended for survival.

(4) The Ashikaga shoguns relied heavily on Zen monks for the conduct of diplomacy and commerce.[19] To provide funds for the construction of Tenryūji, Ashikaga Takauji sent a trading mission to Yuan China. Yoshimitsu went on to develop an active tally trade with Ming China. Temporarily suspended by Yoshimochi, the fourth shogun, the China trade was revived by Yoshinori (1394–1441), the sixth shogun, and continued sporadically until the mid-sixteenth century. Zen monks were indispensable to the successful conduct of this trade. They were familiar with conditions on the continent, well versed in Chinese language and bureaucratic and business methods, able to translate and draft documents, and to entertain and negotiate with Chinese delegations. Most important, those monks involved in foreign trade had acquired considerable financial expertise in the management of monastic finances.

(5) The Ashikaga used the *gozan* as an important source of regular income and occasional loans. Fees collected at the registration of monasteries in the official system and at the appointment of monks to the office of abbot in the *gozan* network provided a substantial annual supplement to the *bakufu* treasury. The *bakufu* also extracted loans from the financially adroit bursars of monasteries like Tenryūji and Shōkokuji who had amassed considerable private capital through successful estate management and money-lending.[20]

(6) The fortunes of the Ashikaga and the *gozan* were so inextricably interrelated that growing *bakufu* weakness in the fifteenth century exposed the *gozan* to attack as inevitably as Ashikaga prestige in the fourteenth had brought prosperity to the official Zen monasteries.

With these general considerations in mind, let us look in greater detail at the institutional development of Zen under the Ashikaga.

TAKAUJI AND TADAYOSHI

Ashikaga Takauji, as the founder of the Muromachi *bakufu*, is usually given credit for shaping Ashikaga policies towards Zen. In fact, in this, his younger brother Tadayoshi played a more active role.

Although he was a generous patron of Musō Soseki, Chu-hsien Fan-hsien (Jikusen Bonsen, 1292–1348), and other Zen monks, Takauji had only a very limited interest in Zen and Chinese culture.[21] A rough and ready warrior, his religious sentiments found their natural outlet in devotion to the saving and protective deities Jizō, Kannon, and Kangiten. The rigors of Chinese learning and culture repelled him. His cultural preference was for the emotion of Japanese poetry and the bucolic entertainment of popular comic mime (*dengaku*). Tadayoshi, in contrast, had unbounded admiration for China, scant respect for the Japanese tradition. He was a devoted student of Chinese Zen and well versed in Chinese culture, thought, and institutions.[22]

Tadayoshi, like his brother, patronized Musō. But, whereas Takauji liked Musō's eclectic, Japanized Zen, Tadayoshi, it has been argued, found it defective. The *Muchū mondō* (Questions and answers in dreams) records questions about Zen asked by Tadayoshi and answers by Musō. The work is frequently cited as an indication of the closeness of the bond between Tadayoshi and Musō. Professor Tamamura Takeji, however, has suggested that Tadayoshi, in their encounters, was deliberately exposing the didactic character of Musō's Zen.[23] This may be unfair to Musō. It is true, however, that, although Tadayoshi and Musō cooperated in matters relating to the Zen institution, Tadayoshi did not practice Zen with Musō. He preferred to study with Chinese masters, or those Japanese monks who best preserved the tradition of Sung Zen.

The early Muromachi *bakufu* was a composite organ in which

power was divided between Takauji and Tadayoshi. Takauji held supreme military and seigniorial authority, while delegating a considerable degree of executive power to his brother. Satō Shin'ichi, analyzing the types of official documents issued by the brothers, has found that those issued by Takauji were either certificates of reward (*ateokonaijō*) or letters of appointment (*buninjō*) of *shugo*. Tadayoshi's household offices issued certificates of confirmation of land rights (*andojō*), judicial rulings (*saikyojō*), customs-barrier permits (*kasho*), and regulatory codes for monasteries (*kinsei*).[24] Satō concludes that a very clear-cut division of function existed, with Takauji holding the rights of feudal military command and granting of rewards for loyal service, Tadayoshi exercising wide-ranging civil, judicial, and economic powers. On the basis of his findings, Satō graphs the early Muromachi *bakufu* power structure provisionally as in Chart 1.[25]

From our point of view, the most interesting thing about the chart is the location of the office of the Commissioner for Zen and Ritsu Monasteries (*Zenritsugata*) under Tadayoshi's direct control. With his greater interest in and knowledge of Zen and Chinese institutions, it was perhaps natural that Tadayoshi should assume primary responsibility for the management and direction of the growing Zen institution. Moreover, the importance he accorded this role is indicated by the prominence the office of *Zenritsugata* held within his household government. It was Tadayoshi, therefore, not Takauji, who issued the first Ashikaga *bakufu* regulations for Engakuji in 1340 which set the tone for the *bakufu* control of Zen. Tadayoshi seems also to have been the driving force behind the construction of Tenryūji and Tōjiji, the building of the Ankokuji and Rishōtō, and the elaboration of the *gozan* system. It was Tadayoshi who saw most clearly the political advantages to the *bakufu* of creating a powerful nationwide system of government-sponsored Zen monasteries.

THE BUILDING OF TENRYŪJI AND ASHIKAGA POWER

Go-Daigo died at Yoshino in the late summer of 1339. Shortly

CHART 1   Dual Power Structure of the Early Muromachi
Bakufu

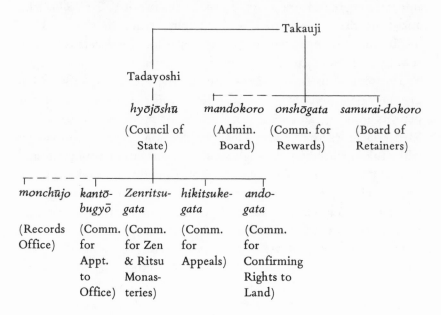

Dotted lines indicate conjectural relationships.

before the emperor's death, Musō had a dream in which he saw
Go-Daigo riding in state into the Kameyama palace in Kyoto. The
monk persuaded Takauji and Tadayoshi that it would be both
fitting and politic to build a memorial where the spirit of the
emperor could be venerated and laid to rest.[26] The Ashikaga
welcomed the proposal. The retired Emperor Kōgon, a devotee
of Zen, was prevailed upon to offer the Kameyama detached
palace in the west of Kyoto for conversion into a Zen monastery,
of which Musō would serve as founding abbot (*kaisan*). Ashikaga
Takauji, Tadayoshi, and Kōgon designated *shōen* in the provinces
of Hyūga, Awa, and Tanba to provide funds for construction. A
master carpenter and twelve assistants were appointed and the
work of construction began.

Work proceeded slowly. The designated funds proved insufficient. In the winter of 1341, Tadayoshi suggested to Musō that a trading mission similar to one sent by the Hōjō in 1325 to raise funds for the rebuilding of Kenchōji be sent to China to raise additional funds. Over the strenuous objections of Enryakuji monks and their supporters among the court aristocracy, it was eventually decided to send two trading vessels. Musō recommended the Hakata merchant Shihon as commander of the venture. Tadayoshi agreed and ordered the merchant to make preparations. Shihon, for his part, issued a declaration in which he promised, regardless of the success or failure of the mission, to provide 5,000 *kanmon* for the monastery. In return for a share of the profits, the *bakufu* agreed to protect the mission from pirates. It was the *bakufu* in the person of Tadayoshi, not Musō or Tenryūji, that confirmed the leader of the mission, fixed the number of vessels, and set the date for departure. The *Tenryūji-bune* set sail from Hakata in the autumn of 1342 and returned in the following summer. According to the *Tenryūji kinen kōryaku*, Shihon made a considerable profit and earned the undying gratitude of Musō. In all probability, the promised 5,000 *kanmon* were added to the building fund.

By 1344, Tenryūji was virtually completed. A proposal was made that Kōgon should attend the seventh anniversary services for Go-Daigo to be held at the new monastery in 1345. When Enryakuji monks, who had no desire to see the Zen sect flourishing in Kyoto or usurping Enryakuji claims to court patronage, got wind of this, they descended on the city in an armed appeal (*gōso*), demanding that the "evil monk" Musō be banished and Tenryūji razed. In the face of Enryakuji threats to bring the sacred portable shrine (*shin'yo*) into the city, and to call up the support of soldier-monks from Kōfukuji and Tōdaiji, Kōgon decided not to attend the Tenryūji ceremonies.

The Ashikaga, however, eager for any chance to assert their control over Kyoto and break the grip of Enryakuji on the city, took a hard line. They threatened to confiscate all the resources of Enryakuji monks if they brought the shrine into Kyoto. The memorial ceremonies and feasts went ahead. The Ashikaga thus used Tenryūji as Yoritomo had used the rebuilding of Tōdaiji, as the occasion for a show of strength, affluence, and benevolence. In the eighth month of 1345, Takauji and Tadayoshi, with their leading generals Yamana Tokiuji and Kō no Moronao, headed a procession of many hundreds of armed warriors to a great celebration feast at Tenryūji. According to such contemporary chronicles as the *Kōmyōin shinki* and the *Entairyaku,* the streets of the city were thronged from early morning with townspeople hoping to catch a glimpse of the military pageantry. It was impressed upon the city that the *bakufu,* not Enryakuji, was the military master of Kyoto and that henceforward Zen was to be the privileged Buddhist school within the capital.

The privileged status of Zen and its intimate relation with the Ashikaga were further symbolized by the rebuilding of Tōjiji in 1336 close to the seat of the *bakufu* in the center of Kyoto.[27] Until Yoshimitsu built Shōkokuji in 1382, Tōjiji served as the Ashikaga family temple (*bodaiji*) in Kyoto. Its first abbot was Kosen Ingen (1295–1374) who studied Zen in China from 1318 to 1326 and was patronized especially by Tadayoshi. After Tadayoshi's fall from power in 1350, Kosen moved to Kamakura. Tōjiji was made a branch temple (*matsuji*) of Tenryūji. The monastery was then restricted to monks of the Musō lineage. Together with Rinsenji and Tenryūji, Tōjiji became a major center of Musō school influence in Kyoto. In spite of its being a "closed" monastery, it was subsequently ranked as a *jissatsu* in the official *gozan* system. The fact that Tōjiji was permitted to retain its exclusive character while being included as an official monastery set a precedent under which the Zen family temples (*ujidera*) of local magnates could be raised to the status of official monastery.

ANKOKUJI AND RISHŌTŌ

At the same time that Takauji and Tadayoshi were using Zen as an instrument in their assertion of control over Kyoto, they were also making use of Buddhist monasteries in their pacification of the rest of the country. This strategy is decribed in a number of articles by Professor Imaeda Aishin.[28] By the spring of 1337, resistance by supporters of Go-Daigo was crumbling. Pro-Ashikaga forces were clearly gaining the upper hand. Although the fighting was not over, many felt that a time had come to try to heal some of the wounds opened in the years of civil war. Musō Soseki proposed that a pagoda and temple should be built in each of the provinces of Japan where prayers could be offered for the spirits of warriors who had fallen in battle and for lasting peace. This suggestion was taken up by Takauji and executed by Tadayoshi. Although the plan resembles the ancient Japanese network of official temples, the Kokubunji system, the direct inspiration was derived by Musō and Tadayoshi from Sung China.[29]

In 1338 and 1339, Tadayoshi ordered the provision of funds in the form of *jitō shiki* for the construction (in some case reconstruction) of five-story pagodas in the Kumedadera in Izumi province, the Jōdoji in Bingo, the Tōmyōji in Hizen, and the Eikōji in Noto. Of these, the Jōdoji actually petitioned the *bakufu* to be allowed to build such a pagoda. In the eighth month of 1338, the community of monks at the Gakuonji in Iga province also requested the *bakufu* to be permitted to build a pagoda in their temple. According to their petition, Niki Yoshinao, the local *shugo*, an Ashikaga appointee, had fortified the Gakuonji and used it as a strongpoint in his struggles with warrior supporters of Go-Daigo in Iga. Gakuonji monks, in support of their claim, protested that they had actively supported Yoshinao and amply demonstrated their loyalty to the Ashikaga.

In 1344 the *bakufu* declared that the pagodas were to have the title of Rishōtō (Pagodas of the Buddha's Favor) and that the temples would be known as Ankokuji (Temples for Peace in the Realm). Ankokuji and Rishōtō were separate institutions. The pagodas were established not in Zen monasteries but principally in powerful provincial Tendai and Shingon monasteries. Ankokuji were designated from among existing Zen monasteries belonging to the *gozan* lineages, especially the Musō and Shōichi lineages. Both the Ankokuji and the monasteries containing the Rishōtō were patronized by *shugo*. In many cases, the Ankokuji were the clan temples (*ujidera*) of their *shugo* patrons and thus the most influential local Buddhist foundations. As leading provincial Zen monasteries, Ankokuji were also rapidly incorporated into the middle and lower tiers of the expanding *gozan* network of official Zen monasteries. Although very few Ankokuji or Rishōtō buildings survive today, Professor Imaeda, on the basis of careful research of contemporary documents, has concluded that, by 1350, Ankokuji and Rishōtō had been established in every province of Japan, with the possible exception of Yamato, where entrenched Kōfukuji power may have prevented the establishment of a rival Zen Ankokuji.

Inspired initially by religious impulse, the policy of building Ankokuji and Rishōtō rapidly assumed political and military implications in the eyes of the Ashikaga. Tsuji Zennosuke has suggested that the foundation of a temple represented an assertion of territorial control by its patron. If this is so, then the successive creation of Ankokuji and Rishōtō provides an index of the growing authority of the Ashikaga and of their claim to exercise benevolent rule over the whole of Japan. Ankokuji and Rishōtō were strategically sited within the areas of *shugo* jurisdiction. The example of Gakuonji in Iga suggests that *shugo* and *bakufu* planned to use these religious centers as military fortifications and centers of surveillance.

Through the Ankokuji and Rishōtō the *bakufu* was able to supervise and support the *shugo* and to tie localities more closely to the center of power in Kyoto. Since monasteries and their local patrons themselves petitioned for the grant of Ankokuji or Rishōtō status, there was obviously considerable incentive. This was partly economic—the grant of additional land rights to the value of two or three hundred *kanmon* per annum. Their enthusiasm was also spurred by a desire for local prestige and the advantages of a direct tie with the Ashikaga. Through the granting of the Rishōtō title, Tadayoshi skillfully maintained the support of powerful monasteries belonging to the older Buddhist sects. At the same time, through the Ankokuji, he was promoting the nationwide diffusion of the *gozan* Zen lineage, and encouraging *shugo* to follow the lead of the Ashikaga in patronizing Zen.

With the death of Musō in 1351, the assassination of Tadayoshi in 1352, and the death of Takauji in 1358, the Rishōtō—which no longer served a vital military function, had no self-sustaining central organization, and were a financial burden to the *shugo* responsible for their upkeep—were allowed to fall into neglect. Ashikaga Yoshimitsu devoted his energy to reorganizing, expanding, and centralizing the *gozan* system into which most of the Ankokuji were eventually absorbed.

GOZAN, JISSATSU, AND SHOZAN

Articulation and centralization of the *gozan* system, which had been set in motion by the Hōjō, was continued by Takauji and Tadayoshi and, after a number of revisions, virtually completed by Yoshimitsu; more accurately, under Yoshimitsu by his advisers (*kanrei*) Hosokawa Yoriyuki and Shiba Yoshimasa.[30] Ashikaga interest in the elaboration of this system of official monasteries, like their interest in the Ankokuji and Rishōtō, was inspired by political and economic as well as religious and cultural considerations.

Chart 2 illustrates the development of the *gozan* tier. It has already been suggested that the surviving documentary evidence relating to the character and organization of the monasteries designated as *wu-shan* (*gozan*), *shih-ch'a* (*jissatsu*), and *chia-ch'a* (*kōsatsu*) in China is very fragmentary. That such a network existed by the early fourteenth century, however, is implied by the brief references to *wu-shan* and *shih-ch'a* by the early Ming dynasty scholar-official Sung Lien (1310–1381) in sections 15 and 20 of his *Sung-wen-hsien-kung-ch'üan-chi* and from the writings of contemporary Japanese Zen monks like Kokan Shiren (1278–1346). In the Chinese "Five Mountains system"—as that "system" was understood in medieval Japan—only five monasteries were included in the topmost *wu-shan* category.

In Japan, in the completed system, there were eleven full *gozan*

CHART 2   Changes in Rankings of *Gozan* Monasteries in Kamakura and Kyoto between 1333 and 1386 (Kyoto monasteries are marked *).

	1334–36 (Go-Daigo)[a]	1341 (Tadayoshi)[b]	1358 (Yoshiakira)[c]	1380 (Yoshimitsu)[d]	(1386) (Yoshimitsu)[e]
Gozan-no-Jō (superior gozan)					Nanzenji
Gozan 1	Nanzenji* (Daitokuji)*	Kenchōji Nanzenji*	Kenchōji Nanzenji*	Kenchōji Nanzenji*	Tenryūji* Kenchōji
Gozan 2	Tōfukuji*	Engakuji Tenryūji*	Engakuji Tenryūji*	Engakuji Tenryūji*	Shōkokuji* Engakuji
Gozan 3	Kenninji*	Jufukuji	Jufukuji	Jufukuji Kenninji*	Kenninji* Jufukuji
Gozan 4	Kenchōji	Kenninji*	Kenninji*	Jōchiji Tōfukuji*	Tōfukuji* Jōchiji
Gozan 5	Engakuji	Tōfukuji*	Tōfukuji* Jōchiji Jomyōji Manjuji*	Jōmyōji Manjuji*	Manjuji* Jomyōji
Jun-gozan (associate gozan)		Jōchiji			

Notes: [a]Rankings during the period of Go-Daigo's restoration are doubtful. [b]Idea of five mountains gives way to five grades plus "associate *gozan*" category. [c]Five monasteries each from Kyoto and the Kantō in uneven ranking. [d]Evenly balanced dual structure.

[e]Intrusion of Shōkokuji leads to promotion of Nanzenji following the example of the contemporary Ch'an monastic system in Ming China. (Documents from Kamakura monasteries continue to list Kenchōji, Engakuji, and the other Kantō *gozan* above their Kyoto counterparts).

monasteries, divided equally between Kyoto and Kamakura, with Nanzenji set at the apex. All monasteries were carefully ranked. Although formal equality was maintained, the Kyoto *gozan* became increasingly influential as the *bakufu* settled into the capital. Moreover, within the Kyoto *gozan*, monasteries like Tenryūji and Shōkokuji, which were controlled by the Musō lineage and had close ties with the Ashikaga, were most influential.

Shōkokuji, for instance, was built as a symbol of the power and pretensions of Ashikaga Yoshimitsu, and his success in ending the civil war and reuniting the Northern and Southern courts. In 1382 Yoshimitsu set aside a large area close to his Muromachi residence as the site for a new Zen monastery. Musō Soseki was posthumously named founder (*kaisan*) and Shun'oku Myōha appointed first abbot. Yoshimitsu was enthusiastic: levies were laid on the various *shugo*, and the shogun himself symbolically carried earth for the foundations. In 1384 the Buddha hall was completed. In 1386 the still incomplete monastery was introduced into the *gozan* immediately below Tenryūji.

The building work was completed in 1392 when Yoshimitsu sponsored an elaborate celebration at the monastery. Two years later, fire reduced much of Shōkokuji to ashes. Undeterrred, Yoshimitsu immediately ordered reconstruction. By 1396, the Buddha hall had been restored, and work on the Dharma hall was under way. Yoshimitsu also built a 7-story, 70-meter high pagoda in the compound to soar arrogantly above the city. To celebrate the completion of the pagoda, a lavish ceremony known as a *gosaie* was held in the ninth month of 1399. One thousand monks from Tōji, Tōdaiji, Onjōji, and other non-Zen monasteries as well as the Zen *gozan* participated. The curious are reported to have come from as far afield as Kyūshū and the Kantō to watch Yoshimitsu lead a gorgeously arrayed procession of warriors and nobles through the city from the newly completed Kitayama palace to Shōkokuji. The return to the palace under the flickering lights of hundreds of lanterns was equally impressive.[31]

While Zen monasteries belonging to the Musō lineage and favored by the *bakufu* were in the ascendant, other Rinzai monasteries

FIGURE 8   Document Signed by Hōjō Takatoki (1303–1333),
Buddhist Name Sūgan

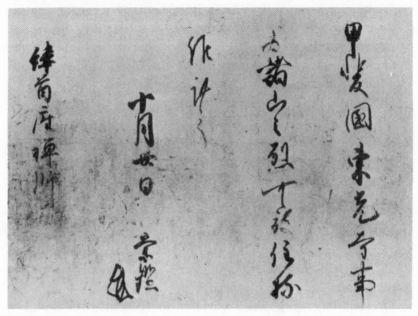

In this document Takatoki raises to the rank of shozan *the Zen temple of Tōkōji in the province of Kai and stipulates that its "chief seat," the monk* I shuso *should serve as abbot (jūji). The Tokōji is said to have been founded by Lan-ch'i Tao-lung and must have been among the first provincial Zen temples to be ranked as a* shozan.

Photograph courtesy of The Historiographical Institute, Shiryōhensan-jo, Tokyo University, taken from Komonjo jidai kagami.

were being demoted in rank. Daitokuji, which, as the creation of Hanazono and Go-Daigo, had strong imperial connections, was excluded from the *gozan* category by the Ashikaga, being reduced to *jissatsu* status. Eventually, on the grounds that it wished to remain a "closed" monastery, Daitokuji requested to be allowed to leave the *gozan* system altogether. This was clearly not a compelling reason. The Chinese ideal that public or official monasteries (*kanji*) should be open to talented monks from any school had already been vitiated by the Ashikaga in the case of Tenryūji, Tōjiji, Rinsenji, and Shōkokuji. Similar accommodation could presumably have been made for Daitokuji had it been welcome in the *gozan*. Tōfukuji, one of the oldest Zen monasteries in Kyoto

and the center of the most populous *gozan* lineage, was also reduced in rank. It was too important and powerful to be excluded
completely from the *gozan* rankings, but its insistence on remaining closed to monks other than those belonging to the Shōichi
lineage and, more important, its connections with the imperial
court and Kyoto *kuge* society alienated it from the Ashikaga.
Kenninji, the third-ranking Kyoto *gozan,* also remained independent of the Muromachi *bakufu* in spirit, being particularly conscious of its debt to the Kamakura *bakufu* and not being an
enclave of the Musō lineage.

The second tier of the *gozan* system was made up of large provincial Zen monasteries referred to as *jissatsu,* literally "ten
temples" (Chart 3). In China, this category included only 10
monasteries. In Japan, however, inflation set in, and in the fifteenth century an increasing number of local Zen monasteries—
and their *shugo* patrons—were honored by inclusion. Yoshimitsu
began the expansion when he added 6 "associate" *jissatsu* in 1380.
In 1386 he established a balanced double system of 10 monasteries each for the Kansai and Kantō. By the end of the fifteenth
century, 46 monasteries, many of them Ankokuji, had been raised
to the status of *jissatsu,* and the category was still expanding.

Changes among the *jissatsu* naturally followed changes in the
upper *gozan* tier. When Jōmyōji, the burial place of Takauji's
father, was made a *gozan* in 1358, Zenkōji, which had been
founded by Lan-ch'i, moved to the top of the Kamakura *jissatsu*
ranking. In the assessment of *jissatsu* rank-order regional balance,
association with the Musō lineage, and ties with the Ashikaga or
their leading vassals were decisive factors. Of the Kyoto *jissatsu,*
Tōjiji was built as an Ashikaga family temple and controlled by
followers of Musō. Rinsenji was built originally by Go-Daigo for
Musō. Half a dozen other *jissatsu* in Kyoto and Kamakura were
either exclusive preserves of the Musō lineage or claimed some
connection with Musō. Daitokuji and its branch-temple, Ryūshōji, were included at the bottom of the 1386 Kyoto ranking.
They withdrew from the *gozan* completely in 1341.

Expansion of the *jissatsu* category served as one means of

CHART 3 Changes in Major *Jissatsu* Ranking 1341–1386

1342 (Tadayoshi)	1358 (Yoshiakira)	1380 (Yoshimitsu)	1358 (Yoshimitsu) KYOTO	KANTŌ
Jōmyōji	Zenkōji	Tōjiji*	Tōjiji	Zenkōji
Zenkōji	Shōfukuji (Chikuzen)	Zenkōji	Rinsenji	Zuisenji
Shōfukuji (Chikuzen)	Manjuji (Kamakura)	Shōfukuji	Shinnyoji	Tōshōji
Manjuji*	Tōshōji	Tōshōji	Ankokuji	Manjuji
Tōshōji	Chōrakuji	Manjuji	Hōdōji	Taikeiji
Manjuji (Kamakura)	Shinnyoji*	Chōrakuji	Fumonji	Kōseiji
Chōrakuji	Ankokuji*	Shinnyoji*	Kōgakuji	Tōzenji
Shinnyoji*	Manjuji (Bungo)	Ankokuji*	Myōkōji	Zenpukuji
Ankokuji*	Seikenji	Manjuji (Bungo)	Daitokuji	Hōsenji
Manjuji (Bungo)	Rinsenji*	Seikenji Jun- jissatsu Rinsenji* Hōdōji* Zuisenji Fumonji* Hōrinji Kokuseiji	Ryūshōji	Chōrakuji

*denotes Kyoto monasteries.

Monasteries having close ties with Musō or the Musō lineage are underlined.

extending both *bakufu* patronage and Rinzai Zen into the provinces. It was also increasingly used as a device to increase *bakufu* income. All monasteries included within the official *gozan* system paid for the privilege. Their abbots also paid a substantial fee upon appointment, and their 20 or so officers paid a small fee at each annual changeover. Obviously, the more monasteries the *bakufu* enrolled and the more rapidly their abbots and officers circulated, the greater the profit to the *bakufu*.[32]

The third and lowest tier of the Chinese Five Mountains system of officially designated Zen monasteries is said to have been eventually made up of about 35 provincial monasteries known as "major temples" (*chia-ch'a*). These were generally referred to as *shozan* (various temples) in Japanese documents. In Japan, granting of *shozan* status was initiated by the Hōjō. The earliest recorded grant of the title was to the Kantō monastery of Sūjuji in 1321. This tier of the hierarchy was more flexible than the *gozan* and *jissatsu* grades. There was no traditional restriction as to the number of monasteries that could be included, and there was also less consciousness of niceties of rank among the individual *shozan* monasteries. The relative standing of any monastery depended upon the reputation of its abbot and the influence of its patron. *Shozan* proliferated under the Ashikaga who granted the title liberally to those temples—or their *shugo* and *jitō* patrons— who were prepared to pay for the honor of inclusion in the official Zen system. Professor Imaeda's research shows that, by the mid-fifteenth century, there were more than 250 *shozan* scattered throughout Japan. These carried *gozan* school Zen teachings and Kyoto cultural values into the remotest parts of the country.

REGIONAL DISTRIBUTION

The mature Japanese *gozan* network, as it existed at the outbreak of the Ōnin War in 1467, was thus made up of some 300 official monasteries. If their numerous sub-temples (*tatchū*) and branch-temples (*matsuji*)—some of which were wealthier and more influential than the parent foundations—are included, the total number of *gozan* affiliates numbered several thousand.

With the exception of large clusters around Kyoto and Kamakura, these Zen monasteries were scattered fairly evenly over the whole country, with an Ankokuji, one or two *jissatsu*, and several *shozan* in almost every province. Those provinces where *gozan* Rinzai Zen had put down the deepest roots were naturally those where it was longest known or had found the most powerful patrons. The provinces of Chikuzen, Hizen, Mino, Shinano, and Ise each contained ten or eleven official monasteries. *Gozan* Zen was weakest where the older Buddhist sects were strongest and where loyalty to the Southern court ran deepest. There were, for instance, no official Zen monasteries in Kōfukuji-dominated Yamato, and very few in Shima, Sado, Oki, or Buzen.[33]

Relatively few of the official *gozan* monasteries were original Zen foundations. Many were clan temples (*ujidera*) which had been converted from Shingon, Tendai, or Jōdo Buddhism to Zen, frequently on the orders of a locally powerful warrior-ruler. Most of these provincial monasteries were "closed" monasteries (*tsuchien*), restricted to members of one or other of the *gozan* lineages. Of the 300 monasteries, more than 70 were affiliated with the Shōichi lineage and another 70 with the Bukkō transmission (derived from Wu-hsueh) which included the Musō lineage.[34] The sectarian affiliation of any local monastery was largely determined by the wishes of its secular founder-patron who chose the first abbot and thus set the pattern for subsequent development.

To the provincial warrior hegemon the most desirable attributes in a Zen monk—apart, of course, from his spiritual attainments—were that he should have been to China, that he should belong to the Musō line which had the special favor of the Ashikaga, that he should be familiar with the latest cultural trends in the capital, and that his Zen should be sufficiently eclectic to be easily accessible to the patron and his family. Except in unusual circumstances, smaller patrons were unlikely to be able to attract to local monasteries the more eminent members of the Musō and Shōichi lineages who combined all these desirable qualities in the highest degree.[35]

CENTRALIZATION AND CONTROL OF THE GOZAN BY THE ASHIKAGA

The Ashikaga shoguns maintained fairly tight personal control over the increasingly systematized and centralized hierarchy of official Zen monasteries, while delegating administrative responsibility to warrior officials or Zen monks. The *gozan* was supervised by *bakufu* officials until 1379. Thereafter administrative control was transferred to the Registrar General (*sōroku*), an office monopolized by the leading prelates of the Musō line. The incumbents of the *sōroku* office also served as religious, cultural, and political mentors to the shoguns, who were thus able to maintain direct control over the Zen institution.

The Hōjō regents had taken a close personal interest in Zen. They sent invitations to Chinese Zen masters, made grants of land for building sites and monastic domain, supervised the work of monastery construction, authorized the building of sub-temples (*tatchū*), selected and appointed abbots, and issued detailed regulations governing the lives of Zen monks. As Zen monasteries and monks proliferated in the opening decades of the fourteenth century, however, the Hōjō found it necessary to create a subordinate bureaucratic mechanism to handle the day-to-day administration relating to Zen monasteries.

The "Engakuji seifu jōsho" (1327) refers to a warrior-official known as the *gyōji*, whom the abbot was to consult on secular matters affecting the monastery, and who was to be informed before the appointment of the major monastic officeholders. Although it is unclear how the office of *gyōji* was staffed, how it operated, and what powers it had, there is no doubt that, before the demise of their regime, the Hōjō had given wide supervisory powers over the *gozan* to a secular official.[36]

Ashikaga Takauji, Tadayoshi, and Yoshiakira (1330–1367), the second Ashikaga shogun, continued the Hōjō practice of making major policy decisions relating to Zen monasteries themselves, while systematizing and extending secular administration. They appointed two kinds of *bakufu* officials. The senior of these were known as Overseers of Zen and Ritsu monasteries (*Zenritsugata tonin*). They were assisted by Commissioners of Zen and Ritsu monasteries (*Zenritsu bugyō*).[37]

The *Zenritsugata* office was originally part of Tadayoshi's household government (Chart 1). The first overseer was Ōtaka Shigenari, who was in office at least between 1342 and 1353. Shigenari was a high-ranking warrior, an intimate of Tadayoshi and Musō, and a devotee of Zen. He was succeeded as Overseer by Sasaki Takauji (1306–1373), who was appointed in 1364. Sasaki was a powerful warrior close to the center of power in the *bakufu*. He had served the Hōjō until 1331, when he gave his allegiance to Ashikaga Takauji. Sasaki's military support was crucial in the establishment of the Muromachi *bakufu*, and he also helped to draft the *Kenmu shikimoku* (1336), the basic legal code of the Ashikaga. *Shugo* of Ōmi, Kazusa, Izumo, Oki, and Hida, as well as the holder of a number of senior *bakufu* posts, Sasaki was also a man of wide cultural interests. He composed *waka* and *renga*, patronized Ōmi *sarugaku*, and practiced Zen. Akamatsu Norisuke (1314–1371) was appointed Overseer in 1370. He too was a local warrior-hegemon, the *shugo* of Harima, Mimasaka, and Bizen. In his youth, he had taken the tonsure and been known as "Akamatsu the Ritsu Master." Later in life, he became a fervent patron of Zen. He studied under the monk Tettō Gikō and built the Hōrinji in Harima for Sesson Yūbai (1290–1346). From these brief biographies, it is evident that the *Zenritsugata tōnin* was chosen from among the most influential supporters of the *bakufu*, a leading warrior who could be expected to foster and regulate the development of the *gozan*.

The *Zenritsu bugyō* were lower-ranking, regular *bakufu* officials. They corresponded in status to such commissioners for Shintō shrines and the older Buddhist sects as the Iwashimizu Hachiman *bugyō*, Sanmon (Enryakuji) *bugyō*, Tōji *bugyō*, and Nanto (Tōdaiji and Kōfukuji) *bugyō*. The first known appointee was the Confucian scholar Hino (Fujiwara) Arinori, who was certainly in office in 1345 and may have been in the post prior to 1341. Others who served in this office were Fuse Shōchin, appointed in 1371, and Iio Sadayuki, who was appointed in 1378.

Together, the *tōnin* and *bugyō* acted as a conduit between the shogunate and the *gozan*. They dealt with litigation involving the official monasteries, confirmed monastic rights and holdings, selected and appointed abbots, determined *gozan* rankings, supervised the collection fees for certificates of appointment, and drafted disciplinary regulations.

THE TENKA SŌROKU AND THE INRYŌSHOKU

Ashikaga Yoshimitsu in 1379 transferred responsibility for the administrative supervision of the *gozan* from secular officials to *gozan* Zen monks when he granted to Shun'oku Myōha (1311–1388), his religious advisor, the title of Registrar General of Monks (*tenka sōroku*).[38]

The *sōroku* system was an institutional import from China. An office of Registrar General of Monks (*seng-lu*), staffed by monks under the civil Commissioners of Religion, had existed in China since at least the T'ang dynasty. According to Japanese scholars, the *seng-lu* office was reformed and expanded in the early Ming dynasty; and it was this reformed office that provided the model for the Japanese *sōroku*. The *seng-lu* office had been a major bureaucratic organ with a substantial secretarial staff who handled the administration of the whole Buddhist institution under the supervision of the civil bureaucracy. The Japanese *gozan sōroku*, however, had jurisdiction only over official Zen monasteries. The office did not have authority to make decisions for non-*gozan* Zen monasteries like Daitokuji and Myōshinji, or the many Sōtō-school monasteries. It was also small, staffed only by the incumbent and his immediate monk disciples, assisted by a scrivener (*kumon bugyō*) who drew up official documents.

It is not entirely clear why Yoshimitsu made the sudden change. Mere reform of the Buddhist control system in China is unlikely to have been a sufficient stimulus. In general terms, it was an expression of his devotion to Zen and desire to honor Shun'oku. It was also a recognition that the *gozan* monasteries were mature, docile, responsible, and no longer in need of warrior protection and surveillance. Moreover, the transfer of administrative responsibility to Shun'oku, far from weakening shogunal control, may actually have worked to strengthen it by making the *gozan* a direct extension of the shogun's private chambers. This administrative change certainly did nothing to prevent Yoshimitsu and his successors from interfering in Zen monastic affairs or from drawing on the *gozan* as a source of advisors, income, and loans.

It is likely that the direct initiative for the establishment of the *sōroku* office came jointly from Shun'oku, who would have been familiar with any Ming institutional changes, and his disciple and patron, the warrior Shiba Yoshimasa (1350–1410), who, in 1379, ousted Hosokawa Yoriyuki (1329–1392) to become regent (*kanrei*) himself.[39]

Hosokawa Yoriyuki had made himself extremely unpopular in Kyoto *gozan* circles, especially with Shun'oku and other leading members of the Musō lineage.[40] In an effort to check growing tendencies towards luxury, secularization, and deterioration of monastic practice in the *gozan*, he issued a stream of regulations and prohibitions. Prohibitions relating to the appointment of abbots of *shozan* monasteries ("Shozan juen kinsei jōjō," 5 articles, 1368/2/13), for instance, forbade newly appointed *shozan* abbots to invite the abbots (*chōrō*) of other *shozan* to their installation ceremonies. They also strictly forbade the mutual exchange of lavish gifts by Zen abbots and warriors or *bakufu* officials.[41] Many Zen prelates were angered by Yoriyuki's interference. Gidō Shūshin was one of the few to agree that some kind of purgation was essential if the ills of the *gozan* were to be cured.

Yoriyuki aroused even greater antagonism among *gozan* monks by his handling of the Nanzenji Gate incident.[42] Nanzenji had been allowed to build a barrier as a source of funds for the rebuilding of its great gate. The Tendai monasteries of Onjōji and Enryakuji resented this privilege. In 1367, an Onjōji novice who tried to force his way through the barrier without paying was killed in a scuffle. Onjōji followers retaliated by attacking the barrier and killing two Nanzenji monks.

Early in the following year, Jōzan Sozen, the abbot of Nanzenji, launched a polemic in which he asserted that Zen alone was the true Buddhist doctrine and that Tendai and the other Japanese Buddhist teachings were base perversions. In the course of this, he described Enryakuji monks as "apes, who merely resemble humans" and the Onjōji monks as "toads, the lowest of creatures." Tendai followers were naturally enraged. Enryakuji monks demanded of the court that Shun'oku Myōha and Jōzan Sozen be banished from Kyoto and that the Nanzenji Gate be pulled down. The Northern court, supported by such *bakufu* officials as the warriors Yamana Tokiuji, Akamatsu Norisuke, and Sasaki Ujiyori, was in favor of acceding to Enryakuji demands. Initially, Hosokawa Yoriyuki alone supported Shun'oku's contention that to give in to Enryakuji demands would not only weaken Zen but also erode the authority of the court and *bakufu*.

In the summer of 1368, soldier-monks from Enryakuji descended on Kyoto bearing their sacred portable shrine. The court petitioned the *bakufu* to order the banishment of Sozen. Yoriyuki reversed his position and ordered the expulsion of Sozen from Kyoto. This, however, did not satisfy Enryakuji. In the following year, Enryakuji monks again forced their way into the city. Few *bakufu* warriors were prepared to make a firm stand against the *sōhei*. Yoriyuki again capitulated and ordered carpenters to demolish the great gate at Nanzenji. Enryakuji was finally satisfied. Zen monks felt that they have been betrayed by Yoriyuki.

Bad feelings between Yoriyuki and Musō-lineage monks led by Shun'oku festered. In 1371 Shun'oku was banished from Kyoto by Yoriyuki. At the same time, members of Shun'oku's faction among Musō's followers were dismissed from their positions as abbots of Kyoto *gozan* monasteries. Shun'oku, and those monks who supported him, looked increasingly to Shiba Yoshimasa to restore their position and the fortunes of *gozan* Zen. Whereas Hosokawa Yoriyuki, who had little personal interest in Zen, had always been more sympathetic to the eclectic "Japanese" faction within the Musō lineage, Shiba Yoshimasa, a devoted practitioner of Zen, developed close ties with the progressive "Chinese" faction led by Shun'oku, Gidō, and Zekkai. No sooner had Shiba ousted Hosokawa than Shun'oku was recalled to Kyoto, made abbot of Nanzenji, and appointed *sōroku* with supreme authority over the *gozan*. Together, Shiba and Shun'oku instituted reforms in Zen monastic practice. They institutionalized some longstanding Japanese practices while introducing recent developments from Ming Chinese Zen monasteries. The *sōroku* system itself was one of these new developments. Under the skillful leadership of Shun'oku and with the determined support of Shiba Yoshimasa, the *gozan* recovered much of the ground it had lost during the Nanzenji incident. The incident, however, had exposed the basic weakness of Zen and its dependence on *bakufu* support.

The duties of the *sōroku* office were those hitherto performed by the secular overseers and commissioners. The *sōroku* was responsible for the appointment and promotion of abbots and monastic officers, collection of fees, ranking of monasteries, granting of monastic domain, and maintenance of standards of monastic life. In addition to these administrative functions, incumbents also instructed the shoguns in Zen and Chinese culture, organized Buddhist ceremonies, mediated between the *bakufu* and *shugo*, and drafted documents for the Ming trade. The *sōroku* was therefore an influential office. After Shun'oku, it was held by Zekkai Chūshin (1336–1405), Kūkoku Meiō (1328–1407), Zuikei Shūhō (1392–1473), and other leading members of the Musō lineage. Control of this office ensured the Musō line's continued domination of the *gozan* Zen institution and its maintenance of political influence.

Towards the end of his life, Yoshimitsu built, in the grounds of Shōkokuji, a sub-temple called the Rokuon'in to use as a private Zen hall. Zekkai Chūshin was appointed abbot. The Rokuon'in later served as Yoshimitsu's burial place, and its abbots were traditionally granted the *sōroku* title. It was this small sub-temple within Shōkokuji, not the great monastery of Nanzenji, that served as the administrative nerve center of the *gozan* network. The Rokuon *sōroku* survived until the seventeenth century, when the Tokugawa put Zen monasteries under *bakufu* control and the *sōroku* title was conferred on Ishin Sūden (1569–1633) and his successors as heads of the Konchi'in sub-temple in Nanzenji. Long before that, however, the *sōroku* had lost its vitality. During the later fifteenth and sixteenth centuries, as the sons of emperors, shoguns, and aristocrats found their way to the top in the Musō lineage, the *sōroku* office suffered increasing aristocratization and enervation until it was eclipsed in influence by the subordinate office of the Inryōken.[43]

The Inryōken was a small hermitage within the Rokuon'in. It was established as a private retreat by Ashikaga Yoshimochi. Yoshimochi used Chūhō Chūshō, the head priest of the Inryōken, as a personal attendant and means of communication with the *sōroku*. This office, like the *sōroku*, was monopolized by Musō's disciples, many of whom were the sons of the Akamatsu, Hoso-kawa, and other leading *bakufu* retainers. Their family back-grounds gave them political connection and expertise. Their closeness to the shoguns provided an opportunity for them to ex-ercise real power. In addition to their administrative and advisory functions within the *gozan*, some holders of the Inryōken office were given charge of shogunal granaries (*kura*) and performed other purely secular functions. Together, therefore, the offices of the *sōroku* and the Inryōken served the *bakufu* in substantially the same way as its regular *bugyōnin* officials.[44]

ZENITH AND DECLINE

The *gozan* institution was at its zenith in the late fourteenth and early fifteenth centuries. Under the enthusiastic patronage of sho-guns Yoshimitsu and Yoshimochi (1386–1428), and of provincial warrior-rulers[45] and Kyoto nobles—many of whom put offspring to train as Zen monks and nuns—*gozan* monasteries enjoyed nearly a century of unprecedented material prosperity and cultural activity. Their Dharma and Buddha halls provided the setting for elaborate Buddhist ceremonials; their abbots' halls (*hōjō*) and sub-temples (*tatchū*) were centers for the enjoyment of poetry, ink painting, tea ceremony, and garden design. Zen monks lectured to emperors and nobles and served as political advisors to shoguns and warrior-rulers. Zekkai Chūshin, for instance, was sent by the *bakufu* to negotiate with the rebellious warrior Ōuchi Yoshihiro during the Ōei disturbance in 1399. Hakudō Bon'i performed a similar function in a rebellion by Uesugi Zenshū in 1416. Zen monks were also active in the Ming trade and in Kyoto commerce and moneylending. While an increasingly impoverished *bakufu* sought to tap the growing wealth of the *gozan* through the expansion of opportunities for the gathering of fees and forced loans, at the same time official Zen monasteries were allowed tax privileges and given immunity from division of estates (*hanzei*). In this favorable environment the *gozan* naturally flourished.[46]

Zen monasteries, however, did not possess significant military strength of their own. The prosperity of the great Kyoto and Kamakura *gozan* monasteries was assured only as long as their principal patrons, the Ashikaga shoguns, were able to protect them and their scattered estates. This ability declined in the fifteenth century. The assassination of Yoshinori, the sixth Ashikaga shogun, in 1441 was an early indication of Ashikaga weakness.[47] *Gozan* domains scattered throughout the country began to suffer intrusions by *shugo* and local warrior-leaders eager to extend their territorial control. Zen monastic domains also suffered considerable depredation in the upsurge of peasant uprisings (*tsuchi ikki*). The Ōnin War brought destruction to the metropolitan monasteries themselves. In ten years of sporadic fighting, almost all the major Kyoto *gozan* were plundered and put to the torch.

Zen was embroiled directly in the contemporary political turmoil in Kyoto by Kikei Shinzui, the chief priest of the Inryōken who, in his eagerness to advance the fortunes of his family, the Akamatsu, interfered in succession disputes within the Hatakeyama and Shiba families. He also became deeply involved in the political struggles surrounding the succession to Ashikaga Yoshimasa which sparked the Ōnin War. Politically partial, the Kyoto *gozan* became targets for rival factions. Of the Kyoto *gozan,* Nan-zenji, Shōkokuji, Tenryūji, and Kenninji were all burned to the ground. Tōfukuji managed to preserve its main buildings, but the majority of its sub-temples were destroyed. Of the score of *jissatsu* and *shozan* in the Kyoto area, most were destroyed, never to be rebuilt.[48]

After the war, Yoshimasa encouraged rebuilding programs, and the *gozan* showed signs of recovery, but it was never to regain its former influence. The eonomies of the great Kyoto Zen monas-teries had been shattered beyond restoration. When Yoshimasa requested loans from the bursars of Kyoto *gozan* in 1486 to cele-brate the coming of age of his son Yoshihisa (1465–1489), they were unable to comply. In the provinces, warrior incursions into *gozan* estates continued. The *gozan* did not collapse, however; the form survived long after the substance had withered. The Christian missionaries who came to Japan in the mid-sixteenth century found it still an impressive monastic organization. But it was then only a shadow of its earlier self. Even before the Ōnin War, monks were leaving the *gozan* monasteries for Daitokuji, Myōshinji, and their provincial offshoots, which came into their own after the mid-fifteenth century.[49]

THE EMERGENCE OF DAITOKUJI AND MYŌSHINJI

Modern Japanese Rinzai Zen derives not from the medieval *gozan* lineages but, via the Zen master Hakuin (1686–1769), from the Zen traditions of Daitokuji and Myōshinji.

After withdrawing from the *jissatsu* in 1431, Daitokuji earned a reputation as a monastery where an austere, meditation-centered Zen monastic life was practiced. Monks like Yōsō Sōi (1376–1458) and Ikkyū Sōjun (1394–1481) who were dissatisfied with the eclectic Zen, ceremonial pomp, and cultural preoccupation of the *gozan* monasteries could find in the monks' hall of Daitokuji the stern, unrelenting Zen they were seeking.

Deprived of its status as an official monastery, and thus of Ashikaga patronage, Daitokuji eventually found three new sources of economic support: the merchant community of the city of Sakai, the emerging Warring States barons (*sengoku daimyō*), and, third, the tea masters (*chajin*), linked-verse masters (*rengashi*), *nō* actors, and other arbiters of contemporary culture who were familiar with Zen monks, consorted with merchants, and served powerful *daimyō*.[50]

Many Sakai merchants were prepared to invest profits in the acquisition of culture and good taste. They looked to Zen monks for guidance in aesthetics, the appreciation of Chinese painting and calligraphy, and the spirit of *nō* and the tea ceremony. Bonds between Daitokuji and Sakai merchants were forged by Yōsō Sōi and Ikkyū Sōjun, both of whom lived for a time in Sakai. Ikkyū scathingly criticized Yōsō for prostituting Zen by selling his sermons, written in simple Japanese script, to nuns and towns-people, and for certifying their enlightenment in return for finan-cial contributions. Ikkyū's own approach was more indirect but no less effective. He castigated the single-minded greed of the merchants. But his scornful tone, far from alienating his audience, convinced many of his honesty.

Sakai merchants proved generous patrons of Daitokuji. The Dharma hall was rebuilt after a fire in 1453 with funds provided by a Sakai merchant known by the Zen name of Sōkan. The mon-astery again suffered in the Ōnin War. It was rebuilt and enlarged through the strenuous efforts of Ikkyū and Sakai merchants like Owa Shirozaemon and Awajiya Jugen, both of whom practiced Zen with Ikkyū. Daitokuji thus emerged from the war larger and more prosperous than it had ever been. It continued to flourish. Ten years after Ikkyū's death, Owa Shirozaemon and other Sakai merchants built the beautiful Shinjuan sub-temple as a memorial to their irreverent mentor. The documents recording the con-tributions made at the thirteenth and thirty-third anniversary ceremonies for Ikkyū list many donations by Sakai merchants.

Tea masters, writers of *nō* and *kyōgen*, poets of linked verse, and other leaders in the arts had access to the sub-temples and abbot's hall of Daitokuji. There they discussed Zen and the arts with Yōsō, Ikkyū, and their disciples. The same contribution list records generous donations by contemporary tea masters, *dengaku* masters, and *rengashi*. The monk and tea master Murata Jukō (d. 1502) practiced Zen under the guidance of Ikkyū and contributed generously to Daitokuji. The lower story of the surviving great gate at Daitokuji was built by the *rengashi* Saiokuken Sōchō (1448–1532), who had studied Zen with Ikkyū. Saiokuken is said to have raised the money by selling a precious early copy of *The Tale of Genji*, and by gathering donations as he wandered from poetry meeting to poetry meeting. The second story was later added by the tea master Sen no Rikyū (1522–1591), who aroused Hideyoshi's anger by having his own statue enshrined there.

Sengoku daimyō who patronized Daitokuji and the monks of the growing Daitokuji lineage included the Hōjō in the Kantō; the Takeda, Uesugi, Hatakeyama, Oda (Nobunaga), Toyotomi (Hideyoshi), Ishida, and Maeda in central Japan; the Sasaki, Miyoshi, Hori, and Gamō in the Kyoto region; the Ōuchi, Kobayakawa, and Yoshikawa in western Japan; and the Kuroda, Ōtomo, and Hosokawa in Kyūshū. Of these, Hatakeyama Yoshitsuna (d. 1545), Ōtomo Sōrin (1530–1587), a Christian *daimyō*, and Miyoshi Nagayoshi (1523–1564), who controlled Sakai and the provinces around Kyoto, were especially generous to Daitokuji. With the wealth of Sakai and the patronage of powerful warlords to sustain it, the Daitokuji lineage expanded rapidly during the sixteenth century. As it spread into the provinces, it even took over defunct *gozan* monasteries, a clear demonstration of the reversal of fortunes within the Zen institution.

The Kyoto monastery of Myōshinji was founded by Kanzan Egen (1277–1360).[51] Kanzan studied Zen under Nanpo Jōmyō (1235–1308) and his disciple Shūhō Myōchō (Daitō Kokushi), the founder of Daitokuji. With Shūhō's death in 1337, retired Emperor Hanazono invited Kanzan to be his instructor in Zen. At the same time, Hanazono granted a detached imperial villa for conversion into the Zen monastery of Myōshinji. Kanzan's Zen was, if possible, even more frugal, severe, and meditation-centered than that of Daitō. Kanzan had little interest in fine buildings and no time for the elaborate ceremonies and literary diversions already becoming evident in *gozan* monasteries. Myōshinji tradition has it that the roof of Kanzan's quarters always leaked, and that, when the eminent Musō Soseki visited Myōshinji, Kanzan, instead of preparing delicacies, offered his guest only a few meager roasted rice cakes.

Myōshinji, unlike Daitokuji, was never included in the *gozan*. The history of the monastery and the Kanzan line very nearly ended in 1399 when Ashikaga Yoshimitsu, on the grounds that Setsudō Sōboku, the abbot of Myōshinji, was in league with the rebel Ōuchi Yoshihiro (1356–1399), confiscated the lands making up the monastery compound as well as its provincial domains. Myōshinji's name was changed, it was made a branch temple of a sub-temple of Nanzenji, its monks were scattered, and its buildings allowed to fall derelict.

In 1432, Yoshinori returned some of the monastery's domain. Under the leadership of the abbots Myōkō Sōei, Nippō Sōshun (1358–1448), and Sekkō Sōshin (1408–1486), and with the patronage of the Ōuchi, and Hosokawa Mochiyuki (1400–1442) and Katsumoto (1430–1473), the monastery recovered and began to attract monks who were dissatisfied with *gozan* monastic life. It was at this time that Myōshinji established both its characteristic system of rotating the abbacy of the main monastery among four major provincial branches, thus allowing it to draw talented monks from anywhere in Japan, and its strictly supervised accounting system. All Zen monasteries had reputations for careful estate management and monastic account keeping. Myōshinji, anxious to preserve its independence but lacking a large financial base, was especially scrupulous in this respect. Among Myōshinji documents there is a uniquely detailed record of the finances of the monastery and its branches from the mid-fifteenth century until the eighteenth.[52]

Besides the Hosokawa and Ōuchi, other *sengoku daimyō* patrons of Myōshinji included the Saitō of Mino, the Imagawa of Suruga, the Takeda, and Oda Nobunaga. Through the *kanrei* Hosokawa Takakuni (1484–1531) and the nun Saitō Ritei-ni, Myōshinji was brought closer to the imperial court and, like Daitokuji, awarded the privilege of the imperial grant of purple robes to its abbots. At the same time, monks of the Myōshinji lineage began actively to proselytize among the common people. The Myōshinji line of Zen grew rapidly during the sixteenth century, outpacing Daitokuji and taking over at least 50 defunct *jissatsu* or *shozan* rank monasteries. This rapid expansion was achieved, however, only by drastic dilution of Zen with popular beliefs, prayers for secular intentions, and funeral ceremonies. Dynamic Zen discussion (*mondō*) between master and disciple degenerated into a secret verbal transmission in which "answers" to *kōan* were passed on from one generation to the next. Moreover, by the end of the sixteenth century, at Myōshinji, the monks' hall, the powerhouse of any Zen monastery, was derelict. Monastic life was fragmented with the proliferation of sub-temples. Myōshinji Zen was only revived from this spiritual torpor by Hakuin.

Before closing this account of the development of Rinzai Zen in medieval Japan, we should as least mention the Genjū lineage comprising the followers of Japanese monks like Kosen Ingen (1295–1374) and Muin Genkai (d. 1358) who had journeyed to Yuan dynasty China to study Zen under the monk Chung-feng Ming-pen at his hermitage, the Huan-chu-an (in Japanese, Genjū'an). The pioneers of this lineage in Japan prized Chung-feng's reclusiveness, advocated his blend of Pure Land and Zen, and quit the official *gozan* monasteries for provincial retreats where they acquired reputations for severe Zen meditative practice. By the late fifteenth century, monks of this lineage had attracted a wide following and enjoyed the patronage of *sengoku daimyō*. Since monks of this lineage were permitted to hold dual *inka*, that is to inherit other Zen transmissions concurrently with the Genjū lineage transmission, with the growing popularity of this branch of Rinzai Zen, many monks affiliated with the Genjū lineage were invited to head the very *gozan* monasteries early members of the lineage had left in disgust because of their formalized and literary character.[53]

PART TWO

The Structure of the Institution

FOUR

The Zen Monastic Life and Rule

Nowadays, in contrast to former times, people do not enter the temple
life. In the old days a man who felt called on to establish the moral life
went in to the temple, whereas now they're all leaving. One look shows
us priests with no intellect who find *zazen* a bother and who refuse to
apply the techniques, men who rather prefer to be connoisseurs of pots
and such and who ornament their *zazen* with ostentatious pride. These
men don priestly garments out of vanity and though they wear the
clothing they are simply dressed-up laymen. Even as they put on the
robe and the cloak they tell us they are in torment, that the robes bind
like cords and the cloaks are heavy as lead.[1]

—Ikkyū Sōjun (1394–1481)

And so these philosophers will never contend or argue with another,
but leave everything to the contemplation of each one so that he may
attain by himself to knowledge by using these principles. They do not
instruct disciples. Thus the monks of this sect are of a resolute and de-
termind character, without any indolence, laxity or effeminacy. As
regards the care of their own persons, they do without a great number
of things which they consider superfluous and unnecessary. They maintain that a hermitage should first of all be frugal and moderate, with
much quietness, peace of soul and exterior modesty.[2]

—Joao Rodrigues (1561–1634)

THE DEVELOPMENT OF THE RULE

Meditation (*zazen*) is at the core of Zen. For centuries, this Zen meditative quest has been pursued within the framework of a distinctive monastic life, regulated in every detail to maximize the practice of meditation. Although the disciplined character of Zen community life is frequently ignored in discussions of the history of Zen, the existence of a strict, clearly defined yet flexible rule gave strength and longevity to the Ch'an schools in China and added to the attractiveness of Zen in the eyes of the Japanese ruling elite. The importance of the rule in the Zen tradition is clearly demonstrated by the fact that, for most of the great Ch'an and Zen masters, concern for discipline and meditation went hand in hand.

While *zazen* and the meditative experience may be considered intrinsically timeless, the Zen monastic life and the regulations that govern it have been responsive to the pressures of time and place. Changes in the character of Zen monastic practice have resulted both from developments within the Zen schools themselves and from the changing relationship of Zen, as an institution, with Chinese and Japanese society.

The characteristic Zen communal life—stressing communal meditation, active debate between master and disciples, frugality, and manual labor—was taking shape by the T'ang dynasty. Thereafter, while other Buddhist sects succumbed to persecution or religious inertia, Ch'an gained in strength. By the time Japanese pilgrim monks began to travel to China again in the Sung dynasty, Ch'an had emerged as the most vital and influential form of monastic Buddhism in China. In the intervening centuries, a detailed body of Ch'an monastic regulations was established (Chart 4). The compilation of this corpus was both cause and effect of the newfound dominance of Ch'an in Chinese Buddhist circles. The composition of new monastic codes gave strength and cohesion to the Ch'an monastic institution and injected vitality into the Ch'an monastic life. At the same time, the promulgation of elaborate, distinctively Ch'an codes was undoubtedly the product of a sense of sectarian maturity and independence. The corpus was later transmitted to Japan to provide the foundation of Japanese Zen monastic life.

CHART 4   Composition and Transmission of Major
            Zen Monastic Codes

China	(Transmitted)	Japan
Pai-chang ch'ing-kuei (?)		
"Ch'an-men kuei-shih" (1004)		
Ch'an-yuan ch'ing-kuei (1103)	c. 1200	Eisai, *Shukke taikō* (1195)
Ju-chung jih-yung ch'ing-kuei (1209)	c. 1300	Dōgen, *Eihei shingi* (1237–)
Chiao-ting ch'ing-kuei (1274)	c. 1300	Lan-ch'i, *Jōrakuji kishiki* & *Kenchōji kishiki* (1278)
		Enni, *Tōfukuji jōjōgoto* (1280)
Ch'an-lin pei-yung ch'ing-kuei (1311)	c. 1330	Shinchi, *Seido'in jōjō kishiki* (by 1298)
Huan-chu-an ch'ing-kuei (1317)	c. 1330	Keizan, *Keizan shingi* (1325)
		Ch'ing-cho, *Taikan shingi*
Ch'ih-hsiu Pai-chang ch'ing-kuei (1336–1343)	c. 1350	Musō, *Rinsen kakun* (1339)
		Tettō, *Daitokuji hatto, Tokuzenji hatto* & *Shōden'an hatto* (c. 1368)
		Ōbaku shingi (1672)

Source: Imaeda Aishin, "Shingi no denrai to rufu," *Chūsei Zenshū-shi no kenkyū,* pp. 56–72.

Zen codifiers were not trying to break new ground. Their avowed aim was always to restate the essentials of Zen monastic practice, to root out abuses, to return to the ideals of Pai-chang, the acknowledged architect of the Zen monastic life. Unwittingly, however, each restatement of the tradition sanctified recent practices born of changing religious, social, and political conditions. Although the major Chinese codes all describe the same institution and the same basic tradition, each of these codes clearly reflects significant changes in the character of the institution. When

Zen was introduced to Japan, the Japanese and Chinese monks who were active in the transmission sought to recreate a mirror image of the Chinese traditions of Zen monastic life by applying Chinese codes and regulations wherever possible, and by writing their own codes for the particular circumstance of their school or lineage. Because the transmission was based on written regulations as well as personal observation, it was remarkably successful. Yet, when we examine the various codes written for Japanese Zen monasteries, we quickly see evidence of accommodation with the religious, social, and political environment of warrior-ruled Japan.

In this chapter, by analysing some of the major Zen monastic codes or "pure regulations" (*ch'ing-kuei, shingi*), we shall try to get inside the medieval Zen monastery to observe the principal components of the monastic life and look at some of the problems confronting Zen monastic legislators. Beginning with a brief outline of the development of *ch'ing-kuei* and their transmission to Japan, we shall then look in detail at the *Rinsen kakun*, a personal "house code" written in 1339 by Musō Soseki to regulate the lives and conduct of his disciples at the monastery of Rinsenji in Kyoto. Finally, in an attempt to set the Zen monastic rule in a broader social context, we shall compare some of the issues raised in the *Rinsen kakun* with those raised in contemporary *bakufu* regulations for Zen monasteries.

THE PROBLEM OF THE PAI-CHANG CODE

The monk Pai-chang Huai-hai (d. 814) is revered both as the author of the Zen work ethic—"No work, no food"—and of the Zen monastic rule. Zen tradition maintains that Pai-chang established Ch'an as an independent sect by providing Ch'an monks with their own monastic regulations, thus releasing them from dependence on the monasteries and rules of the Lü sect. This debt is acknowledged in the *Sung kao-seng-chuan* [3] (Sung biographies of eminent monks) in the "Ch'an-men kuei-shih" (1004),[4] and subsequent codes. By the Sung dynasty, Pai-chang was venerated as one of the central figures, alongside Bodhidharma and Hui-neng, in the Ch'an patriarchal pantheon.

Although the origins and early development of the Ch'an school are obscure, there is reason to think that Pai-chang may have played a somewhat less crucial and singular role than that commonly attributed to him.[5] It is unlikely that early Ch'an communities were "confined" to Lü school monasteries and rules prior to Pai-chang. It seems very much more likely that early Ch'an practitioners were either mendicants or members of isolated communities of like-minded meditating monks.[6] Zen masters before Pai-chang, including Hui-neng and his predecessor, the fifth patriarch, are recorded as having established such independent communities where a meditation-centered, regulated communal life developed naturally.[7] Many of these communities were isolated and of necessity economically self-sufficient. Although Pai-chang may have coined the phrase "A day without working should be a day without eating," he was not the first Ch'an master to stress manual labor as a vital part of Ch'an community life and practice. Likewise, while Pai-chang may have added regulations to a growing Ch'an corpus he was almost certainly not the first Ch'an legislator. Nor is there any solid evidence that he compiled the first written Ch'an code, frequently, but misleadingly, referred to as the *Pai-chang ch'ing-kuei.*

No such code exists. Nor was it in existence in the Sung dynasty when the most comprehensive Ch'an codes were compiled. It may have existed but been lost in the centuries after Pai-chang's death, but this, too, seems unlikely. The *Ch'ih-hsiu Pai-chang ch'ing-kuei* (Imperial compilation of the Pai-chang Code), although it has Pai-chang's name in the title and is frequently referred to as the *Pai-chang Code,* is a Yuan dynasty synthesis of the major Sung dynasty codes. It contains nothing that can be traced directly to Pai-chang.[8]

The *Ch'an-yuan ch'ing-kuei,* 1103 (Ch'an compilation) is the oldest surviving full-scale Ch'an monastic code and the first to use the term "ch'ing-kuei" in its title. Although the preface to the

Ch'an-yuan Code pays tribute to Pai-chang as a Ch'an legislator, no mention is made of a *Pai-chang "ch'ing-kuei"*.[9] Volume 10 of the *Ch'an-yuan Code* contains a section entitled "Pai-chang kuei-sheng-sung" (Commentary on the rules of Pai-chang). On examination, the rules described here turn out to be a section of the *Ching-te ch'uan-teng-lu,* 1004 (Transmission of the lamp) known as "Ch'an-men kuei-shih" (Ch'an monastic rules), supplemented with a commentary by Sung-i, the compiler of the *Ch'an-yuan Code.* Although the "Ch'an-men kuei-shih" claims to provide the essence of the regulations of Pai-chang, it makes no mention of a *Pai-chang Code*, nor does the expression "ch'ing-kuei" appear.

The brief "Ch'an-men kuei-shih" and the short biography of Pai-chang in the Sung biographies of eminent monks are the closest we get to the elusive *Pai-chang Code.* They seem also to contain some of the earliest references to Pai-chang as codifier. Those Japanese scholars who have recently searched the copious Buddhist printed literature of the late T'ang and Five Dynasties for mention of a *Pai-chang Code* have so far found none.[10] In the writings of Pai-chang's contemporaries and disciples there seems to be neither mention of a *Pai-chang ch'ing-kuei* nor even of Pai-chang's having compiled any Ch'an monastic regulations. Even Pai-chang's memorial inscription, written in 814 by Ch'en-hsu, makes no mention of either a full-scale code or individual regulations. In view of Pai-chang's subsequent reputation and the importance, in Ch'an monastic tradition, of Pai-chang's regulations to the independence of Ch'an, this silence is remarkable. Had Pai-chang been the codifier and architect of independence that he was later believed to be, it seems inconceivable that his contemporaries and disciples would not have regarded this as one of his most noteworthy achievements and left some mention of the rules in question.[11]

THE CH'AN-MEN REGULATIONS AND THE CH'AN-YUAN CODE

The earliest reliable description of Ch'an monastic life in China still extant, is the short sketch given in the "Ch'an-men kuei-shih."[12] The work opens with a declaration of Ch'an independence:

> Master Pai-chang felt that after the founding by the first patriarch, Bodhidharma, through the time of the sixth patriarch, Hui-neng, and later, members of the Ch'an school mostly resided in Lü (Vinaya) school monasteries where, although they had their own separate compounds, they did not act in accord with rules of their own on such matters as the expositions of Ch'an teachings by the abbot or the transmission of leadership. Because he was always concerned with this deficiency, Pai-chang said: "It is my desire that the Way of our founders should spread and enlighten people in the hope of lasting into the future. Why should our school follow the practice of Hinayana regulations?" One of his disciples interjected: "But there exist such Mahayana regulations as those included in the *Yoga-śāstra* and the *P'u-sa ying-lo-ching* (Necklace sutra). Why not rely on these and follow them?"
>
> Pai-chang replied: "What our school believes should not be bound either by Hinayana or Mahayana. Neither should it arbitrarily differ from them. Our aim should be to take a broad view and synthesize at the middle ground in establishing the regulations and making sure of their being appropriate for our needs. Thereupon the Master instituted his ideal of establishing Ch'an monasteries separately.

The "Ch'an-men kuei-shih" goes on to describe some of the principal features of what we immediately recognize as the characteristic Zen monastic life. The communal, meditative life of the monks' hall is emphasized:

> Irrespective of their numbers or of their social status, those who have been permitted to enter the community to study should all reside in the monks' hall (*seng-t'ang*), arranged strictly according to the number of summers since their ordination. Meditation platforms should be built [along the sides of the hall] and a stand provided for each monk to hang up his robes and personal belongings. When resting, monks should lay their headrests at an angle to the lip of the platform and lie down on their right sides with their hands supporting their heads in the posture of the Buddha reclining. They rest only briefly even though the meditation sessions have been long. This should not be thought of as sleep but as reclining meditation.

Together with meditation and private visits to the abbot's chamber for guidance, public debate between the abbot and the monks in the Dharma hall is stressed:

> The whole community should gather in the Dharma hall for the morning and evening discussions. On these occasions the abbot enters the hall and ascends the seat. The monastic officers and the body of monks stand in files, listen attentively to the lecture, and engage their master in debate, thus exposing the essence of Ch'an teachings.

If there is a monks' hall and Dharma hall, the monastery does not need a Buddha hall:

> Not to construct a Buddha hall, but only to build a Dharma hall is to demonstrate a proper respect for the abbot as the mind-to-mind inheritor of the teachings of the Buddha and the Ch'an patriarchs.

The Buddha hall later became a central feature of the classical Zen monastic ground plan. The deliberate rejection of the Buddha hall in the "Ch'an-men kuei-shih" probably derived from four basic considerations: a strong strand of iconoclasm in Ch'an thought, a sense of Ch'an sectarian identity, a fear that energy would be drawn from meditation and Zen practice into elaborate ceremonial functions in the Buddha hall (involving a shift from the struggle to attain enlightenment by one's own efforts to reliance on prayers and devotions) and, finally, a fear that, through these ceremonies, dependence on the state and the patrons who sponsored Buddha hall ceremonies and memorial services would be unduly increased.

The "Ch'an-men kuei-shih" indicates that a Ch'an monastic bureaucracy was developing but that manual labor was still regarded as a duty for all:

> In carrying out the universal practice of labor (*p'u-ch'ing*), all members of the community, high and low, must work equally. Ten offices or chambers should be established.[13] In each of these offices one monk should be appointed to supervise several others. Each member of the office is responsible for the diligent performance of the duties allotted to him.

Those who broke the rules of the community were to be severely punished:

If there should be somebody who falsely claims an official title, who falsely acts like an officer, thus confusing the good members, or who otherwise causes quarrels and disputes, he should be disciplined at the monks' hall by the registrar (*wei-no*) who should remove the offender's belongings from his place and expel him from the monastery. This is to maintain tranquility among the good members. When a monk is guilty of a major breach of the regulations, he should, as a mark of his disgrace, be beaten with the master's stick, have his robes, bowl, and other belongings burned before the assembled community, and then be expelled through a side gate.

Where the "Ch'an-men kuei-shih" offers us little more than a tantalizing glimpse into the basic organization of the Ch'an community prior to the year 1000, the *Ch'an-yuan ch'ing-kuei*, is a comprehensive code regulating almost every conceivable aspect of Ch'an monastic activity. It provides a very comprehensive picture of the organization of the large Ch'an communities of the early Sung dynasty. The code was widely used in Ch'an monasteries during the Sung dynasty. As the oldest surviving Ch'an code, it provided the model for subsequent Chinese and Japanese Zen codes, and even for *Ch'ing-kuei* of other Buddhist schools. The more than seventy sections of the code cover such areas as:

The proper reception and strict observance of the Buddhist precepts (both Hinayana and Mahayana): "The practice of Zen begins with the precepts" (sections 1 and 2).

The monk's costume, equipment, and essential documents. The proper method of packing the bundles of belongings when traveling from monastery to monastery. The correct procedure when requesting to stay overnight at a monastery or when seeking to enroll for a season in a monks' hall (sections 3–6).

The etiquette to be observed during meals and tea ceremonies (sections 7 and 8).

The procedure for requesting the abbot's spiritual guidance and for the private interviews (*ju-shih*) in the abbot's chamber (sections 9 and 10).

The forms of regular monastic activities, including the morning and evening assemblies, ceremonies for state and monastic intentions, ceremonies for the opening and closing of the summer retreat, etc. The manner of the regular tours of inspection of the monastery halls by the abbot. The correct procedure for entertaining Buddhist dignitaries and secular officials (sections 11–18).

The manner of appointment and the duties of the two ranks of monastery officers and their assistants. The *Ch'an-yuan Code* mentions 10 principal officers: 4 stewards and 6 prefects assisted by more that 40 sub-prefects (sections 19–40).

The details of special monastery tea ceremonies and feasts (sections 41–50).

The regulations for the daily sutra reading. Sound signals. Correct epistolary forms for official monastery correspondence. Procedures to be followed in the case of sickness of an abbot or monk. Personal hygiene and latrine etiquette (sections 51–60).

Details of the obsequies for a deceased monk. The monastic and civil procedures for appointing a new abbot. Installation of the abbot. The proper attitude of mind of the abbot. Obsequies for an abbot. Formalities upon the retirement from office of an abbot (sections 61–68).

Disquisition on the spirit of the Ch'an monastic life and the importance of the abbot and the monastery officers, remembering that they are there for the sake of the community not vice versa (section 69).

The practice of meditation (section 70).

One hundred and twenty questions for monks to test the depth of their religious lives. The detailed form of the ordination ceremony. The training of postulants. The duties of monastery servants. The encouragement of monastery patrons. Rules for lay people in giving feasts for monks. Commentary on the Pai-chang rules (sections 71–78).[14]

The principal components of the Ch'an religious life outlined in the "Ch'an-men kuei-shih" were meditation, unscheduled private interviews, public assemblies, and communal manual labor. The "Ch'an-men kuei-shih" gives no indication of how many hours were actually devoted to meditation each day. It says simply, "With the exception of entry to the chamber and lectures, practice should be left to the will of the student." This could imply that meditation was not emphasized. It is equally likely that the compiler felt no need to single out meditation for specific regulation, that monks were assiduous.

The *Ch'an-yuan Code,* likewise, does not specify times for

meditation. We can perhaps assume from this silence that meditation practice was still sufficiently dedicated to need no special regulation. During the Southern Sung dynasty, however, communal meditation sessions were held 4 times daily: from about eight to nine P.M., three to four A.M., nine to ten A.M. and three to four P.M. Each "hour" was measured with a burning stick of incense. The term "four hours' meditation" first appears in Ch'an codes in the *Pei-yung Code* (1311).[15] That this practice had been established well before this code was compiled is clear from the fact that both Eisai and Dōgen, who were in China a century earlier, used the expression in their regulations to describe the standard practice they had observed. Although "four hours' *zazen*" (*shiji no zazen*) remained the ideal, in some Chinese and Japanese Zen monasteries, by the fourteenth century, only 3 daily sessions of meditation were being held, with prayers or sutra readings substituted for one of the hours.

The "Ch'an-men kuei-shih" states that assemblies were to be held morning and evening. The implication seems to be every morning and evening. We have no way of knowing, however, whether these assemblies were, in fact, held daily in early Zen communities. By the time the *Ch'an-yuan Code* was compiled, assemblies were being held 6 times per month each. The "great assemblies" were normally held in the Dharma hall on the mornings of the 1st, 5th, 10th, 15th, 20th, and 25th days of the month. Evening assemblies, known as "small assemblies," were held in the abbot's chamber at his convenience. They were normally held on the 3rd, 8th, 13th, 18th, 23rd, and 28th days of each month.[16] If the abbot was busy or indisposed, the assembly would be "released."

Twelve assemblies per month, in addition to the individual guidance of large numbers of monks and the administrative responsibility for the running of the monastery, must have imposed a severe strain on Ch'an abbots. This contributed to a gradual reduction in the stipulated number of assemblies. From later Southern Sung and Yuan dynasty codes, it is clear that the morning assemblies had been reduced to 4 per month. The mornings of the 1st and 15th days of the month were given over to prayers and ceremonies for monastery intentions and the welfare of the imperial family respectively.[17] The "small" evening assemblies were reduced from 6 times per month on the "3rd and 8th days," to 3 times per month on the "three eights," i.e., 8th, 18th and 28th.[18] Since there does not seem to have been a compensating increase in private contact between the abbot and individual monks, this can only be seen as a reduction in the instructional content of the traditional Ch'an monastic life. As in the case of meditation, active debate between the master and his disciples was increasingly replaced by devotional practices and state-sponsored ceremonies.

There was a similar reduction over time in the emphasis on the value of labor as an integral part of Zen practice. The Ch'an work ethic still finds expression in the *Ch'an-yuan Code*. In volume 3 in the section describing the duties of the *wei-no*, the code states that, except for the two officers responsible for guarding the monks' hall and reading room, all monks must engage in labor. The abbot is excused if he is unwell or has official guests. If he fails to appear without good reason, however, his acolyte must be held responsible and expelled from the monastery.[19]

Labor, in the *Ch'an-yuan Code*, is stressed as religious value—a potential source of enlightenment—rather than as strict economic necessity. By the time the *Ch'an-yuan Code* was compiled, Ch'an monasteries had long since shifted from self-sufficient agrarian production, where labor meant rough field work for community survival, to reliance on donations from powerful, high-ranking patrons and carefully organized support groups. Donations from the latter were gathered by specially appointed fund-raising monks sent out by the monastery.[20] It is also clear from the *Ch'an-yuan Code* that the large Northern Sung dynasty Ch'an monasteries had developed sophisticated monastic bureaucracies responsible for handling all the details of monastic life. Opportunities for ordinary monks to engage regularly in manual labor were restricted. These developments notwithstanding, the ideal of labor is very much alive in the *Ch'an-yuan Code*. In later codes this ideal seems to be neglected. One does not read of Zen monks from the Kyoto *gozan* sweating in the fields. With the possible exception of estate officials, their labors, apart from meditation, were primarily ceremonial, administrative, literary, and artistic.

Looked at in terms of meditation, assemblies, and labor, the *Ch'an-yuan Code*, in spite of many indications of bureaucratization, gives a much stronger impression of vigorous, disciplined, meditation-centered monastic life that the later *Pei-yung* or *Ch'ih-hsiu Codes*, where the daily monastic routine seems increasingly to have centered on formal, ceremonial activities.

INTRODUCTION OF THE CH'AN MONASTIC RULE
TO JAPAN

One powerful impulse behind the resurgence of Buddhism in the Kamakura period was dissatisfaction with the laxity of the established sects. This dissatisfaction provoked one of two responses: either complete rejection, or vigorous reaffirmation of the monastic life and rule. Shinran, Nichiren, and Ippen, each in varying degrees, rejected the rule and the celibate, exclusive, monastic life. They moved among the common people, preaching salvation for all through absolute reliance on the saving grace of Amida or the *Lotus Sutra*. How, they argued, could men hope to attain salvation by their own efforts, or even aspire to keep the precepts, in an age of degeneration of the Buddha's teaching (*mappō*)? Far safer to rely on the *nenbutsu* or the *Lotus*, both of which transcended precepts and regulations.

Zen pioneers adopted a more conservative approach. Where the founders of the popular Buddhist schools moved among the common people of Japan, the founders of Zen journeyed to China, the traditional source of Japanese Buddhism, in search of texts and regulations on which to base a revitalized monastic life. Men could find salvation, they argued, only by leaving the world (*shukke*), by devoting themselves single-mindedly to meditation, and by strict observance of the Buddhist precepts and rules of monastic life. In Dōgen's case, for instance, immediately after his return from

China, he taught the possibility of salvation for all—rich and poor, men and women, monks and laymen—through meditation.[21] After moving to Eiheiji, however, Dōgen increasingly stressed the traditional monastic ideal, stating that, while even a bad monk might possibly attain enlightenment, good laymen and women had no hope of doing so.[22]

When Eisai, Dōgen, Shōichi, and other Japanese monks enrolled in the great monasteries of Sung China, they were impressed by the vitality of the Ch'an monastic life and rule. The *Ch'an-yuan Code* still regulated the monastic life and it was natural that the Japanese monks should seek to introduce both the code and the forms of monastic practice it described to Japan. They carried copies back to Japan, quoted it extensively and produced their own regulations under its influence. Moreover, the importance of the *Ch'an-yuan* was reemphasized by the Chinese monks who came to Japan later in the thirteenth century. Lan-ch'i and his successors had all been trained under this code and they used it as the basis for monastic practice in the new Zen monasteries in Kamakura and Kyoto.

In seeking to understand the character of medieval Japanese Zen monastic life, one should remember that, while pursuing a gradually divergent course of its own, it remained in constant contact with China and reflected the latest developments in Chinese Ch'an monasteries. As recompilations of the *Ch'an-yuan* were made in Chinese monasteries, they too were quickly introduced to Japan. The famous *Ch'ih-hsiu Code* (1336–), for instance, was probably introduced by the mid-fourteenth century.[23] It set the pattern for monastic practice in the mature *gozan* system, its state-conscious tone being perfectly appropriate to the *bakufu*-sponsored Japanese *gozan*.

Eisai is best known as the monk who introduced Rinzai Zen teachings to Japan and popularized the use of tea. A lesser known, but equally important, aspect of his life and thought was his interest in the Buddhist precepts and rules of monastic life. To understand Eisai fully we must see him not simply as an exponent of eclectic Zen thought but as a monastic legislator. Immediately after returning from his second visit to China, Eisai began to introduce Chinese monastic practices into those monasteries he established. He was convinced that Zen was the true tradition of Buddhism and that its diffusion in Japan could only benefit the country and its rulers as well as the established Buddhist sects. Eisai also believed that it must be practiced in the proper disciplined monastic environment. The propagation of Zen in Japan presupposed the creation of such an environment.[24]

All Eisai's later writings stand on a double foundation—Zen and the precepts. The two are inseparable in his thought. This conviction derived from the *Ch'an-yuan Code* and his general experience in Chinese monasteries. In the *Kōzen gokokuron*, Eisai quotes with approval the statement in the *Ch'an-yuan* that "the practice of Zen begins with the precepts."[25] Moreover, the *Kōzen gokokuron* is not simply a plea for Zen as a system of metaphysics or meditation practice. It is also a plea for the full-scale adoption of the forms of the Ch'an monastic life. The eighth section, for instance, is entitled "Regulations of the Zen school."[26] It describes the basic features of the Ch'an monastic practice that Eisai had experienced in China. Here Eisai stresses the importance of observance of the precepts, both Mahayana and Hinayana, and of the "four hours' *zazen*." He encourages frugality and strict monastic discipline and outlines the daily and annual round of prayers, feasts, and ceremonies. Many of the practices he advocates were entirely new to Japan and must have seemed alien to disciples and detractors alike. His only major concessions to Japanese circumstances were the acceptance of certain Tendai and Shingon buildings and ceremonies, and an extreme deference towards the secular authorities, whose support was vital if Zen was to take root in Japan.

Dōgen was deeply impressed by the disciplined monastic life he experienced under Eisai at Kenninji. Disappointment with the laxity he found in the same monastery after his return from China contributed to Dōgen's determination to found his own community in which the Ch'an monastic life he had learned in China would be faithfully practised. Dōgen, like Eisai, must be seen as a

Zen codifier as well as Zen master. His writings provide not only one of the finest expositions of Zen philosophy; they also offer one of the most comprehensive statements of the ideal and practice of the medieval Zen monastic life. Of the 90 or more chapters of the *Shōbō genzō*, nearly a third are devoted wholly or in part to the detailed regulation of such everyday monastic activities as meditation, prayer, study, sleep, dress, the preparation and taking of meals, and bathing and purification.

In addition to those regulations included in the *Shōbō genzō*, Dōgen also compiled a series of regulations later gathered together to make up the *Eihei shingi* (Eiheiji Code). These include: "Tenzo kyōku" (Instructions for the monastery cook), 1237; "Taidai kohō (Deference toward seniors), 1244; "Bendōhō" (Regulations for the monks' hall), 1245; "Chiji Shingi" (Regulations for monastery officers), 1246; "Fushuki hanpō" (Method of taking meals), 1246; and "Shuryō shingi" (Regulations for the reading room), 1249.[27]

In his regulations, Dōgen always explains not only what should be done but how and why it should be done. He emphasizes a constant mindfulness that makes even the simplest of actions, whether washing the face, cleaning rice, or cutting vegetables, as conducive to Zen enlightenment as meditation, prayer, or sutra reading:[28] "Under the Buddha-Dharma the methods of washing—washing the body, washing the mind, washing the face, washing the eyes, washing the two functions of urination and excretion, washing the hands, washing the bowl, washing the robe, washing the head—are all carefully prescribed. All these actions express the right Dharma of the Buddhas and Patriarchs of the three eras" (*Shōbō genzo,* "Senmen"). Or "Bear this in mind: The meanest vegetable feeds the seeds of Buddhahood and nurtures the buds of the Way. Do not disdain or neglect it " ("Tenzo kyōkun"). Pai-chang is Dōgen's ultimate authority. Dōgen's regulations consciously seek to inculcate what the Japanese monk understood to be the spirit of Pai-chang's monastic practice. However, although Dōgen refers on occasion to Pai-chang's regulations, there is no reason to suppose that he ever saw a *Pai-chang Code*. The quotations he attributes to Pai-chang all derive from the *Ch'an-yuan Code*.[29]

Emphasis in the transmission of the orthodox Ch'an monastic life and rule continued after Dōgen's death. Shōichi (Enni) is said to have brought back to Japan a copy of the *Ch'an-yuan*, and later produced his own regulations for Tōfukuji.[30] Lan-ch'i compiled regulations for Jōrakuji and Kenchōji, including a document imposing severe penalties on those monks who shirked the regular meditation sessions. Wu-hsueh, I-shan, Ch'ing-cho, and other Chinese monks all stressed the strict observance of the rules of monastic life as well as meditation and kōan study. By the close of the Kamakura period, because of this steady emphasis on the monastic rule, monastic life in the major Japanese Zen monasteries hardly differed in detail from that in continental monasteries. Sung-style Zen monastic life had taken firm root in Japan, largely on the basis of the *Ch'an-yuan Code*.[31]

THE RINSENJI CODE

Returning from exile on the island of Oki, Emperor Go-Daigo entered Kyoto in triumph in the early summer of 1333 to inaugurate what was to prove a short-lived Imperial Restoration. One of his first actions was to summon Musō Soseki from Kamakura. The emperor formally took the robe, thus becoming Musō's disciple. He granted the monk the title of "National Master" (*Kokushi*) and bestowed on him the monastery of Rinsenji in the Saga-Arashiyama district northwest of the capital.[32]

Rinsenji, or "temple overlooking the river," had been an imperial residence. It was converted into a Zen monastery as a memorial to one of Go-Daigo's sons, Prince Sera Shinnō (the Totoku Shinnō of the code), a devoted student of Zen. After Go-Daigo's departure from Kyoto in 1336, Musō remained at Rinsenji. In 1339 he moved to the smaller retreat at Saihōji, now familiarly known as the Moss Temple. After Go-Daigo's death in 1339, Musō urged the building of Tenryūji on a site near Rinsenji as a memorial to his imperial benefactor. Until Musō's own death at Rinsenji in 1351, he divided his time between Saihōji, Rinsenji, and Tenryūji.

Although these three temples were all closely connected with Musō and his disciples and were included in the *gozan* network, each temple had its own unique character. Tenryūji was built on a lavish scale. When completed, it was immediately raised to the status of full *gozan* and rapidly became one of the most influential monasteries in Japan. Musō, as its founder-abbot, stressed that Tenryūji, befitting an offical *gozan* monastery, should be "open" to the monks of any line. To prevent monopoly control by his own disciples, he restricted the number of sub-temples (*tatchū*) that could be built. He also provided that Tenryūji should have all the traditional Zen monastic buildings and that the assemblies and ceremonies be fully in accord with the *shingi*. Saihōji, on the other hand, was a small and very private retreat where Musō and a few carefully chosen disciples engaged in concentrated meditation in a perfect natural setting. From the *Saihōji ikun* (1345), it is clear that Saihōji had a complement of only 20 or so: an abbot, 16 monks, an acolyte or personal attendant to the abbot, and 1 or 2 novices and postulants. In these regulations, Musō stated that the abbot should be selected for his devotion to meditation, that he should not hold a joint abbacy with some other monastery, and that, once appointed, he should remain at Saihōji until his death.

Rinsenji combined the private characteristics of Saihōji with the public quality of Tenryūji. As the burial place of Musō, it provided a focus for the proliferating Musō lineage. Rinsenji was gutted in the Ōnin War and survives today only as a sub-temple of Tenryūji, which is also greatly reduced in scale. Maps of Rinsenji made prior to the Ōnin War show a large-scale, independent monastery spreading along the banks of the Ōi River. It was very much larger than Saihōji, and its rank as a major *jissatsu* suggests that the community may have numbered between 200 and 500.

Rinsenji was a closed monastery (*tsuchien*). When Go-Daigo bestowed the monastery on Musō, he stipulated that it be restricted in perpetuity to Musō's disciples. Rinsenji was also patronized by Ashikaga Takauji. The fact that it was a closed monastery did not prevent its being ranked by the *bakufu* as a *shozan* in 1336 or its elevation to the status of *jissatsu* in 1353. In 1377 it was briefly made a full *gozan*, ranking immediately below Tōfukuji. The prestige was probably not unwelcome, but leaders of the main stream of the Musō lineage, led by Shun'oku Myōha, were concerned that being ranked as a full *gozan* might lead to the loss of Rinsenji's exclusive character. They petitioned the *bakufu*, and in 1379 the monastery was returned to the *jissatsu*, where there was less pressure for conformity with traditions observed in Chinese official monasteries.

Musō himself intended that Rinsenji should serve as a base for his growing following. To provide cohesion and continuity after his death, he established within Rinsenji a memorial sub-temple known as the San'e-in. This sub-temple consisted of three main chambers, the central chamber containing an image of Maitreya, flanked by halls housing the tombs and images of the secular patron, Prince Sera Shinnō, and of Musō, the religious founder. The San'e-in had its own chief priest and small community. It was clearly intended to serve as a vital nerve center for Rinsenji and to have a large measure of control over the Musō line. Important decisions affecting Rinsenji and its branch temples were to be made before the founder's memorial in the San'e-in. For security, documents and treasures were to be kept there, and its chief priest was to have an important voice in the selection of abbots for Rinsenji and its branches.

In 1339, Musō issued two sets of regulations, one for the San'e-in, the other for Rinsenji. The *San'e-in ikai* (Final instructions for the San'e-in) regulates the duties of the chief priest of the sub-temple and describes various ceremonial activities. The San'e-in was not to number more than 20 persons including the head monk, 3 assistant monks, 3 novices, and 3 monastery servants. Musō especially admonished the chief priest not to indulge in elaborate ceremonies. The *Rinsen kakun* (Rinsenji House Code) provides a more detailed picture of the organization and operation of a medieval Zen monastic community. It offers an insight into the problems confronted by Zen legislators, and shows Musō as a conscientious monk-administrator. The use of the term *kakun* in the title suggests that the code is close to the tradition of warrior and aristocratic house codes.[33] As a Zen code, the *Rinsen kakun* is in the tradition of the smaller Chinese codes compiled to regulate the activities of a single school or monastery. Yanagida Seizan has pointed out that the *Rinsen kakun* can be compared to the *Huan-chu-an ch'ing-kuei* compiled by Chung-feng Ming-pen in 1317.[34] Elsewhere Musō also quoted the larger *Pei-yung ch'ing-kuei*, compiled in 1311, indicating that, although he never visited China, he was aware of recent administrative developments in Chinese monasteries. It is also significant that the *Rinsen kakun* and *San'e-in ikai* were compiled in 1339, while the *Ch'ih-hsiu Pai-chang ch'ing-kuei*, which was to set the tone for the mature Japanese *gozan* system, was being compiled in China. The *Rinsen kakun* can also fruitfully be compared with the *Daitokuji hatto, Tokuzenji hatto,* and *Shōden'an hatto* compiled by Tettō Gikō in 1368.

As they stand, the 32 articles of the *Rinsen kakun* do not have an immediately apparent logical progression. They seem rather to be ad hoc responses by Musō to particular problems. For convenience, they have here been grouped topically under three general headings: the monastery, the community, and monastic life.[35]

I. THE MONASTERY

San'e-in

This monastery was established through the earnest devotion of Totoku Shinnō. Having chosen a suitable site, we are building a memorial tower to Totoku and to one side of it erecting a monument to mark the foundation.[36] Between them there is to be a miroku hall to act as an illuminated hall (*shōdō*) for the two memorials. Accordingly, the new complex is called Temple of the Three Ceremonies (San'e-in). This place should be thought of as community property. Apart from the above buildings, do not build private retreats within the monastery grounds or in the vegetable garden. I am afraid that someone may lay out a landscape garden to the east of San'e-in, invading the vegetable garden. Buy a piece of land nearby and use it for the purpose. (article 22)

Branch Temples

The heads of our branch temples should be elected. The abbot of Rinsenji, the superior of San'e-in, and the older monks of our school should discuss the matter and select a suitable monk. If there is nobody suitable among the community, then they should invite somebody from another monastery. Rules and regulations in the daughter houses should be patterned after those in effect in the main house. Those who are acting as abbots must not do just as they like. There is an old saying, "Monks of a single generation should bear in mind the thousand-year legacy." (article 27)

Do not think of the main house and its branches as qualitatively different. They should assist each other and thus keep alive the light of their founders. This is my sincere wish. All too often the main house treats its branch temples as *shōen* and draws tax tribute from them. By this the daughter houses languish and the main house invites criticism for improper appropriation. Neither side gains. It is essential to exercise restraint. (article 28)

Documents

Documents that concern the affairs of the main house or the branch houses should be kept in San'e-in. I am afraid that otherwise they may be lost. (article 29)

Private Kitchens (kuri)

The living quarters of many monasteries nowadays are equipped with individual kitchen-sitting rooms (*kuri*). This shows a desire for comfort and does not follow the basic principles of monastic life. In addition, there is the danger of fire. This tendency should be stringently checked. Monks should be satisfied with simplicity, not seekers after ease and conviviality, and when guests are present they, too, should share the frugality. (article 21)

Instructions concerning kitchens (*kuri*) are given separately. I shall say no more on that subject here. (article 30)

No Need for a Dharma Hall (hattō)

It is not essential to establish a Dharma, or preaching, hall (*hattō*). In monasteries in the past, those monks of penetrating insight were made Dharma masters. These "dragons and elephants" of the community, in the rank of prefect (*chōshu*), assisted the abbot in his training of the other monks. Because of them, the practice of Zen was fruitful, and going to the lecture hall had some meaning. However, in monasteries today, the Way is fallen below the standards of the past. Even in large monasteries, it is difficult to find capable abbots, and the problem is that much greater in smaller houses. When those in authority, unenlightened and wanting in wisdom, merely ape the style and vocabulary of the great Zen masters of the past, embellishing their instruction with witticisms and bright but superficial phrases, they are not only deceiving themselves; they are leading others astray. It is much better, in these circumstances, for the abbot and *chōshu* to do *zazen* with the other monks, participating in an unrelenting, life-or-death Zen. If the abbot truly has the capacity of the great masters of the past, then he may sit squarely in his own quarters and instruct those who visit him there. How can you say there is no *hattō*? (article 12)

Management of Monastery Estates

The administration of monastery lands (*shōen*) in distant provinces should be handled by an estate overseer (*shōsu*). Fields adjoining the monastery should be managed with the aid of the prior (*tsūsu*) (or the comptroller [*kansu*] or assistant comptroller [*fusu*]). The estate overseer should not be carelessly appointed. Great pains should be taken in finding a suitable person. When an overseer is appointed and whenever there is a change of overseer, the candidates' qualities should be evaluated by the abbot, the senior members of the two ranks, and the older monks. With regard to the tax tribute from the *shōen*, at the time for collecting the rent, so as not to cause those living in the monastery hardship, there should be careful discussion to plan in detail for the provision of the following year's food supply and repair work. The abbot and the monks responsible for administration should not decide the disposal of revenue on their own initiative. This will only serve to invite suspicion on the part of the other members of the community. (article 8)

II. THE COMMUNITY

The Abbot

The chief monks (*jūji*) of this temple should not be chosen carelessly. The head monk of San'e-in and the senior monks, after discussing the matter carefully, should select and appoint an able monk. If no suitable candidate for the office is to be found among the members of this community, then a renowned and virtuous monk from some other monastery may be invited. Do not necessarily be bound by the forms of selection procedure prevailing in other monasteries. (article 1)

Whether he comes from this or from some other lineage, the community of monks should select the head. The degree of his lenience in dealing with the community should be comparable to the gathering of the tax tribute from the monastery estates. Many abbots nowadays, whether from kindness or from a sense of pity, take little note of the disturbance and waste about the monastery and are too easy with their monks. This type of attitude contributes to monastic decline and is very undesirable. According to an old saying, "Monks should not be treated softly. When, out of the daily food supply a surplus is always saved, then energies are not depleted." This precept has much truth in it and should certainly be followed. (article 2)

Everything concerning the installation of a new abbot (*juen*) should be done simply. The ceremony should follow the ancient regulations. Nowadays the old rules are neglected, and the ceremony has become a gaudy show. This puts patrons to considerable bother and expense, and is a drain on the monastery. You should reflect on this carefully. The Japanese way is to invite some respected monks from other monasteries to act as witnesses. Although it is said that in the T'ang ceremony they did not invite anyone, sometimes the new appointee was accompanied by acquaintances who came for the occasion, attended the ceremony, and acted as witnesses. Afterwards the most eminent of these was asked to officiate as "white mallet" (*byakutsui*).[37] This must have been very meaningful. However, since we have simplified the *hattō* ceremonies for installation in this monastery, there is no need for a *byakutsui*, still less for anything else. (article 31)

Entering the monastery gate, offer incense (there should be a short sermon [*hōgo*]). Next, going to the Buddha hall (*Butsuden*), offer incense and prayers (there should be a sermon here). Then go to the guardian deity hall (*dojidō*) and the patriarchs' hall (*soshidō*) (no sermon here). Then going to the monks' hall (*sōdō*), perform the registration (*kata*). (In the old regulations, the procession went to the *Butsuden* after registration; now the way is to go in sequence to the *Butsuden*). After this, entering the abbot's quarters, take possession of the room (there should be a sermon here). You should then go once more to the *Butsuden* and offer incense to the sages of Buddhism, and incense for the succession to the Dharma.[38] Pai-chang drew up regulations covering everything. If these were practiced, there would be no reason for the activities of the monastery not to proceed smoothly. However, nowadays there are many eminent monks who make different rules. This is only to keep in step with the times with the aim of leading people by giving examples and adjusting the standards. How, then, can anybody question my drawing up simplified rules as the house code of a small monastery? Those who enter the monastery should incline to the judgment of the superior and not refuse to do what should be done. If they do not like this, they are free to look for some place more to their liking. The world is wide, there is really no need for them to remain here wrinkling their noses in disgust! (article 32)

The Officers

There should not be more than 10 monks in the 2 ranks (*han*).[39]

Four should be appointed acolytes to the abbot (*jisha*). Those who are so requested and refuse may be permitted to escape the obligation if they offer some valid reason. If they refuse but give no reason, they should withdraw from their places in the monks' hall and leave the monastery. It is important that monks should experience this position at least once, and they should not be permitted casually to shirk the obligation. It is difficult enough to get a sufficient number of *jisha* in large monasteries and much more so in a small monastery like this. If, when a monk has completed his appointed term as *jisha*, there is no one to take his place, the abbot should request him to remain in the position. If he objects vigorously, he may be excused, in which case the grade should be left open until a successor is available. The offices of dormitory head (*ryōgen*),[40] sick-room head (*dōsu*), sanitation steward (*jinjū*),[41] and monks' hall acolytes (*shōsō jisha*)[42] should not be left vacant. The office of *ryōgen* should be given only to those who have been monks for 20 years. Holders should alternate every half month. As *dōsu*, monks of generous disposition who will be patient and compassionate in their charge of sick monks should be appointed. If there are no volunteers for the offices of *jinjū* and *shōsō jisha*, the duties may be given to monks of less than 10 years' standing. Holders should serve alternately a month at a time. In cases where there are old monks of few years' standing, they may be excused from these duties. (If there is a shortage of monks in the 10-year category, the range of choice may be extended and those of up to 15 years' standing called upon.) (article 5)

The Monks

Older monks, whether from Rinsenji or from other monasteries, whatever their status, should take places in the hall and join the community in reciting the sutras and doing *zazen*. They should not try to be different from other monks. Monks of abbot rank, whether former abbots of other monasteries (*seidō*) or former abbots of this monastery (*tōdō*), and monks who, because of their age, cannot bear the daily regimen, may act at their own discretion. (article 6)

With regard to seniority in the community, there should be no squabbling between older monks and their younger fellows. Such matters should be settled on the basis of a proper balance between age and the time elapsed since ordination. Retired superiors, from this or other temples, and very elderly monks should of course be considered senior to other monks. It says in the *Bonmōkyō* (Sutra of the Brahma's net), "Those who were ordained earlier should sit in front, those who were ordained later should sit at the rear.[43] Shaka Nyorai gave this explanation because he wanted monks to respect the various codes. Nowadays, in the Zen school, however, ordination ceremonies are, in many cases, little better than mere formalities. Young monks, asserting that more years have passed since their ordination, seat themselves ahead of older monks. This would seem to be in accord with the *Bonmōkyō* quotation, but their behavior displays a lack of respect for older monks. Shaka Nyorai's regulations should not be interpreted to insist exclusively on the time of ordination. For this reason I do not decide seniority simply on the basis of the time of a monk's ordination. In the case of monks of the same age, I regard as senior the one who was ordained earlier. In the case of those who were ordained at the same time, I regard the elder as senior. In the case of monks of the same age who were ordained at the same time, seniority should depend on who was registered (*kata*) first. If there is more than 10 years' disparity in their ages, the older man should be considered senior. However, if a younger monk was ordained 10 or more years before an older monk, then the older monk should not be regarded as senior. I have practiced this as an expedient in my training of monks. Of course in the Dharma Realm of Absolute Reality (*shinnyo hokkai*), there is no "self" and no "other"; how then, can there be any ranking? Each individual, entering the state of harmonious, single-minded concentration (*mujō sanmai*), strives to comprehend the Buddha, True Person of No Status. (article 7)

Itinerant monks who are not already known to a member of the community should not be permitted to stay overnight. Those who are known should not stay more than one night. In cases where, because of inclement weather or for some other pressing reason, visiting monks stay for a longer period, they must always obtain the permission of the head monk. Furthermore, the monk in charge of the kitchens (*tenzo*) should not go out of his way to prepare extra food for them. Monasteries have traditionally maintained dormitories where visitors were received, and that tradition should be respected. However, with the world in its present degenerate condition, there are many who, though they appear to be monks, are not in fact true monks. They are a drain on the resources of the monastery and, worse, have a destructive influence on the purity of the monks within the community. Problems of this nature occur when rules which were in the past used to regulate the treatment of guests are neglected. (article 4)

Novices and Postulants
The registration of novices (*shami*) and postulants (*kasshiki*) should not exceed 5 in number. It is not permitted for them to become monks before the age of seventeen. (article 3)[44]

III. THE MONASTIC LIFE
Ritual versus Practice
Monastic rules and regulations should be directed towards the practice of essentials. Do not be too ready to follow the example of big monasteries. In many monasteries nowadays, there is a tendency to give priority to rituals while neglecting the actual practice of the Way. How can they so lose the meaning of the founders in establishing regulations and organizing rituals? If one were absolutely thorough, no amount of ritual would be an obstacle to sincere practice. People of these later generations, however, are incapable of such range and must reject everything but single-minded concentration on cultivation of the Way. (article 9)[45]

Four Daily Sessions of Zazen
With the exception only of bath days[46] and those days on which there are meetings with the abbot, four daily sessisions of *zazen*

(*shiji no zazen*) must be held, even at the hottest and coldest periods of the year. Even during the New Year and the summer Bon festivities[47] there must be no cessation (if during *zazen* something arises that requires immediate attention, then you may interrupt the sitting). The abbot Jōshū (778–897) had this to say: "I was for thirty years in the southern regions doing *zazen* continuously except for two meal periods—this (that is, the time spent eating) was secondary."[48] Jōshū is saying that time given to meals had to be taken from time he would have preferred to devote to his principal object, but that, apart from this, he allowed no distractions to interfere. This old monk was enlightened almost from birth, yet his practice of Zen was like this. You can imagine what those who are not yet fully self-enlightened have to do! There is an old saying, "The non-enlightened must strive as if he were mourning his parents; the enlightened, too, must strive as if he were mourning his parents." Here we see the well-intentioned severity of the ancient masters. In the light of these ideals, how is it that monks limit the number of days, shorten the time, and do not meditate sincerely? Seekers after the Way in the past, choosing remote valleys and craggy ledges, sat on rocks and under trees. What else was there for them to do? Foregoing sleep, forgetting food, they single-mindedly pursued the Way. After Pai-chang established his monastery, there was considerable temple-building work and domestic duties to be taken care of. But, since the monks who gathered there were all earnest seekers, training and meditation were not interrupted by secular concerns. In the centuries since Pai-chang's death, monastic discipline has been gradually declining, but monks seem to feel little regret about this. In the past, *zazen* at fixed times (*gyakuhan zazen*) was instituted.[49] This method was adopted only as an expedient by Dharma masters to assist and encourage idle monks. Those born in these later ages still dislike 4 daily sessions and sometimes wish to reduce them. What could be more regrettable and shameful than this? (article 10)

Special Prayer Ceremonies
When, whether in obedience to imperial command or in response

to the orders of the military rulers, other monasteries offer special prayer ceremonies, then this monastery too should hang up prayer banners and participate sincerely. However, you should not offer such prayers at the request of monastery residents or wealthy patrons. The thrice-daily reading of the sutras and chanting of prayers is for peace in the world and tranquillity within the monastery. If daily prayer is ineffective, can the offering of special prayers be expected to produce results?[50] There are two kinds of prayer: the prayer of the worldly who, out of the depths of their secular craving, beg Buddha or the *kami* for happiness through prosperity and the prevention of disasters; and the prayer of those seeking to shake off the world's dust whose bodies and minds, instruments for pursuing the Way, are not to be lightly thrown away. The latter pray in order to seek the compassion and mercy of the Three Treasures[51] and the Heavenly Deities, and with this assistance advance in cultivation of the Way, striving to allow nothing to interfere with their progress. When one looks at the manner in which people express their belief in the Dharma or pay their respects to the *kami*, there are many who offer only worldly prayers. Monks, too, ensnared in worldliness, offer prayers for fame or profit. Can this be said to be proper? If monks and their followers neglect their principles how can Buddha and the *kami* be merciful? Though some trifling temporary profit may result, this may be the very cause of the loss of greater, truer benefits. Can there then be any reason for them not to be prudent? Zen people should neglect everything to concentrate on the root. This is the proper prayer by which to repay the Four Obligations[52] and assist the Three Realms of Existence. (article 11)[53]

The Observance of the Precepts

Pungent foods and *sake* must not be brought into the monastery. They must not be used even for cooking. Even if there are secular guests, they should not be permitted to eat after noon. Monks at leisure in their quarters, too, should not eat after mid-day. If, for the sake of their illness, it is necessary to have meals at special times, they must return to the infirmary (*enjudō*). It is said that there are two kinds of monk: *bodhisattva* monks and *śrāvaka* monks.[54] But as I see it, all "round-headed, square robes" (that is, monks) are merely *śrāvaka* monks. As it says in the sutra, "In the Buddha Law there is no separate *bodhisattva* monk." That is to say, The Buddha's coming into the world was only to carry on the tradition of the Law by taking the form of a *śrāvaka*. For this reason, when Shaka Nyorai went to Mṛgadāva he appeared in the form of a monk. Also Mañjuśrī (Monju) and other Mahayana *bodhisattvas* shaved their heads and dyed their clothes and appeared in the same guise as the Buddha. This is exactly what is described in the *Lotus Sutra*, "internally a *bodhisattva*, externally a *śrāvaka*." However, many present-day Zen monks complain that practitioners of the Mahayana Way are trammeled by petty prohibitions and regulations. Alas, those who express this view are very far from understanding Shaka Nyorai's intention in making his disciples take the same *śrāvaka* form as himself. Did Pai-chang draw up his code for the benefit of scholars of Hinayana? With Buddhism in a state of decline, it is difficult to observe the three thousand regulations and the eighty thousand detailed practices, but is it too much to expect monks to observe a few simple regulations and instructions? If you can't observe the rules, then it is better to relinquish the form of a monk and do Zen as a layman. What is there to prevent this? (article 17)

Absence from the Monastery

Wandering about idly, revisiting old haunts, going out in the evenings, and staying away overnight should be restrained. If a monk wishes to go outside the monastery precincts, it is essential for him to get the advance permission of the abbot or the registrar (*inō*). (article 13)

Women

It is forbidden for monks to enter the hermitages of nuns or the homes of widows except when invited for Buddhist functions. When they are invited, they must not go without a companion. (article 14)

Nuns and laywomen are forbidden to enter the monastery precincts except when coming to hear the exposition of the Dharma. When meals are donated to the monks, women must not take tea or eat in the monks' quarters. (article 15)

Frivolous Behavior
It is very bad for monks who have gathered in the abbot's or monks' rooms for religious purposes to end the day eating cakes, sipping tea, and indulging in frivolous conversation. This type of behavior is only permitted after a Buddhist memorial service. But even when a great feast is held for a memorial service, there should not be more than two varieties of cakes served. (article 16)

Leave
Requests for leave of absence must be limited to at most 50 days. If you are going far and can't return before the expiry of the time limit, you must request permission to re-register. Whether this request is granted or not should depend entirely on the abbot. (article 18)

Dormitory leave should not exceed 7 days. If, after that period, the monk has still not recovered, he must take sick leave and rest in the sickroom. He should not be in other places. (article 19)

Those on sick leave should stay in the infirmary. If they wish to convalesce elsewhere, they should take leave of absence and leave the monastery. If their leave exceeds the time limit (that is, 50 days), they must relinquish their places and, after resting, request re-registration. Whether they are accepted or not is up to the abbot. Only during illness are extraordinary (after noon) meals permitted, but pungent foods and wine are not permitted. In some monasteries, in the treatment of sickness, they forbid the provision of extra meals but permit the use of the pungent foods. They have their reasons for doing this. What I control is opposite to this and I, too, have my reasons. The use of wine to take medicine in, or the addition of a little onion to medicines is not forbidden. Otherwise you should follow Nyorai's instruction that one should rather die than violate the rules. Do not say that *sake,* meat, and the five pungent foods can preserve the body and extend life. In the secular world, of those who eat such foods, there are none who have escaped death through longevity. That monks should care for their bodies in order better to pursue the Way was not forbidden by the ancient sages and, fortunately, there are medicines that may be taken; but to want to take sinful medicines is the height of idiocy. The preservation of life is difficult; there are many who die though they are suffering from no disease; how much more likely to die are those who are sick. Do not say, "First relieve my sickness, then I'll engage in the Way!" There is an old expression, "Hardship and ease alternate; the Way lies therein." You should realize that, in time of sickness or grief, there is only the Way. (article 20)

Quarreling and Discipline

Keep a tight rein on your thoughts and your tongue, and do not quarrel. What is called a *sangha* in Sanskrit is here called a "harmonious assembly." If monks, harboring in their hearts self-assertion and arrogance, disrupt the harmony of the community with harsh words and quarrels, how can this be called a *sangha?* Monks have gathered for the sake of the Way. If, even on doctrinal matters, discussion should not degenerate into argument, how much the more so should this not happen over trivial matters. However, monks are human, and it is hard to forbid all feelings of joy or anger. When small quarrels take place, the abbot, chief seat (*shuso*), or *inō* should encourage the parties to make peace. If things reach the level of insults and blows, then, without going into the rights and wrongs of the affair, both parties should be expelled from the monastery. (article 23)

When a monk is accused by the community of committing repeated offenses, whether they be verified or unverified, he must not be permitted to continue to live in the community. The abbot should talk to him privately and get him to withdraw from his place and leave the monastery. Do not make a public record of this. (article 24)

Luxury

The furnishings and equipment of the monastery should all be modest, and the clothing of monks must not be luxurious. Luxury not only interferes with the pursuit of the Way; it also invites robbery. (article 25)

Weapons

In monasteries nowadays, in order to prevent robbery, they store a variety of weapons. This is a major cause of decline in the Dharma and should not be countenanced. Lately, robbers take monks' lives as well as their belongings, simply because monks have weapons within their monasteries. The best means of preventing robbery is not to accumulate riches but rather to observe the Buddhist regulations. The only thing to be concerned with is grasping the fundamental truths of the Buddha and making them one's obligation. Do not cherish the ills of the secular world. If you follow the true Way, the gods and spirits will protect you. What need is there to rely on weapons? If you wander from the Way and invite disaster upon yourselves, then any number of weapons won't help you. (article 26)

BAKUFU REGULATION OF THE GOZAN

So far, we have looked at the regulation of the Zen monastic life from within—by monk legislators. Zen monasteries were also subject to close regulation and control by the secular authorities. The official Zen monasteries and nunneries in Japan included thousands of able-bodied men, enjoyed considerable wealth, held large tracts of land, exerted influence at all levels of society, and played a role in the *bakufu* political power balance. Unlike the older Buddhist sects, Zen was dependent on warrior support from the outset, and regulation went hand in hand with patronage. While the warrior authorities were eager to see Zen grow, they were not anxious to see it grow out of control. The Hōjō and later the Ashikaga issued comprehensive regulations for individual Zen monasteries and for the growing *gozan* institution as a whole. These regulations clearly reveal the kinds of problems in the developing Zen institution that attracted the attention of the secular authorities. The following pages provide a simple content analysis of 7 *bakufu* codes, 3 compiled under the Hōjō, 4 under the Ashikaga, together with the *Rinsen kakun*.[55] The results are summarized in Chart 5.

The 110 articles in the 8 codes can be reduced to 11 problem areas: (1) prodigality, (2) wandering, (3) contact with women, (4) novices and postulants, (5) total number of inhabitants, (6) weapons, (7) abbots (*jūji*), (8) the two ranks of officers, (9) economic affairs, (10) religious matters, (11) miscellaneous.

(1) *Prodigality* includes such items as prohibitions against luxurious monastic furnishings or monks' robes, lavish feasting on Buddhist holidays, provision of banquets for wealthy patrons or their retainers, giving farewell or welcoming parties for monks going on, or returning from, long journeys, extravagant seasonal gift-giving to other monasteries, and taking meals at odd hours (after noon). Several of the codes try to curtail the practice of eating cakes (*tenjin*). The secular codes referring to *tenjin* state that only one variety may be taken. Musō permits two. Musō also expressly forbids the use of pungent foods and *sake* within the monastery.

(2) *Wandering* covers all excursions outside the monastery without permission. There are repeated efforts to block what seems to have been a much-used escape route: supposedly sick monks wandering out of the infirmary. Some of the absenteeism seems to have been simply to search for flowers (1294 code); some was, no doubt, less innocent.

(3) *Women* were permitted to enter Zen monasteries on special memorial days "to listen to the Dharma," as Musō puts it. While there, they were not to take tea or food in the monks' quarters. Monks, for their part, were forbidden to visit nunneries or the homes of widows unless accompanied by other monks.

(4) Regulations relating to *novices* and *postulants* deal either with the age at which these boys could enter monasteries (not

CHART 5 *Bakufu* Regulation of the *Gozan*

	Sadatoki 1294 12 articles	Sadatoki 1303 7 articles	Takatoki 1327 18 articles	Musō 1339 32 articles	Tadayoshi 1340 7 articles	Tadayoshi 1342 5 articles	Motouji 1354 12 articles	Yoshimitsu 1381 16 articles
Prodigality	XXXX	XXX	XXX	XXXX				
Wandering	XXXX	X	XXX	XXX			X	
Women	XX		XX	XX				
Novices		X	X	X		X		X
Total numbers		X	XX		X		X	X
Weapons		X	X	XX	XX		X	
Abbots			XX	XXXX		X	XXXXX	XXXXXX
Officers			XX	XXXX	X	X	XXX	XXXXXXX
Economic matters			XX	XXXXXX	XX	XX	X	
Religious life				XXXX				X
Miscellaneous	XX			XXX	X			

Each "X" indicates a reference to that particular problem.

before 15), the obligation to have the permission of a guardian before enrolling, and the number allowed at any one time (not more than 5 for a medium sized monastery).

(5) The references to the problem of the *total number* of monks illustrate clearly the kind of expansion taking place within *gozan* monasteries in the fourteenth century. The code of 1303 for Engakuji limits the complement of monks for that monastery to 200; in 1327, the maximum is 250; in 1340, it is 300; and the code of 1381, which relates to *gozan* monasteries in general, has this to say: "The total number of monks in large monasteries should not exceed 500. There are cases, however, of 700 or 800 or even 1,000 or more." The concern is not merely for the absolute size of monasteries. The codes make it clear that, in official thinking, size should correspond to the resources available in land and rents.

(6) The prohibition against *weapons* within Zen monasteries appears in most codes. The *bakufu* code of 1354 has this to say: "We are constantly hearing about monks wounding one another with swords or staves. This is reprehensible. The injured party should be summarily expelled; there is no need to go into the rights and wrongs of his grievance. The monk who perpetrated the act should be closely questioned and then expelled. He should not be permitted to enter other communities. If it is discovered that searching inquiries have not been made into these disputes, future pleas from that monastery will be disregarded." The repeated prohibitions against weapons do not necessarily imply that Zen monasteries were becoming military enclaves like Hieizan and other older monasteries with their armies of soldier-monks. They do indicate, however, that medieval Zen communities were not always havens of meditative tranquillity.

(7) Regulations affecting *abbots* deal mainly with appointment and conduct in office. The senior monks of individual monasteries were expected to select 3 candidates on the basis of ability and present these names to the *bakufu*, where a final choice would be made, if necessary, by drawing lots. Monks, however talented, proposed by powerful secular patrons should not be considered

for office. The installation ceremony for abbots should be simple, and presents for the new abbot restricted to one kimono, a sheaf of paper, and a silver sword. Abbots should serve at least two years. Able men should be permitted to serve for longer periods, and exceptionally able men might hold the position of abbot in different monasteries concurrently, if no suitable candidate was available for one of the posts. Abbots should not behave arbitrarily but should consult appropriate monastic and secular officials when making major decisions. They should avoid personal luxury and be strict yet humane towards their monks. One code (1327) mentions the possibility of expulsion of an abbot as a last resort, to be done only after careful discussion among senior monks and upon consultation with *bakufu* officials.

(8) *The eastern and western ranks:* these two bodies, made up of 5 or 6 senior monks each, were responsible for the day-to-day running of the monastery. Broadly, the eastern rank had charge of administration, while monks of the western rank were more directly concerned with Zen practice and ceremonial. Regulations in *bakufu* codes referring to the officers relate to such things as duration of service and honesty in handling monastic funds (the 1354 code insists that annual accounts be kept, and shown to the *bugyō*). Associated with the two ranks were the abbot's acolytes (*jisha*). The 1381 code forbids boys under 16 to be made *jisha*. Musō's code implies that monks were frequently reluctant to serve in some of the more menial offices or unable to pay the fees required. Other regulations under this heading relate to the place of older monks within the community. In principle, those who had completed the term in office were expected to return to the monks' hall. In practice, many senior monks moved into private sub-temples. Repeated but unavailing efforts were made by legislators to check this tendency. Musō, we have seen, admonishes these older monks to do *zazen* with their fellows, and take an active part in the life of the monastery.

(9) *Economic matters* do not receive very detailed attention in the sample used. There were other channels than the codes for dealing with such matters as grants of land, rents and taxes,

moneylending, and inter-monastic disputes. The relevant articles refer to such things as taking care to appoint honest estate over-seers, eliminating peculation by monks in the eastern rank, and treating branch temples fairly. A fairly common item included under the economic heading relates to the building of sub-temples (*tatchū*). The requirements to be met before commencing building became increasingly more stringent, indicating that the *bakufu* was trying, without success, to check an epidemic of *tatchū* building.

(10) Until Yoshimitsu's code of 1381, there is little effort by the *bakufu* to regulate the religious life of Zen monasteries. This was left to Zen abbots. From the late fourteenth century, how-ever, *bakufu* codes indicate a growing secular concern that the practice of monastic life was in decline.

From Chart 5 it appears that there was a shift from a primary concern by the Hōjō for what can be described as decorum to an interest on the part of the Ashikaga in closer regulation of the administration of Zen monasteries. This is in keeping with the development of the *gozan* under Tadayoshi and Takauji and their successors. However, there is an ad hoc quality to most of the codes, and the fact that the later codes make few references to such problems as prodigality, wandering, and contact with women probably does not mean that these particular problems had been overcome but simply that bureaucratic concerns were now upper-most.

One interesting point emerging from Chart 5 is the question of the relationship between the *Rinsen kakun* (1339) and Tadayoshi's codes of 1340 and 1342. Tadayoshi was active in the promotion of Zen and a confidant of Musō. It is possible that he consulted Musō before promulgating his own codes. He can hardly have been unaware of the existence of the *Rinsen kakun* and may even have prompted its compilation. We should probably see a close correla-tion between the repeated attempts by Zen monks to keep their house in order and prodding and control from outside by secular authorities.

FIVE

The Monastery and Its Sub-Temples

Those monks, Japanese pilgrims and Chinese émigrés, who were instrumental in establishing the Zen schools in Japan during the thirteenth century were eager to introduce to Japan not only the teachings and meditation practices of the great Sung monasteries, but the full Zen monastic life under correct Zen regulations in the proper setting—the Zen monastery.

In China the Ch'an-oriented monastery had evolved slowly over the centuries between the early T'ang dynasty and the Southern Sung in step with the development of the characteristic teachings, practices, and ceremonies of the Ch'an schools. The monastery was not a haphazard jumble of buildings. Each building and its furnishings were intricately related to the religious and social needs of the community. Some of the most important Ch'an buildings, the Dharma hall (*fa-t'ang, hattō*) and monks' hall (*seng-t'ang, sōdō*), had no precise counterpart in the monasteries of other Buddhist schools in China or Japan. Ch'an monastic regulations are detailed, and the everyday activities of monastic life as well as the elaborate ceremonial functions called for quite distinctive furnishings, equipment, and ceremonial objects.

The Zen monastery and its lifestyle are today so accepted as Japanese that it is difficult to realize how exotic the new Zen monasteries must have seemed in the thirteenth century. Not only were monastery buildings different in style, disposition, and furnishing from anything existing in Japan; the robes of Zen monks, their manner of walking and bowing, their etiquette before and after eating, bathing, and even defecating were also distinctive. So too were the sounds of the Zen monastery: the signals on bells, clappers, and gongs that regulated the meditative pattern of daily life; the musical accompaniment of the ceremonies and chants; even the style of sutra chanting. The vocabulary of Zen monastic life included hundreds of terms unfamiliar to Japanese ears. And, as a final reminder of the foreign origin of the institution, spoken Chinese was heard frequently in Japanese metropolitan *gozan* monasteries until the end of the thirteenth century, and the Chinese literary flavor continued to thicken in the fourteenth. The new Zen monasteries were outposts of Chinese religion and culture in medieval Japanese society.

TRANSMISSION OF THE GROUND PLAN

Early Japanese Zen practitioners and their secular patrons were naturally anxious that Japanese Zen monastic practice should inherit the lamp of the Ch'an tradition and that the new Japanese monasteries should be faithful to their Chinese models. But how did they go about translating the complexities of the Ch'an monastery from China to Japan? How were the artisans who built the new monasteries able to work with confidence and dispatch? And how can we, from our remote historical vantage point, know to what degree, if at all, they succeeded in their task of duplication?

Eisai, Dōgen, and Enni each spent four or five years enrolled in Chinese monasteries. Their writings reveal that they took an active, observant interest in Ch'an monastic buildings, their furnishing and use, as well as in every other area of Ch'an practice, teaching, and ceremonial. During their years in the monks' halls of Chinese monasteries, Japanese monks were expected to do their share of the routine jobs, thus familiarizing themselves with every aspect of monastic activity. Eisai, while in China, is reported to have helped with the building of a great gate and Kuan-yin

(Kannon) hall at Wan-nien-ssu and a Thousand-Buddha Pavilion at T'ien-t'ung-shan.[1] The chapters in Dōgen's *Shōbō genzō* devoted to bodily hygiene and washing the face or cleaning the teeth, for instance, explain the correct Zen etiquette and attitude of mind to be adopted by monks in performing these simple everyday activities. These chapters also demonstrate on Dōgen's part an extremely detailed architectural knowledge of the design and furnishings of the washstands and latrines of Sung monasteries.[2] During his stay in China, Dōgen had clearly been at pains to familiarize himself with the material as well as the spiritual aspects of Ch'an monastic life. Even if, after their return to Japan, Eisai and his successors did not themselves clear sites, cut and haul timbers, lay stone platforms, or shoulder roof beams and tiles, they would certainly have kept a knowledgeable eye on the work and given advice and instruction.

Although it is difficult to document, there is a strong tradition that Chinese artisan-builders, skilled in the construction of Ch'an monastic buildings, came to help direct the early building work in Japan, and that Japanese master builders were sent by the Hōjō to observe the structure of Chinese monasteries. Eiheiji still preserves a wooden statue, dating from the middle ages, of a man in the costume of an artisan-builder, mallet in one hand, chisel in the other. The figure is said to represent Kuro Genzaemon Morishige, a Ch'an master builder whom Dōgen is alleged to have brought back with him from China. A family line of Zen master builders who lived near Eiheiji from medieval times and directed the construction of Zen monastic buildings there and elsewhere in Japan traced their ancestry to Morishige.[3]

A similar family of specialist Zen artisans attached to Kenninji for many generations also traced their genealogy to a medieval master builder, Yokoyama Gonnokami Yoshiharu, who, according to records of the Yamanoue family, received imperial permission to visit China to study the building techniques used at Ching-shan and on his return directed the building of Kenninji.[4] These family traditions do not seem far-fetched when it is recalled that there was close and friendly contact between Japanese and Chinese monasteries from the very beginning of Zen monastic development in Japan.

Chinese mentors and colleagues of Japanese monks showed great interest in the fledgling Zen communities in Japan and actively encouraged their growth. Wu-chun, for instance, is said to have been so pleased at the news that his disciple Enni, on his return to Japan, was building a Zen monastery near Hakata in Kyūshū that he sent pieces of his own calligraphy to be used as models for the plaques to be hung over the entrances to the various monastery halls. Known as *gakuji*, these inscribed tablets are an important feature of any Zen monastery, giving the names of buildings, offices, or monastic functions. Among *gakuji* in the Wu-chun style still held by Tōfukuji are those reading *jōdō* (ascending to the hall), *shōsan* (small assembly), *fusetsu* (general lecture) and *sekkai* (explanation of the precepts).[5] Enni, for his part, sent timber from Hakata to Ching-shan to be used in the re-building of the Buddha hall there which had been destroyed by fire.[6]

There is no record that Eisai, Dōgen, or Enni went so far as to make sketches of Chinese monasteries themselves. Among their disciples, however, were some who did make detailed group plans and drawings of Sung monastic buildings and their furnishings. Fortunately, a number of early copies of these ground plans survive, providing us with a remarkably clear picture of the scale and principal features of some of the leading Chinese Ch'an monastic centers as they were in the mid-thirteenth century.

The earliest and most comprehensive of such ground plans is owned by the monastery of Daijōji in Kanazawa. Known as *Gozan jissatsu zu* (Illustrations of the Five Mountains and Ten Temples), the surviving 2-scroll document is a mid-Muromachi period copy of an original thought, on internal evidence, to date from about 1250. There is doubt as to the author of the original, but there could be some truth in the tradition which says that it was brought back to Japan by the monk Tettsū Gikai (1219–1309), a disciple of Dōgen and the founder of Daijōji, who was sent to China in 1259 to make, or acquire, plans of major Chinese monasteries to be used in the completion of Eiheiji.[7]

Whatever their origin, such plans were in great demand in Japanese Zen monasteries. At least half a dozen monasteries still preserve copies of the Daijōji plans. Tōfukuji has a slightly different version, also a mid-Muromachi period copy, perhaps derived from the same original as the Daijōji series. There are numerous later copies of this Tōfukuji version and also of a later Eiheiji version.

The Daijōji *Gozan jissatsu zu* is in 2 scrolls totaling 72 illustrations. The illustrations include:

(1) Full ground plans of several Chinese "mountains": T'ien-t'ung-shan, Pei-shan, and T'ien-t'ai-shan (Wan-nien-ssu) but not, unfortunately, Ching-shan.

(2) Ground plans of individual buildings from various monasteries: monks' halls, a reading room, bathhouse, washstands, and latrine.

(3) Elevations of buildings: the 2-storied Dharma hall at Ching-shan, the 2-storied Buddha hall (*fo-tien, Butsuden*) at Chin-shan-ssu.

(4) Diagrams of furnishings and ceremonial objects: an altar used in a Buddha hall; a dais from which the abbot addressed the community and stands for the great drums used in the Dharma hall; different ceremonial chairs and screens used by the abbot in the monks' hall and abbot's building (*fang-chang, hōjō*); a bronze "cloud sheet" hung at the entrance to the kitchen and used to signal meals; the mallet and block used to signal the beginning and ending of meals or meditation sessions in the monks' hall; miscellaneous bell-shaped window frames, door-hinges and sockets, incense burners, bells, revolving sutra wheels, and so forth.

(5) Diagrams of agricultural equipment, notably the water-powered milling machinery at Pi-shan-ssu.

(6) Diagrams of ceremonial and daily functions: the correct seating order for the reading of sutras in the Buddha hall; the seating order during the ceremony of "offering incense" by new entrants to the monks' hall; the order of precedence for the thrice-monthly invocations and circumambulation

FIGURE 9 Ground Plan of T'ien-t'ung-shan, near Hangchow

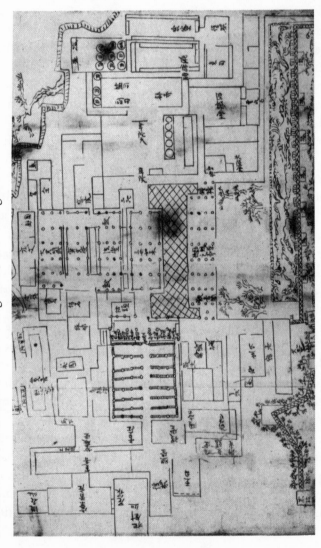

This illustration, from one of the scrolls known as Illustrations of the Gozan and Jissatsu, details the principal architectural features of the T'ien-t'ung-shan as it was in the late thirteenth or early fourteenth century. The scale of buildings was indicated by the small circles showing the spacing of pillars, which were set one ken (1.82 meters) apart. The titles of the various monastic officers are written in against their seating positions in the outer chamber of the monks' hall. Diagrams like this were helpful in recreating the Sung Ch'an monastery in medieval Japan.
Photograph courtesy of Daijōji Temple, Kanazawa, and Komazawa University Library, Tokyo.

of the various halls; together with schematic diagrams of the various bell and drum signals used to set the pace of monastery life.

(7) Sample documentary and calligraphic forms: for the reading of the Ten Buddha Names during the circumambulation ceremonies; and for the wooden tablets assigning officers and monks to their places during ceremonies.

This is far from being a complete inventory of the contents of the Daijōji *Gozan jissatsu zu.*[8] Sufficient has been given, however, to indicate that the diagrams and illustrations cover the most characteristic features of Ch'an monastic life. The illustrations vary in detail. Some are hardly more than sketches. Most are very detailed, drawn to approximate scale, labeled, and including basic measurement. There can be no doubt that they were drawn by somebody familiar with the details of Ch'an monastic architecture. To a skilled carpenter they would have served as a comprehensive and reliable source of reference.

As the title of the document suggests, the plans illustrate the large official Ch'an monasteries in the Five Mountain or Ten Temple categories. Ching-shan, the senior "mountain," was most frequently used as a model, followed by T'ien-t'ung-shan, Pei-shan, and A-yü-wang-shan. These plans suggest that a very small number of Chinese monasteries shaped the development of Japanese Zen monastic life.[9]

With this kind of illustration to assist them, reinforced by the guidance of those monks and the few artisans who were familiar with Ch'an monasteries, and by reference to such documents as monastic codes (*ch'ing-kuei*), where buildings and their furnishings are frequently mentioned, the builders of the early Zen monasteries in Japan could feel confident they were producing a fair facsimile of the Chinese model.

Illustrations also survive which allow us to see clearly what the earliest medieval Japanese Zen monasteries were like, and to gauge their faithfulness to their continental models. Of these, the earliest and most detailed is the *Kenchōji sashizu* (Kenchōji ground plan).[10] The history of this document is checkered. In 1319 a fire destroyed many of the buildings at Tōfukuji in Kyoto. To help them in their work of reconstruction of what was to be a pure Zen monastery with no tincture of Tendai or Shingon, the Tōfukuji artisans in 1331 made a copy of a master plan of the recently rebuilt Kenchōji. Kenchōji lost its master plan in a disastrous fire early in the fifteenth century, and later (1723) Kenchōji monks recopied the copy handed down in the family of the Tōfukuji artisans. It is this later version that survives.[11] Although it does not show the earliest form of the monastery, it does show Kenchōji as it was at the peak of its prosperity in the early fourteenth century. Since the Kenchōji style of layout was copied by Tenryūji and other Japanese Zen monasteries, as well as the rebuilt Tōfukuji, the ground plan, which is very detailed, can be said to reflect the classical stereotype of the fully articulated medieval metropolitan Zen monastery.

Other helpful early Japanese illustrated documents include the *Engakuji keidai ezu* (Plan of the Engakuji compound), a ground plan showing the layout, setting, and boundaries of this compound in about 1330;[12] the *Sanshōji garanzu* (Sanshōji ground plan), showing Sanshōji, an affiliate of Tōfukuji, in the late fourteenth century;[13] the *Eiheiji garanzu* (Eiheiji ground plan)[14] and the detailed painting, attributed to Sesshū, of Tōfukuji in the second half of the fifteenth century.[15] When these sources are combined with the Kenchōji ground plan, it is possible to build up a very clear picture of the layout and furnishing of medieval Zen monastic buildings. The authenticity of these early plans is attested by the fact that they tally very closely with the descriptions of these monasteries and their buildings given in contemporary diaries, *shingi*, and other written documentary sources.

The reader may wonder why so much reliance has to be placed on reconstruction through documentary evidence when so many Zen monasteries still stand in Japan. Zen monastic buildings dating from before the Ōnin War do survive. The Buddha reliquary (*shariden*) at Engakuji (c. 1285),[16] the Buddha hall of Kōzanji (Yamaguchi prefecture, c. 1320),[17] the monks' hall (c. 1340), bathhouse (1459), and latrines (Muromachi period)

FIGURE 10   Ground Plan of Kenchōji, Kamakura

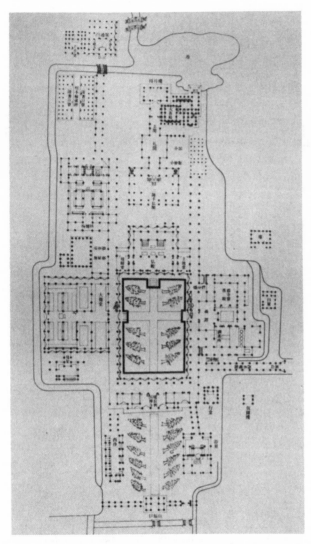

This is thought to be an early copy of the original ground plan, depicting Kenchōji as it was shortly after its foundation. The layout is clearly based on Chinese monastic centers like T'ien-t'ung-shan. From the outer gate an avenue of trees led to the two-storied great gate which bore the legend "Kenchō kōkoku zenji" (The Kenchō Zen monastery for the prosperity of the country). Walking north between more pine trees, the visitor would come to the Buddha hall. To his left would be the great monks' hall, to his right the administrative buildings in the kitchen-office. To the north of the Buddha hall lay the two-storied Dharma hall and the abbot's building.

Photograph courtesy of Shogakkan Publishing Company, Tokyo, and Kenchōji, Kamakura.

at Tōfukuji,[18] the small sub-temple abbot's building of the Ryūg-in'an (Tōfukuji, 1389),[19] the Kannon hall (c. 1314) and founder's hall (1352) of Eihōji,[20] and other surviving medieval Zen buildings undoubtedly constitute an invaluable surviving architectural record. Unfortunately, they are scattered, belong to monasteries of different scale, and are not fully representative of the whole range of monastic buildings in use in medieval Zen monasteries. No large medieval *hōjō* survives, for instance, nor is there any early surviving example of a Zen monastery reading room (*shuryō*) or of the large kitchen-office building (*kuin*). The one medieval monks' hall surviving at Tōfukuji is internally in disrepair. Fire has been the worst scourge, aggravated by warfare, intersectarian feuding, earthquakes, and typhoons.

Abbots of Zen monasteries naturally felt an obligation to try to rebuild their monasteries after each fire and to restore buildings that had fallen into disrepair. If funds could be found, artisans and monks were on hand who could quickly reproduce lost buildings. During the late thirteenth and the fourteenth centuries, while metropolitan Zen was in the ascendant, a timely fire, as at Kenchōji, might even provide an opportunity for the building of new or larger structures. During the fifteenth and sixteenth centuries, however, the Ashikaga, the principal patrons of *gozan* Zen, found themselves in increasingly straitened economic circumstances, with little to spare for the expensive work of monastery building. Thus, the great medieval *gozan* foundations in Kyoto never fully recovered from the destruction they suffered in the Ōnin disturbances. Those Rinzai monasteries that went from strength to strength after the Ōnin War,—Daitokuji, Myōshinji, and their branches—were able to do so only because they had tapped new sources of economic support, and even with this support were smaller in scale than the leading *gozan* had been.

Quite apart from the reverses caused by fires, warfare, and ups and downs of patronage, other factors were at work to alter, slightly but significantly, the character of the Zen monastery. The Rinzai emphasis on the *kōan* as an instructional device tended to focus attention on the person-to-person interviews between the monk and his master at which the *kōan* were given and discussed. This, in turn, gave increasing prominence to the *hōjō* where these encounters took place. In time, this led to the decline of the reading room, since formal study was held to be useless for the resolution of *kōan*.

These developments were compounded by the emergence and proliferation of sub-temples (*tatchū*) around major monastic complexes from the late thirteenth century. This was a uniquely Japanese development. As Professor Tamamura Takeji has pointed out, it is vital to understand the significance of the sub-temples in order to grasp the character and development of the medieval Japanese Zen schools.[21] As monks gathered around favored masters in the smaller more intimate milieu of the sub-temples, the central monks' halls were emptied, and the great kitchen-office buildings which had served them fell into disuse. Thus, when reading rooms, monks' halls and kitchen-office buildings of the central complex, and the corridors which had connected them, were destroyed by fire, they were either not replaced at all, or, after the sixteenth century, replaced in a modified form under the influence of the newly imported Ōbaku style in which the great monks' hall (*sōdō*) had become a small Zen hall (*Zendō*). Sub-temples also tended to encroach physically on the central compound, altering its shape by overflowing into spaces left by lost buildings.

Existing Zen monasteries, therefore, although they contain individual early buildings and preserve the basic features of the lifestyle of the Zen monastery as it was inherited from Sung dynasty China, are not perfect facsimiles of the medieval monastery but derivations of the early-modern Zen monastery—a somewhat different style of compound. Daitokuji and Myōshinji in Kyoto, for instance, both preserve fine, whole complexes. Few of their buildings, however, predate the Tokugawa period. To know the great metropolitan monastic centers as they were in their heyday in the mid-fourteenth century—and to know the medieval monastery is to begin to know medieval as opposed to post-Hakuin Zen—the surviving architectural evidence has to be supplemented by close reference to whatever medieval documentary evidence can be found.

THE SETTING

Every Zen monastery includes in its formal title the name of a mountain. Shōkokuji, for instance, which stands on level ground in the city of Kyoto, has the mountain name of Myriad Year Mountain (Mannenzan) after a Chinese monastery with that mountain name. Nature has always had a central place in Ch'an consciousness. Many early Ch'an masters are portrayed as recluses who sought enlightenment through solitary meditation and seclusion in nature. T'ang dynasty Ch'an communities are thought to have settled in remote areas, providing for themselves by mendicancy or the labor of their own hands. Some of these communities, like certain other Chinese Buddhist communities, may have lived in isolated mountain fastnesses. There is a possibility, however, that the mountain conceit was somewhat exaggerated under the reclusive influence of Taoist or Confucian thought and that early Ch'an centers were less isolated than is generally assumed. Certainly by the beginning of the Sung dynasty, when the general picture is much clearer, Ch'an monasteries were being built close to, or in the midst of, centers of population, and most monasteries were dependent for their survival on local patrons and the local economy. Wherever the monastery was built, however, it was conceived of as a mountain retreat: a total spiritual environment in which monks could practice Ch'an as the early masters had practiced. Deliberate efforts were therefore made to include in the surroundings and grounds features of natural scenery. This is evident from a glance at the ground plan of T'ien-t'ung-shan.[22]

This concern for an appropriate natural setting was carried over into Japan and further refined there. Zen monasteries always embraced a number of scenes or "grounds" (kyōchi). These included trees, ravines, rocks, streams, bridges, and ponds within the compound, and the borrowed scenery of nearby rivers or surrounding mountain slopes, as well as notable monastery buildings. At times the scale was grand. The "ten grounds" (*jukkyō*) of Tenryūji took in the whole sweep of Arashiyama.[23] Or it could be as condensed as the tiny stone garden at Daisen'in (Daitokuji).[24] Whatever the scale, the natural features encompassing the monastery were as important as the monastery buildings and contributed to make a whole world. A flat stone under a moonlit tree was considered to be as fitting a place for meditation and enlightenment as the meditation platform of the monks' hall.

Although the natural environment was further reshaped and refined in the gardens designed by monks like Musō Soseki (1275–1351),[25] it is clear from the plans of the earliest Japanese Zen compounds that the skillfully contrived incorporation of nature into the monastery was present from the very beginning of Zen monastic life in Japan.[26]

In their concern for a harmonious balance between symmetry of form and compromise with nature, Japanese Zen monasteries took a middle path between the severe symmetry but aloofness from nature of the great Nara monasteries on the one hand, and the straggling mountain-crest centers of Kōyasan and Hieizan on the other. Zen monasteries were usually sited on the lower slopes of forested hillsides, where nature was abundantly at hand but a clearly defined monastic form could still be preserved. This preference was itself a mark of the mellow sophistication of Sung Zen. Wherever possible, Zen monasteries observed the north-south axial norm of the traditional Buddhist monastery. The north-south axis could be sacrificed, however, for a particularly fine site, as at Tenryūji and Nanzenji which face east and west respectively.

One other important factor in the siting of Japanese Zen monasteries was that of political patronage. It was no accident the the most important *gozan* Zen monasteries were located in the two major political centers or their outskirts.

THE LAYOUT

The irreducible core of the Zen monastery is commonly referred

to as the seven halls (*shichidō* or *shichidō garan*). When earlier
applied to the monasteries of the Nara sects in the eighth century,
the seven halls had included the pagoda (*tō*), golden (Buddha)
hall (*kondō*), lecture hall (*kōdō*), bell tower (*shōrō*), sutra repository (*kyōzō*), monks' dormitories (*sōbō*) and refectory (*jikidō*).
The courtier statesman, Shintō scholar, and Buddhist monk
Ichijō Kanera (1402–1481), who was one of the first to apply
the term "seven halls" to a Zen monastery, listed them as: "the
mountain gate (*sanmon*), Buddha hall (*Butsuden*), Dharma hall
(*hattō*), kitchen-office (*kuin*), monks' hall (*sōdō*), bathhouse
(*yokushitsu*), and latrine (*tōsu*)."[27]

Not only is the Zen list different from the earlier seven, the
disposition of the various halls was also rather different. At a
much later date, Mujaku Dōchū (1653–1745), a Rinzai monk and
scholar of Zen monastic history and organization, the author of
the *Zenrin shōkisen,* depicted the seven halls and their layout
thus:

Dharma hall
(head)

Buddha hall
(heart)

Monks' hall		Kitchen-office
(left arm)		(right arm)
Latrines	Mountain gate	Bathhouse
(left leg)	(privates)	(right leg)

This anthropomorphic conception of the Zen monastery was
common in Mujaku's day. In a contemporary Sōtō school document of the kind given by a master to a recognized disciple
to pass on secret lore, the seven halls are shown even more
graphically:

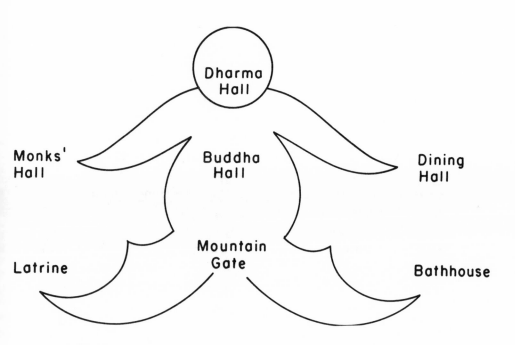

The positioning of a refectory opposite the monks' hall betrays this document as being heavily influenced by the style of the Ōbaku school monastery and somewhat out of step with the style of monastery and monastic life advocated by Dōgen. These pictorial representations of the monastery are later innovations. They are not found in medieval documents. Since a number of these diagrams have also been found in the family handbooks of Zen temple builders (*Zen daiku*) from the beginning of the early-modern period, there is a possibility that this version developed among artisans as a convenient pictorial mnemonic.

A glance at the *Kenchōji sashizu* and other early Japanese ground plans shows that this type of representation is not inappropriate for Japanese monasteries. If we neglect the abbot's building and the corridor system, then the monastery does consist basically of a central line of three imposing ceremonial buildings, the great gate, Buddha hall, and Dharma hall, flanked by two balanced pairs of buildings, latrines and bathhouse; monks' hall and kitchen-office.

It is also obvious, however, that the seven halls constitute no more than the essential minimum skeleton of the Zen monastery. The *Kenchōji sashizu*, for instance, also shows an outer gate (*sōmon*), attendants' hall (*andō*), bell tower (*shōrō*), mortar room (*usuya*), storehouse (*kura*), reading room, abbot's building, elderly monks' hostel (*kikyūryō*) and Kannon hall (*senjudō*). There were also a pagoda and several sub-temples which are not shown. All these buildings were essential in the daily life of the monastery. From the *Ch'an-yuan Code* it is clear that, in China, some Ch'an monasteries in the Northern Sung dynasty (early twelfth century) had as many as 30 or 40 buildings.

The term "seven halls" does not seem to have been applied to Chinese monasteries. Neither the term itself nor the later anthropomorphic mnemonic variant were quite so applicable. Ground plans of T'ien-t'ung-shan and Ling-yin-ssu (Pei-shan) show the characteristic central axis of great gate, Buddha hall, Dharma hall, front and inner abbot's chambers, with the monks' hall and kitchen-office building to left and right of the Buddha hall.[28] To this extent, the layouts of Sung and Japanese monasteries were identical.

The balanced positioning of the latrines and bathhouse, however, and their inclusion within a seven-hall stereotype seems to have taken place in Japan. In T'ien-t'ung-ssu, the bathhouse was situated to the left of the great gate and conveniently near the monks' hall. The main latrine was located just behind the monks' hall. In Ling-yin-ssu, the bathhouse was to the right of the great gate towards the back of the kitchen-office complex, and the latrine was at the back of the monks' hall. Function, rather than form or symbolic value, obviously still determined the location of these two buildings in Chinese monasteries. Nor do Chinese descriptions of the components of the Ch'an monastery normally include these buildings as basic features.

Comparison of the layout of Chinese and Japanese monasteries, as shown in their ground plans, also suggests that the Japanese monasteries were more vertically oriented and neater in outline. The verticality may have been encouraged by the nature of the terrain, the narrow valleys in which many Japanese monasteries were built. Restriction of space may also have influenced the neatness of their outline, though this tidiness was also due to the smaller scale of the Japanese monastery: T'ien-t'ung-shan, for instance, had 40 or more interlinked buildings arranged in a compact but very intricate layout. The monks' hall at T'ien-t'ung-shan had many more satellite buildings than that at Kenchōji. These included dormitories, reading rooms, needle rooms, laundry areas, washstands, and latrines.

The cluster of buildings to the right of the main gate at T'ien-t'ung-shan provided accommodation for itinerant monks: those monks who were merely seeking accommodation for a night or two at the monastery but had no intention of registering for a season in its monks' hall. This important area of the Chinese monastery is not shown in Japanese ground plans, suggesting either that the practice had not developed, or that the few itinerants who came were accommodated elsewhere, perhaps in the guest section (*kyakuden*) of the kitchen-office.

One other important area of the Sung Ch'an monastery which appears in more vestigial form in Japanese monasteries is the assistants' hall (*anjadō*). *Anja* were lay novices over the age of 16 who had either not completed the training, or had not acquired the official documents required of somebody taking the full vows and tonsure of a monk. They did much of the manual work around the monastery and had their own extensive quarters referred to as the "monk selection hall" behind the kitchen-office building. This area included a meditation hall, a communal reading room, latrine, and washstand. An attendants' hall (*andō*) is shown on the Kenchōji ground plan, but it is small in comparison with the other buildings.

Differences of scale and complexity were to be expected: the Japanese monasteries illustrated in these ground plans were still within the first century of their development; those in China had 500 or 600 years of history behind them. Comparison shows that, in layout, the Japanese Zen monastery followed the Chinese model as closely as circumstances in Japan permitted. Japanese monks may also have deliberately sought to isolate the essential symbolic and practical core of what they believed to be the traditional Ch'an monastery.

GATES

In Japanese Zen monasteries today, the most impressive structures are the great gates or *sanmon*. These are beetling-eaved, 2-storied structures (the only genuine 2-storied buildings surviving), standing on stone platforms.[29] The weight of the upper story and the heavy tiled roof is carried on 3 rows of massive timber columns: 3 rows of 6 columns each for a large 5-bay gate, 3 rows of 4 each for a 3-bay gate. Heavy wooden doors still hang in the central bays of many *sanmon*, and one occasionally finds standing in the two outer bays the statues of the Guardian Kings, a conspicuous feature of such gates in medieval Japanese and Chinese Zen monasteries.

In Rinzai monasteries, the great gates now stand detached, linked to no walls or corridors of any kind, only to rather unlikely looking staircases at either end of each gate, which give access to the upper story. The visitor can either walk through the central doorways into the compound or he can simply skirt the gate.

This was not the case in the medieval monastery. The early ground plans of Japanese and Chinese monasteries show that this gate was the principal entrance to the monastery proper, the only break in the encompassing outer walls of the central corridor system. To enter or leave the monastery, monks and visitors had to pass, under the watchful eye of a gatekeeper, through this gate or, in some monasteries, a small gate let into the wall beside it. According to Eisai:

> There is no difference between large and small monasteries, for all derive from the model of the original monastery built by Shudatsu (Sudatta) for the Buddha himself. There should be walled cloisters on all four sides with no side gates and only a single gate to permit entrance and exit. The gatekeeper must see to it that the gate is closed at dusk and opened at dawn. Nuns, women or evil people should on no account be

permitted to stay overnight. All degeneration of the Law begins with women.[30]

In the word for this gate, *sanmon*, the *san* could be written with either the character for "mountain" or "three." The great gate was more than simply the entrance to a particular Zen mountain or a bulwark against moral pollution. It was, in a more positive sense, the ultimate boundary between the secular and the religious worlds, between the realms of attachment and liberation. The mountain was a realm of Buddhist search, the ground of Nirvana. The great gate, with its 3 doorways, was a conscious symbol of the 3 gates offering liberation from the bonds of illusion and suffering in the 3 worlds (*sangedatsu mon*): the gate of the realization of the non-substantiality of self and Dharma (*kū-mon*), the gate of realization of the non-existence of phenomena (*musōmon*), and the gate of the realization of the non-existence of desire (*musamon*). Although the terms "triple gate" and "mountain gate" were both in use in Sung and Japanese medieval monasteries, with "mountain gate," if anything, becoming the more popular, the term "triple gate" is older and more expressive.

The great gate was therefore an integral and important part of the monastery. As such, it provided the setting for a number of monastic ceremonies, among them the formal reception of a new abbot. At the appointed hour, the officers and members of the community, wearing their formal stoles (*kesa*), gathered at the gate to welcome their new mentor and guide. Here he offered incense and delivered his first formal address (*hōgo*) before proceeding to enroll, like any ordinary monk, in the monks' hall, and then to assume temporary custodianship of the *hōjō*.

In keeping with the symbolic and ceremonial character of the gate, the chambers of the upper story were decorated with gilt and azure, and housed gilded statues or brilliant color scrolls depicting "seekers" of Nirvana: usually Śākyamuni, attended by Getsugai Chōja (Somachattra) and Zensai Dōji (Sudhana), and flanked by statues or paintings of the 16, or 500, Arhats.

The very human Śākyamuni and the semi-mythic Arhat sages had a very important place in the life and thought of the Zen monastery. They exemplified the struggle for enlightenment each monk had to live through for himself within the framework of the monastic life and rule. Regular ceremonies were held in the upper chambers of the great gate, and many medieval monasteries also had an additional Arhat hall (*rakandō*). These figures, however, were not adored as gods, simply revered as exemplars.

The great gate and the realm within were shielded from unwelcome contact with the outside world by 2 smaller, though still imposing, outer gates. Unlike the 3 gateways giving access to the earlier Nara monasteries, which all straddled the central axis of the monastery, the outermost gates of the Zen monastery were usually off this axis, so that anybody approaching the monastery had to do so indirectly, his view of the main gate and central compound obscured until he was almost upon it. The medieval Zen monastery was not open to casual entrance. Set well back behind its walls, gates, and outer ponds and gardens, it was designed to preserve the seclusion and tranquillity essential for monastic life.

THE BUDDHA HALL

The *Eiheiji garanzu* shows the Buddha hall (*Butsuden*) as an imposing 5-bay building located near the center of the compound. Since the *Kenchōji sashizu* and the ground plans of the major Sung monasteries show Buddha halls of similar scale in the same position, we can assume that this hall was a major feature of the Southern Sung and medieval Japanese Zen monastery.[31]

In the medieval monastery, the Buddha hall was flanked by two separate buildings or annexes, a guardian deity hall (*dojidō*) and a patriarchs' hall (*soshidō*). The patriarchs' hall, as the name implies, had as objects of devotion statues of one or more of the Ch'an patriarchs, frequently Bodhidharma or, in Japanese Rinzai monasteries, Lin-chi, or Pai-chang. The guardian deity hall housed a statue of one of the protective Buddhist deities: Daigon Shuri Bosatsu, Bonten, or Gohō Myōō. The patriarchs' hall and guardian deity hall were important buildings in the early medieval monastery, with their own sub-prefects to supervise the various ceremonies. In time, however, both these halls were absorbed into the Buddha hall as altars (*dojidan* and *soshidan*) at the back of the hall.[32]

The Zen Buddha hall corresponds to the golden hall (*kondō*) of the Nara period monastery, serving as the devotional center. In Zen monasteries, the principal deity revered in this hall is most commonly Śākyamuni in the role of the Buddha of the Present World, flanked by statues of the Buddhas of the Past and Future Worlds; or Śākyamuni attended by two disciples. Kenchōji, which was built on the site of an execution ground, has always had as the principal deity (*honzon*) in its Buddha hall a statue of the compassionate *bodhisattva* Jizō, who was believed to guide the souls of the dead out of their torments in hell.[33] One also occasionally finds Shingon deities left in the Buddha halls of former Shingon monasteries taken over by the Zen schools. The most common *honzon*, however, is the seeker Śākyamuni.

The statues are set on pedestals on an altar platform (*shumidan*) symbolizing Mt. Sumeru, the center of the Buddhist cosmos. Above the *honzon* hangs a gilt or purple drapery, frequently bearing the characters meaning "invocation" (*kitō*). In front of the deity stand 3 lacquered wooden tablets. The central tablet bears an inscription meaning "Long Live the Emperor." Those on either side are inscribed "Prosperity and Good Fortune to Patrons" and "Felicitations to Nan-fang-huo-te, Lord of Fire." These tablets are a tangible expression of the historic dependence of the Zen monastery upon powerful patrons, and an indication of the accommodation that took place between the Zen schools and the ruling authorities in China and Japan.[34]

Since illustrations of these tablets are included in the scrolls illustrating the furnishings of the Chinese Five Mountains, we can be fairly certain that they were in use in Chinese monasteries in the Southern Sung dynasty. In the Yuan dynasty, when Ch'an monks found it expedient to be particularly obsequious towards the imperial court, some monasteries displayed tablets reading

"Long Live the Emperor," "Gracious Years to the Empress" and "A Thousand Autumns to the Crown Prince."

It is not known when the first set of such tablets was brought to Japan, but the monk Seisetsu Shōchō is recorded as having brought a set to Japan in 1326. He is said to have placed them on the altar of the Zenkyo'an, a sub-temple of Kenninji. By this time, they were almost certainly a standard feature of all Zen Buddha halls. In the Tokugawa period, at least one Kamakura monastery replaced the tablet dedicated to the "Lord of Fire" with one bearing the more mundane, but probably more useful, invocation "Long Life and Prosperity to the Shogun."

We have already suggested that Musō Soseki blamed the Mongol invasions for the common acceptance by Zen monasteries of the Shingon-Tendai practices of offering prayers and invocations (*kitō*) for the intentions, political as well as religious, of powerful patrons. He complained that time given to such prayers had led to a decline in the practice of meditation (*zazen*). The Mongol crisis did much to increase the accommodation of the metropolitan Zen monasteries with the Japanese state, but, well before the Mongol threat, the obligation of making some return for patronage had existed. Eisai's defense of Zen and plea for its promotion in Japan in the *Kōzen gokokuron* implied a contract: in return for official recognition, an independent Zen sect would contribute to the restoration of religious values and the well-being of the country by its rigid observance of the Buddhist precepts (*kairitsu*), by the austere practice of meditation (*zazen*), and by prayers (*kitō*). Impressed by the grandeur of the great Sung Ch'an centers, a grandeur paid for in part by regular prayers and ceremonies for imperial and aristocratic intentions and by the acceptance of a considerable measure of official control, Eisai must have visualized a similar relationship in Japan. Between the completion of the *Kōzen gokokuron* and the foundation of Kenninji, Eisai served as family prelate (*kitōsō*) to the shogunate, offering prayers for their intentions and welfare. Although Kenninji did not have a Buddha hall in Eisai's lifetime, prayers, invocations, and sutra chanting were conducted in the Shingon

and Tendai (*shikan*) halls in the intervals between meditation.

Dōgen saw clearly that, behind the impressive facade of the
Sung Ch'an monastic institution, there were flaws and weaknesses.
Dislike of the secularization and aristocratization he saw in
Chinese monasteries prompted him to reject official patronage
in Japan and to forsake the eclectic atmosphere of Kyoto. There
is no reason to suppose, however, that he objected to the time-
honored Buddhist practice of offering thanks to those who had
contributed to the maintenance of the community. Although he
felt that the monks' hall was the most important building, he did
not object to the presence within the monastery of the Buddha
hall: "The cardinal monastic buildings are the Buddha hall,
Dharma hall, and monks' hall . . . the monks' hall is most vital."[35]

The Buddha halls of the Ch'an monasteries that Dōgen visited
in China were in constant use. During the daily chanting of sutras,
prayers were offered for the welfare of the ruler, the peace of the
nation, and the prosperity and security of patrons. In addition,
on the first and fifteenth day of each month and around the
anniversary of the emperor's birthday, a special ceremony of
invocation for the imperial well-being was held.

The Buddha hall, however, had not always had such an assured
position in the monastery. In fact, there was a strong strain in
Ch'an thought that argued it had no place there at all. We have
seen that the "Ch'an-men kuei-shih" (1004), which claims to
express the intentions of Pai-chang, the accepted founder of
Ch'an as an independent sect under its own rule, states flatly that,
with the elder (*chōrō*), the living embodiment of the Buddhas
and patriarchs, and a Dharma hall in which he could instruct and
engage in discussion the members of the community, there was no
need for a Buddha hall. Ch'an master Lin-chi I-hsuan (d. 867)
was critical of the Buddha hall, and master Te-shan Hsuan-chien
(780–865) is said to have demolished those he found standing
in monasteries over which he presided.

Behind this rejection of the Buddha hall—and behind the strong
tinge of seeming iconoclasm in Ch'an expressed in such anecdotes

as that in which the Ch'an master T'ien-jan Ch'an-shih (738–824), the monk from Tan-hsia, burns a statue of the Buddha to warm himself, or Yun-men Wen-yen (864–949) describes the Buddha as an anal stick—lay the experiential emphasis of the concept of "sudden enlightenment" espoused by Hui-neng and the Southern school of Ch'an. Moreover, the Buddha hall symbolized the ritualistic, textual, and scholastic aspect of Chinese Buddhism against which early Ch'an had been in revolt. Its acceptance by Ch'an could only mean a loss of independence and dilution of meditation, as Ch'an monasteries, in return for patronage, became vehicles for the satisfaction of secular intentions.

In spite of this resistance, Buddha halls were in use in some Ch'an monasteries even before the end of the T'ang dynasty. They are mentioned frequently in the later sections of the *Ching-te ch'uan-teng-lu* (1004), which describes the lives of eminent T'ang monks. By the time the *Ch'an-yuan Code* (1103) was written, they were an accepted, though, to judge by the relatively low status in the monastic hierarchy of the monk in charge, not yet a central part of the monastery. The hall received full formal acceptance for the first time in the *Ju-chung jih-yung Code* (1209), compiled between the time of Eisai's final departure from China and Dōgen's arrival.

During the thirteenth century, this hall became steadily more important. The *Chiao-ting Code* (1274) lays down in great detail the ceremonial to be observed during the twice-monthly imperial birthday services and gives the Buddha hall a central place in the ceremonies for the induction of a new abbot. With these developments still taking place in China, it was hardly surprising that, when Engakuji was established towards the end of the thirteenth century, one of the first buildings to be completed should be the Buddha hall.

THE DHARMA HALL

Although the Buddha hall was slow to win full acceptance, the Dharma hall (*hattō*) was accepted as a vital element in the Ch'an monastery from a very early date.[36] We have seen that the "Ch'an-men kuei-shih" (1004) laid particular emphasis on this building. The Dharma hall had some of the characteristics of the lecture halls of other Buddhist sects. It differed from them, however, in that it was not intended simply as a place for erudite lectures on the sutras but as a forum for discussion and questioning (*mondō*) between the abbot and the members of the community. In the Ch'an Dharma hall, there was no need for the images found in the lecture halls of other sects. The abbot spoke as the Buddha to his disciples.

In the Sung dynasty, the Dharma hall was in regular use. It was the scene of the formal, morning assembly known as "ascending to the hall" (*shang-t'ang, jōdō*) or "great assembly" (*ta-ts'an, daisan*). It was also used for the less formal "explanations" (*p'u-shuo, fusetsu*) and some of the occasional 'little" evening assemblies (*hsiao-ts'an, shōsan*). The pattern adopted at the assemblies was for the abbot to deliver an introductory address on some aspect of Ch'an teaching or to offer an illustrative anecdote, then to invite discussion. The original intention behind these assemblies had no doubt been to provide the opportunity for give-and-take discussions aimed at clarifying basic problems encountered by the monks during meditation, study, or the everyday practice of the monastic life.

The "Ch'an-men kuei-shih" implies that these assemblies took place morning and evening daily. There is little evidence that they were ever held quite so frequently. In the medieval monastery, these assemblies were still taken seriously and held several times each month. Signs would be posted at the entrance to the Dharma hall in advance, and all monks, with the exception of those on duty in the monks' hall and reading room, were expected to attend. During the later Southern Sung and Yuan dynasties, however, assemblies were held less frequently, usually only on auspicious or ceremonial occasions. They tended, therefore, to become increasingly formalized.

Attendance by the whole community, in some monasteries 500 or 600 monks or more, called for a building of generous proportions. Dharma halls at T'ien-t'ung-ssu, Ling-yin-ssu, and Kenchōji were at least as imposing as the Buddha halls in those monasteries.[37] The oldest surviving Dharma hall in Japan is the fine building at Shōkokuji, rebuilt by Hideyoshi and now used as a combined Buddha hall and Dharma hall. The Dharma halls at Myōshinji and Daitokuji give a very good idea of the large pure Dharma hall. That at Manpukuji is an example of the smaller Ming dynasty style of hall.

Like the Buddha hall and the other buildings in the continental style in the compound, these halls stand on stone platforms. Inside they are tiled with stone flagstones. The interior, designed to accommodate the whole community, is empty except for signal drums in the northern corners and a signal block and mallet. The principal furnishing of the hall is a dais (*shumidan*) approached by 3 flights of stairs, that at the front reserved for the abbot, those on either side used by acolytes during formal ceremonies. The dais in the Shōkokuji Dharma hall bears statues of Śākyamuni with attendants, that at Kenchōji a Thousand-Armed Kannon. These two halls are now used for devotional as well as instructional purposes, but this is a later development. In the Myōshinji and Daitokuji halls, the only item of furniture on the dais is the abbot's Dharma chair (*hōza*). This is in keeping with the traditional character of the hall, which was not intended as a place of worship. In medieval halls, white lions (*shishi*), companions of Monju (Mañjuśrī) were sometimes placed on either side of the abbot's chair.

The Dharma hall shown in the *Kenchōji sashizu* is labeled "Two-story, Thousand-Buddha Pavilion," indicating that this hall, like the Buddha hall and many other buildings in the medieval Zen monastery, was 2-storied. The upper story was used for devotional purposes. The Tōfukuji *Sōshobun* (1250) describes the then existing Dharma hall at Tōfukuji as a 5-bay-by-5, 2-storied building, the upper story housing a 10-foot statue of Monju flanked by full size statues of the 16 Arhats, and smaller statues of the 500 Arhats.[38]

Although surviving Japanese Dharma halls appear from outside to be 2-storied, they are all single-storied buildings. Painted within the high circular "mirror ceilings" of the Dharma halls of Tōfukuji, Daitokuji, and Myōshinji and the Buddha hall at Sennyūji (Kyoto) are dragons, a popular symbolic motif in Zen art and thought, auspicious creatures of legendary spiritual energy. [39]

THE ABBOT'S BUILDING

The abbot's building in a Zen monastery is known as the "ten-foot square" (*fang-chang, hōjō*). This term was in use from the T'ang dynasty to describe the private chambers of a Buddhist dignitary or the retreat of a lay scholar recluse. Chinese T'ang and Sung dynasty sources trace the origin of the term to the tradition that the Chinese pilgrim Wang Hsuan-ts'e, while en route to India in 660, passed the ruins of a cottage in which the Buddhist layman-sage Vimalakīrti was said to have instructed 32,000 disciples and debated with the *bodhisattva* Mañjuśrī. Wang Hsuan-ts'e, surprised that such a modest cottage could have been the scene of such momentous instruction, is said to have measured the foundations and found them to be only 10 feet square. [40]

Although it is very difficult to establish a clear picture of the place of the *fang-chang* in the T'ang dynasty Ch'an monastery, frequent uses of the term in Ch'an texts and anecdotes indicate that it was used to refer both to the abbot's quarters and to the abbot himself.

The "Ch'an-men kuei-shih" stresses the public, instructional function of the *fang-chang*:

> One who is gifted with insight into the Way, and worthy to act as guide, is given the title of elder, just as in India elderly and experienced followers of the Way were referred to as *Subhūti*. Already the "master of instruction" (*hua-chu*), the elder has his quarters in the ten-foot square. This chamber, like that of Vimalakīrti, is not to be used simply as a private retreat. [41]

From the "Ch'an-men kuei-shih" and the *Ch'an-yuan ch'ing-*

FIGURE 11 The Buddha Hall at Chin-shan

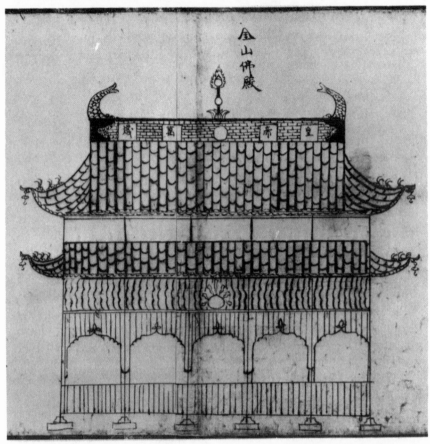

This illustration from the Gozan jissatsu-zu shows the elevation of a five-ken, two storied Buddha hall, characteristic of Sung and Yuan dynasty Ch'an monasteries. Many of the features were quickly adopted in Japan, including the stone pedestals for the wooden columns, the gracefully arched windows, the curved wooden trellis work, and the sweeping tiled roofs. The Chinese characters printed on the roof ridge read "Ten Thousand Years to the Emperor."
Photograph courtesy of Daijōji Temple, Kanazawa, and the Komazawa University Library, Tokyo.

kuei, it is possible to build up a picture of the various functions of the *fang-chang* in the early Sung dynasty. It was here that the incumbent abbot slept, studied, practiced private meditation, instructed the monks individually in the private interviews known as "entry to the chamber" (*ju-shih, nisshitsu*) and "asking for instruction" (*ch'ing-i, shōeki*), and held some of the occasional general evening assemblies known as the "little assemblies," here that he conducted the day-to-day administrative and organizational business of the monastery in discussion with the various monastery officers, and here that he entertained local Buddhist dignitaries, monastery patrons, and officials of the civil bureaucracy. Since the building had to be capable of accommodating the whole community for evening assemblies or occasional tea ceremonies and be appropriate to the entertainment of ecclesiastical and civil dignitaries, there is little doubt that, by the twelfth century at least, the *fang-chang* was an imposing building or group of buildings.

On the mid-thirteenth century ground plans of Ch'an monasteries, the *fang-chang* is shown as comprising three component buildings located directly north of the Dharma hall. At T'ien-t'ung-shan, there were two front *fang-chang*, an inner *fang-chang* and a meditation chamber and at Wan-nien-ssu (T'ien-t'ai-shan) a front *fang-chang*, *fang-chang*, and inner *fang-chang*.[42] Of these, the innermost building was used as the residential chambers of the abbot, the outer buildings as formal public reception and ceremony chambers. Taken as a block, these three buildings made up a very substantial area of the monastery. Around the ceremonial chambers and the abbot's residential section were the offices of the monastery acolytes (*shih-che, jisha*) and rooms for assistants (*hsing-che, anja*).

In medieval Japanese monasteries, the *hōjō* occupied the same position to the north of the Dharma hall; however, the main area of the building tended to be off the central axis. At Sanshōji, the *hōjō* proper was set within its own compound to the northeast of the front *hōjō*, which in turn was linked by a corridor to the rear entrance of Dharma hall.[43]

The *Kenchōji sashizu* shows a ceremony chamber (*raima*), corresponding to the foremost *fang-chang* of the Chinese monasteries, immediately north of the Dharma hall. In other medieval Japanese monasteries, this building was also known as a tea hall (*sadō*) or rest hall (*shindō*). North of the ceremony chamber lay the great guest pavilion (*daikyakuden*) and 2-story inner pavilion known as the "moon-gaining tower." These corresponded to the inner *fang-chang* of the Chinese monastery, comprising formal reception and guest chambers and the abbot's private quarters.

These inner buildings were approached by a covered and flag-stoned passageway with a double folding door at its center known as the "gateway to the mysterious" (*genkan*). The word *genkan* has now passed into everyday Japanese speech to mean a hallway or entrance porch, and few people are consciously aware of the strong Taoist-Zen overtones of its components "mysterious realm" and "barrier." The word was in use among Taoist-influenced T'ang poets; adopted by Ch'an as a fitting term to describe the entrance to the august presence of the Ch'an masters; transferred to Japan and later borrowed from the Zen monastery by aristocrats and warriors, becoming part of the aesthetic vocabulary of the Muromachi period.[44] It is not too far-fetched to assume that this term played some small part in shaping Zeami's consciousness of *yūgen*, "mysteriousness," nor to suggest that the *nō* actor, moving slowly along the bridge onto the stage, felt something of the sense of awe a monk might feel passing through the *genkan* to enter the chamber of his spiritual guide.

Perhaps the most striking feature of the *hōjō* of Japanese Zen monasteries is that, from a very early stage, they were built in the Japanese aristocratic residential *shinden-zukuri* or *shoin-zukuri* styles of architecture, whereas all other buildings in the compound were in the continental style. The Kenchōji ground plan of the inner *hōjō* clearly shows the vertically opening wooden shutter doors of the kind known as *shitomido*, a characteristic feature of *shinden-zukuri* architecture. There is also the suggestion of a fishing pavilion (*tsuridono*) built out over the pond. The inner *hōjō* at Sanshōji and Engakuji were also built in the Japanese manner on wooden supports, not on a stone pediment. The early Tenryūji *hōjō* is said to have been originally the residential section (*shinden*) of one of the palaces of the Emperor Kameyama and would certainly have been in the aristocratic Japanese style, with board floors and the rooms divided by the sliding paper-panel doors (*fusuma*), which provided a natural surface for ink, and later gilt, painters.

At least one part of the Kenchōji inner *hōjō* was 2-storied, the "moon-gaining tower." The 2-storied *hōjō* was a common feature of medieval Zen monasteries. The Kenninji, Nanzenji, Sanshōji, and Engakuji *hōjō* all had upper chambers, as did the *hōjō* of many prominent sub-temples. That these upper chambers were carefully decorated and used by the abbots as studies or guest chambers is indicated by references in the *Inryōken nichiroku* to the shogun admiring the view of Kyoto's eastern hills from the *hōjō* pavilion at Kenninji. Although no 2-storied *hōjō* pavilions survive, the founder's hall (*kaisandō*) at Tōfukuji probably gives an accurate impression of what they looked like.

It was these elegant Zen monastic buildings with their fine views over gardens, ponds and into mountains, and with their moon-viewing platforms and airy rooms, that provided the model for those two symbols of Muromachi period culture, the Golden and Silver Pavilions.

The *hōjō* was thus the instructional and administrative center of the monastery or sub-temple. It was also, in Sung and Japanese *gozan* monasteries, a cultural matrix. It was around the *hōjō* of the great monasteries and their sub-temples that the characteristic Zen garden developed. In its elegantly simple rooms the tea ceremony and art of flower arrangement were cultivated. Its alcoves and screens provided space for talented calligraphers, ink painters, and painters of Zen portraits (*chinsō*). And it was here that the study of Chinese poetry and thought was encouraged. It is probably to the *hōjō* of the metropolitan monasteries, to their incumbent abbots and their guests, rather than to some abstract notion of "Zen," that we should look if we are to understand the precise nature of the influence of Zen on the art and culture of the Muromachi period.

THE BATHHOUSE, LATRINES, AND WASHSTANDS

The *Kenchōji sashizu* shows the monastery bathhouse (*yokushitsu*)

to the southeast of the main gate, linked to the other buildings of
the monastery by a short corridor. The latrine, referred to at
Kenchōji as "western purity" (*seijin*), but in most other monasteries as the "eastern office" (*tōsu*), was located in a corresponding position to the southwest of the main gate. From the ground
plans of other medieval monasteries, it is clear that the locations
of these two buildings were formalized in Japanese monasteries,
although their positioning had been somewhat more functional in
Sung monasteries. To the south of the monks' hall was a small
building housing washstands referred to as the "rear stands"
(*goka* or *kōka*). The importance attached to these buildings in
the Zen monastery is indicated by the facts that the bathhouse
and latrine were included among the Japanese list of the basic
seven halls, and that Zen monastic codes devote considerable
attention to the etiquette and attitude of mind to be maintained
in using these buildings.[45]

The bathhouse at T'ien-t'ung-shan in the mid-thirteenth century
was a building 7 bays wide by 4 deep, situated to the southwest
of the main gate.[46] Over the door hung a plaque reading "clarity"
(*hsuan-ming*), a reference to the lay Buddhist sage Bhadrapala
who, with 16 followers, attained enlightenment and was granted
*bodhisattva*hood through contemplation of water while bathing.
Bhadrapala is the accepted patron figure in Zen bathhouses.

Above the entrance to the bathhouse proper hung another
plaque reading "perfumed sea," perhaps a reference to the perfumed water used in the traditional purification ceremony of
bathing a statue of the Buddha. A statue of Bhadrapala was set
on an altar table near the entrance. Before it stood an incense
burner, with candleholders at either side. To the right of the
altar was a hand-washing basin, to the left a large washtub. Left
and right of these again were towel racks and stoves for airing
damp towels. Platforms around three walls served as places for
monks to disrobe and put on their bathing wraps. They hung their
outer robes and the cloth wrappers containing their under-robes
over the trellises around the bath.

The bath, consisting of two large basins, was heated by a stove

FIGURE 12 The Bathhouse at T'ien-t'ung-shan

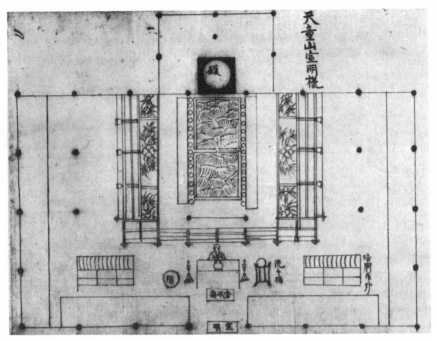

This building, which is fully described in the text, was seven ken *wide by four* ken *deep, with an extension at the rear for the water-heating stove.*

Photograph courtesy of Daijōji, Temple, Kanazawa, and the Komazawa University Library.

in an annex at the rear of the building. This was the domain of the bath steward, who would fuel the stove or add cold water according to signals on wooden clappers from the bathhouse: "One for more hot water, two for more cold, three when satisfactory." To judge from the accounts of bathing etiquette in the *Ch'an-yuan* and other codes, monks in medieval monasteries did not get bodily into the bath. They took water from the bath in one of the tubs provided, crouched beside the bath and, cupping their hands, dipped water over their bodies.

Although smaller in scale, the bathhouse at Kenchōji in the early fourteenth century was very similar to that at T'ien-t'ung-shan, and we can assume that this type of bathhouse and style

FIGURE 13 The Latrine at Chin-shan

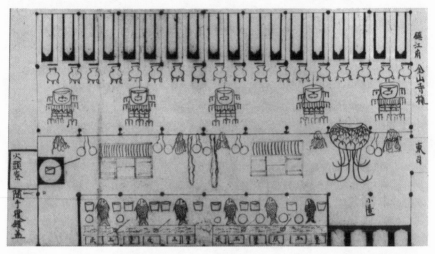

Photograph courtesy of Daijōji Temple, Kanazawa, and Komazawa University Library, Tokyo.

of bathing was standard in medieval Zen monasteries. By the sixteenth century, however, fashions were changing. Surviving bathhouses at Tōfukuji (Muromachi period, but frequently repaired), Daitokuji, and Myōshinji (both seventeenth century) all contain steam baths (*karaburo*) into which the bather stepped bodily.

The principal latrine at the Chinese monastery of Chin-shanssu, as shown on the *Gozan jissatsu zu*, was a building 9 bays long by 4 wide, linked to the monks' hall by a corridor.[47] Over the door hung a plaque reading "eastern office" (*tung-ssu, tōsu*). Along the right-hand wall were 18 cubicles, each with an incense burner at the door. Another large "octopus" incense stand was placed at the center of the hall. The incense, used as part of the ritual etiquette, served also to keep the air fragrant. Along the left-hand wall, just inside the front door, were a number of urinals and further along the wall basins of water, dippers, and wooden tubs used for carrying water to purify the receptacles before and after evacuation. Here also were placed the fish-shaped pumice stones and the containers of ashes, earth, and bean-powder used for cleansing the hands afterwards.

A rail running down the length of the center of the hall served as a place to hang towels and outer robes, with tags provided for identification. Damp towels could be dried and aired over the stoves and drying racks. In the interior of the hall was a furnace and cauldron of hot water for final hand-washing. This was superintended by the "stoker," whose office is shown beside it. Five lanterns along the center of the hall provided illumination when needed. The patron deity of the Zen latrine was Ususama Myōō (Uccusma), whose compassion for those in the bonds of life was such that he was prepared to enter and purify the foulest places. Before using the latrine, monks were required to remind themselves of his virtue.

The Kenchōji ground plan is less detailed. It does, however, show the same kind of long, narrow building with cubicles along one wall and what looks like a stove and wash place in the southeast corner. The only surviving Japanese Zen monastery latrine (*tōsu*) is that at Tōfukuji in Kyoto, a long single-storied building to the south of the monks' hall.[48] The interior of the building is now in disrepair, making it difficult to reconstruct its original appearance. However, a plan of the building made before deterioration shows rows of cubicles on both sides of the entrance door, urinals farther in, and a cauldron and washstand at the far end of the building. There is little doubt, therefore, that the furnishing and use of the latrine in the medieval Japanese Zen monastery followed the Chinese model very closely. Dōgen's description of the proper etiquette and attitude of mind to be observed while using this building, included in the regulations he compiled for his Japanese disciples,[49] echoes the descriptions given in earlier Chinese codes and tallies precisely with the illustration of the latrine at Chin-shan-ssu.

The "rear stands" (*goka* or *kōka*) was a building in which monks washed their faces and cleaned their teeth in the mornings, and washed their legs and feet before entering the monks' hall after a journey.[50] This wash house was always located very near the monks' hall, either directly behind it or, as at Kenchōji, immediately to the south of it. Originally the building was nothing but a wash house. By the Southern Sung dynasty, however, it became, in some monasteries, an outer annex to the latrine. An early stage in this transition can be detected on the Kenchōji ground plan. By the sixteenth century, the word *kōka* had passed into colloquial Japanese as a synonym for *kawaya*, meaning latrine.

The plan of the "rear stands" at A-yü-wang-shan in the mid-thirteenth century shows a large washstand, "two feet six inches high," in the middle of the room.[51] At the center of this stand was a bath containing cold water, and arranged around this several dozen washtubs and some containers for tooth-cleaning powder. Hot water, if needed, was taken from a cauldron at one end of the stand. A smaller stand held water pitchers and bowls of salt and ginger for cleaning mouth and teeth. Although there is no sign of them, the split willow twigs used for brushing the teeth were probably also kept here. In this building, too, stoves and trellises were provided for drying and airing towels.

These, then, were the carefully arranged and furnished hygienic facilities of a medieval monastery. In some larger Chinese monasteries, where 600 or 700 monks and as many attendants (*anja*) were in residence, separate latrines and wash houses were also provided for the assistants and itinerants. The abbot's building would also have had its own self-contained conveniences. The product of the latrines, gathered in huge earthenware jars, was used to fertilize the monastery lands.

THE MONKS' HALL

The monks' hall (*sōdō*) was the spiritual powerhouse of the medieval Zen monastery. Where the monasteries of other Buddhist sects housed their monks, as at Tōshōdaiji (Nara), in individual cells built in blocks around the central lecture and worship halls, Ch'an regulations, from an early date, stressed that all monks should live a communal life in a single open hall.[52] In the space of the single mat allotted to him, each monk sat for long hours in meditation, took his meals in silence, and stretched out for the few hours of rest allowed.

Since it was on the meditation platforms of the monks' hall that "Buddhas were made," the hall was frequently referred to as the "place for the selection of Buddhas" (*senbutsujō*). And since it was to this hall that monks came from all directions "like clouds and vapors" to pursue their individual struggles for enlightenment in communal meditation around their patron, the "holy monk" (*shōsō;* usually represented by a figure of Monju, the *bodhisattva* of intuitive wisdom), the hall was also referred to as the "cloud hall" (*undō*) and the "hall of the holy monk" (*shōsōdō*).

The origins of the monks' hall are as obscure as the origins of the Ch'an sect. The generally accepted model of early Ch'an monastic development is that, for the first few generations after Bodhidharma, Ch'an practitioners moved from place to place as solitary mendicants or in small groups who meditated out of doors or used the facilities of the monasteries of other sects. From the fourth and fifth generations, the number of Ch'an devotees increased sharply and more settled communities began to appear, frequently in remote areas, with their own distinctive pattern of monastic life. It was probably at this stage that the monks' hall began to develop as a communal center for meditation and that rules for the conduct of Ch'an monastic life were first laid down. Pai-chang (749–814) is usually given credit for drawing up the first Ch'an code of rules, for liberating the sect from dependence upon the buildings and regulations of monasteries of the Vinaya (Lü) school. We have already suggested that there is little concrete evidence to support this assertion.

One of the earliest unequivocal descriptions of the Ch'an monks' hall is to be found in the *Ch'an-men kuei-shih* (1004).[53] Thus, although we cannot pinpoint the precise origin of the Ch'an monks' hall, there is no doubt that, before the Sung dynasty, it had already taken on a very characteristic form and was regarded, together with the abbot's building and Dharma hall, as one of the most essential Ch'an monastic buildings.

The *Ch'an-yuan Code* (1103) stresses the priority of the monks' hall and makes frequent reference to the activities conducted there. The first volume of the code, for instance, after emphasizing the importance for Ch'an monks of receiving and keeping the Vinaya precepts, goes on to describe the equipment needed by monks in the monks' hall, the correct way to pack and carry this equipment, the procedure for entering the itinerant monks' hall, the procedure for enrolling in the monks' hall, and the manner in which meals should be taken there. In a later section of the code, the procedure and posture for meditation are described in detail. Moreover, newly appointed abbots, like any ordinary monks, were instructed by the code to go first to the monks' hall and enroll:

> The new abbot enters the monastery. At the great gate he offers incense and delivers a sermon. He then proceeds to the monks' hall, in front of which he takes off his bundles, goes to the washstands and washes his feet, then enters the hall, salutes the "holy monk," and offers incense. When he has completed enrollment in the monks' hall he may proceed to the great hall . . .[54]

During the Southern Sung dynasty, the centrality of the monks' hall in the monastery seems to have been eroded. Later Ch'an codes are more concerned with the niceties of organization of ceremonial functions conducted in the Buddha hall than with strict monks' hall practice. The *Ch'i-hsiu Pai-chang Code* regrets that monks' halls had been adversely affected by the development of private retreats (*tu-liao* or *tan-liao*) set up by monks who, on retirement from office, not only declined to return to the monks' hall themselves but also used monks from the hall as assistants or servants. These independent halls are already mentioned in the *Ch'an-yuan Code* as guest quarters for dignitaries but not yet condemned as a cause of degeneration of the communal life and discipline of the monks' hall.[55]

In spite of these hints of declining vigor, the monks' hall was still a dominant feature of Southern Sung Ch'an monasteries and was copied faithfully in Japan. This is clear from a comparison of illustrations of the monks' halls at Ling-yin-ssu and Ch'ing-shan with those at Kenchōji and Tōfukuji.

The *Kenchōji sashizu* provides a very detailed plan, with

measurements, of the monks' hall at Kenchōji in the early four-teenth century. The hall was situated to the west of the central axis of the monastery, between the great gate and the Buddha hall and linked to both by the western corridor system. At Ken-chōji, this hall was known as the "great attainment hall" (*daitetsu-dō*). The three characters making up the name were engraved on a wooden plaque and hung above the front entrance, which opened to the east. Externally, the building was 7 bays wide by 8 deep (exclusive of the encompassing corridors). Internally, it was divided into an outer hall (*gaidō*), linked by a passageway to an inner hall (*naidō*). Between the inner and outer halls were 2 light wells (*mindō*).

The most prominent features of the inner hall were the knee-high meditation platforms arranged in blocks around the walls and in the body of the hall. On these platforms the monks who were formally enrolled in the hall sat in meditation, took their meals, and slept. In Japanese monasteries, the platforms were surfaced with *tatami* mats. In Chinese monasteries, rush matting was used in summer and rugs in winter. Since the long northern and southern platforms were counted as double blocks, the Kenchōji monks' hall would be described as a 12-block hall. Single blocks were each 2 bays long. At 5 *tatami* mats to a bay (the average at Tōfukuji) this would have allowed 10 monks to a block, making a total seating capacity for the Kenchōji hall of about 120 monks.

The platforms were just deep enough to allow monks to stretch out and sleep. Against the rear walls were shallow cupboards into which were put bedding, under-robes, the blade used for shaving, and the monks' few other possessions. Each monk's set of bowls used for eating and taking tea was placed on a ledge above this cupboard and his spare outer robes on a rail running the length of the back wall. The outer edge of the platform was made of a length of polished, but untreated, timber about 12 inches wide running the length of the platform. This lip was treated with the greatest respect. During meditation, the monks' *kasāya* (*kesa*) rested on the lip. It was also used as a meal table and as a headrest at night. All Ch'an codes stress that monks should be careful not to set foot on this "pure area" when getting up onto or down from their places. During meditation, monks sat on cushions facing the back wall. For meals they turned and faced the body of the hall, laying out their bowls in a carefully prescribed manner on the lip of the platform before them. Above each monk was a tablet bearing the four characters making up his name. While he was on the platform he left his sandals neatly under it.

Other features of the inner hall were a central altar dais and the abbot's chair. The altar bore an image of the patron and spiritual leader of the hall. This was always referred to as the "holy monk" (*shōsō*). In most monks' halls, the figure represented was Mañjuśrī (Monju), dressed in the robes of a monk and armed with the sword of perception. The "holy monk" faced east, that is towards the front door of the hall. Before the dais was an altar table bearing an incense burner, flanked by candles and flowers, and on the southern side of the dais a wooden block and mallet used to signal meals or the beginning of meditation sessions or hall ceremonies. Movements in the hall, as elsewhere in the monastery, were done to prescribed sound signals. There was thus little cause for speech or confusion.

The abbot's meditation chair was placed just inside the northern portal of the entrance to the inner hall. He sat facing the "holy monk." A screen stood behind his chair; a small table set in front of it was used at meal times. The order of seating position in the hall was determined in relation to the "holy monk." Those platforms in front of the altar dais were known as front hall (*Zendō*), those behind as rear hall (*godō*), those to the left of the "holy monk" as upper places (*jōkan*), those to the right as lower places (*gekan*).

The senior officers in the hall thus sat on the platform to the right of the abbot's chair; other hall officers and senior monks sat on the platform to his left and on the "upper" and "lower" platforms at the rear of the hall. Other monks were placed in order of the length of time since their ordination. In a large hall, new entrants would thus be placed on the platform just behind and to the right of the "holy monk" and would "move up" in serpentine fashion as monks above them left the hall.

The abbot made his entrances and exits through the front door, always using the upper, northern side. Ordinary monks used the back door, or, if they should use the front, were careful to use the lower, southern side. To avoid jostling or stumbling and to encourage constant mindfulness, the codes direct that, when entering the hall, monks should raise the left foot over the lintel first.

The inner hall was reserved for monks who had formally enrolled (*kata*) in the monks' hall for the season. Even the abbot was not exempt from this requirement. The administrative officers (*chiji*) of the monastery, whose duties meant that they had to be elsewhere in the monastery for much of the time, sat on the inner platforms of the outer hall. They were required to return to the platforms of the inner hall when they had finished their term in office, though, as we have seen, some did not do so but set themselves up in private retreats. Monks in charge of sound signals, itinerant monks, monks who intended to enroll but had not yet done so, elderly monks, and lay visitors used the platforms just inside the front door of the outer hall. Since those who used the platforms in the outer hall did so only for meditation or meals, and slept elsewhere, the platforms in this area were only half the depth of those in the inner hall.

In the open space in the center of the outer hall stood trestle tables upon which the tubs of rice, soup, and vegetables and the pitchers of hot water and urns of tea carried from the kitchen by the assistants (*anja*) were rested before the meal and between servings. When not engaged in distributing food, the servers stood beside the tables. The only other furnishings of the outer hall were the drums and bells for signaling assemblies, meals, washing, bathing, and other daily activities.

The spaces on either side of the passage linking the outer and inner halls were intended to allow more light and fresh air to reach the inner hall. Even so, the interior of the inner hall was always gloomy. This half-light was conducive to meditation. Moreover the hall was not intended for study but for Zen practice through meditation; meditation carried on during meals and into slumber. Deepening of the understanding acquired through meditation and discussion with the elder by study of sutras and the writings of earlier Zen masters was done in the reading room, not in the monks' hall.

The main doorway of the outer hall gave directly onto the western corridor of the monastery. On its other three sides, the hall was bounded by a covered corridor used for walking meditation (*kinhin*) to ease the legs during extended sessions of seated meditation (*zazen*). The corridor also served to insulate the hall against any extraneous noise. Monks going to the washstands, bathhouse, latrines, or one of the other halls normally made their exit from the rear door of the inner hall. The section of the corridor between the rear door and the washstands was known as the illuminated hall (*shōdō*) because extra windows were provided to relieve the near-darkness of this out-of-the-way corner. This section of the corridor was also occasionally used by monks' hall officers to lecture to the monks.

The basic similarity of the Kenchōji monks' hall with the monks' halls of Ling-yin-ssu and Ching-shan is evident from a glance at the plans of the monks' halls in these monasteries. However, the inner hall at Ling-yin-ssu was a 16-block hall, bigger than anything known in Japan, capable of accommodating upwards of 200 monks. This in turn necessitated a larger outer hall. The hall at Ching-shan was a massive 20 blocks, capable of accommodating between 300 and 400 monks.[56]

The Ching-shan monks' hall plan is particularly valuable, since it gives the seating positions of the various monastery officers and functionaries as well as the basic measurements of the hall.[57] North of the abbot, on the first platform sat the prefects (*t'ou-chu, chōshu*): the chief seat (*shou-tso, shuso*), scribe (*shu-chi, shoki*) and the eastern and western sutra hall stewards (*hsi-ts'ang, seizō* and *tung-ts'ang, tōzō*). Senior monks who did not hold formal office, known as the western hall (*hsi-t'ang, seidō*), sat

FIGURE 14 The Monks' Hall at Ching-shan

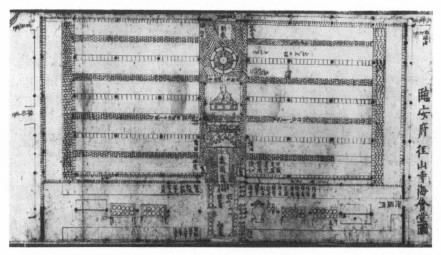

Photograph courtesy of Daijōji Temple, Kanazawa, and Komazawa University Library, Tokyo.

on the second southern platform. At the northern end of this platform was a space used by the "caller of meals" (*ho-shih, kas-shiki*), a postulant who "called" each course as it was served, setting the pace so that monks throughout the hall could keep time, know what they were eating, and know who had donated it. The rear hall chief seat (*hou-t'ang shou-tso, godō shuso*), who was responsible for supervising monks at the rear of the inner hall, sat at the head of the third platform.

Places in the outer hall were also precisely delegated. The administrative officers (*chih-shih, chiji*), including the prior (*tu-ssu, tsūsu*), comptroller (*chien-ssu, kansu*), assistant comptroller (*fu-ssu, fūsu*), registrar (*wei-no, inō*), cook (*tien-tso, tenzo*) and labor supervisor (*chih-sui, shissui*), had their places at the southern end of the upper northern platform. North of them sat the 5 acolytes (*shih-che, jisha*). When meals were served, the acolytes stood between the tables to supervise the attendants (*hsing-che, anja*), who stood ready to carry in the food. To judge from the number of tubs and the number of *hsing-che* written in beside them, more than a score of servers were required to cope with a meal if the hall was full. Those prefects, such as the guest prefect (*chih-k'o, shika*), bath prefect (*chih-yü, chiyoku*), and so forth, who had duties outside the hall sat at the northern end of the inner southern platform. Visitors, elderly monks, and those responsible for sound signals and music sat on the platforms just inside the outer door. It is, of course, very difficult to know how many monks were actually sitting in these halls at any one time. That they were sometimes packed to capacity and over is clear from the fact that some monasteries built a second, or even a third hall to take the overflow. Moreover, 600 or 700 monks enrolled in the monks' halls of a monastery, and a constant flow of itinerant monks called for several hundred assistants to serve as a commissariat for the monks' halls and for the itinerant monks' hall. Thus, the references to 2,000 inhabitants at Ching-shan during the Southern Sung dynasty do not seem incredible. While the populations of individual Japanese Zen monasteries never reached this figure, *gozan* Zen monasteries with 600 or 700 enrolled monks and a total population of over 1,000 inhabitants existed in medieval Japan.

There is some doubt as to whether monks' halls in the Southern Sung manner were part of the earliest Rinzai complexes at Kenninji and Tōfukuji. Eisai and Enni, with their firsthand knowledge of Ch'an monks' halls, naturally wished to build the same in Japan. The need to tread cautiously vis-à-vis the older schools, however, prevented the immediate introduction of a building as blatantly different as the monks' hall. The first Sung-style monks' hall in Japan was, therefore, probably built by Dōgen at Eiheiji. Upon completion of the hall in 1244, Dōgen was able to say with pride: "This mountain now has a monks' hall. It is the first that has been heard of (in Japan), the first seen, the first sat in."[58]

Monks' halls in the Sung style were being built in Rinzai monasteries by 1250. Lan-ch'i-Tao-lung, who came to Kamakura in 1248, built a Chinese-style monks' hall at Jōrakuji. When he subsequently moved to Kenchōji, one of his first concerns was to build a monks' hall there, for which he produced Draconian regulations. In his testament (*ikai*), he stressed the importance of this building: "The Sung-yuan school enforces monks' hall regulations and stresses *zazen* about everything."[59] The precise form of the first Kenchōji monks' hall is not known, but it was probably not dissimilar to its successor shown on the *Kenchōji sashizu*.

Well before the end of the thirteenth century, the communal Ch'an style monks' hall in which monks sat in meditation, slept, and took their meals was firmly established in Japanese Zen monasteries. This hall remained the center of monastic life and Zen practice until the fifteenth century, when the proliferation of sub-temples (*tatchū*), the shift of emphasis to the abbot's building, and the soldier's torch all contributed to its virtual disappearance. In the seventeenth and eighteenth centuries, efforts were made by leading Rinzai and Sōtō school monks to revive the traditional monks' hall. A number of halls were re-opened, but in most cases, under Ōbaku sect influence, as small meditation halls (*Zendō*), rather than as true monks' halls in the full communal sense.

THE READING ROOM

Although restored reading rooms (*shuryō*) can be seen in some Sōtō school monasteries in Japan today, none survive in Rinzai monasteries. Rinzai emphasis on the *kōan*, the resolution of which calls for intuitive rather than discursive understanding, and the decline of the monks' hall as the sub-temple rose to prominence meant the extinction of the reading room which had been an extension of the monks' hall.[60] That reading rooms were an important feature of all large medieval Zen monasteries, Rinzai as well as Sōtō, is clear from early ground plans.

The word *shuryō* can be translated "community hall" or "community dormitory," and this may well have been the original function of the building—a communal center where monks from the hall could rest, take tea, wash and repair their robes, store their belongings, and be given their duties for the day. The hall still preserved this character when the *Ch'an-yuan Code* was com-

FIGURE 15 The Reading Room at Chin-shan

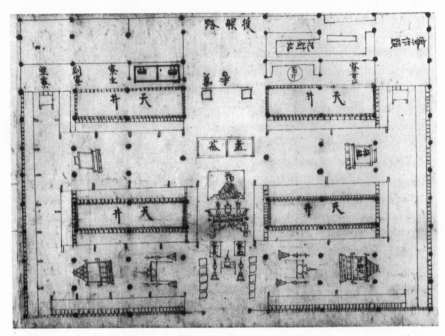

Photograph Courtesy of Daijōji Temple, Kanazawa, and Komazawa University Library, Tokyo.

piled. However, the code mentions that lecterns were in use in the hall, suggesting that it was at least beginning to assume the character of a reading room. By the time the ground plan of Chin-shan-ssu was drawn in the mid-thirteenth century, the building had become primarily a reading room, although its original recreational function had not been entirely lost.

The Chin-shan-ssu ground plan shows a building not unlike the monks' hall in scale and furnishing.[61] The most noticeable difference is the presence in the reading room of 4 light wells (*t'ien-ching*) and full-length windows on three sides of the hall, opening not onto a surrounding corridor but to the daylight. Platforms similar to those in the monks' hall (though shallower, since they were not used for sleeping) were built around each of the light wells and under the windows around the sides of the hall. Monks sat on these platforms, their backs to the hall, to study at the lecterns placed against the windows or light wells. The reading platforms at Chin-shan-ssu could seat upwards of 160 monks.

In the center of the hall was an altar table and dais bearing a statue of Kuan-yin (Kannon). Immediately behind this were tables bearing tea and tea bowls, suggesting that the hall still had a recreational function. Four sutra stands stood in the open spaces between the light wells. One of these contained copies of the *Avatamsaka sutra (Kegon-kyō)*, another held "Ch'an classics" (*Ch'an-tien*). No indication of the contents of the other two stands is given.

Like the monks' hall, the reading room had its own supervisory staff. At Chin-shan-ssu, these included a chief seat (*liao-shou-tso, ryō-shuso*), chief prefect (*liao-chu, ryōshu*), assistant (*fu-liao, fukuryō*), supervisor (*wang-liao, bōryō*), and attendant (*liao-tso, ryōsaku*). Their offices were located in the annex at the back of the main hall, which also housed a stove, needle-room and laundry area.

The importance of the reading room in the Southern Sung dynasty Ch'an monastery is indicated by the fact that Dōgen, who was concerned to transmit orthodox Ch'an practice to Japan, stressed the importance of the building and laid down detailed regulations for its use:

> In the monks' hall, monks should read nothing, not even Zen texts. There they should pursue understanding (*ri*) and strive in the Way (*bendō*). Illuminating the mind (*shōshin*) through the study of the ancient texts should be done under the illuminated windows [that is, in the reading room].[62]
>
> In the reading room one should study the Mahayana texts and the writings of the Ch'an patriarchs, striving to bring oneself into accord with their instructions for illuminating the mind.[63]

Medieval Kenchōji, like other Rinzai monasteries, also had a large reading room. That at Kenchōji was known as the "sandalwood grove" (*sendanrin*). The basic layout obviously followed the Chinese model, although the hall was smaller than that at Chin-shan-ssu, seating about 120 monks. Here there were two supervisory officers: a reading room chief prefect (*ryōshu*) and a reading room supervisor (*ryōgen*) with their offices located in the rear annex which bore a plaque reading *shōshin*—"Illumine the Mind."

THE KITCHEN-OFFICE

The preparation of two meals a day—three from the Southern Sung dynasty when the practice of taking an evening meal was accepted—for 500 or more monks in the monks' hall and elderly monks' buildings and for the hundreds of novices and assistants, even if these meals consisted of little more than rice, pickled vegetables, and soup—called for large, well-staffed kitchens. Moreover, in addition to those monks actually preparing the food, this requirement also called for administrative officers who would organize the provision of basic necessities from the monastery's own lands, by sending out mendicants, by persuading patrons to contribute, or, if necessary, by buying food. Keeping monks meditating in the monks' hall and the rest of the community fed from day to day was a vital task, and the kitchen-office, where these culinary and administrative functions were carried out, was a busy and important building.[64]

The Kenchōji ground plan shows the kitchen-office (*kuin*) located between the great gate and the Buddha hall, to the east of the central axis and directly opposite the monks' hall, to which it was linked by a corridor.

The ground plan also shows a smaller kitchen building to the north of the Dharma hall. This building, known as the (small) kitchen (*kuri*) served the abbot's building and guest quarters. Over the centuries, this smaller kitchen gained in importance, while the great kitchen-office buildings fell into ruin, and eventual extinction, since the decline of the monks' halls in the later middle ages also meant the decline of the large kitchen-office buildings which had served them.

The functions of the *kuin* were transferred to the *kuri* which, with the abbot's building, became the administrative core of the monastery. Sub-temples handled their own business affairs and were equipped with their own kitchens (*kuri*). The large kitchen-office was never restored in Rinzai monasteries. When efforts were made in the Tokugawa period to revive the monks' hall, part of the *kuri* in Rinzai monasteries was set aside as a dining area (*jikidō*). The Sōtō school had also allowed the great kitchen-office to decline. In a more self-consciously traditional revival of the monks' hall as a place in which monks slept and ate as well as meditated, large kitchen-office buildings on the medieval model were rebuilt in some Sōtō school monasteries.

Looking more closely at the great kitchen-office building shown on the Kenchōji ground plan, we see that the building was divided internally into a southern kitchen section and a northern office section. These two areas were separated by an open hall in which was an altar and statue of the patron deity of the hall, normally Idaten.

The kitchen section included an area for the preparation of food and a wood-fueled cooking range with a row of large cauldrons. The kitchen was presided over by the cook (*tenzo*), one of the most responsible offices in the monastery. Every monastery ran to a tight schedule geared to the activities of the monks' hall, and food had to be ready on time. The cook was therefore helped by rice, gruel, vegetable, water, fire, and dish sub-prefects and by a number of *anja*. The planning of meals was a careful, cooperative effort between the cook and those administrative officers whose offices were in the north of the same building and who had charge of monastery finances and resources: "Consult the administrative officers (*chiji*) in the kitchen-office building, deciding the next day's flavors and the kinds of tea and gruel to be made."[65] The administrative offices in the northern section of the kitchen-office building at Kenchōji were those of the comptroller (*kansu*) and prior (*tsūsu*). A guest hall (*kyakuden*) is also shown. Here the administrative officers entertained patrons, dealt with estate managers, and perhaps negotiated with local merchants. In Chinese monasteries of the period, the labor supervisor (*shissui*) and assistant comptroller (*fūsu*) also had offices here. Behind the Kenchōji *kuin* was a store, where commodities like rice, salt, pickles, and spices were kept, and a mortar chamber (*usuya*), where rice or grain could be ground. Some Southern Sung monasteries had mills using water-powered milling equipment. It is not clear what kind of equipment was used at Kenchōji. Both the storehouse and mill were under the general supervision of the administrative officers and staffed by sub-prefects.

This completes our survey of the medieval monastery. Although many buildings have been neglected, enough has probably been said to give an impression of the complex but highly ordered setting within which the medieval Zen monastic life was practiced.

SIX

The Community

In 1283, Hōjō Tokimune made the recently founded Engakuji a shogunal invocatory temple and for its maintenance awarded it rights (*jitō shiki*) over two substantial tracts of land in the provinces of Owari and Kazusa. The earliest records of the tax income in rice, vegetables, and cash from these lands provide an unusually detailed picture of the population of the newly-established Engakuji.[1]

POPULATION

Out of a total tax-rice income of 1569 *koku* and 8 *to*, 360 *koku* were allocated to feed 100 monks for the year, a daily allowance of 1 *shō* (approximately 1.8 liters) per monk.[2] A similar amount was earmarked for the sustenance of 100 assistants (*anja*) and laborers (*ninku*). A further 72 *koku* were set aside for the 20 attendants (*shōji*) and lay officers (*yakunin*), an allowance of 3 *to* (approximately 54 liters) per person per month. Fourteen *koku* and 4 *to* were allocated, on the same scale, for 4 launderers (*sen'e*); 21 *koku* and 6 *to* for the 6 assistants attached to the abbot's building (*hōjō anja*), and a further 136 *koku* and 8 *to* for the 38 servants (*shimobe*). Altogether, therefore, 964 *koku* and 8 *to*, (61 percent) of a total rice income of nearly 1600 *koku*, were set aside for the annual needs of 268 inhabitants, of whom less than half were classified as monks.[3]

Engakuji expanded rapidly. So many monks flocked to the monastery to receive the instruction of I-shan I-ning, who came to Japan in 1299, that he was forced to institute an examination in the composition of verse in Chinese to select those most capable of benefiting from his instruction.[4] In 1303, Hōjō Sadatoki stipulated that the maximum monk population of Engakuji should not exceed 200.[5] The regulation cannot have been enforced very strictly for, in 1323, 350 monks from Engakuji attended the memorial services marking the thirteenth anniversary of Sadatoki's death.[6] The total population of the monastery at this time was probably about 700. In 1327, Takatoki, the last of the Hōjō regents, again tried to restrict the numbers of monks in Engakuji, this time to 250, but without much success.[7]

The destruction in 1333 of the Hōjō family, which had hitherto been its exclusive patrons, did nothing to halt the growth of Engakuji. During Go-Daigo's brief restoration (1333–1336), the focus of patronage shifted temporarily to the Kyoto Zen monasteries of Nanzenji and Daitokuji, with their strong imperial connections. However, the victory of Ashikaga Takauji in 1336 meant a new lease on life for the Kamakura Zen monasteries. In the case of Engakuji, its ties with Musō Soseki, who had studied under I-shan I-ning, helped win it the sympathy and special favor of both Go-Daigo and the Ashikaga, and guaranteed its successful transition to the Muromachi period.[8] Engakuji was raised by Takauji to the second rank of the *gozan* and remained the second-ranking Kamakura *gozan* monastery throughout medieval and early-modern times.[9]

In regulations for Engakuji drawn up in 1340, Ashikaga Tadayoshi tried to limit the complement of monks to 300.[10] By 1363, the permitted maximum had been raised to 400,[11] and it is reported that, in 1383, 1,145 hall monks and 375 senior monks from Engakuji and its 20 or so sub-temples attended the memorial services held on the thirty-third anniversary of the death of Musō.[12] This was the high point of Engakuji's growth. The Ashikaga shoguns had by this time settled into Kyoto and were devoting more of their patronage to the Kyoto *gozan*. A symbolic moment in the history of Engakuji and the Kamakura *gozan* occurred in 1396 when Yoshimitsu ordered the transfer of the Engakuji Buddha relic to Kyoto.[13] From about this time, too, the Engakuji landed domain began to dwindle. The Kamakura *gozan* survived, but the spotlight had returned to Kyoto.

In the century after its foundation, the monk population of Engakuji and its sub-temples had thus risen from 100 to well over 1,000. By the end of this period, the inhabitants of the whole complex must have numbered nearly 2,000. Monastic population declined in the fifteenth century. This tendency was hastened by the Ōnin War and by the gradual weakening of the Ashikaga *bakufu*. Many of Engakuji's sub-temples, however, continued to flourish, and the monastery's fortunes recovered somewhat under the Tokugawa.[14]

The 4 other monasteries of *gozan* status in Kamakura more or less matched Engakuji in scale. Kenchōji, the senior Kamakura *gozan*, sent 388 monks to the memorial services for Sadatoki in 1323, some 30 more than Engakuji.[15] Its total population at this point was probably in the region of 800. Since Kenchōji maintained its preeminent position in the Kamakura *gozan* rankings throughout the medieval and early-modern periods, it is safe to conclude that its population was normally at least equal to that of Engakuji.

Jufukuji, Jōchiji, and Jōmyōji, the remaining Kamakura *gozan* (1386 ranking), were smaller than Engakuji and Kenchōji but still substantial communities. Jufukuji sent 260 to the 1323 memorial service, Jōchiji 224, and Jōmyōji, which was still ranked as a *jissatsu*, 51.[16] Thus, even the smaller Kamakura *gozan* had, by 1323, monk populations of over 200 or so. If these monasteries had followed anything like the growth curve of Engakuji, they would have doubled in population by the end of the century.

The Kyoto *gozan* were larger than their Kamakura counterparts. Nanzenji, the capstone set above the other 10 monasteries of *gozan* rank, had, already by the late Kamakura period, 700 monks and 130 novices and postulants.[17] Its total population throughout the middle ages was therefore probably in the region of 2,000. Tenryūji, Shōkokuji, and Tōfukuji[18] were on a similar scale, while Kenninji and Manjuji matched the larger Kamakura monasteries. However, the monks, assistants, and monastery servants were, by the fourteenth century, no longer concentrated in the central core of monastic buildings. They had been increasingly absorbed into the sub-temples (*tatchū*) which had developed around the main complex. Some of the larger of these sub-temples were monasteries in their own right with several hundred inhabitants.

On the basis of these figures, we can estimate that, during the later fourteenth and the fifteenth century, the total population of the 5 Kamakura *gozan* was between 5,000 and 7,000. (Two thousand and twenty monks from 38 Kamakura monasteries attended Sadatoki's memorial service in 1323. Of these, over 1,000 were from the 5 *gozan* monasteries.) During this time, some 10,000 may have been attached to the 6 Kyoto monasteries of *gozan* status.

The second tier of the hierarchy of official monasteries was known as the Ten Temples (*jissatsu*). Initially, there were only 10, but by the end of the fourteenth century (1386), the number had risen to 20, 10 each for the Kansai and Kantō. More large provincial monasteries were ranked as *jissatsu* during the fifteenth century.[19] The category included 46 monasteries by 1489 and over 60 by the early sixteenth century.

Monasteries of *jissatsu* status represented at the memorial services for Hōjō Sadatoki included Jōmyōji, which sent 51 monks; Zenkōji, 92; Taikeiji, 83; Tōshōji, 53; Manjuji, 75; and Zenpukuji, 66.[20] By the early fourteenth century, the population of a monastery of *jissatsu* rank was thus between 50 and 100 monks, with a total population of between 150 and 200. Fifty monasteries on this scale would have accounted for at least 5,000 inhabitants, perhaps as many as 8,000. Like the upper tier of the *gozan* hierarchy, these monasteries tended to grow in population with the rise to dominance of the *gozan* schools during the fourteenth century.

The lowest rank of the official hierarchy was made up of

smaller local temples, known as *shozan*, scattered throughout the country. These monasteries probably had no more than a score of monks and perhaps a total of 40 or 50 inhabitants. They made up in numbers, however, for their small size. By the end of the medieval period, 230 monasteries had been given *shozan* status.[21] At 30 inhabitants per monastery this would bring within the *gozan* population another 6,600 persons.

The major *gozan* monasteries and their sub-temples had numerous branch temples (*matsuji*). There were an estimated 5,000 *gozan* branch temples by the late fifteenth century.[22] Each of these was small in population, perhaps accommodating no more than 10 or 12 people in all, but collectively they swelled the *gozan* ranks considerably.

For the *gozan* network as a whole, therefore, it seems reasonable to suggest that, by the Ōnin period, the population of all *gozan* monasteries and their affiliates was at least 50,000 persons. Outside the *gozan*, but within the Zen monastic institution, were also the Rinzai monasteries of Daitokuji and Myōshinji and their branches, which grew rapidly from the fifteenth century,[23] as well as the many hundreds of Sōtō school monasteries and temples.[24] And in considering the overall scale of the medieval Zen institution, Zen nunneries, of which there were many (Rinzai nunneries later established their own *gozan* network), should be taken into account.

How do we explain this rapid and considerable population growth in Zen monasteries during the first five or six decades of the fourteenth century? Undoubtedly Zen, especially the burgeoning *gozan*, attracted many monks who would, in an earlier age, have entered the monastic centers of Nara, Kōyasan, or Hieizan. In some instances whole communities of Shingon or Tendai monks gave their allegiance to Zen en masse. But there was also a very new element in the population growth of the Zen monastic institution: its roots were deeply embedded in warrior society.

Unfortunately we do not have a very precise picture of the social origins of medieval Zen monks. The only biographical

compilations are the *Enpō dentōroku*, giving biographical
sketches of 1,000 illustrious Zen monks and lay devotees, compiled by the Rinzai monk Mangen Shiban (1626–1710) between
1650 and 1678 and the *Nippon tōjō rentōroku*, listing the biographies of Dōgen and Sōtō school masters, compiled by Reinan
Shūjo (1675–1752) and published in 1742. These, of course,
account for no more than a small sample of the well-known Zen
masters of the medieval and early modern periods. Other information can be gleaned from diaries and documents, but the record
remains far from complete.

We have already seen that some imperial princes and aristocrats were put into the large *gozan* monasteries, especially those
connected with the Musō school. On the basis of the *Enpō
dentōroku*, it is assumed that the majority of Zen monks were
the younger sons of *bushi* families. If this was the case, the Zen
cloister was helping to take the edge off the developing system
of unigeniture in warrior society by offering a refuge to the
disinherited sons of *bushi* families. Young samurai found in the
Zen monastery rigid discipline, a high level of education and
culture, the possibility of the eventual exercise of real authority,
and the attainment of social prestige as well as, perhaps, spiritual
enlightenment. Since Zen was new and fostered most vigorously
by the Kamakura and Muromachi *bakufu*, the way to the top in
the *gozan* hierarchy, at least in its early days, was probably easier
for a man of *bushi* origin than it was in the *kuge*-dominated
monasteries of the older Buddhist sects. This is not to say that
families entrusting their younger sons to the life of the Zen monk
always calculated career opportunities. They could feel assured,
however, that, in committing children to official monasteries
sponsored by the *bakufu* and patronized by *shugo* and powerful
local warrior-rulers, they were not giving hostages to fortune.

The use of the Zen monastery as a safety valve to relieve pressures in *buke* society naturally increased tensions within the
monastery. A Zen monastery is both superbly egalitarian and
rigidly authoritarian. In principle, the single criterion of seniority
has always been the length of time since ordination: those entering

the *saṅgha* first, irrespective of their age or secular status, being senior to those entering later.[25] In general, this system was preserved in the *gozan*, but it was possible at certain critical points in the monastic career for some monks to be advanced faster than others in the bureaucratic hierarchy.

Decisions on when to give a novice the full vows, when to make the young monk an acolyte, when to appoint him to the various senior offices, when, and where, to appoint him abbot all had an impact on the rapidity and extent of the monk's progress in the administrative hierarchy of the *gozan*. At such moments, a number of factors were involved in the decision: the monk's progress in Zen, his experience of monastic life, his personality, his intellectual suitability for the position, the availability of other talent, and the monk's family and social connections.

This last factor should not have been included in the equation, but there is evidence that in *gozan* monasteries social connections played a significant role in the career patterns of monks. Appointment to any office in the official monasteries involved the payment of a fee, the amount rising in relation to the desirability of the office. Moreover, service as an abbot could involve heavy personal expenses. A monk without substantial private means or the backing of a powerful patron could not expect to become the abbot of a major monastery or prestigious sub-temple, if that was his hope. If he was profound, or glib, he might quickly win such backing. If he did not, he would have had to reconcile himself to a simpler life than his better-connected fellow monks.

Zen monasteries do not seem to have developed the rigid status hierarchies found in many Tendai and Shingon monasteries whereby some monks, because of their origins, were totally excluded from the higher monastic offices. Nevertheless, the social and economic distinctions of aristocratic and warrior society were reflected in the formation of cliques and stratifications within *gozan* monasteries and their sub-temples. It has been suggested, for instance, that one factor in the decision of the monk-painter Sesshū (1420–1506) to quit Shōkokuji was his realization that higher office was closed to him because of the modest status of his family, middling *bushi* from the province of Bitchū.[26] No doubt there were *gozan* monks who were indifferent to advancement in the institutional hierarchy and continued their private quest for spiritual awareness by wandering from monastery to monastery, master to master, never seeking security or office. Sesshū's departure from Shōkokuji may have been motivated as much by this kind of spiritual concern as by any feelings of frustration. On the other hand, there were plenty of monks who were critical of the secularization of the *gozan*. Some, like Ikkyū Sōjun, expressed their criticism in writing. Other monks expressed it silently, by quitting *gozan* monasteries for private rural retreats or for the monks' halls of Daitokuji and Myōshinji.

With this as introduction, let us now look at the structure of the medieval *gozan* monastery, the career pattern of its monks, and the bureaucratic mechanism by which it was regulated.

Basically, the medieval Zen monastic community was divided into those who had taken the 250 Mahayana *bodhisattva* precepts of the fully-fledged monk and those who had not. The category of monks included the abbot, the dozen officers who assisted him in administering the monastery, the 5 acolytes who acted as his personal assistants and the body of ordinary monks who, with only minor duties or none at all, spent their days in meditation, prayer, study, and labor.

THE ABBOT

Abbots (*jūji* or *chōrō*) were appointees. In the thirteenth and early fourteenth centuries, appointments were made by emperors and retired emperors, courtiers, and powerful *bushi*, as well as by the shogunate. Appointment to Nanzenji, Daitokuji, and Myōshinji was, for many years, the prerogative of the imperial house. The headship of Tōfukuji, until the late fourteenth century, was in the gift of the Kujō branch of the Fujiwara family. Abbots of many provincial Zen monasteries were appointed through the influence of local warrior-rulers. By the mid-fourteenth century, however, all appointments of abbot to the several hundred official monasteries were made either through the office of the Commissioner for Zen and Ritsu Monasteries (*Zenritsugata*) or through the office of Registrar General of Monks (*sōroku*) when that body was established in 1379.[27]

Although the ultimate decision was made by the shogun and his religious advisors, and individual *gozan* communities had little say in the selection of their abbots, minimum standards of achievement were maintained. Abbots of Zen monasteries were appointed only from among suitably qualified monks who had undergone the many years of Zen monastic training. Gifts of sinecure Zen abbacies or high monastic offices to princes of the imperial blood, courtiers, or warriors who had no monastic training were not made, and Zen monasteries were not included in the *monzeki* system.[28]

A monk was normally considered eligible for a first appointment as abbot in one of the official monasteries when he had attained the office of chief seat (*shuso*) at the head of the western rank of monastic officers and had passed the qualifying test known as "holding the whisk" (*hinpotsu*). In this test, which was held twice each year, senior monks of the status of sutra prefect (*zōsu*), secretary (*shoki*), or chief seat (*shuso*) took the place of the abbot and engaged in Zen questions and answers with younger monks who were themselves seeking accreditation as senior acolytes (*jisha*). Their performance was evaluated by the assembled community.

In recognition of his services and his success in the *hinpotsu* encounter, the senior monk was given a formal certificate of thanks (*jago*) by his abbot. The certificate, which implied acceptance as a proficient instructor, together with the experience in guiding other monks in meditation and monastic discipline acquired in the office of the chief seat, were considered the essential minimum qualifications for appointment. From the fifteenth century, there were occasional cases of the forging of *hinpotsu* credentials or of monks being excused from this requirement in return for a generous contribution to the *bakufu* or some monastery. These cases were recognized as aberrations and condemned within Zen circles. The attainment of *hinpotsu* remained the prerequisite to promotion to the status of abbot.

A qualified *shuso* was first appointed by the *sōrōken* to a monastery of *shozan* rank. Here he was formally referred to by the title of "western hall" (*seidō*) appended to the final two characters (the *imina*) of his name. The stipulated term of office in an official monastery was "three years or two summers." Successful performance of his duties in one of the small *shozan* would normally lead to promotion to the rank of abbot of a larger provincial monastery of *jissatsu* rank. Here he would be referred to formally by the first two characters of his name (*azana*), accompanied by the title of *seidō*. If he was eventually appointed to one of the great *gozan* monasteries in Kyoto or Kamakura, he would be referred to as "eastern hall" (*tōdō*) and, for the first time, by the courtesy title of "venerable" (*oshō*). Within the *gozan* grade itself, abbots worked their way up from smaller monasteries like Jōmyōji in Kamakura or Kenninji in Kyoto to Tenryūji and Nanzenji, the foremost official monasteries in Japan.

At each level of the *gozan* system, monks of abbot status were distinguished by the color of their robes. Ordinary hall monks wore black robes and black stoles (*kesa*). Monks who had attained the status of abbot of *shozan* monasteries were permitted to use colored tie-strings and ring on the *kesa*. Abbots of *jissatsu* monasteries wore yellow *kesa* over black robes. Abbots of full *gozan* monasteries were permitted to wear yellow robes. Abbots of Nanzenji, the senior *gozan*, with imperial connections, wore deep purple robes, and those of Tenryūji, the second ranking *gozan*, robes of pale purple. The non-*gozan* monasteries of Daitokuji, Myōshinji, Eiheiji, and Sōjiji also applied for, and were granted, the right of their abbots to wear purple robes.

In public monasteries in China, including the officially designated Ch'an centers, the rule of open appointment of abbots (*shih-fang chu-ch'ih, jippō jūji*) was enforced.[29] When a vacancy occurred in any monastery within the official network, the best available candidate, irrespective of his Buddhist doctrinal affiliation, was appointed. This principle was well known in Japan. It was practiced in Zen monasteries during the Kamakura period and remained an ideal throughout the middle ages, but, from the mid-fourteenth century, was eroded in practice by the *gozan* schools and their *bakufu* patrons. Claiming to respect the wishes of their founders, a number of important *gozan* monasteries accepted as abbots only monks who belonged to the same Zen lineage. Such "closed" monasteries included Tōfukuji, founded by Shōichi Kokushi and restricted to monks from his line, and the important Musō-lineage dominated monasteries of Tenryūji, Shōkokuji, and Rinsenji, all of which were high in the *gozan* system and had close ties with the Muromachi *bakufu*. Of the non-*gozan* monasteries, Daitokuji and Myōshinji also asserted this prerogative. The acceptance of "closed" monasteries within the official *gozan* system is one interesting example of the way in which Chinese bureaucratic principles were bent to conform to the social reality of feudal Japan, where personal relations were paramount.[30]

Irrespective of the rank of the monastery or whether it was "open" or "closed," all appointees to the abbacy of a *gozan*-affiliated monastery had to have certificates of appointment (*kujō* or *kumon*) from the *bakufu*.[31] A fee was charged in relation to the importance of the appointment. As monks passed the *hinpotsu* examination and advanced to the position of front hall *shuso*, their monasteries informed the *sōroku*. When the abbacy of a *shozan* monastery fell vacant, the *sōroku* listed the suitably qualified candidates and sent the list to the shogun who decided the candidate to be appointed. The list was then returned to the *sōroku*, where a certificate of appointment (*kujō*) was drawn up. This document was again sent to the shogun who added his official cipher (*kaō*) and returned it to the *sōroku* for dispatch to the selected appointee. Appointments to all Kyoto official monasteries and to the two senior Kamakura *gozan*, Engakuji and Kenchōji, were made through the office of the Muromachi *bakufu* in Kyoto. Appointments to Kantō *shozan* and *jissatsu* and to the three lower Kamakura *gozan* were confirmed by the office of the Kantō Governor (Kantō *kanrei*) in Kamakura.

Once a monk was appointed abbot, he was expected to take up residence in the specified monastery after a formal ceremony of entry or inauguration (*juen*). The details of this ceremony were prescribed in detail in Zen monastic codes.[32] The new abbot entered via the main gate (*sanmon*) and visited the more important monastery halls, offering incense and making an oration (*hōgo*) at each before engaging in his first formal Zen debates (*mondō*) with the community and its officers. He was then expected to reside in the monastery for the term of his appointment, to train its monks to manage its business affairs, and to satisfy the religious needs of its patrons. When the term of his appointment was over, he would be considered for promotion and, in time, would be issued with a new certificate of appointment.

The installation of a new abbot could be a costly business for the abbot himself, for his monastery, and for its patrons. He had not only to find the money to pay for the official fee (*kansen*) for his certificate of appointment—between 5 and 50 *kanmon* depending on the rank of the monastery—and to make an offering of thanks to the Registrar General (*sōroku*) and the office of the Inryōken. In addition, he, or the monastery, had to bear the costs of accommodation and gifts for the witnesses and companions who came to assist with the installation ceremonies. The various meals given after the inauguration for local Zen dignitaries, patrons, officers, and members of the community had to be paid for. Money had also to be found to meet the costs of restoring or decorating buildings in readiness for what was always one of the most important ceremonial occasions in the Zen monastic calendar.

Many monasteries spared no expense in the conduct of installation ceremonies. *Bakufu*- as well as Zen-inspired regulations from the early fourteenth century onward frequently forbid excesses Yoshimitsu's regulations of 1381 were repeating a well-known refrain in stating:

> At installation ceremonies, gifts should be given to only one witness (*byakutsui*). Moreover, these gifts should be limited to one silver dirk, one short-sleeved kimono, and one sheaf of Sugawara paper. Gifts

other than this to abbots of other monasteries, to warrior representatives (*daikan*), or officials (*bugyō*) must be curtailed.[33]

The frequency with which regulations seeking to curb gift-giving and feasting are repeated in *bakufu* and monastic regulations suggests that, when abbots, monasteries, and patrons could afford to be lavish, frugality was neglected. For one installation ceremony at a large *gozan* monastery in about 1460, the maigre feast on the day of the inauguration, a tea ceremony (*tenjin*) on the following day, and invitations to the community and officers later, cost 120 *kanmon*, a sum equivalent to the total annual income of some small temples.[34]

If these ceremonies had been held only once in two or three years, the expense involved might have been justified. During the fifteenth century, however, the three-year residence regulation was relaxed, and the turnover of incumbent abbots became much more rapid at all levels of the *gozan*. Two incumbents a year were not uncommon, and there were instances of abbots entering the monastery to which they were appointed for only five days or even a single night. Even if the full installation ceremonies were not held on each occasion, still expenses were entailed. The *bakufu* protested such reductions in the term of actual residence but, since it gained financially from each changeover, its objections were, at best, half-hearted. Ashikaga Yoshimochi (1386–1428) tried hard to correct this and other irregularities in a series of strict codes for the *gozan*. He was not entirely successful, and after his death irregularities went largely unchecked.[35] Some smaller monasteries, too poor and ill-equipped in buildings to bear even the privilege of the three-yearly installation, were, upon petition, spared the burden of actual entry and given a contribution by the appointed abbot, who continued to reside elsewhere.

Absentee appointments to wealthy monasteries, whereby monks were sold certificates of appointment but never entered the designated monastery, were also made. Certificates of appointment, known as *zakumon* or *inari kumon*, were issued irrespective of whether the abbacy of the monastery in question was vacant or not. In some cases, there were several simultaneous nominal incumbents of a single post.[36]

Although it did not carry the prestige—or the responsibilities and financial burdens—of residence, the absentee certificate did advance its holder's formal status in the *gozan* hierarchy. It gave him the title of *seidō* or *tōdō* and permitted him to wear the appropriate colored robes. He was, in time, recorded as a former absentee abbot of that monastery. This in turn brought some reflected glory to his own monastery or sub-temple and its patrons.

Absentee certificates, although condemned by leading Zen monks, were sold in increasing numbers from the early fifteenth century. By the end of the century, many senior monks in some monasteries held title to the headship of their own as well as several other prestigious official monasteries. Certificates of absentee appointment to Nanzenji and other major *gozan* monasteries were, by the sixteenth century, being sold at the rate of four or five a year. There was no shortage of applicants. Behind this phenomenon lay both a weakening of *gozan* discipline and a worsening of *bakufu* finances. Whether the holder of a certificate of appointment entered the monastery or remained a ghost abbot, he still paid the stipulated fee (*kansen*) to the *sōroku*. Some of this money was used by the *sōroku* for the repair of *gozan* buildings or the financing of Ming trading ventures, but most if it found its way into *bakufu* coffers.

Some absentee titles to the office of abbot were disposed of very cheaply. Known as "merit certificates" (*kudokunari*), they awarded the title of abbot of a specified monastery to suitably qualified monks, who agreed to conduct a cycle of memorial observances for the founder of the monastery or the welfare of its secular patrons. These merit certificates were entirely free of tax. Moreover, the donation expected by the *sōroku* was much smaller than that for a regular taxed certificate. Merit certificates were, therefore, much in demand by monks too poor to afford more elaborate credentials and by elderly monks who had failed to get ahead in the *gozan* hierarchy. By the mid-fifteenth century, these certificates were being given to some *gozan* monasteries for disposal in batches of 20 or 30.[37]

Although merit certificates helped provide memorial services that would otherwise have had to have been paid for through other means, they did not bring in much income to the *sōroku* or *bakufu*. The other two types of certificates, of actual and absentee appointment, did, however, provide a very substantial source of finance. The scale of fees for *kumon* and *zakumon* naturally varied with the rank of the monastery and fluctuated as the fortunes of the *gozan* and the Ashikaga, its principal patrons, wavered in the fifteenth and sixteenth centuries. On average, each appointment to Nanzenji or Tenryūji involved a basic fee of some 30–50 *kanmon*; other monasteries of full *gozan* rank, 20 *kanmon*; and *jissatsu* and *shozan*, 10 *kanmon*.

Individually, these amounts may seem modest. But if one third of the 300 *gozan* installed a new abbot each year at the lowest average of 10 *kanmon* per appointment this would represent a minimum annual income of 1,000 *kanmon*, most of which went to the *bakufu*. This is less spectacular than the 5,000 to 10,000 *kanmon* profit the *bakufu* might make from a single venture in the China trade. Income from the *gozan*, however, was steady, whereas the profits from overseas commerce were irregular.

The income derived by the *bakufu* from the *gozan* (or from *shugo* and *gōzoku* via the *gozan*) seems more impressive when it is recalled that certificates of absentee appointment were being sold in increasing numbers in the fifteenth century, while the duration of incumbent appointments was decreasing and income from this source, too, consequently increasing. Moreover, in addition to fees derived from the appointment of abbots, the *sōroku* received a small fee, perhaps 1 *kanmon*, for each appointment of a monastic officer.[38] With 12 officers in 300 monasteries taking up office annually this would add another 3,600 *kanmon* to the annual total. Some of this money found its way into the *bakufu* treasury. In 1340, Ashikaga Tadayoshi decreed that monks should remain in office for two seasons, that is six months, thus doubling this source of income at a stroke. The five acolytes in each monastery were also obliged to pay a fee of from 3 to 5 *kanmon* on appointment.

For the Muromachi *bakufu*, therefore, the *gozan*, far from being simply a purely religious institution or an expensive cultural ornament, was one of the stronger pillars in a weak economic structure. To judge by the shortening of terms of appointment of abbots, the increase of *gozan* affiliates, the consequent increase of sales of regular and irregular certificates of appointment, the shortening of terms of office-holders, all of which became very prevalent from the mid-fifteenth century, the *bakufu* leaned more heavily on this pillar as its other sources of financial support began to collapse.[39]

THE OFFICERS

Intensive spiritual guidance and administrative direction of a community of several hundred monks is a heavy burden for one man. Buddhist communities, like their Western monastic counterparts, developed a variety of organizational patterns to cope with this problem. Many T'ang dynasty Chinese monasteries were headed by three senior elected officials: the abbot (*shang-tso*), rector (*ssu-chu*), and superintendent (*tu-wei-no*). These were assisted by such lesser elected officers as the controller (*tien-tso*), accountant (*chih-sui*), steward (*k'u-ssu*), and monastery supervisor (*chien-ssu*).

Ch'an monasteries forged, out of earlier Chinese Buddhist monastic organization and the examples of the Chinese government bureaucracy, a distinctive symmetrically balanced authority structures of 2 ranks with 5 or 6 officers in each (Chart 6).[40] It is clear from Ch'an monastic codes that this structure had developed in China well before the twelfth century. It was introduced to Japan by Eisai, Dōgen, Enni, and émigré Chinese monks during the thirteenth century and imitated by the Jesuits in setting up their mission in Japan in the sixteenth century.[41] It survives, in vestigial form, in Japanese Zen monasteries to this day. Parallel to the 2 ranks of officers who conducted the public business of the monastery, a third group of 5 young monks, known as acolytes (*jisha*), served the abbot as private attendants.

Because of the positions in which they sat in the Dharma hall during assemblies, the 2 groups of officers were referred to as the eastern and western ranks. In principle, all officers were equal under the abbot. The holders simply acted as his temporary assistants in serving the community. In theory, there was freedom of movement between the eastern and western ranks. In practice, however, in both Chinese and Japanese monasteries, offices within each of the ranks quickly assumed the characteristics of a progressive hierarchy and each rank tended to become self-contained with its own functions, traditions, and types of personnel.

It has already been noted that the term of office was for one year until 1340, when Ashikaga Tadayoshi reduced it to six months. On appointment, each officer paid a small fee which was collected by the monastery. New officers were selected for appointment by the abbot and his senior advisers. Hōjō Sadatoki's regulations for Engakuji state, however, that the approval of the monastery's major patron must be had for appointment to the three important offices of chief seat (*shuso*), prior (*tsūsu*), and registrar (*inō*).[42] In 1340, Ashikaga Tadayoshi extended this requirement to all offices. Thus, although the monastery had the right of selection, secular authorities maintained a veto power which could, on occasion, be used to secure the appointment of a favored candidate.

The grouping of 2 ranks with 6 officers in each, as shown in Chart 6, is the basic stereotype. In small monasteries some offices were not filled, the duties of each such office being performed by another officer. In large monasteries, additional officers were created by splitting one office. Moreover, some officers might have a number of other monks or sub-prefects to carry out various minor tasks. In a very large monastery of 500 or 600 monks there could easily be 30 or 40 sub-prefects. Acolytes, likewise, were assisted by lay attendants attached to the abbot's building (*hōjō anja*).

The western rank of prefects (*chōshu*) were responsible for assisting the abbot in training the community in meditation, Zen monastic discipline, the study of Zen and other Buddhist texts, and the details of monastic ceremonies. With the exception of the guest master (*shika*) and bath prefect (*chiyoku*), their duties kept them in the monks' hall, reading room, or nearby Buddha and Dharma halls.

The chief seat (*shuso*) derived his title from his place next to the abbot on the meditation platforms. He was the principal monk in the hall and the leader of meditation. In large halls, there were sometimes 2 monks with this title, front-hall and rear-hall chief seats (*Zendō shuso, godō shuso*), responsible for supervision of the sections of the hall before and behind the "holy monk" (*shōsō*), normally a statue of the *bodhisattva* Mañjuśrī (Monju) located near the center of the hall. Of the two, the front hall chief seat was senior and was in line for appointment as abbot. Both, however, were experienced monks who had spent ten or more years under monastic discipline and were capable of guiding others in all aspects of monastic life.

The second officer of the western rank, the scribe (*shoki*), was responsible for the production of all official monastery documents, including the announcements of monastic functions, reports to the abbot, letters, and official communications sent to patrons, government offices, and other monasteries. Since the scribe composed and wrote these documents himself, familiarity with documentary styles and decent calligraphy were basic requirements for appointees to this office.

The sutra prefect (*zōsu*) was responsible for supervision of the sutra repository, for the acquisition and preservation of sutras and texts, and the provision of copies for the various monastic ceremonies. The office naturally called for familiarity with the whole range of Buddhist literature used in the Zen monastery. The guest prefect (*shika*) entertained official visitors and took care of itinerant monks. Since he spent much of his time dealing with secular guests, monastic codes warn that care should be taken to appoint a monk who would not be swayed into worldli-

CHART 6 The Zen Monastic Bureaucracy

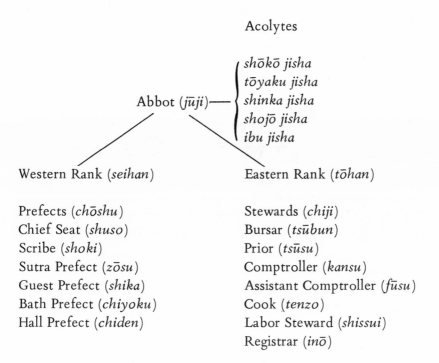

Acolytes

Abbot (*jūji*) —
- *shōkō jisha*
- *tōyaku jisha*
- *shinka jisha*
- *shojō jisha*
- *ibu jisha*

Western Rank (*seihan*)

Prefects (*chōshu*)
Chief Seat (*shuso*)
Scribe (*shoki*)
Sutra Prefect (*zōsu*)
Guest Prefect (*shika*)
Bath Prefect (*chiyoku*)
Hall Prefect (*chiden*)

Eastern Rank (*tōhan*)

Stewards (*chiji*)
Bursar (*tsūbun*)
Prior (*tsūsu*)
Comptroller (*kansu*)
Assistant Comptroller (*fūsu*)
Cook (*tenzo*)
Labor Steward (*shissui*)
Registrar (*inō*)

ness. The bath prefect (*chiyoku*) supervised the preparation of baths and discipline in the bathhouse, while the hall prefect (*chiden*) was responsible for preparing the various halls, especially the Buddha hall, for ceremonial functions.

The 6 stewards (*chiji*) of the eastern rank had overall responsibility for the economic affairs of the monastery. The comptroller (*kansu*) and assistant comptroller (*fūsu*), under the supervision of the prior (*tsūsu*), kept the monastery accounts and drew up the annual budget. They collected, recorded, and re-allocated the annual tax rice and cash income from the monastery's estates, solicited donations from patrons, handled the occasional proceeds of trading ventures, took charge of the collection and payment of appointment fees to the *sōroku*, and made applications for assistance with rebuilding. They also supervised the provision of food, vegetables, oil, robes, incense, paper, ink, and the hundred and one other items needed for the daily life of the monastery. Zen monastic documents relating to economic matters normally bore the signatures and ciphers of all 3 officers in addition to those of the abbot and, in some cases, the principal monastery patron. Zen codes naturally stress integrity and the spirit of service to the community for holders of these offices and occasionally hold up for condemnation examples of financial officers who engaged in private speculation or collusion with other officers to defraud the monastery.

These 3 officers had their rooms in the main kitchen-office building. Of the remaining stewards, the cook (*tenzo*) consulted them before preparing meals or feasts for the community, and the labor supervisor (*shissui*) conferred with them before assigning tasks to the monks or monastery attendants. The registrar (*inō*), an important officer, had his office near the monks' hall. New arrivals who wished to enroll for a season in the monks' hall registered with him first. As an administrative officer, he organized the daily timetable and supervised discipline. His duties as registrar and chanter of invocations during services in the Buddha, Dharma, and monks' halls, however, gave him close ties with the prefects of the western rank. In Japanese Zen monasteries, these 6 stewards were generally supervised by a seventh, known as the bursar (*tsūbun*).

The *Ch'an yuan Code* (1103) made provision for only 4 stewards, one of them, the prior (*kan'in*), being responsible for financial matters. By the time Dōgen visited China a century later, 6 stewards were the norm: "In monasteries there have always been 6 stewards."[43] The 2 additional stewards were both financial officers, the duties of the *kan'in* having been divided among a *tsūsu, kansu,* and *fūsu*.

This development suggests that, during the Southern Sung dynasty, not only had formalization of Ch'an monastic bureaucratic structure taken place—6 stewards to balance 6 prefects—but, more important, a single financial officer had been insufficient to cope with an expansion in the volume and complexity of economic affairs as Ch'an monasteries were drawn more intimately into a monetized local economy.[44] This triumviral system of financial management was carried over into Japan where, in *gozan* monasteries, the 3 officers were placed under the supervision of a bursar (*tsūbun*). Appointment to *tsūbun* was normally made from among those monks who had already served as *tsūsu*. On retirement from office in the main monastery, *tsūbun* frequently moved into one of the *tatchū* to manage its business affairs.

Japanese *gozan* monasteries depended for survival upon two main sources of income: donations made by patrons for the performance of Buddhist memorial services or prayers for intentions, and income in the form of rice, vegetable, and cash rents from land. Some monasteries benefited from foreign trade, but this was sporadic, not regular, income. The most important single source of support was land. Zen was a relatively late arrival on the Japanese religious scene and, even with the energetic patronage of the *bakufu*, Zen monasteries never succeeded in acquiring the kind of massive landed base held by long-established monasteries like Tōji, Tōdaiji, and Kōyasan. To augment this deficiency, Zen monasteries were obliged to husband and manage what landed resources they did possess as carefully as possible.

Where the older Buddhist monasteries had relied on lay representatives to manage their estates for them, Zen monasteries sent out estate overseers (*shōsu*) from the monastery itself. The overseers were under the supervision of the eastern-rank stewards. Although, in principle, any monk was eligible for appointment as an overseer, in practice, since the aim was maximization of income, this office was monopolized by those officers most skilled in financial matters, especially by the bursars (*tsūbun*).[45]

To supplement income from land, it also became common, from the mid-fourteenth century, for the bursar and other financial officers to engage in moneylending activities of the kind already common in the monasteries of other Japanese Buddhist sects and in Ch'an monasteries in China. *Bakufu* efforts to curtail this practice were unavailing. As positive financial support by the *bakufu* for the *gozan* dwindled during the fifteenth century, monasteries had no alternative but to seek other sources of in-

come. Far from rooting out moneylending, the *bakufu* found
itself relying on loans derived from the proceeds of speculation
by the more successful bursars of monasteries like Shōkokuji
and Tenryūji. Financial officers of the eastern rank, therefore,
were not only vital to the prosperity or survival of their own
communities; they also came to play an increasingly important
role in *bakufu* financial affairs.[46]

The functions of the two ranks of officers, especially of their
senior members, were thus quite different. It was natural that, in
time, the two groups should have hardened into two quite distinct
elites. Religious, intellectual, and cultural activities were the
exclusive preserve of the western rank of prefects. They provided
the supply of abbots, and their monks formed the coteries of
poets and painters who contributed to the output of *gozan* literature and ink painting.

Although monks of the eastern rank were generally excluded
from these activities, the power of the purse was a compensating
source of pride and exclusiveness. Effective service in the upper
reaches of the eastern rank called for specialized administrative
skills, and this requirement naturally contributed to the gradual
development of self-perpetuating "guilds" of financial officers,
in which senior stewards trained as their successors younger monks
with an aptitude for administration. In China, by the Sung
dynasty, men who were unsuccessful in gaining entrance by
examination to the civil bureaucracy were finding scope to
exercise their administrative and financial talents within Ch'an
monastic bureaucracies, which had increasing need for their
skills.[47] There was no equivalent of the Chinese examination
system in Japan, but the very nature of the duties involved encouraged, over time, the development of a body of specialized
monk-administrators.

For its day, the Ch'an bureaucratic structure provided an
effective instrument of monastic management. Not only were Zen
monks much in demand by secular patrons as economic advisors,
but the bookkeeping methods and documentary forms derived
from Chinese bureaucratic practice via the Zen monastery had

a considerable influence on the development of *bakufu* bureaucratic methods.

ACOLYTES

Talented—or well-connected—young monks were appointed to serve as acolytes or personal attendants (*jisha*) to the abbot in the abbot's building and in the ceremonial functions in the various halls.[48] Five acolytes were normally appointed from among those who had recently taken the Mahayana *bodhisattva* precepts. The senior acolyte was known as the incense acolyte (*shōkō jisha* or *jikō*), a title derived from the prominent role this monk played in ceremonial functions as the bearer of the incense box. Holders of this position were expected to have passed a qualifying test in public Zen debate (*Zenkaku*) with the abbot or one of the senior prefects. The hot water and herb acolyte (*tōyaku jisha* or *jiyaku*) carried the offerings of hot water, tea, or rice cakes made during ceremonial functions. The guest acolyte (*shinka jisha* or *jika*) received the abbot's personal guests. Since these included warrior-rulers, courtiers, and Buddhist dignitaries, graciousness and a sense of decorum were important qualifications. The private secretary (*shojō jisha* or *jijō*) handled the abbot's private correspondence, while the fifth acolyte, who was known as the robe and bowl acolyte (*ibu jisha* or *jie*), kept the abbot's personal accounts.

Experience as an acolyte was an important part of a young monk's training: he was under the direct supervision of the abbot, from whom he could learn much about the spirit and practice of Zen monastic life; he gained insight into the organization of the abbot's building, its finances, guests, and religious, intellectual, and social life; and he was also given the opportunity to memorize the intricate details of the various monastic ceremonies.

The fee of 5 *kanmon* for appointment to the position of acolyte may have been too much for some monks to raise. But, if the youth or his family was ambitious, it was well worth the cost. As an acolyte in any of the official monasteries, the young monk

had his feet firmly planted on the first rungs of a ladder of prefer-
ment which could take him up through the western-rank offices
of his own monastery to become eligible for appointment as an
abbot.

Acolytes who had successfully negotiated the *Zenkaku* barrier in
public disputation would normally be appointed sutra repository
prefect (*zōsu*). In this office, they would gain deeper acquaintance with the Buddhist texts used in the daily life of the monastery. A period as scribe (*shoki*) would further familiarize the
young monk with the documentary and literary forms of Zen
monastic expression. The final and most testing stage of his
training involved the responsibility for leading others in meditation, first as rear-hall chief seat then as front-hall chief seat. Once
he had been appointed *zōsu*, the monk could take the *hinpotsu*
test which opened the way to ultimate appointment as abbot.

Not all *gozan* monks who later became abbots followed this
course precisely. In the thirteenth and early fourteenth centuries,
some renowned *gozan* abbots served as officers in the eastern
rank. Depending on the numbers enrolled and the special circumstances of individual monasteries, there was occasional repetition
in office. In the fully articulated *gozan* system of the late fourteenth and fifteenth centuries, however, the course from acolyte
to abbot via the western rank was well defined. Monks who did
not follow this path could work their way up to the higher offices
of the eastern rank if they had the necessary administrative
talents.

In large monasteries, the bulk of the precepted monks were
neither senior officers nor acolytes. They sat silently in meditation, worked on the *kōan* given to them by their spiritual director,
took part in ceremonies in the Buddha hall and assemblies in the
Dharma hall, performed minor duties, and labored in the monastery grounds. Some monks would spend one or two seasons in
a hall and move on looking for deeper insight under another
master in a different monastery or leave the *gozan* for the monks'
halls of the non-*gozan* sects. Some would stay long enough in a
monks' hall to be considered for appointment to office in their

turn as they moved slowly up the platforms in the hall. (Even those who advanced fairly quickly up the hierarchy still spent many years in training as an ordinary hall monk.)

Attention has so far been confined to monks, those members of the community who had taken the 250 *bodhisattva* precepts. Something should also be said about the large non-monk segment of the monastic population.

Of those who had not taken the full precepts and the tonsure, there were many who would never do so. These included the assistants (*anja*) attached to the various halls, attendants (*shōji*), lay officers (*yakunin*), artisans (*ninku*), and laborers (*ninriki*).[49] In a large monastery, there might be several hundred persons in these various categories. They helped with the preparation and serving of meals, the cleaning and repair of buildings, the tidying of the grounds, and with work in the monastery mill or fields. The ideal of T'ang dynasty Ch'an masters had been that the whole community of monks should labor to sustain themselves. This remained an ideal. But in Chinese monasteries in the Southern Sung dynasty and in the *gozan* monasteries of Japan, ceremonial activities and literary avocations increasingly militated against the rigorous practice of labor by monks.

POSTULANTS AND NOVICES

Also in the category of those who had not taken the full vows were postulants (*kasshiki* or *katsujiki*) and novices (*shami*).[50] They would in time, however, become monks. We have already encountered the *kasshiki* as the young assistants who "called the meals" in the monks' halls of Chinese monasteries. As an *anja*, the *kasshiki* should not, in principle, have become a monk. In medieval Japanese monasteries, however, *kasshiki* was the title given to boys between the ages of 5 and 7 or 8 who were taken into the monastery as postulants to begin their training in reading and chanting Buddhist and Chinese classical texts and learning monastic ceremonies under the personal supervision of the abbot. *Shami* were youths in their early teens who had taken the tonsure, robes, and 10 vows of the novice. They continued their studies under the abbot in preparation for eventual reception of the 250 precepts and entry to the monks' hall.[51]

The numbers of these youths varied from monastery to monastery. At Nanzenji, before the end of the Kamakura period, there were 130 *shami* and *kasshiki* as against 700 monks. Most regulatory codes for *gozan* monasteries include at least one article on the subject of postulants and novices. Almost without exception, these articles state that numbers of *shami* and *kasshiki* should be kept to a minimum. In 1303, Hōjō Sadatoki stipulated that only those youths who had received permission from the monastery patron should be accepted as postulants or novices by Engakuji. Hōjō Takatoki's regulations for the same monastery in 1327 state that there should not be more than 5. Musō Soseki's regulations for Rinsenji drawn up in 1339 also restricted the number to 5, but Ashikaga regulations for the *gozan* in the mid-fourteenth century allowed 20 in large monasteries.

The presence of these youths created numerous problems for Zen monastic legislators. Although *shami* had their hair cropped, *kasshiki* wore their hair shoulder length and modishly. By the Muromachi period, their childish features were being decorated with white powder. In contrast to the somber black robes of the *shami* and precepted monks, *kasshiki* were dressed in finely wrought silken robes and vividly colored variegated under-robes.

The *Inryōken nichiroku* and other monastic regulations repeatedly warn that postulants and novices were to wear "robes of a single color; and that not to be scarlet." However, the frequency with which these regulations were repeated and their increasing detail suggest that they were not observed. Tōfukuji regulations of 1463 stipulate that under-robes for postulants and novices were not to be made of such luxurious materials as fine silk gauze, satin, or embroidered cloth; that they should not be scarlet or parti-colored, crested, or decorated with gold or silver thread.

The presence of large numbers of children in the monastery could adversely affect standards of discipline. Rivalries in conspicuous consumption indulged in by wealthy *bushi* families were carried on within the Zen cloister by their sons. The flaunting of luxurious robes by some young postulants could hardly fail to arouse envy among their less fortunate fellows and undermine Zen traditions of simplicity and frugality. Gorgeously arrayed youths became the center of admiration in lavish monastic ceremonies that were far in spirit from the simple, direct search for self advocated by the early Ch'an masters. In some cases, the youths became the focus of homosexual affection and rivalry. Poems were written by *gozan* monks to attractive *kasshiki* or *shami*;[52] and the beauty of the Zen postulant was sufficiently celebrated to find expression in a mask known as the *kasshiki* used on the *nō* stage.[53] It would be misleading to leave the impression that medieval Zen monastic life was totally disrupted by the presence of these young people. Contemporary documents, however, make it very clear that they caused much concern to monks and secular officials responsible for maintaining monastic discipline.[54]

SEVEN

The Zen Monastic Economy

Buddhist monasteries in T'ang dynasty China are known to have
held extensive estates and to have been thriving centers of commercial and entrepreneurial activity. Their estates, built up
through donation, reclamation, or purchase, were farmed by tenants or serfs, and excess produce in tax-rent was sold in local
markets. Lowlands produced cereals, vegetables, and mulberries.
Mountain valleys provided timber and bamboo. In addition,
monasteries received generous donations in cash and kind, charged
fees for memorial services, drew profits from the milling of grain
and the operation of oil presses, and ran shops, pawnshops,
hostels, mutual financing associations, and "inexhaustible treasuries." It was largely the wealth and privilege of the major monasteries, and the allegedly parasitic lives of their inhabitants, that
made the Buddhist church the target of criticism, regulation, and
persecution during the T'ang dynasty.[1]

CH'AN COMMUNITIES IN CHINA

The above description is less applicable to the Ch'an communities,
most of which were still in a formative stage during the T'ang
dynasty, than it is to the mature T'ien-t'ai, Fa-hsiang, and Hua-yen
monasteries. The early institutional history of Ch'an in China is

still very obscure, but Japanese scholars who have examined the development of the early Ch'an communities are in fairly general agreement that the Ch'an economy in the T'ang dynasty differed significantly from that of other branches of Buddhism, especially in that Ch'an communities had not accumulated vast estates prior to the persecution of 845. A regulation made by the disciples of Pai-chang in 814 expressly forbade the acquisition of such estates and their cultivation by tenants for rent. Of course, the very fact that such a ruling had to be made explicit implies that such a trend was already evident.[2] Early Ch'an communities did depend upon landholdings. These, however, were probably the aggregate of the allocations of 30 *mou* (about 5 acres) per monk permitted under the equal-field system, supplemented by land reclaimed by the community, rather than estates donated by wealthy patrons. If early Ch'an injunctions and codes can be relied upon, community land was farmed not by tenant cultivators or serfs but by the monks themselves, including their abbot. The ideal of labor for all—"A day without work should be a day without food"—was probably realized in most communities.

The picture that is emerging of the economic life of the early Ch'an communities is thus one of largely self-contained, self-sufficient agricultural activity, perhaps augmented by occasional local medicancy. Opinion is divided, however, on the degree of self-sufficiency and the relative importance of donations and secular sponsorship. Earlier research by Ui Hakuju and Nakamura Hajime tended to stress the virtually complete self-sufficiency of early Ch'an economic life.[3] More recently, Shiina Hiroo has shown that early Ch'an communities at Tung-shan were heavily dependent on secular patronage.[4] Kondō Ryōchi allows for some degree of dependence on lay patrons—T'ang dynasty Zen masters certainly had powerful secular sponsors—but he stresses that the principal component of Ch'an economic life until the mid-ninth century was self-sufficient agriculture.[5] This relative economic simplicity, the remoteness of many Ch'an monasteries from urban centers, and the stress on productive labor by Ch'an monks helped the Ch'an school to survive the Hui-ch'ang persecution unscathed.

From the mid-ninth century, however, according to Kondō, Ch'an monasteries moved steadily in the direction of greater dependence on wealthy secular patrons and of integration with the local commercial economy. On the basis of his research into the biographies of Ch'an monks mentioned in the *Sung kao-seng-chuan* (988) and the *Ching-te ch'uan-teng-lu* (1004), he concludes that, of famous Ch'an masters active after the mid-ninth century, most had their monasteries donated to them instead of building them themselves, as monks of the early T'ang dynasty had done. The donated monastery buildings were frequently accompanied by gifts of land, serfs, and draught animals, which provided the basis for the development of substantial estates. This trend was encouraged by the growing popularity of Ch'an, especially among wealthy provincial families and with the local military governors (*chieh-tu-shih*) who had grasped economic as well as military power. As Ch'an monasteries became increasingly dependent on patronage, the self-sufficient economy was undermined and the need for manual labor by all monks reduced. From the late T'ang dynasty on, Kondō detects a steady decline in the number of references to the "universal practice of labor by all monks." Instead, there are frequent references to specialized monastic officers responsible for directing the labor of others, frequently monastery servants. These changes in the character of the Ch'an community life were taking place within the context of a rapid growth in commerce and the extension of a money economy in China. Once remote Ch'an monasteries were being drawn within this network of secular economic activity.

Analysis of the *Ch'an-yuan ch'ing-kuei* (1103) shows how far this shift from self-sufficiency to dependence had gone, at least in large monasteries, by the Northern Sung dynasty.[6] The kind of monastic economy described in the *Ch'an yuan Code* clearly rested on two principal pillars: income in tax-rent and the proceeds from the sale of surplus produce of monastery estates on the one hand, and income in the form of solicited donations from a broad spectrum of patrons on the other.

The code refers to estate overseers (*chuang-chu*), whose duties included the collection of rents and taxes in cash and kind from peasant cultivators, as well as supervision of the monks, monastery attendants, and slaves who ran the mills, oil presses, stables, and fruit and vegetable gardens.[7] To judge from the large number of such assistants named, and the variety of outbuildings, agricultural implements, and produce mentioned, the economies of the larger Ch'an centers were well developed by the Northern Sung dynasty and integrated with local markets. The *Ch'an-yuan Code* states that excess produce from the estates, gardens, mills, and oil presses was to be sold by monastery officers known as the chief factors (*hsieh-yuan-chu*), who also acted as negotiating agents with local government officials.[8] The activities of the estate overseers and factors were supervised by senior monastery officers, including the prior (*chien-yuan*) and the storehouse prefect (*k'u-t'ou*).

The *Ch'an-yuan Code* also outlines a carefully articulated, two-pronged fund-raising organization within Ch'an monasteries. The code devotes considerable attention to the selection, appointment, and responsibilities of the officers known as chief solicitors (*hua-chu*).[9] These solicitors were carefully selected monks who were sent to distant regions to secure donations from wealthy individual patrons and support groups. The importance attached to this office is evident from the fact that the solicitors were seen off and welcomed back in elaborate ceremonies involving the abbot and the whole community. They were provided with letters of introduction from the monastery to prominent officials and laymen of the region to which they were sent, and were accompanied by monastery servants to protect them and the funds they collected. In addition to this permanent office, whose incumbents were rotated regularly, the *Ch'an-yuan Code* also provides for a dozen or more occasional mendicant monks whose duty it was to solicit donations of rice, vegetables, charcoal, oil, or whatever else was in short supply, by begging from door to door or by lecturing on the sutras to groups of local patrons.[10]

The kind of large-scale Ch'an monastic economy described in the *Ch'an yuan Code*, based on the management of estates worked by tenant cultivators, dependent on the sale of excess produce to local markets and the active solicitation of donations from support groups, and run by specialized monk-bureaucrats, seems a far cry from the small, self-sufficient economies that are presumed to have supported the early Ch'an communities.

JAPAN: ZEN MONASTIC DOMAINS

To turn now to Japan, it is evident from the *Taiheiki* that Zen monasteries had, by the fourteenth century, acquired a reputation for wealth and opulence:

> They [Zen monks] adorn themselves with five-colored robes; they gorge themselves on the eight delicacies; with their private fortunes they scheme to become abbots and achieve their ends under the guise of donations. When one looks at Zen in its present state the contrast is plain: where once the hermitages of the sages had pine gates and bark roofs, Zen monasteries today have jeweled pagodas and gilded halls; where the sages lived on simple food and wore rough clothing, Zen monks now must have rare foods and gorgeous robes.[11]

In medieval Japan, as in T'ang and Sung dynasty China, land was the foundation of the Zen monastic economy and of monastic wealth. Cash donations by warriors, nobles, and emperors were helpful in constructing or restoring monastery buildings, and in providing memorial ceremonies and feasts, but they were rarely sufficient to sustain communities of hundreds of monks and monastery servants on a permanent basis. By the fifteenth century, some Zen monks were engaging in foreign trade or money-lending. On the whole, however, these activities were either undertaken for private gain or to augment dwindling returns from land as Zen monasteries were deprived of their holdings in the disturbed years of the later fifteenth and early sixteenth centuries. The growth of the *gozan* monasteries, their prosperity, and social prestige were all directly proportional to their access to land and its produce in the form of goods and taxes. This access in turn hinged upon the political fortunes of their principal patrons, the Hōjō regents, the Ashikaga shoguns, and the imperial house.

The following pages examine the changing economies of three Zen monasteries; Engakuji, Nanzenji, and Daitokuji. These three have been selected for purposes of contrast. Engakuji was a Kamakura monastery that enjoyed the special favor of the Hōjō regents and limited support from the Ashikaga shoguns. Nanzenji was the principal Kyoto *gozan* monastery and enjoyed the enthusiastic support of Emperor Go-Daigo and the Ashikaga. Daitokuji was favored by Go-Daigo but neglected by the Ashikaga and eventually dropped out of the *gozan* system. The landholdings of all three monasteries are copiously documented, and all have been the subject of careful studies by Japanese scholars.[12] A full study of the medieval Zen monastic economy would take into account Sōtō as well as Rinzai monasteries, provincial as well as metropolitan centers, and sub-temples and branch temples as well as the main monasteries. This, however, would far exceed the scope of a single chapter. It is hoped that investigation of the economic life of these three monasteries will also shed some light on the economies of other Zen and non-Zen Buddhist monasteries in medieval Japan. At the outset, however, we should perhaps remind ourselves that Zen monasteries were established at a time when landed estates (*shōen*), the principal source of wealth of absentee central proprietors, including nobles, temples, and shrines, were being eroded by local warriors, brought within the domains of *shugo* and *sengoku daimyō*, and subjected to occasional eruptions of peasant unrest. Buddhist monasteries naturally did all in their power to resist these pressures, to cling to their holdings, and to develop new sources of income to compensate for lost rights in distant *shōen*. While the Muromachi period saw the protracted and painful demise of *shōen*, it also witnessed the growth, especially in the Kinai region, of a vigorous commercial economy and profitable continental trade. Some temples were able to take advantage of these new commercial opportunities directly, through the sponsorship of guilds and markets, from barrier charges and money-lending, by the sale of produce, or by engaging in the China trade. Many more benefited indirectly, enjoying the patronage of those warriors and merchants who grasped the new wealth. Thus, although its landed base was being severely undercut, the Buddhist institution as a whole still remained a powerful economic force in medieval society.[13] It is against this backdrop that we should view Zen monastic landholdings and economic activity.

THE ENGAKUJI ECONOMY

Engakuji was established by Hōjō Tokimune in 1282. The original core of Engakuji holdings consisted of rights (*shiki*) in 3 pieces of domain: Tomita-no-*shō* in Owari, 4 districts, or administrative villages (*gō*), in the neighboring Tomiyoshi-no-*shō*, and the Kameyama *gō* in Ahiru-no-*shō*, Kazusa.

The surviving map of Tomita-no-*shō*, dated 1327, shows a substantial tract of land embracing a dozen hamlets, together with several temples and shrines.[14] Stewardship of the *shōen*, the *jitō shiki*, was bestowed on Engakuji by Tokimune in the third month of 1283, three months after Wu-hsueh's installation.[15] Engakuji was raised to the status of shogunal invocatory temple and the grant of land confirmed by the *bakufu* in the seventh month of the same year.[16] In the document of commendation, Tokimune ordered the dispatch of inspectors to Tomita-no-*shō* to clarify Engakuji's rights. This was essential in contemporary *shōen* where a welter of overlapping *shiki* were shared by a hierarchy of claimants. These might include an absentee guarantor (*honke*) and proprietor (*ryōke*) in Kyoto, such local estate officials as agents (*azukari-dokoro*) and military stewards (*jitō*) who administered the *shō*, kept order, and collected the tax-rents and, beneath them, various levels of cultivators.

Older monasteries like Tōdaiji and Tōji, which had held their lands since the beginnings of *shōen* development, generally held *honke* or *ryōke* privileges. By the late Kamakura period, however, a saturation point had been reached in *shōen* growth, and even a warrior-ruler as powerful as Tokimune could not conjure up new *shōen* proprietorships to confer on favored monasteries. The best he could do was grant some of the many scattered rights the Hōjō had accumulated, *jitō shiki* for the most part, and then try to ensure that the monastery received every grain of rice or copper cash to which it was entitled. The more of a *shōen*'s tax output that went to the holder of the *jitō shiki*, the less that was available for the nominal proprietor. Most *shōen* in the Kamakura period were the scenes of protracted and bitter disputes between holders of *jitō shiki*, whether warriors or newly emerging temples, and absentee proprietors. Buddhist monastic domains, for their part, naturally reflected the landholding powers and privileges of their principal patrons, and fluctuated over time in relation to the changing fortunes of those patrons. In the case of Tomita-no-*shō*, the proprietor (*ryōke*) was the Konoe (Fujiwara) family. By the early thirteenth century, the Hōjō had acquired the *jitō shiki* and assumed virtually complete control over the estate. It was this *shiki* that Tokimune conferred on Engakuji. The rights in the Tomiyoshi *gō* and Kameyama *gō*, probably also *jitō shiki*, were also conferred on Engakuji in the summer of 1283.[17]

From Tomita-no-*shō* in 1283, Engakuji was receiving the very substantial annual income of 1,428 *koku* 8 *to* of tax rice and 1,506 *kan* 868 *mon* in cash.[18] This was a very large *shōen* tax yield, and Engakuji was clearly receiving the bulk of the available income from the *shōen*. According to a document of 1327, the proprietor (*ryōke*), the Konoe family, was receiving only 110 *kanmon* from the *shōen*.[19] No separate record of income from the Tomiyoshi *gō* survives but, since they were contiguous to Tomita-no-*shō*, it is probable that their rice and cash yield were included with those of Tomita-no-*shō*. Kameyama *gō* provided 141 *koku* of tax rice and 68 *kan* 580 *mon* in cash, plus 200 *koku* of soybeans, 3,960 horse loads of firewood, and 500 horse loads of charcoal. Kazusa (within present-day Chiba prefecture) was much closer to Kamakura than Owari, and the Kameyama domain was clearly expected to provide most of the daily necessities other than rice for Engakuji. The cash and rice income from these two domains provided a solid economic foundation for the new community, which numbered 268 persons in 1283. From the point of view of the economic history of medieval Japan, it is interesting to note that in the late Kamakura period the *shōen*-based economy of this Zen monastery rested almost as heavily on cash income as it did on income in rice and other commodities. Engakuji thus provides one indication of the extent to which imported coinage had gained acceptance by the late thirteenth century.

We have already seen that, under Hōjō patronage, the Engakuji community grew rapidly, reaching more than 350 monks by the 1320s and continuing to expand until after mid-century. Moreover, Engakuji was ravaged by fires in 1287, 1289, and 1293. Extra resources, therefore, had to be provided to support the costs of rebuilding, as well as to feed the growing community. The Hōjō were generous patrons, however and, until the end of the Kamakura period, expansion of Engakuji domain more than kept pace with the growth of the monastery and its community. By the time the Hōjō regime collapsed in 1333, Engakuji had rights, mostly *jitō shiki*, in eighteen holdings scattered over Japan. The following paragraphs will trace the fortunes of four or five of these additional holdings.[20] The details are perhaps difficult to digest but essential to convey an impression of the fluid, shifting nature of monastic estate holdings and the Zen monastic economy.

In 1293, Engakuji was granted temporary privileges in the Shinoki-no-*shō* (Owari) as *zōeiryō* to help with rebuilding expenses.[21] This *shōen* belonged to the Chōkōdō and was part of the domain of the Jimyō'in line of emperors. In 1295, Engakuji secured a more permanent interest in the *shōen* by forcing a compromise settlement (*wayo*) on the proprietor.[22] In return, the monastery agreed to pay the reluctant proprietor a mere 760 *kan* in back taxes over several years.[23] The Yamamoto-no-*shō* (Echizen) was bestowed on Engakuji in 1286, probably as *zōeiryō*. In a document of 1323, it is again designated as *zōeiryō*, this time for the rebuilding of the Dharma hall on the occasion of the thirteenth year Buddhist memorial services for Hōjō Sadatoki.[24] At this time, Engakuji was deriving at least 1,000 *kanmon* a year in *nengu* from this domain.[25] In 1306, the novice Gakuzō and 15 other signatories conferred on Engakuji the title to the Imamura Fukumanji temple in Owari.[26] The annual tax yield was small, 3 *kan* 500 *mon* at a rate of 100 *mon* per *tan*, but no doubt Engakuji was pleased to extend its Owari holdings. This process was continued in 1322 when two villages, Hayashi *mura* and Agara *mura* in Owari, were conferred on Engakuji by the novice Jōen and five others.[27] This grant was made reluctantly. From the statement accompanying the donation, it is apparent that the grantors only agreed to send in the tax registers and pay *nengu* under duress from Engakuji, whose claims they contested.[28] They must have known, however, that they had little hope of success in a dispute with a powerful monastery that had substantial holdings in Owari and was assured of the support of the *bakufu*. Eager to extend its holdings, Engakuji was unresponsive to their protests. From the tax register for the two villages, we learn that the tax assessment of Hayashi *mura* amounted to 9 *kan* 350 *mon*; that on Agara *mura* to 650 *mon*. *Nengu* was levied at the rate of 130 *mon* per *tan*.[29] This was 30 *mon* per *tan* higher than the rate at Imamura Fukumanji; presumably the land around these two villages was higher yielding.

The political transition from the Hōjō, under whose patronage Engakuji had prospered, to the Kyoto-based governments of Go-Daigo and the Ashikaga brought uncertainty to Engakuji and instability to its domains. In 1333 and 1334, Go-Daigo issued imperial directives (*rinji*) reaffirming the holdings of the But-sunichi'an sub-temple and Engakuji interests in the Yamamoto-no-*shō* in Echizen.[30] At the same time, the emperor tried to deprive Engakuji of its valuable rights in Tomita-no-*shō* and to bestow them on one of the court ladies.[31] Engakuji objected. The *jitō shiki* was restored, but there was trouble in the domain, and division (*chūbun*) of the *shōen* seems to have been attempted by Engakuji. In the summer of 1334, Go-Daigo issued directives that division of Engakuji domains in Tomita and Shinoki-no-*shō* should cease and that Engakuji should pay *nengu* to the proprietors of both *shōen*.[32] The monastery was having troubles of a different kind in its holdings in the Yamamoto-no-*shō* in Echizen. Although Engakuji's rights had been confirmed by Go-Daigo, the *shōen* was invaded by a local warrior, Yuasa Sōken. Engakuji protested, and Go-Daigo's Court of Pleas (*zasso ketsudansho*) issued an order to Nitta Yoshisada, the *shugo* of Echizen, directing him to restrain Yuasa and protect Engakuji's interests.[33]

Under the early Ashikaga, during the war-torn decades of the mid-fourteenth century, Engakuji recovered temporary control over much of its domain and even added some new rights in the Kantō. It suffered increasingly heavy erosion from the periphery, however, so that, by the end of the century, *bakufu* support notwithstanding, it was losing control of many of its more important holdings.

Ashikaga Takauji entered Kyoto early in 1336. Later in the same year, he confirmed Engakuji in holdings taken from it during the Kenmu Restoration and in its existing holdings.[34] This document is unspecific. Engakuji's holdings under the first Ashikaga shogun are clarified, however, in a document issued the following year by Ashikaga Tadayoshi, who had assumed general oversight of the Zen monastic institution. This document confirmed Engakuji in nine *jitō shiki*: Shinoki-no-*shō*, Tomita-no-*shō*, and the villages of Kokubu and Mizoguchi, all in Owari; the Yamamoto-no-*shō* and the districts (*gō*) of Izumi and Funatsu in Echizen; Maejima in Musashi; Kameyama *gō*, Ahiru-no-*shō*, in Kazusa; two villages in Shimōsa; Kitatamamura *gō* in Kōzuke; and five districts in Dewa.[35]

Although these probably include the most important of Engakuji's earlier holdings, they account for only half the number held under the Hōjō. It is not clear what happened to the other 9. Five of the missing holdings are listed in a 1365 catalogue of Engakuji holdings as non-*chigyō*, that is, lands over which the monastery had a nominal claim but from which, because of warrior intrusion or local unrest, it was unable to derive any income.[36] For the most part, these were precarious rights in villages like Hayashi and Agara that had been acquired under pressure, and only with Hōjō backing. These had probably been lost to Engakuji during the disturbances attending the Kenmu Restoration. Moreover, other forms of income, such as the contributions levied by the Hōjō regents on their retainers to help pay for the monthly memorial services for Tokimune, were naturally lost to the monastery with the fall of the Hōjō. Had Go-Daigo managed to establish an enduring regime, Engakuji would probably have suffered a rapid and irreversible economic decline. The establishment of Ashikaga authority gave it a reprieve. Although Ashikaga government was centered in Kyoto and shogunal patronage was lavished on the Kyoto *gozan* monasteries, the deliberate articulation of a nationwide *gozan* network by Takauji and Tadayoshi also benefited Kamakura Zen monasteries.

In succeeding decades, Engakuji continued to grow and to improve its position in and around the Kantō. During the 1360s and 1370s, leaders of the Imagawa family, *shugo* of Suruga, conferred on Engakuji land rights and tax exemptions in several districts in Suruga, encouraged, no doubt, by the fact that a brother of Imagawa Norikuni had been appointed abbot of Engakuji.[37] Ashikaga Yoshimitsu commended part of the Kaji-no-*shō* in Echigo, and there were a number of similar land grants by other warrior patrons.[38] In addition to these more or less permanent grants, there were awards from the *bakufu* of temporary levies, usually to pay for reconstruction after fire damage. These included: tax levies on districts in Hitachi province;[39] a share in the income from barriers in the Izu and Hakone mountains;[40] household levies (*munebetsu-sen*) of 10 *mon* or a bolt of cloth on households in the Kantō and northeastern regions;[41] similar levies on Kamakura residences and Kamakura *sake* dealers;[42] and, in 1378, sail levies (*hobetsu-sen*) on ports in Musashi province.[43] This was probably piecemeal income, revoked after two or three years, or once the particular need was satisfied, but it was income.

While Engakuji was holding its own, or even improving its economic position in the Kantō, it was experiencing growing difficulties in some of its more vital distant holdings. In Tomita-no-*shō*, Engakuji was involved after 1315 in a boundary dispute over the eastern part of the *shōen*,[44] and in litigation with the proprietor, the Konoe in Kyoto, over unpaid taxes.[45] From the

1350s, the northern part of the *shōen* suffered repeated incursions by a local warrior, the brother of the *shugo* of Owari. Neither orders from shoguns Yoshiakira and Yoshimitsu nor gifts of paintings from the monastery were sufficient to relieve the local pressure on the *shōen*.[46] Eventually, in 1396, in response to a petition from Engakuji, what was left of Tomita-no-*shō* was exchanged for rights in 3 *gō* in the province of Kazusa, nearer to the monastery.[47]

When the cloistered Emperor Go-Fushimi advised his consort Kōgimon'in in 1334 not to revoke Engakuji's *jitō ukesho* in Shinoki-no-*shō*, the monastery seemed to have recovered a secure grip on this domain, in spite of recent intrusions by monks from Daisenji and Enpukuji.[48] In 1336, Engakuji, for its part, made inroads into the holdings of the proprietor, Kōgimon'in.[49] This dispute was patched up in 1338 by cloistered Emperor Kōgon.[50] A year later, the *shōen* was invaded by the intendant of the Atsuta shrine.[51] Thereafter, there is no record of disturbance in the *shō* until the 1380s, when it, like Tomita-no-*shō*, was subjected to mounting warrior pressure and eventually alienated from the monastery.[52]

Yamamoto-no-*shō* in Echizen had been invaded by Yuasa Sōken in 1334. It was restored to Engakuji by the Ashikaga, but the monastery's rights were never very secure.[53] In 1365, Engakuji sent gifts of paintings from the Butsunichi'an to the *shugo* of Echizen, Shiba Takatsune, to win his favor.[54] In spite of this gesture, Takatsune enforced *hanzei* on the two districts, whereby he held back half the tax proceeds. Engakuji appealed and had the *hanzei* repealed by Ashikaga Yoshiakira.[55] In 1384, Engakuji, acting through the monk Shun'oku Myōha, acquired the title to this *shōen* from the *monzeki* abbot of the Shōren'in in return for 3,000 *kanmon*. It is unclear, however, whether this title was to the whole *shōen*, or only part of it, or what connection this transaction had with the two villages.[56] The last mention of Engakuji rights in the domain is in a document of 1388.[57]

We have already suggested that Engakuji's growth had ceased before its Buddha relic was moved to Kyoto in 1396. By this time, Engakuji, in spite of *bakufu* sympathy, was beginning to lose its grip on many of its valuable distant *shōen* holdings. Those that remained were small and confined to the Kantō. Kameyama *gō* in Ahiru-no-*shō*, Kazusa, which supplied the monastery with much of its vegetables and firewood, for instance, was still listed among the holdings confirmed by the Kantō regional governor (*kanrei*), Ashikaga Mochiuji, in 1419.[58] By 1440, however, even these smaller, nearby holdings were being alienated. The last known documentary record of Engakuji *shōen* rights dates from 1447.[59] Since this was a time of nationwide *shōen* dissolution, it is not surprising that this Kamakura monastery should have been buffeted so severely. Yet, in spite of the loss of most of its *shōen* interests, the Engakuji community somehow survived the warfare of the Sengoku period. In 1582, Hideyoshi confirmed Engakuji and its branch temples in their existing active holdings as revealed by cadastral survey.[60] In 1591, scattered Engakuji rights, together with those of its sub-temples, were concentrated in two places near the monastery, and income of 144 *kan* 830 *mon* bestowed on Engakuji by Tokugawa Ieyasu.[61] Although Engakuji may have had additional income from donations, the grant from Tokugawa Ieyasu probably laid the economic base that was to support the monastery and its sub-temples until the nineteenth century. By any standards, this was a very far cry from 1284, when the cash income alone from Tomita-no-*shō* had amounted to more than 1500 *kanmon*. It was also a very much smaller income than the 800 *koku* allowed by Hideyoshi to Nanzenji, or the 1800 *koku* which he awarded Tōfukuji in 1585. The change of fortune would probably appear even starker were price fluctuations taken into account. Engakuji's reverses reflect both a general weakening of the *gozan* monastic economy in the late fifteenth and sixteenth centuries and a relative decline of Kamakura Zen monasteries vis-à-vis their Kyoto counterparts. Kyoto *gozan* monasteries, in an effort to compensate for lost landholdings or waning support from the *bakufu*, engaged in foreign trade, moneylending, and other commercial activities. Such opportunities were largely unavailable to Kamakura Zen monasteries.[62] When their estates were stripped from them, Engakuji, Kenchōji, and other Kamakura monasteries were entirely dependent upon the largesse of powerful warriors.

THE NANZENJI ECONOMY

The pattern of acquisition, consolidation, and attrition of Nanzenji domain was basically similar to that of Engakuji, but modified by the facts that Nanzenji was a Kyoto monastery, that it had close ties both to the Daikakuji imperial line and to the Ashikaga shogunate, and that it was elevated to the apex of the *gozan* system. It was able, therefore, to build up an even more extensive landed base than Engakuji in the late Kamakura and early Muromachi periods, and to hold on to most of its *shōen* rights until the Ōnin War period. Even so, Nanzenji suffered frequent intrusion, dislocation, and alienation of its holdings.[63]

Nanzenji was converted from an imperial palace into a Zen monastery by cloistered Emperor Kameyama. In 1299, with the buildings nearing completion, Kameyama conferred on the monastery, then named Zenrinji, rights in 3 domains: Hatsukura-no-*shō* in Tōtōmi, Kosaka-no-*shō* in Kaga, and the Munakata-no-*shō* in Chikuzen. In 1300 the Kosaka-no-*shō* was exchanged for rights in 3 *shōen*: the Yano and Ōshio-no-*shō* in Harima, and the Ikedera-no-*shō* in Tajima. In 1303 the Munakata-no-*shō* was exchanged by Kameyama for 3 different holdings in the public domain: the Tokuhashi district (*gō*) and the Kasama eastern ward (*ho*) in Kaga, and the Mitsunari *gō* in Bitchū.[64] These 7 holdings, with subsequent additional grants, provided the basis of Nanzenji's economy until the Sengoku period and, at times, sustained a community of over 1,000 persons.

With the weakening of Hōjō authority in the late Kamakura period, there were disturbances in Nanzenji domains as in those of other Zen monasteries. Nanzenji's holding in the Yano-no-*shō* was invaded in 1315 by the local *jitō*. Kaga Tokuhashi *gō* was subjected to intrusion by the *jitō* of Yamanouchi-no-*shō* and his son in 1312 and during the 1320s, and by supporters of local

Shintō shrines. In response to appeals from Nanzenji, the *bakufu* eventually ordered its Kyoto Commissioner (Rokuhara *tandai*) to intervene on Nanzenji's behalf. Such disputes, however, were part and parcel of contemporary domain management. Nanzenji survived them and even managed to consolidate its holdings.[65] Under Emperor Go-Daigo, who was both a grandson of Kameyama and a patron of Rinzai Zen, Nanzenji fared well. The emperor confirmed the monastery's existing holdings and granted 5 new *shiki*, guaranteed in a Daijōkan decree of 1335.[66] Having replaced Go-Daigo, Ashikaga Takauji began by stripping Nanzenji of all the holdings granted to it during the Kenmu Restoration period. This reaction against a monastery favored by Go-Daigo was quickly modified, however, and Nanzenji recovered all its earlier holdings and added new ones.[67] Musō Soseki and other abbots of Nanzenji won the respect of the Ashikaga shoguns, and the monastery played a major role at the apex of the rapidly developing *gozan* hierarchy. It reached a pinnacle of influence and prosperity in the late fourteenth and early fifteenth centuries under the shoguns Yoshimitsu, Yoshimochi, and Yoshinori.

At the height of its prosperity, Nanzenji was deriving from its holdings an income equivalent to that of many provincial warlords. In 1392 the tax rice (*nengu*) from its Kaga domains totaled 2,035 *koku*, 7 *to*, 2 *shō*. Of this, 736 *koku*, 1 *to*, 2 *shō* came from Tokuhashi *gō*; 243 *koku*, 2 *to*, 2 *shō* from Sano village; 167 *koku*, 2 *to*, 8 *shō* from Sara village; and 889 *koku* and 2 *to* from the Kasama ward.[68] From the Tōtōmi Hatsukura-no-*shō*, the monastery derived in 1387 a total *nengu* of 929 *koku*, 5 *to*, 2 *shō*.[69] In 1453 it was obtaining 1,000 *koku* from its holdings in Harima and Bitchū.[70] Nanzenji income from these holdings in Kaga, Tōtōmi, Harima, and Bitchū thus amounted to nearly 4,000 *koku*. In addition, Nanzenji was receiving *nengu* from the Shinjo district (*gō*) in Tōtōmi, from the Kosa and Ikedera districts in Tajima, and from the Mori-no-*shō* in Owari. Although no records survive for these domains, it seems reasonable to estimate that income from these sources would have pushed Nanzenji's total annual tax rice receipts well above 5,000 *koku*.[71] If we take

CHART 7 Tax Income from Tenryūji Domains, 1386

Province	Landholding	koku	Income kan	mon
Tanba	Mutobe-no-shō	594	602	
	Kawayara-no-shō	770	139	
	Yuge-no-shō	266	423	
Yamashiro	Mozume-no-shō	341	20	
	Toyotomi-no-shō	99	79	
	Nagai	18		
Harima	Matobe gō		295	
Kaga	Yokoe-no-shō	567	122	
Awa	Nakayama-no-shō		882	
Tōtōmi	Murakushi-no-shō		302	
Wakasa	Jisai gō		257	
Bitchū	Seiu-no-shō (etc.)		1,447	
	Total tax rice payment:	2,402 koku		
	Total cash payment:		5,721 kanmon	
	COMBINED TOTAL INCOME:	8,123 kanmon (on the assumption that 1 kan was equivalent to 1 koku)		

Notes: Based upon *Tenryūji monjo*; cited by Imatani Akira, *Sengoku-ki no Muromachi bakufu*, p. 54. Totals do not tally in the original document.

Nanzenji's sub-temples and branch temples into account, the greater Nanzenji complex may have been deriving as much as 15,000 *koku* annually from its scattered *shōen* holdings. In addition, the monastery was also enjoying a substantial income in cash and commodities other than rice.

The examples so far raised, Engakuji, Nanzenji, and Tenryūji (Chart 7), should convey some impression of the extensive landholding rights and great wealth of some of the major *gozan* monasteries in the late fourteenth and early fifteenth centuries. This, however, was merely the tip of the iceberg of the prosperity and landed interests of the whole *gozan* network. In addition to the 3 monasteries mentioned above there were 8 other full *gozan* monasteries, each probably having a dozen or more *shōen* holdings. Many of the 30 *jissatsu* monasteries—for instance Rinsenji, Chōfukuji, Hōdōji, Rokuō'in—had rights in 10 or more *shōen* holdings, while each of the several hundred *shozan* probably had at least 2 or 3 local domains. Collectively, therefore, the *gozan* network was one of the most extensive and powerful landed proprietors in Muromachi Japan. Moreover, while the shogun-*shugo* alliance continued to provide a viable political basis for Muromachi government, *gozan* monasteries enjoyed official protection and a variety of privileges and immunities. *Gozan* holdings, for instance, were frequently explicitly exempted from temporary provincial tax levies (*yakubuku-mai* or *tansen*) imposed for palace and shrine reconstruction or to pay for coronations. Local officials and agents of *shugo* were prohibited from entering *gozan* domains to collect taxes or corvée; much *gozan* tax rice and other commodities were exempted from barrier charges. In disputes involving *gozan* monasteries and non-*gozan* litigants, the *bakufu* tended to favor its *gozan* protégés. Zen moneylending funds (*shidōsen*) were excluded from debt moratoria laws (*tokuseirei*) and Kyoto *gozan* monasteries physically protected against peasant and townspeople anger at the exactions of usurers. These various forms of protection and immunity were of incalculable assistance in the accumulation and maintenance of Zen monastic wealth in the early Muromachi period.[72]

In 1442, Nanzenji still held nearly 30 domain rights in Kaga and half a dozen other provinces. The assassination of Yoshinori, the sixth Ashikaga shogun, in 1441, however, marked the beginning of a downturn in the fortunes of the Ashikaga, and heralded a slackening of Nanzenji's grip upon its domains. *Shugo*, their deputies (*hikan*), and local warrior leaders (*kokujin*) intruded into weakly defended domains as they tightened their grip over their localities. In 1457, the head monk of the Inryōken appealed to Yoshimasa to recover lost Nanzenji rights in alienated domains in Tōtōmi and Harima. Yoshimasa duly issued the requested directives, but it is doubtful whether his writ carried sufficient weight actually to secure the return of the domain.[73] Nanzenji was also faced with a surge of peasant unrest in its holdings. In 1445, for instance, peasants of the Hatsukura-no-*shō* petitioned Nanzenji for a reduction in the rate of the tax levy.[74] There were frequent demands for relief from interest payments due on loans. Even before the outbreak of the Ōnin War, the Kyoto *gozan* were the target of mobs protesting against the exactions of usurers. The Ōnin War, however, took a particularly heavy toll. With the exception of Tōfukuji, all the major *gozan* and their sub-temples were pillaged and completely razed; nor did the *jissatsu* and *shozan* monasteries within the city escape the flames.[75] Like other *gozan* monasteries, Nanzenji was put to the torch; the community scattered. Those of the monastery's domains that fell within the *bakufu* sphere of control were designated as public land to provide military provisions. Those controlled by anti-*bakufu* forces were confiscated for the same reasons.[76]

After the war, in 1478, Yoshimasa ordered the return of all Nanzenji domain.[77] By this time, however, the *bakufu* was little more than one among many competing provincial authorities. *Shugo daimyō* or the emerging *sengoku daimyō*, who were struggling to preserve or extend their local authority, paid scant heed to directions from Kyoto that conflicted with their interests. An entry in the *Inryōken nichiroku* for 1488, ten years after Yoshimasa's intervention, makes it clear that Nanzenji's claims to its former holdings in Kaga, Owari, Tajima, Harima, and Tōtōmi were all contested; and that only the Mitsunari-no-*shō* in Bitchū was held securely.[78] More rights were recovered by the end of the century. A catalogue of holdings compiled in 1501 shows that the monastery had recovered some domain rights in Kaga, Harima, and Bitchū; but the same document also notes that the Ikedera district in Tajima, the Hatsukura and Shinjo districts in Tōtōmi, the Mori-no-*shō* in Owari, and holdings in Ōmi all remained under the control of local *shugo*.[79] Before long, the Bitchū holdings were also lost, and all that finally survived of Nanzenji domains were those in Kaga. As late as 1546, however, Nanzenji monks were still being sent out as estate supervisors to the Kaga holdings, suggesting that the monastery managed to cling to at least a few of its distant *shōen* interests through the unsettled Sengoku period. At the same time, in an effort to compensate for the loss of distant *shōen* rights, Nanzenji and its sub-temples, which had suffered a similar decline, tried to accumulate domain *(tōchigyō)* and to buy or otherwise acquire small-holding rent rights *(kajishi)* in and around the city of Kyoto. From the surviving documents it is impossible to know how successful Nanzenji was in accumulating *kajishi* rights. But even at their best, these could only have been a poor substitute for the extensive *shōen* holdings the main monastery and its subtemples had hitherto controlled.[80]

Although the sparse documentary record suggests that Nanzenji was at the nadir of its fortunes in the Sengoku period, it made a substantial recovery in the late sixteenth century under the patronage of Hideyoshi, and the leadership of the monks Genpo Reisan (d. 1608) and his disciple Ishin Sūden (1569–1633).[81] In 1591, Hideyoshi confirmed Nanzenji holdings in and around Kyoto worth 592 *koku*, 7 *to*, 2 *shō*.[82] This was later raised by Tokugawa Ieyasu to 892 *koku*, and additional funds were made available for the repair of the Dharma hall and other devastated buildings.[83] Nanzenji's recovery was completed by Ishin Sūden who, as the confidant of Tokugawa Ieyasu, Hidetada (1579–1632), and Iemitsu (1604–51), played a major role in the councils of the Tokugawa *bakufu*. In 1615, Sūden was designated head of the *sōroku* office, which was shifted from the Rokuon'in (Shōkokuji) to his sub-temple, the Konch'in, within Nanzenji. The Konch'in was allocated a fief of 1,900 *koku* and given a rank equivalent to that of a *daimyō* with a fief of 100,000 *koku*.[84] Thus, although Nanzenji had suffered heavy material loss during the Sengoku period, being reduced to perhaps one tenth of the scale and income it had achieved in the early Muromachi period, under the patronage of Hideyoshi and the early Tokugawa shoguns it recovered some of its lost wealth and, with the Konchi'in at its core, remained an influential monastery throughout the Edo period.

THE DAITOKUJI ECONOMY

So far, we have looked at Zen monastic holdings as sources of income. But how was this income used once it had reached the monastery? What were some of the economic priorities of medieval Zen monastic organization? How did Zen monasteries and their sub-temples adjust to the loss of their distant *shōen* holdings? And how did they respond to the growth of commerce and foreign trade in the Muromachi period? To find answers to these questions we must look at the changing economy of Daitokuji and its sub-temples, for which the surviving documents are most plentiful and revealing.[85]

Chart 8, based on the "Daitokuji jiyō gegyō sadamebumi," provides a fairly detailed statement of accounts for the monastery in 1371.[86] In that year, Daitokuji had an income of only 433 *kanmon*, derived almost entirely from 2 *shōen*. This Kyoto monastery, which had enjoyed the special favor of Emperor Go-Daigo, been ranked as the leading *gozan*, and in 1334 claimed full control and immunity (*ichien fuyu*) in 6 *shōen* holdings,[87] had fallen on hard times with the collapse of the Kenmu Restoration and the advent of the Ashikaga, who were indifferent to its welfare. A rough index of its relative penury is revealed by comparing it with Tenryūji (Chart 7), which was collecting more than 8,000 *kanmon* annually from its estates in the late fourteenth century.[88]

Apart from the 100 *kanmon* set aside for building expenses and the 30 *kanmon* devoted to the entertainment of secular officials, the bulk of Daitokuji's outlay was consumed in sustaining the small community of 30 or so monks and attendants. The basic allowance per monk was in the region of 3.5 *kanmon* a year. Over and above this, additional allotments were made to the abbot (30 *koku*), the 8 officers (1 *kan* 500 *mon* each), the estate overseers (3 *kan* to each of the overseers of the Oyake-

no-*shō*, and 1.5 *kan* to the *shōsu* of the Yuge-no-*shō*). The relatively large allowances made to the attendants and laborers can
perhaps be accounted for by the fact that they were laymen and
may have had families to support. The fact that the largest single
allotment, after that made to the abbot, went to the monastery
representative (*zasshō*), a well-placed layman, is an indication of
the importance accorded this secular agent of monastic interests.
The abbot's allotment was worth about 21 *kan* at 1370 prices.
The basis for the distinction made in the document between
regular and occasional outlay is not entirely clear. Some of the
items listed under the heading "Occasional" would seem to have
been disbursed regularly. It is possible that the regular category
was seen as basic, unalterable outlay, while items in the occasional
category might have been reduced or increased in relation to
annual fluctuations in income. There is little indication that
Daitokuji was, at this stage, involved with the developing commercial economy of the Kinai region. There seems to have been
little or no surplus produce for sale; rather some of the outlay
went to purchase supplementary rice. No mention is made of
moneylending or *shidōsen*, and no figure is given for rental income
from property around the monastery.

The overall picture that emerges from this document is of a
severely circumscribed budget, meticulous management of meager
resources, restricted ceremonial and building activity, limited
gift-giving, tight control over monks and their incomes, and a
general air of frugality; all in rather stark contrast to the financial
leeway then being enjoyed by many of the larger Kyoto *gozan*
monasteries, a number of which were embarking on major construction programs.

In a reorganization of the *gozan* system by Ashikaga Yoshimitsu
in the seventh month of 1386, Daitokuji was brought back into
the *gozan* network, but ranked a lowly ninth among the *jissatsu*
monasteries. It was, however, uncomfortable as an official monastery, and in 1431 the *bakufu* acceded to a request by Daitokuji
to be permitted to leave the *gozan* system, on the grounds that
the monastery wanted to preserve the intent of its founder and

CHART 8   Statement of Accounts for Daitokuji ("Daitokuji jiyō
gegyō sadamebumi") 1371/10/22

	kan	mon
Income from active domain		
Tax income (*nengu*) from Oyake-no-*shō*:	350	
Income from summer grain, Oyake-no-*shō*:	30	
(Abbot's allotment: 30 *koku*, estate overseer's allotment: 6 *kan*)		
Donation of 30 *koku* from Uragami Zenmon:		
Tax income from Yuge-no-*shō*, Mino:	50	
sub-total (delivered to Kyoto):	430	
Income from Kyoto smallholdings		
Rents (*jishi*) from Higuchi-Horikawa:	–	
Income from vegetable gardens:	3	
TOTAL INCOME:	433 *kanmon*	
Outlay for Regular Consumption and Offerings		
Cash equivalent of 149 *koku* of rice:	124	200
Of this, 144 *koku* was disposed of in 40 personal allotments to the principal monastery deities, the founder's image, 20 monks, 5 attendants, 5 laborers, and the Shōden'an sub-temple. The remaining 5 *koku* constituted a gift to Myōkakuji.		
Cash equivalent of 40 personal allotments of salt, soy, firewood:	35	
sub-total	159	200
Occasional Outlay		
Monastery ceremonies:	19	495
These included: New Year ceremonies (2 *kan* 730 *mon*), three seasonal tea ceremonies (2k 100m), reading of the *Mahaprajnaparamita-sutra* by 15 monks (4k600m), Kasuga sutra reading (669m), monthly Kannon ceremonies (2k400m), Three Buddhas, One Patriarch ceremonies (1k 766m), Founder's hall ceremonies (1k200m), Founder's memorial ceremonies (2k800m), former abbots (–), memorial ceremonies for shogun		

Yoshiakira (630m), ceremonies for other lay patrons (600m).		
Gifts and contributions:	35	80
Including: seasonal gifts to the Imamiya Shrine (1k600m), New Year gift to abbot of Tokuzenji (250m), New Year gift to master sculptor (90m), fee to master sculptor for cleaning Buddha hall (1k), gifts to master carpenter (340m), levy (*kajishi*) on land at monastery gates (800m), charcoal bags for tea ceremonies (1k), entertainment of officials and members of court (30k).		
Stipends and allotments:	161	500
Including: allowance for the overseer of Yuge-no-shō (1k500m), stipend to the monastery representative (*zasshō*) (12k), expenses for office of construction (100k), contributions to carpenters (3k), robe allowances for the 8 monastery officers, finance office (*nassho*), garden prefect, acolytes, sanitation steward, hall steward, building repair supervisor (22k500m), robe allowances for 5 attendants (15k), robe allowances for 5 laborers (7k500m).		
Heating and lighting:	12	170
Including: firewood for baths (7k), oil for various halls and offices (2k700m), charcoal (2k470m).		
Miscellaneous:	16	980
Including: supplementary rice provision (13k), unaccounted for (3k980m)		
sub-total	245	225
TOTAL REGULAR AND OCCASIONAL OUTLAY:	404	425

its charters from Hanazono and Go-Daigo that it remain exclusive to members of Daitō's Zen lineage. The Daitokuji economy remained at a low ebb during these decades.

Economic recovery began under the leadership of the monks Yōsō Sōi (1376–1458) and Ikkyū Sōjun (1394–1481) from the mid-fifteenth century, continued throughout the Sengoku period, and culminated in a golden age for Daitokuji in the late sixteenth and early seventeenth centuries. This recovery rested on the one hand on the enthusiastic support of new types of patrons—Sakai merchants, tea masters, and *sengoku daimyō*—and on the other of the attainment of new sources of income to supplement dwindling returns from *shōen* holdings. A few examples will suffice to convey the enthusiasm of Daitokuji's new-found patrons and the changing character of its economy. After a severe fire at Daitokuji in 1453, a Sakai merchant with the Buddhist name of Sōkan paid for the rebuilding of the Dharma hall. Some twenty years later, another Sakai merchant, Owa Shirozaemon Sōrin, a devoted follower of Ikkyū, bore most of the cost of rebuilding the abbot's building, Buddha hall, and some of the older *tatchū* after the Ōnin destruction. He also persuaded other Sakai merchants to contribute to the establishment of the Shinju'an as a memorial temple for Ikkyū and bequeathed mortuary funds (*shidōsen*) to Daitokuji.[89] Patronage of Daitokuji by Sakai merchants and tea masters was sustained by the city's growing commercial importance during the sixteenth century.

Of the more than 20 Daitokuji sub-temples established prior to 1600, at least half were built during the sixteenth century by *daimyō*, combined the character of *daimyō* family temple (*bodaiji*) with that of memorial temple (*tatchū*), and were generously supported, at least while their warrior-patrons were successful in the wars and political intrigues of the age. Typical examples of such *daimyō tatchū* include the Ryūgen'in, established in 1504 and supported by the Hatakeyama, Ōuchi, and Ōtomo families, the Jukō'in, established in 1566 and patronized by the Miyoshi family, and the Sangen'in, built in 1586 under the patronage of the Ishida, Asano, and Mōri *daimyō* families.[90] Bonds linking merchants and *sengoku daimyō* with Daitokuji included a common interest in Zen, admiration for the character of Ikkyū and subsequent abbots of Daitokuji, and a passion for the tea ceremony, for which Daitokuji became a leading center. Ironically, the fact that Daitokuji was outside the *gozan* and detached from Ashikaga patronage made it more accessible to these new forces in late medieval society. The patronage of *daimyō* and tea masters was further stimulated by the example of Toyotomi Hideyoshi, who held lavish funeral ceremonies for Oda Nobunaga at Daitokuji in 1582, built the Sōken'in as a memorial sub-temple to Nobunaga, and, in 1585, awarded the monastery an income of 1,545 *koku*.[91] This allowance, which was more generous than those made to most former *gozan* monasteries, set the seal on Daitokuji's recovery and confirmed its leadership in Rinzai Zen Buddhist circles.

At the same time that Daitokuji and its sub-temples began to enjoy the sponsorship of new patrons, the monastery seems also to have found new ways to compensate, at least in part, for its diminished *shōen* holdings. Professor Sasaki Ginya has analyzed the economies of four Daitokuji *tatchū*: Ryūshōji, Nyoi'an, Yōtoku'in, and Shōgen'in. He concludes that, although these sub-temples continued to derive some of their income from consolidated *shōen*-type holdings in distant provinces until well into the sixteenth century, they also developed a variety of alternative sources of income to offset the relentless erosion of *shōen* rights by local warriors. Among the most important of these new sources of support, he argues, were supplementary rents (*kajishi*) paid by the cultivators of numerous nearby smallholdings; rents (*jishi*) from house lots in the city of Kyoto; income siphoned from the holdings of a growing number of provincial branch temples; mortuary funds (*shidōsen*), money left to a temple to pay for memorial services and used either as capital for moneylending or to accumulate rights in local smallholdings; and the sale through markets of such temple produce as rice, bamboo, or lumber.[92] The "mix" of economic activities naturally varied from *tatchū* to *tatchū* and was determined by such factors as the date of foundation and the type of patronage enjoyed by the temple. Some *tatchū* seem to have managed to subsist largely on *shōen* income until the sixteenth century. Others, like the Shōgen'in, relied heavily on mortuary funds or rental from smallholdings; or, like the Ryūshōji, on the sale of commercial produce. All, however, were obliged to respond in some degree to changing economic circumstances in which *shōen* were an increasingly

precarious and inaccessible source of support, while new opportunities were being made available by the growth of commercial
activity in and around the Kinai region. Documentary evidence
for the day-to-day economic life of the main monastery, Daitokuji
itself, in the fifteenth and sixteenth centuries is disappointingly
slight, but we can perhaps assume that it too engaged in the
acquisition of smallholding rights and in moneylending in order
to supplement its meager *shōen* interests.

MANAGEMENT OF THE ZEN MONASTIC DOMAIN

In the preceding pages, an attempt has been made to convey an
impression of the extensive, but shifting, landed base upon which
medieval Japanese *gozan* monasteries flourished and to suggest
some of the ways in which income from *shōen* and other sources
was used to sustain the day-to-day life of the monastic community. For a fuller understanding of the *gozan* economy, however, it is also necessary to take into account the management of
the monastic economy and the close economic ties that developed
between *gozan* monasteries and the Ashikaga shogunate. This, in
turn, calls for more careful scrutiny of the activities of the monks
of the eastern rank (*chiji*) than was provided in the previous
chapter.

In order to maximize their scattered landholding rights, Zen
monasteries employed a variety of strategies. Wherever possible,
for instance, they worked to convert rights in the public domain
(in *gō* and *ho*) into private, *shōen*-type holdings and to extend
control over neighboring, weakly held holdings of non-Zen Buddhist temples and absentee central proprietors.[93] Nanzenji's
rights in Mitsunari-no-*shō*, for instance, were first granted under
the title of *gō*. In 1386, the domain was designated a *shō* and
entry by public officials restricted. Three *ho* in Bizen were later
converted into *shō* with similar immunities. *Gozan* monasteries
were frequently embroiled in boundary disputes with other
religious proprietors and in many cases secured favorable decisions
from a sympathetic *bakufu*. In 1463, for instance, the *bakufu*,

after a protracted boundary dispute between Shōkokuji and
Tōji over rights in the Niimi-no-*shō* (Bitchū), until then controlled
by Tōji, recognized Shōkokuji's claims in the *shōen*. At the same
time, Tōji's holdings in the Kamikatsura-no-*shō* (Yamashiro)
and the Yano-no-*shō* (Harima) were also being subjected to
incursions from neighboring *gozan* holdings.[94]

Another means of maximizing resources was to use the *jitō
shiki* that had been granted as leverage and, with *shogunal* backing,
force a division (*shitaji chūbun*) of the *shōen* in order to establish
an integrated area of absolute control. Engakuji seems to have
attempted this in Tomita-no-*shō* in 1333. Tenryūji later converted
rights that had been granted to provide building expenses into
consolidated domain through *shitaji chūbun*. Most *gozan* monasteries probably attempted this technique at one time or another.
In this, they were simply following the example of *jitō* and other
powerful local *bushi* in physically alienating rights hitherto shared
with a proprietor. Moreover, once rights were secured, they were
hedged about and protected with immunities, of the kind mentioned above, from a wide range of extraordinary levies, thus
guaranteeing that *gozan* monasteries enjoyed the maximum possible tax revenue from their holdings.

Perhaps the most important means of maximizing income,
however, was through careful, efficient management. As we have
already seen, Zen monasteries and monk legislators attached great
importance to effective monastic organization and estate management. By the fifteenth century, some Zen monks had acquired
such reputations as building supervisors, estate overseers, administrators, and financiers that they were being "borrowed"
by monasteries of other sects to supervise rebuilding programs
or manage estates, and by the *bakufu* and *shugo* to serve as deputies (*daikan*).[95] These were all senior monks from the eastern
rank of monastery officers, usually *tsūbun* (bursars) or *tsūsu*
(priors). Since those monks appointed to office in the two ranks
retained their titles after their term in office was ended, the pool
of monks with eastern-rank titles was always much larger than the
six who happened to be in office at any particular time. According

to a Shōkokuji record for 1489, for instance, out of a total of 361 monks, 60 were *chiji*.⁹⁶ There were, therefore, always a number of experienced *tsūbun* or *tsūsu* available for duty. The incumbent *tsūbun* and *tsūsu* resided within the monastery and managed its internal affairs. Aided by the *kansu* (comptroller) and *fūsu* (assistant comptroller), they supervised the operation of the monastery finance office (*nassho*), the office of construction (*shūzōshi*), the personnel office (*shukkan*), and the registry (*mensō*). Ex-officers returned to their own sub-temples, managed the affairs of other sub-temples or branch temples, were appointed estate overseers (*shōsu*), or employed by the *bakufu* or other monasteries.

Surviving documents do not provide a detailed picture of the activities of the incumbent administrative officers or of the operation of the finance office (*nassho*) and related administrative offices.⁹⁷ They do, however, contain many scraps of information about the activities of some of those senior eastern-rank monks who were sent out as estate officials and who, having thus accumulated private fortunes, engaged in moneylending and other financial ventures.

In order to maintain the tightest possible control over their landholdings, and over the officers who managed those holdings, major Zen monasteries dispatched their own carefully selected monks to serve for limited periods as estate overseers. Unlike most monasteries of the older Buddhist schools, Zen monasteries did not delegate the management or supervision of their estates to local warriors. With *bakufu* support, they resisted pressures from secular interests to serve as their *daikan*. Zen codes specifically warned that the utilization of lay estate officials invited the destruction of the Zen monastic economy. Certainly, the eventual alienation of Zen monastic domain was precipitated by the inroads of warriors who had been employed as *daikan*.

Zen estate officials had a variety of titles, including *shōsu*, *zasshō*, and *daikan*. The term "*daikan*" was applied to agents or deputies of *shugo*, the *bakufu*, and temples and shrines of all varieties. The *zasshō* seems to have been a socially well-connected layman, resident in the capital, who represented the monastery's financial interests with the *bakufu* and advised it on economic matters. *Shōsu*, already introduced in connection with the *Ch'an-yuan Code* and in the Daitokuji statement of accounts for 1371 as characteristic within Zen monasteries, were monks, and were actively involved within *shōen*. Most of the *shōsu* mentioned in the *Inryōken nichiroku* were either *tsūbun* or *tsūsu*, reflecting the fact that the appointment was the most responsible one in the eastern rank and the awareness that the survival and prosperity of the community hinged on the integrity and effectiveness of the monks sent out as overseers. In most large *gozan* monasteries, by the fifteenth century, appointment was for five years—not renewable. In Daitokuji, where circumstances were more straitened and control tighter, appointment was for one year. The changeover, in Daitokuji, was made on the founder's memorial day, the 22nd day of the 12th month, before the abbot, the senior monks, and monastery officers, when the incumbent *shōsu* had to produce the tax income they had collected and make a detailed accounting.[98]

Since the office of *shōsu* was one of the most prestigious positions open to monks of the eastern rank, and since appointment opened the way to personal profit, there were numerous cases of squabbling among suitably qualified candidates. There were also cases in which *shōsu* tried to renew their term of office or, though rarely, to hold several such appointments concurrently.[99] Monasteries tried to resist these pressures. In order to keep some kind of rein on peculation, profiteering, and collusion with local interests, Zen regulations stressed that appointment to the office of overseer should only be made after devoted and competent service in other administrative capacities within the monastery. Monasteries occasionally recalled or dismissed *shōsu* for misbehavior, and they tried to reject, not always successfully, appeals for reappointment in the same *shōen*. In larger holdings, *shōsu* were sent in pairs for mutual accountability. In spite of these precautions, *gozan* estate overseers in distant *shōen* had considerable freedom of initiative and economic leeway: 5-year appointments with the possibility of appointment to other *shōen*, if not to the same one. In general, therefore, they had the same character as *daikan* of non-Zen *shōen* holdings. In the *Inryōken nichiroku*, *shōsu* are frequently referred to as *daikan*, and in some instances actually served as *daikan* in *bakufu*, imperial, and non-Zen monastic domain. Like secular *daikan*, too, they were rewarded for their services.[100]

The two *shōsu* of Daitokuji's Oyake-no-*shō* were each allotted 3 *kanmon* a year for their services. This was less than 1 percent of the annual tax yield of that *shōen* received by Daitokuji. Rewards to *shōsu* of prosperous *gozan* monasteries were very much more generous. An entry in the *Inryōken nichiroku* for 1489 indicates that the allotment (*tokubun*) for *shōsu* was one tenth the total income from a domain, roughly equivalent to that of a secular *daikan*.[101] In Tenryūji domains, it ran as high as one third the tax yield.[102] Even a 10 percent *tokubun* represented a substantial income for the overseer, or overseers, especially as Zen monks had no dependents. On a large domain, this kind of personal income could amount to as much as 100 *koku* (70 or more *kan*) per year. This explains the eagerness with which this office was sought.

Some of these personal profits were siphoned off by the shogunate in the form of forced loans and contributions or as gifts of cash or luxury items. Such contributions were being squeezed out of *gozan* eastern-rank monks by the early fifteenth century. They became increasingly important to the shogunate as other sources of income were reduced after the mid-fifteenth century. In 1435, for instance, 1,000 *kanmon* was demanded of Shōkokuji *chiji*. In 1459, the *bakufu* imposed a levy of 2,000 *kanmon* on the *chiji* of the Kyoto *gozan* to help pay for the relocation of the shogun's palace. In 1462, a levy of 1,000 *kanmon* for building expenses was imposed on Zen monastery bursars. In 1465, the eastern-rank monks of Shōkokuji were required to contribute to the inauguration expenses of Emperor Go-Tsuchimikado. On this occasion, Min, Sō, and Tō *tsūbun* each contributed 100 *kanmon*, Sei *tsūbun* donated 500 *kanmon*, and other members of the Shōkokuji eastern rank contributed 1,000 *kanmon* for a total from the monastery of 1,800 *kanmon*.[103]

The Ashikaga shoguns made frequent visits to *gozan* monasteries. On these occasions, in addition to Buddhist ceremonies, discussions of Zen, and the appreciation of poetry, painting, and calligraphy, it was customary for monks of the eastern rank to present gifts in kind or cash to the shogun. Cash contributions ranged from 10 *kanmon* up to several hundred *kanmon*. Other gifts were in the form of luxury gift sets—comprising, for instance, 5 kimonos, a tray, an incense container, a bolt of silk brocade, and a sheaf of paper—worth about 25 or 30 *kanmon*, and probably quickly converted into cash through the office of the *sōroku*. A single visit might produce 100 *kanmon*. By the mid-fifteenth century, it is clear from the *Inryōken nichiroku*, such visits had become almost weekly occasions. In some years, as many as 50 or 60 gifts a year were made, with a total value of several thousand *kanmon*.[104] Together with the income derived from the appointment of *gozan* abbots, mentioned in the preceding chapter, these forced contributions and gifts from eastern-rank monks became a vital, almost regular, item of shogunal income, as important to the shogunate as the 6,000 *kanmon* derived from *bakufu* levies on *sakaya* and *dosō* (1393) or the 10,000 or so *kanmon* derived occasionally from foreign trade. Wealthy non-Zen monasteries also received shogunal visits and were called upon for contributions. The Kyoto *gozan*, however, as officially sponsored monasteries, suffered the heaviest exactions.

To put their profits to work, and to compensate for contributions to shoguns, those *tsūbun* and *tsūsu* who had accumulated capital during their terms of office as estate overseers frequently engaged in moneylending. The career of Sei *tsūbun* of Shōkokuji, who contributed 500 *kanmon* to the *bakufu* in 1465, is probably fairly typical.[105] After serving as overseer in several Shōkokuji domains, he was employed, in 1461, as a *daikan* in *bakufu* domain. It is unclear when his moneylending activities began, but in 1459 he loaned money to a Kyoto temple, the Shōbai'in, and subsequently made loans to other temples and nobles. The pages of the *Inryōken nichiroku* provide the names of, and fragments of information about, at least half a dozen Zen *tsūbun* or *tsūsu* from Kyoto monasteries who used inherited wealth or the proceeds of estate management as capital for moneylending ventures. Although interest rates were high, ranging between 3 and 8 percent per month,[106] there were plenty of temporarily hard-pressed temples, nobles, warriors, townsmen, and even peasants, anxious to avail themselves of the service.

In addition to the private moneylending activities of individual monks, many Zen monasteries engaged in a more public form of moneylending using "mortuary contributions" (*shidōsen*) donated by monastery supporters to pay for memorial ceremonies for deceased relatives. These small contributions were pooled and either loaned directly to applicants or entrusted to merchants or warehouse proprietors (*dosō*) to be loaned by them on the monastery's behalf. This kind of lending of mortuary contributions was common in Chinese Buddhist monasteries from the T'ang dynasty. In Japan it was most prevalent in Zen monasteries, though not unknown in other religious institutions, and was widespread by the fifteenth century. Although there is no evidence that the Kamakura *gozan* engaged in this type of moneylending, their Kyoto counterparts were actively involved, and some sub-temples, such as the Shōgen'in, Daitokuji, relied heavily on interest payments from *shidōsen* loans to support their communities. Compared with the interest rates of between 5 and 10 percent demanded on private loans made by *tsūbun*, interest rates on *shidōsen* were relatively low, 2 or 3 percent per month being common. Since over a year, however, this amounted to well over a 20 percent return on the loan, it is hardly surprising that this enterprise should have been a source of friction between Zen monasteries and their debtors.[107] Daitokuji documents make frequent references to *shidōsen*. In 1502, for instance, the Shinjuan sub-temple made a grant of 100 *kanmon* to Daitokuji on behalf of a certain Sōrin Zenmon, a Sakai merchant, who stipulated that the money was to be used as *shidōsen*, with half the interest accruing to be given to the abbot, the other half to be used to provide vegetarian feasts for the monks officiating at the annual memorial services for Sōrin.[108] At 2 percent a month the abbot would have received 12 *kanmon* a year from the donation of this one patron.

Although the evidence is inconclusive, it is possible that mortuary funds and monastery-sponsored moneylending activities played a relatively more prominent role in the Zen monastic economy as income from land, especially from distant *shōen* holdings, was reduced after the mid-fifteenth century. Since *shidōsen* loans enjoyed the tacit recognition and protection of the Muromachi *bakufu*, where surplus cash was available, this kind of enterprise was a safe and profitable way of putting it to work.

There was considerable demand for *shidōsen* loans. Such activities, however, while they contributed to monastic prosperity, also made Zen monasteries the target of additional levies and loans to the *bakufu* and exposed them to attack in the uprisings (*ikki*) that jolted Japanese society in the fifteenth and sixteenth centuries. Leaders of these risings frequently had among their slogans demands for relief, or *tokusei*, from interest payments due, or overdue, on *shidōsen* loans. The fact that in Kyoto the principal targets of such *tokusei* uprisings were pawnshops (*dosō*), *sake* dealers, and Zen monasteries is a clear indication that, in the popular mind, the Kyoto Zen institution was tarred with the same brush as other commercial moneylending enterprises.

Whenever *tokusei* riots erupted, the *bakufu* was torn between the temptation to buy order by canceling outstanding debts and the desire to protect the substantial income it derived in levies and loans from *sakaya, dosō*, and *gozan* monasteries, an income that would naturally be reduced were they to suffer financial loss. After 1440, the *bakufu* felt obliged to promulgate a large number of debt moratoria edicts. Thirteen were issued in the reign of Ashikaga Yoshimasa alone. Although these laws recognized the reduction or cancellation of debts to pawnbrokers and *sake* merchants, they usually specifically excluded Zen monastic *shidōsen* from cancellation. The *tokusei* law of 1441, for instance, protected *shidōsen* while the interest rate did not exceed 2 percent a month. The exclusion of *shidōsen* from debt moratoria can be seen as yet another indication of the economic importance of the *gozan* to the *bakufu*. *Bakufu* efforts to protect *gozan* monasteries from the social repercussions of usury, however, were not always successful. Even before the depradations of the Ōnin War, Tenryūji, Shōkokuji, and other leading Kyoto *gozan* monasteries had suffered damage at the hands of armed bands of peasants and *bushi* seeking direct redress for their grievances.

The *gozan* and other Zen monasteries were less directly involved in the domestic commercial activities of the age than some of the older Buddhist centers like Enryakuji and Kōfukuji which controlled *sakaya* and *dosō* and sponsored guilds (*za*) and markets. It would be misleading, however, to suggest that the *gozan* remained aloof or detached from the growing commercial activity of the Muromachi period. While Zen monasteries may have produced their own rice and vegetable produce, they were not entirely self-sufficient, and such commodities as building materials, robes, paper, luxury commodities, and artwork and sculpture must sometimes have been acquired commercially. Some of the several hundred *sakaya, dosō*, and *za* in the capital were clustered at the gates of such *gozan* monasteries as Tenryūji, Shōkokuji, and Tōfukuji and catered to their needs. Rinsenji and Tenryūji had a thriving *sake*-brewing industry in their neighborhood. By the fifteenth century, regular markets were being held in some of the *shōen* controlled by Nanzenji, Rinsenji, or Daitokuji where surplus monastic produce could be sold. Although detailed evidence is lacking, we can suggest that the *gozan* network contributed in some measure at least to the commercial vitality of Kyoto and the surrounding provinces in the later medieval period.

One form of commercial activity in which some *gozan* monks and monasteries were particularly conspicuous was the China trade. The trading expeditions sent to China in the fourteenth century to raise funds for the restoration of Kenchōji and the building of Tenryūji have already been mentioned. The considerable profits derived from these two ventures—the Tenryūji vessels yielded 5,000 *kanmon* for the monastery—may have encouraged Ashikaga Yoshimitsu to develop his positive foreign trade policy. They also sparked the interest of Kyoto Zen monasteries in this potentially lucrative enterprise. Zen monks acted as the envoys-in-chief of most, if not all, of the 19 trading missions sent to China by the *bakufu*, the Ōuchi, and the Hosokawa between 1401 and 1547. Vessels sponsored by Shōkokuji were included in the 1432, 1434, and 1436 ventures. Three Tenryūji vessels were included among 9 that sailed in 1451.[109]

According to the Boshi nyūminki (1468), a record of the mission that set sail in 1465 led by the Zen monk Ten'yo Seikei, abbot of Kenninji, that particular expedition comprised 3 vessels— one sponsored by the *bakufu*, one by the Ōuchi, and one by the Hosokawa. Ten'yo, as envoy-in-chief, traveled on the *bakufu* vessel. He was assisted by 2 monks, a *tsūbun* and a *tsūsu*, from the eastern rank of Shōkokuji. According to the diary, there were more than 80 crew members, monks, and "passengers" aboard. Thirty-six passengers were listed, on the basis of the scale of their investment in the voyage, in two groups of 18: a 1,000-*kanmon* group and a 500-*kanmon* group. Since these "passengers" included many members of Hyōgo merchant houses, they were almost certainly merchants. Among them were 8 monks, most of them from the eastern rank of Shōkokuji.[110] This leaves little room for doubt that Zen monks of certain favored and wealthy Kyoto *gozan* monasteries were actively engaged in the Ming trade as merchants, not simply as diplomats and guides. They may have acted officially on behalf of their monastery or the *bakufu*, but no doubt made substantial profits for themselves in the process. Some of these profits were used to acquire Chinese luxury items (*karamono*); others provided capital for money-lending ventures.

Successful participation in the China trade, as with other financial activities of eastern-rank monks, ultimately depended upon the authority of the *gozan* as an institution and on the active support of the *bakufu*. When these faltered, as they did in the late fifteenth century, Zen monasteries were excluded from the Ming trade. By the close of the fifteenth century the missions to Ming were dominated by the Ōuchi and Hosokawa families rather than the *bakufu*. Zen monks continued to be used as envoys, but the profits of the trade were skimmed off by the *daimyō* sponsors and the merchants associated with them.

Summarizing the foregoing rather extended discussion of the economic life of the medieval *gozan*, we can, I think, make the following points. First, the *gozan* economy, like that of most other medieval Buddhist institutions, was based upon the possession of extensive *shōen* rights, mostly *jitō shiki*, scattered throughout Japan. When we take into account the fact that a large metropolitan *gozan* monastery might have had as many as 20 or 30 *shōen* interests, a *jissatsu*-rank monastery between 10 and 20, and a *shozan*-rank monastery 3 or 4, and bear in mind that Zen sub-temples (*tatchū*) and branch temples (*matsuji*) also had landed interests, then it is evident that at its zenith the several-hundred-strong *gozan* network was, collectively, one of the largest landed proprietors in late medieval Japan, with an annual income of tens of thousands of *kanmon* in cash and *koku* in rice. These holdings, however, were acquired at a time when the landed holdings (*shōen*) of the central proprietors, nobles, temples, and shrines, were being subjected to increasing intrusion and erosion by local warriors. Although some of the more powerful *gozan* monasteries managed to cling to some of their *shōen* rights, and to derive part of their income from *shōen*, until the land reforms of Hideyoshi in the late sixteenth century, on the whole, distant *gozan shōen* holdings were drastically reduced during the disturbances of the Sengoku period. In an effort to replace declining income from *shōen* proprietorship, Zen monasteries tried to accumulate, by gift or purchase, large numbers of rights to de facto rent (*kajishi*) from the cultivators of small holdings in the vicinity of the monastery. Many Japanese medievalists have pointed out the phenomenon whereby, during the period of *shōen* dissolution, between the fourteenth and sixteenth centuries, wealthy peasant cultivators and local samurai began to buy rights to receive rents from other cultivators, becoming, in effect, small

landlords.[111] From the rather fragmentary documents relating to
medieval Zen monastic landholding arrangements, it is clear that
gozan monasteries, Daitokuji, and their sub-temples, like the
monasteries of the older Buddhist schools, were active in accumulating such rental rights. Since, however, the rental from
such plots averaged only about 10 *mon* per *tan*, and the average
size of a single "holding" was usually a few *tan* at most, a monastery would have had to acquire hundreds of such holdings in
order to derive an income equivalent to that from even a small
shōen interest. It is, therefore, unlikely that *kajishi* rental income
offset the losses sustained with the erosion of *shōen* proprietory
rights.

Second, Zen monasteries, like the older Nara and Kyoto monasteries, tried to take advantage of new opportunities offered by
the diffusion of coinage and the development of domestic commercial activity and foreign commerce between the fourteenth
and sixteenth centuries. Income from moneylending, ventures
in the Ming trade, and the sale of surplus produce all contributed
to the great wealth and cultural vitality of the Kyoto *gozan*
monasteries in the mid-fifteenth century. Although Daitokuji
was excluded from direct participation in the Ming trade, it may,
later, have benefited indirectly by helping to finance ventures
by Sakai merchants. Zen monasteries, however, do not seem to
have established strong footholds in such areas of commercial
activity engaged in by other non-Zen Buddhist monasteries as
guild and market sponsorship, or the control of strategically
placed toll barriers. Although the gradual erosion during these
centuries of their *shōen* income was a chronic and debilitating
problem for medieval Buddhist monasteries, Zen and non-Zen
alike, the reduction of land-tax income (*nengu*) was at least partially mitigated by active involvement in moneylending and other
forms of commercial activity. However, while these commercial
activities were important in sustaining the economic influence of
the Buddhist institution, it is unlikely that they were sufficiently
extensive to compensate fully for dwindling estate income. Nor
did Buddhist monasteries have unrestricted access to commercial

enterprises. The Ashikaga *bakufu* and *sengoku daimyō* worked to loosen the control of Enryakuji and other powerful monasteries over warehouses, guilds, transportation facilities, and toll barriers. In the case of the *gozan* network, quasi-commercial activities were most conspicuous in the higher-ranking Kyoto *gozan*, and at the apogee of their prosperity in the first half of the fifteenth century. The destruction of Zen monastic buildings in the Ōnin War, the curtailment of income from distant landholdings, and the exclusion of *gozan* monasteries from active participation in the Ming trade after the mid-fifteenth century all contributed to reduce the capital available for moneylending or the accumulation of *kajishi* rights. Without more complete data for the Sengoku period, we can only assume that these alternative or supplementary economic activities played a much larger relative role in the shrinking Zen monastic economy of the late fifteenth and sixteenth centuries than they had in the solidly *shōen*-based economy of the thirteenth, fourteenth, and early fifteenth centuries.

Third, it should be evident that medieval Zen monastic economies were thoroughly and scrupulously managed, that Zen monasteries set high standards of administrative and economic organization, and that some monks of the eastern rank took a frank, professional interest in the accumulation of wealth for their monasteries or sub-temples and for themselves. In this they were encouraged by Zen monastic codes which provided for an efficient administrative structure and placed a premium on the efficient management of meager resources. The eastern rank *tsūbun* and *tsūsu* or *gozan* monasteries were adept in exploiting the opportunities presented by more than a century of generous Ashikaga patronage and by the growth of domestic commerce and foreign trade. The accumulation of wealth by these monks laid the financial foundations for the rich material culture of the fourteenth and fifteenth century *gozan* expressed in lofty ceremonial buildings, numerous *tatchū*, carefully landscaped dry-stone gardens, ink-paintings, tea rooms, and fine ceramics. While many eastern-rank monks may have remembered that their primary aim was the rigorous search for personal enlightenment through meditation and that their administrative functions were intended only to provide an environment in which they and their fellows in the community could devote themselves wholeheartedly to the pursuit of Zen, there were other eastern-rank monks who neglected Zen practice and became little more than merchants in the robes of monks. In this sense, it seems reasonable to suggest that the very expertise and success of *gozan* administrators contributed to the sapping of the vigor of Zen practice and to the secularization of *gozan* monasteries which became pronounced in the fifteenth century.

Finally, it must be stressed that the economic fortunes of the *gozan* monasteries, and of Daitokuji and Myōshinji, were tied closely to the political fortunes of their principal patrons. In this respect, Zen monasteries were less independent than such older Buddhist centers as Enryakuji, Kōyasan, Tōji, and Negoro or such new religious forces as Honganji. While the Hōjō regents and Ashikaga shoguns were in the ascendant, *gozan* monasteries enjoyed donations of buildings and lands, fiscal and physical protection, exemptions from many taxes and levies, and a privileged participation in trade and moneylending. However, as the Ashikaga shogunate declined politically and economically after the assassination of Yoshinori in 1441, it leaned more heavily on the *gozan* for financial support, canceled many of the exemptions and privileges, treated *gozan* landholdings as its own domain, and pressed the monks of the eastern rank for gifts and loans until their coffers were exhausted. Moreover, the weakening of Ashikaga authority over the country exposed central and provincial *gozan*, *jissatsu*, and *shozan* monasteries to the full force of the storms of the Sengoku period. The uncertainty confronting the *gozan* system was compounded by the fact that many provincial *shugo*, who had been the principal patrons of *jissatsu* and *shozan*, were toppled by local warriors, many of whom had little sympathy with the centralized, Ashikaga-sponsored *gozan* system and had established close personal ties with Zen monks of non-*gozan* lineages. The Sengoku period was, thus, a painful century for the *gozan* network, as monasteries were pillaged and burned and monastic economies severely reduced. It did not, however, see the demise of the system, and a partial recovery was made under the patronage of Toyotomi Hideyoshi in the late sixteenth century and Tokugawa Ieyasu in the early seventeenth century, for both of whom *gozan* prelates acted as diplomatic and cultural advisors in much the same way as they had for the Hōjō regents and Ashikaga shoguns. Nanzenji, Shōkokuji, and Tōfukuji were awarded domains with assessed values of 600, 1,320 and 1,800 *koku* respectively by Hideyoshi,[112] who also contributed generously to the restoration of their monastic buildings. Although economic recovery did not necessarily bring spiritual renewal to the great Zen monasteries, the leading *gozan* monasteries remained substantial institutions in the Tokugawa period. Shifting currents of patronage were no less crucial to the prosperity of the Daitokuji and Myōshinji lineages. Deprived of the favor of the Ashikaga and excluded from the *gozan* system, at least in part because of their sympathies for Go-Daigo and the Southern court, these two monasteries, despite some destruction of buildings in the Ōnin War, came into their own during the sixteenth century under the patronage of Sakai merchants and *sengoku daimyō*. By the end of the sixteenth century, they were as wealthy, influential, and active as any of the major *gozan* monasteries. The late fifteenth and sixteenth centuries also witnessed the rapid, nationwide expansion of the various branches of Sōtō Zen, largely under the patronage of *sengoku daimyō*.[113]

EIGHT

Conclusion

The aim of this book has been to present Zen Buddhism, especially the *gozan* branches, as a vigorous and pervasive institution in medieval Japanese society. One striking feature of the Zen monastic institution in medieval Japan was its scale. The 3 tiers of the *gozan* network of officially designated monasteries, at their zenith, included more than 300 monasteries, ranging in size from small communities of less than a hundred monks to metropolitan complexes with several thousand inhabitants. In addition, there were sub-temples and branch temples attached to the main monasteries; and by the fifteenth century these may have numbered as many as five thousand. Outside the official *gozan* system were the so-called "provincial temples" (*rinka*), which included the Rinzai monasteries of Daitokuji and Myōshinji and their branches, as well as several thousand Sōtō school temples. Although few records for them survive, there were also a substantial number of Zen nunneries.

These new Zen monasteries and nunneries seem to have been filled largely by the sons and daughters of the newly dominant warrior class, with a sprinkling of nobles and, towards the end of the period, a few offspring of wealthy townsmen. On the basis of the close ties established from the outset between Zen monks and warrior leaders, Zen monasteries were quickly seen as providing an acceptable career channel for *bushi* children. Some

individuals may have entered the Zen cloister on their own voli-
tion, as a result of their personal search for enlightenment; many
more, however, were placed there in childhood by family heads.
Although the relationship has not been analysed, it seems likely
that Zen cloisters swelled in response to an increasing acceptance
of unigeniture in warrior households during this period. Zen
monasteries offered excellent intellectual training as well as
spiritual discipline. With the nationwide articulation of the *gozan*
network, the children of provincial warrior families could aspire
to become influential Zen prelates in the capital. Birth obviously
carried weight in the *gozan* as in other areas of medieval society,
and, in time, the gradations of secular society tended to be reflected in Zen monastic hierarchies; but, still, the offspring of
warrior families stood a better chance of attaining eminence
within the *gozan* or *rinka* monasteries than they did of rising to
the top in one of the older Buddhist centers.

The medieval Japanese Zen monastic system was, of course,
a direct import from Sung and Yuan dynasty China. The principal
models were the great Ch'an centers of southern China headed
by the Five Mountains of the Hangchow region. These Chinese
monasteries served as the womb of both Japanese Rinzai and
Sōtō Zen. Although we do not yet have as detailed a picture as
we would like of Ch'an sectarian development and of Chinese
Buddhist monasticism in general during these centuries, it is
clear that Japanese monks and their secular patrons sought to
transmit Ch'an monastic life faithfully and fully to Japan. The
process of replication was facilitated by the existence of detailed
Ch'an monastic codes and by the willingness of fully trained
Chinese monks to come to Japan and help set the institution on
its feet. There was, until Musō's generation, a constant coming
and going of Chinese and Japanese monks, and the latest Ch'an
regulations, texts, and practices were quickly introduced to
Japan. Thus, Japanese Zen could develop in step with developments in continental Ch'an monasteries. This close contact with
Chinese monasteries intensified the differences between Zen monastic life and organization and that of the established Buddhist

schools in Japan. Metropolitan Zen maintained an exotic flavor, and Zen monasteries, especially the major *gozan* monasteries, remained centers of Chinese religion, learning, and culture in Japan. More accurately, they served as conduits through which the ideas and interests of the Chinese elite flowed into the upper reaches of Japanese society.

But at the same time, while maintaining contact with China, medieval Japanese Zen monasteries also showed signs of accommodation with the society in which they had taken root. This accommodation was probably most obvious in the transformation of Sōtō Zen practice in the generations after Dōgen, but it was also evident in *gozan* Zen. The strong influence of Shingon Buddhism, the proliferation of sub-temples, the interest of some monks in Japanese poetry as well as Chinese, and the political and economic manipulation of the *gozan* by warrior-rulers were only some of the ways in which the pressures of Japanese society were reflected in *gozan* monasteries.

As a new arrival on the Japanese religious scene in the thirteenth century, Zen encountered determined opposition from the established Buddhist schools, especially the Enryakuji branch of Tendai. The Nanzenji Gate incident in the late fourteenth century was only one in a series of clashes between Tendai and Zen monks. Because of its alien character, the novelty of Zen teachings, the unfamiliarity of Zen-related Chinese culture, and the opposition of vested religious interests in Japan, Zen teachings gained ground only slowly at first, through an initial process of accommodation with familiar teachings and practices. It is very possible that Zen would not have developed independently in Japan had it not found powerful protectors, especially the Hōjō and the Ashikaga, who were prepared to invite Chinese monks to Japan, to build and endow monasteries, and to promote the diffusion of the sect.

The motives of these patrons were complex. With few exceptions, they do not seem to have given themselves to Zen as a religious experience. At least as important as any search for Zen enlightenment was the lure of Chinese learning and culture made available by Zen monks and monasteries. This was a particularly

important factor in the patronage of Rinzai *gozan* Zen by powerful warrior leaders who had military power but were uncertain
of their cultural legitimacy. That Zen was stable and disciplined,
upholding the traditional monastic life and rule, gave it added
appeal in an age when the older forms of monastic Buddhism
were lax and unruly and newer forms were socially volatile.

The commonly held view that Zen developed in Japan because
of its intrinsic spiritual appeal to the Japanese warrior mentality
does not go far towards explaining the development of sectarian,
institutional Sung-style Zen in medieval Japan. Although Zen
monks depended heavily on warrior patronage, relatively few
warriors, even the most educated, displayed a very deep understanding of Zen or a sustained commitment to *zazen*. The undiluted Chinese teachings certainly did not appeal to the mass of
semi-literate or illiterate warriors, who were more attracted to the
simpler teachings of Ippen or Nichiren. Popular diffusion of Zen,
whether Rinzai or Sōtō, was only achieved by the dilution of
traditional Zen teachings and monastic practices with more
readily comprehensible elements of traditional Japanese religious
belief, or by the provision of funeral ceremonies and memorial
services.

Although, as is clear from the regulations they issued, there
was a considerable degree of continuity between Hōjō patronage
of Zen and that of Go-Daigo and the Ashikaga, the *gozan* developed
most rapidly in the mid-fourteenth century because of the efforts
of Musō Soseki and Ashikaga Tadayoshi, who combined a deep
personal interest in Zen with the political aim of encouraging the
spread of Rinzai Zen as a counterweight to the influence of the
older schools and as a means of acquiring and exerting influence
over local *shugo* and *jitō* who were the principal provincial patrons
of Zen. Moreover, the building of Ankokuji and Rishōtō was not
simply an expression of piety for those who had died in dynastic
wars. It was part of a carefully conceived policy designed to spread
the influence of the *gozan* Zen lineages and of the Ashikaga, with
whom they were intimately connected, into every province in
Japan. Ashikaga Takauji, who had a more limited understanding of

Zen, but great personal regard for Musō, supported his brother's policies. After their estrangement and death, the policy was allowed to lapse by later shoguns. By then, however, the *gozan* was solidly established as the most influential, if not the most powerful, segment of the Buddhist institution.

Although *gozan* Zen was made up of many different lineages, *gozan* monasteries were dominated by the Shōichi and Musō lineages. As a legacy of the close ties between Musō and Ashikaga Takauji, the most important offices and abbacies in the *gozan* network went to monks of the Musō line. The principal monasteries and sub-temples of that school were granted privileges and exemptions within the official system. And it was to followers of Musō in particular that the Ashikaga shoguns turned for advice on religious, economic, and political matters.

Unlike many of the monasteries of the established Buddhist sects, Zen monasteries, closely regulated by their secular patrons, never developed independent military power. Moreover, their landed base was weak and completely dependent on the prosperity and generosity of their patrons. This twofold weakness was exposed during the fifteenth century when, with the Ashikaga no longer able to provide effective protection, *gozan* Zen domains suffered intrusion and alienation of property. In less than a hundred years, the larger *gozan* monasteries slipped from affluence to near destitution. As their landed base was eroded, some Kyoto Zen monasteries turned to foreign trade, to the sale of certificates to the title of abbot, and to moneylending, in an effort to make ends meet. Indulgence in moneylending, in turn, made the *gozan* monasteries the targets of rioters and looters during the Ōnin War. Daitokuji and Myōshinji, which had been excluded from Ashikaga favor, escaped the ravages attendant upon Ashikaga decline and flourished under the patronage of new social groups, including *sengoku daimyō*, Sakai merchants, and tea masters. It can be argued, however, that this growth, too, had as much to do with the purveying of cultural attainments as it had to do with the encouragement of religious insight.

Looking inside the Zen monastery, we have seen a disciplined monastic life lived under distinctive regulations. Zen monasteries had their own special organization and bureaucracy made up of two ranks of officers under the abbot. Some monks of the eastern rank developed such financial and administrative skills that they were employed by non-Zen monasteries or by the *bakufu*. Some of those monks who were appointed to manage Zen monastic domains or who engaged in foreign commerce were able to accumulate private fortunes which provided both the capital for moneylending and the basis for forced loans for an increasingly indigent shogunate. These private economic activities were also curtailed with the weakening of the Ashikaga and the loss of Zen monastic domain.

While it is impossible to measure the quality of Zen monastic life in China and Japan, there are indications that the material prosperity, social influence, and cultural ethos of the *gozan* monasteries dulled the religious spirit of their inhabitants. Examination of Zen monastic codes indicates that Zen monastic life was still vital in the Northern Sung dynasty monasteries in China and in the new Zen monasteries in Kamakura and early Muromachi period Japan, but that, with time, it became steadily more formalized and lax. The Zen monastery was a human institution, and it was inevitable that there should be problems of the kind discussed by Musō in the *Rinsen kakun*. By the fifteenth century, however, abuses such as buying *hinpotsu* certificates, or certificates of appointment as abbot or estate overseer, which Musō cannot have conceived of, were common practice in *gozan* monasteries and provided justification for Ikkyū's bitter criticisms of those who entered the monastic life for material ends. This problem was compounded in Japan by the proliferation of subtemples. These hastened the decline of the traditional monks' hall, the scene of strenuous communal *zazen*, and encouraged the development of literary and artistic coteries. It remains a matter of debate whether the cultural activities of *gozan* monks and their secular associates, which marked one of the vital peaks of Japanese cultural history, did not also imply the death of Zen as a religious experience. On the other hand, perhaps we should beware of dismissing the entire *gozan* institution as totally degenerate and secularized. Even in its worst days, there were, no doubt, monks who devoted their energies to meditation, and through it found deepened spiritual awareness.

Notes

Bibliography

Glossary

Index

Notes

PREFACE

1. To be accurate, it is important to mention the pioneering essays of Kan'ichi Asakawa in *Land and Society in Medieval Japan* (Tokyo, 1965) and to note that, in recent years, there has been a revival of interest in medieval Japanese religious institutions by American scholars. Valuable contributions have been made by David L. Davis, *"Ikki* in Late Medieval Japan," in John Hall and Jeffrey Mass, eds., *Medieval Japan: Essays in Institutional History* (New Haven, 1974), pp. 221-247; James H. Foard, "Ippen Shōnin and Popular Buddhism in Kamakura Japan," (PhD dissertation, Stanford University, 1977); Elizabeth Satō, "The Early Development of the Shōen," *Ibid.,* pp. 91-108; Michael Solomon, "Rennyo and the Rise of Honganji in Muromachi Japan," (PhD dissertation, Columbia University, 1972); and Stanley Weinstein, "Rennyo and the Shinshū Revival," in John W. Hall and Toyoda Takeshi, eds., *Japan in the Muromachi Age* (California, 1977), pp. 331-358. There is, however, still much to be done. The Nichiren (Lotus) and Ji (Timely) schools of Buddhism have received little attention, and the older schools of Nara and Heian Buddhism, which were still active through the medieval period, have been ignored. Sōtō Zen, too, deserves closer scrutiny. The interaction of Buddhist institutions of all kinds with warriors and nobles, their involvement in commerce, and their contributions to the diffusion of learning also merit investigation. Studies of individual medieval monasteries and their organization and sketches of lesser known, but influential, monks, their social origins, and religious and cultural interests would also help to fill in what is still a very fragmentary picture.

2. The reading of the characters for this monk's name preferred by Japanese specialists in the history of Zen Buddhism is Yōsai. Since, however, he is now firmly established in the Western literature on Zen as Eisai, he will be referred to as Eisai throughout this book.

3. Heinrich Dumoulin, *A History of Zen Buddhism*, translated from the German by Paul Peachey, (New York, 1963; Boston, paperback, 1963), provides a very readable survey of the development of the Zen schools. For a detailed bibliography of works on all aspects of Zen up to 1975, see Patricia Armstrong Vessie, *Zen Buddhism: A Bibliography of Books and Articles in English 1892–1975* (Ann Arbor, 1976). Hirose Ryōkō in *Rekishi kōron 10, 1977, Zen to chūsei bunka*, pp. 130–136, gives a brief, but very helpful bibliography introducing the most important materials for the study of medieval Japanese Zen.

4. A comprehensive listing of the Ch'an monasteries believed to have been included in the various tiers of the Sung dynasty Five Mountains network is provided by Imaeda Aishin, *Chūsei Zenshū-shi no kenkyū* (Tokyo, 1970), pp. 143–146. There are, to my knowledge, no detailed Western-language studies of Ch'an Buddhism as a religious institution in Sung and Yuan dynasty China, and few references to the Chinese Five Mountains. For information on Ch'an in the Ming dynasty, the reader is referred to Kristin Yü Greenblatt, "Yun-ch'i Chu-hung: the Career of a Ming Buddhist Monk" (PhD dissertation, Columbia University, 1973).

5. Sakurai Kageo (Keiyū), *Nanzenji-shi* (Kyoto, 1940); Tamamura Takeji and Inoue Zenjō, *Engakuji-shi* (Tokyo, 1964).

6. Haga Kōshirō, *Chūsei Zenrin no gakumon oyobi bungaku ni kansuru kenkyū* (Tokyo, 1956).

7. H. Paul Varley, "Ashikaga Yoshimitsu and the World of Kitayama: Social Change and Shogunal Patronage in Early Muromachi Japan"; John M. Rosenfield, "The Unity of the Three Creeds: A Theme in Japanese Ink Painting of the Fifteenth Century"; and Toshihide Akamatsu and Philip Yampolsky, "Muromachi Zen and the Gozan System." All three essays are included in Hall and Toyoda, eds., *Japan in the Muromachi Age.*

8. Marian Ury, *Poems of the Five Mountains: an Introduction to the Literature of the Zen Monasteries* (Tokyo, 1977); reviewed by Martin Collcutt, "Gozan Literature: the Practice of Zen and the Pursuit of Poetry," *Monumenta Nipponica* 33.2:201–205 (Summer 1978).

9. Jan Fontein and Money L. Hickman, *Zen Painting and Calligraphy* (Boston, 1970); Yoshiaki Shimizu and Carolyn Wheelwright, eds., *Japanese Ink Paintings from American Collections: The Muromachi Period* (Princeton, 1976).

10. The single exception is the essay by Akamatsu and Yampolsky cited in note 7, above.

11. For works in English on the spiritual and cultural dimensions of Zen, see Vessie, *Zen Buddhism.*

12. *The Rinsen kakun.* This code is translated and discussed below in Chapter Four.

INTRODUCTION

1. These figures are taken from Kawasaki Yōsuke and Kasahara Kazuo, eds., *Taikei Nihon-shi sōsho,* Vol. 18, *Shūkyō-shi* (Tokyo, 1966), p. 219; and Kanaoka Shūyū, ed., *Bukkyō shūha jiten* (Tokyo, 1974), pp. 14, 136, 270.

2. Descriptions of *sōdō* life will be found in Daisetsu Teitarō Suzuki, *The Training of the Zen Buddhist Monk* (Kyoto, 1934); Eshin Nishimura, *Unsui: A Diary of Zen Monastic Life,* ed., Bardwell L. Smith (Honolulu, 1973); Jon Covell and Sōbin Yamada, *Zen at Daitokuji* (Tokyo, 1974); and Janwillem Van de Wetering, *The Empty Mirror* (Boston, 1976). For a fuller listing, see Vessie, *Zen Buddhism*, pp. 74–76.

3. Imaeda Aishin, *Zenshū no rekishi* (Tokyo, 1962), pp. 1–7.

4. Edwin O. Reischauer, trans., *Ennin's Diary: The Record of a Pilgrimage to China in Search of the Law* (New York, 1955), p. 44. Note: Chinese characters included in the text of Professor Reischauer's translation have been omitted in this quotation but are included in the glossary.

5. Reischauer, *Ennin's Diary*, p. 210.

6. Kenneth Ch'en, *Buddhism in China: A Historical Survey* (Princeton, 1964), pp. 389–408. For an introduction to the institutional development of Buddhism in China, see also: Erik Zürcher, *The Buddhist Conquest of China* (Leiden, 1958); Kenneth Ch'en, *The Chinese Transformation of Buddhism* (Princeton, 1973); Dennis Twitchett, "The Monasteries and China's Economy in Medieval Times," *Bulletin of the School of Oriental and African Studies*, 19.3:526–549 (1957). A helpful bibliography of Western studies of Chinese Buddhism up to 1970 is provided by Laurence G. Thompson, *Studies in Chinese Religion: A Comprehensive and Classified Bibliography of Publications in English, French and German through 1970* (California, 1976). For articles on Chinese Buddhism published in Japanese between 1956 and 1969, see Ryūkoku Daigaku Bukkyōgaku Kenkyūshitsu, ed., *Bukkyōgaku kankei zasshi ronbun bunrui mokuroku* (Kyoto, 1971).

7. William Theodore de Bary, Yoshito Hakeda, and Philip Yampolsky, eds., *The Buddhist Tradition* (New York, 1969), pp. 52–72.

8. On Bodhidharma and the early history of Ch'an in China, see Sekiguchi Shindai, *Daruma no kenkyū* (Tokyo, 1967) and Yanagida Seizan, *Daruma no goroku, Zen no goroku 1* (Tokyo, 1969), pp. 1–21. The reader is also referred to a forthcoming volume in the Berkeley Buddhist Studies Series: Lewis Lancaster and Whalen Lai, eds., *The Early History of Ch'an in China and Tibet.*

9. On Tao-an, see Zürcher, *Buddhist Conquest of China*, pp. 184–197; Leon Hurvitz, *Chih-i, Mélanges Chinois et Bouddhiques 12* (Bruxelles, 1962), p. 318; Sekiguchi Shindai, *Tendai shikan no kenkyū* (Tokyo, 1969), pp. 271–374; Stanley Weinstein, "Imperial Patronage in the Formation of

T'ang Buddhism," in Arthur F. Wright and Denis Twitchett, eds., *Perspectives on the T'ang* (New Haven, 1973), p. 276.

10. Yanagida Seizan, "Chūgoku Zenshū-shi," in Nishitani Keiji et al., eds., *Kōza Zen* (Tokyo, 1967), 3, 28.

11. This dispute is discussed by Philip Yampolsky, *The Platform Sutra of the Sixth Patriarch* (New York, 1967), pp. 1-57.

12. On Lin-chi and the development of *kōan*, see Yanagida Seizan, "Chūgoku Zenshū-shi," pp. 88-104; Furuta Shōkin, *Rinzai-roku no shisō* (Tokyo, 1967), pp. 102-113; and Yanagida Seizan and Umehara Takeshi, *Mu no tankyū, Bukkyō no shisō* 7 (Tokyo, 1969), pp. 178-187.

13. The role of Pai-chang in the development of the Zen monastic rule and monastic system is discussed in Chapter Four.

14. Shiina Hiroo, "Shotō Zensha no ritsu'in kyojū ni tsuite," *Indogaku Bukkyōgaku kenkyū* 17.2:325-327 (1969).

15. Yanagida Seizan, "Chūgoku Zenshū-shi," p. 27.

16. Satō Tatsugen, "Hokusō sōrin no keizai seikatsu," *Komazawa daigaku Bukkyōgakubu kiyō* 25:14-28 (1967).

17. An annotated edition of this code is available: Kagamishima Genryū, Satō Tatsugen, and Kosaka Kiyū, eds., *Yakuchū Zen'on shingi* (Tokyo, 1972).

18. Brief outlines of the Chinese Five Mountains system are given by Imaeda Aishin, *Chūsei Zenshū-shi no kenkyū*, pp. 141-146; and Yanagida Seizan, "Chūgoku Zenshū-shi," pp. 95-97. See note 4 to Preface.

19. Hiraizumi Kiyoshi, *Chūsei ni okeru shaji to shakai to no kankei* (Tokyo, 1934) pp. 18-37.

20. Tamamuro Fumio, "Bakuhan ryōshu no shūkyō tōsei," in Tamamuro Fumio and Miyata Noboru, *Shomin shinkō no gensō* (Tokyo, 1977), pp. 46-57; and Tamamuro Fumio, *Shinbutsu bunri* (Tokyo, 1977), pp. 22-33.

21. Kuroda Toshio, "Chūsei jisha seiryoku ron," *Kōza Nihon rekishi 6, chūsei 2* (Tokyo, 1975), pp. 245-295.

22. Hiraizumi, *Chūsei ni okeru shaji to shakai*, pp. 48-49.

23. See below, Chapters Four and Six.

24. For detailed descriptions of the campaigns against Enryakuji, Negoro, and Kōyasan, see Tsuji Zennosuke, *Nihon Bukkyō-shi 7, Kinsei 1* (Tokyo, 1952), pp. 21-39 and 294-310. In English: Michael Cooper, *They Came to Japan* (Berkeley, 1965), pp. 98-99, 322, 329.

25. Takeuchi Rizō, *Jiryō shōen no kenkyū* (Kyoto, 1942), pp. 379-559.

26. Details from the Ōtabumi are taken from Ishii Susumu, *Nihon chūsei kokka-shi no kenkyū* (Tokyo, 1970), pp. 120, 127, 144; and from Kuroda Toshio, "Chūsei jisha seiryoku ron," p. 247.

27. Asakawa, "Life of a Monastic *Shō* in Medieval Japan," p. 316.

28. Kageyama Haruki, *Hieizan* (Tokyo, 1975), pp. 126-132 and, for a list of Enryakuji *shōen* proprietorships, pp. 211-218.

29. For a list of medieval *shōen* by province, see Nagahara Keiji et. al., eds., *Chūsei-shi handobukku* (Tokyo, 1973), pp. 403–445; or Yasuda Motohisa, ed., *Shōen* (Tokyo, 1977), pp. 250–283.

30. Japanese historians' varying evaluations of the process of *shōen* decline are discussed by Nagahara Keiji, "Shōensei kaitai katei ni okeru nanbokuchō nairanki no itchi," *Nihon chūsei shakai kōzō no kenkyū* (Tokyo, 1976), pp. 284–290.

31. Peter Judd Arnesen, *The Medieval Japanese Daimyo* (New Haven, 1979), pp. 127–131.

32. Nagahara Keiji, *Nihon chūsei shakai kōzō no kenkyū*, pp. 302–352.

33. Kōsen Tachibana, "The Codes of Chōsokabe Motochika and the Economy of Buddhist Temples in His Day, 3," *Indogaku Bukkyōgaku kenkyū* 21.1: 470 (1972).

34. Miyasaka Yūshō, *Kōyasan-shi* (Tokyo, 1962), p. 84. Kōyasan holdings in the medieval period are discussed in detail in Egashira Tsuneharu, *Kōyasan shōen no kenkyū* (Tokyo, 1938) and Toyoda Takeshi, ed. *Kōyasan-ryō shōen no shihai to kōzō* (Tokyo, 1977). Hideyoshi's treatment of the Buddhist institution is discussed by Kuwata Tadachika, *Toyotomi Hideyoshi kenkyū* (Tokyo, 1975), pp. 341–358.

35. Asakawa, "Life of a Monastic *Shō*," p. 339.

36. The changing character of the guilds (*za*) in medieval Japan is described by Kōzō Yamamura, "The Development of the Za in Medieval Japan," *Business History Review* 47.4:438–465 (Winter 1973). For a list of medieval *za* and bibliography of research articles in Japanese, see *Chūsei-shi handobukku*, pp. 446–540. Hiraizumi, *Chūsei ni okeru shaji to shakai*, pp. 159–260, also provides extensive information on the economic activities of Buddhist monasteries in this period.

37. Market development in the medieval period is discussed by Toyoda Takeshi, (Zōtei) *Chūsei Nihon shōgyō-shi no kenkyū* (Tokyo, 1957) pp. 302–322; Sasaki Ginya, *Chūsei shōhin ryūtsū-shi no kenkyū* (Tokyo, 1972), pp. 24–26, 124, etc.; and Wakita Haruko, *Nihon chūsei shōgyō hattatsu-shi no kenkyū* (Tokyo, 1969). In English, articles on the commercial development of this period include: Haruko Wakita, "Towards a Wider Perspective on Medieval Commerce," *Journal of Japanese Studies* 1.2:321–345 (Spring 1975), and Takeshi Toyoda and Hiroshi Sugiyama, "The Growth of Commerce and the Trades," in Hall and Toyoda eds., *Japan in the Muromachi Age*, pp. 129–144.

38. Kageyama Haruki, *Hieizan*, pp. 167–172. On *jinaimachi*, see Wakita Osamu, "Jinaimachi no kōzō to tenkai," *Shirin* 41.1: 1–24 (1958).

39. Hiraizumi, *Chūsei ni okeru shaji to shakai*, pp. 209–219. Takeuchi, *Jiryō shōen no kenkyū*, pp. 334–350.

40. Kuroda Toshio, "Chūsei jisha seiryoku ron," pp. 285–290.

41. There is no detailed study in English of the economic policies adopted by

sengoku daimyō. In Japanese see, for instance, essays by Fujiki Hisashi in his *Sengoku shakai-shi ron* (Tokyo, 1974).

42. Mentioned by Tamamura Takeji in the course of conversation.

43. See below, Chapter Six.

44. The nationwide diffusion of these schools is outlined in Nakamura Hajime et. al., *Ajia Bukkyō-shi, Nihon-hen*, Vols. 3, 4, 5, 6 (Tokyo, 1972–).

45. On the *sōhei*, see: Katsuno Ryūshin, *Sōhei* (Tokyo, 1956); Hirata Toshiharu, *Sōhei to bushi* (Tokyo, 1965); Hiraoka Jōkai, "Sōhei ni tsuite," Hōgetsu Keigo Sensei Kanreki Kinenkai eds., *Nihon shakai keizai-shi kenkyū, kodai chūsei hen* (Tokyo, 1967); and Hioki Shōichi, *Nihon sōhei kenkyū* (Tokyo, 1972). In French there is an article by G. Renondeau, "Histoire des Moines Guerriers du Japon," *Bibliothèque de l'Institute des Hautes Études Chinoises* 9: 159–344 (1957).

46. Standard works on the *ikkō-ikki* include Kasahara Kazuo, *Ikkō ikki no kenkyū* (Tokyo, 1954) and Inoue Toshio, *Ikkō ikki no kenkyū* (Tokyo, 1968). There is a more recent study by Minegishi Sumio, "Ikkō-ikki," in *Kōza Nihon rekishi 9, Chūsei 4* (Tokyo, 1976), pp. 127–173. Shingyō Norikazu, *Ikkō ikki no kiso kōzō* (Tokyo, 1975), analyzes the Mikawa *ikki*. For materials in English, see the works by David L. Davis, Michael Solomon, and Stanley Weinstein mentioned in note 1 to the Preface.

47. Tatsusaburō Hayashiya, "Kyoto in the Muromachi Age," in Hall and Toyoda, *Japan in the Muromachi Age*, pp. 30–34.

48. This incident is mentioned by Nagahara Keiji, *Minamoto Yoritomo* (Tokyo, 1958), p. 180. It is analyzed in detail by Kuroda Toshio, "Enryakuji shūto to Sasaki-shi," *Nihon chūsei no kokka to shūkyō* (Tokyo, 1975), pp. 143–168.

49. Ōishi Shinzaburō et al., *Nihon Keizai-shi ron* (Tokyo, 1967), pp. 7–8.

1. JAPANESE ZEN PIONEERS AND THEIR PATRONS

1. Kaiten Nukariya, *The Religion of the Samurai* (London, 1913), pp. 28–46; Masaharu Anesaki, *History of Japanese Religion* (Tokyo, 1963), pp. 210–212; and Daisetsu T. Suzuki, *Zen and Japanese Culture* (New York, 1959), pp. 61–85. John W. Hall, *Japan: from Prehistory to Modern Times* (New York, 1970), pp. 99–101; and H. Paul Varley, *Japanese Culture* (New York, 1973), p. 73, suggest that more mundane factors were also involved.

2. Kawai Masaharu, *Chūsei buke shakai no kenkyū* (Tokyo, 1973), p. 113.

3. Mochizuki Shinjō, et al., *Butsuzō* (*zoku-hen*, Tokyo, 1965), p. 98.

4. Brief discussions of the distinctive character of Sung dynasty Ch'an Buddhism will be found in: Araki Kengo, *Bukkyō to Jukyō* (Kyoto,

1963), Araki Kengo, "Zen," in *Chūgoku bunka sōsho,* 6 *Shūkyō,* ed. Kubo Tokutada and Nishi Junzō (Tokyo, 1968), 106–114; Kagamishima Genryū, *Dōgen Zenji to sono monryū* (Tokyo, 1961), pp. 7–56; Abe Chōichi, "Sōdai Zenshū shakai no haaku ni tsuite," *Rekishi kyōiku* 9.8: 85–92 (August 1961); Tamamura Takeji, "Zen," in *Chūgoku bunka sōsho,* 10, *Nihon bunka to Chūgoku,* ed. Bitō Masahide (Tokyo, 1968), pp. 151–171. Kenneth Ch'en, *Buddhism in China,* pp. 389–400; Heinrich Dumoulin, *A History of Zen Buddhism,* pp. 123–124.

5. For a survey of the manifold religious activity of the Kamakura period, see Imaeda Aishin et al., *Kamakura Bukkyō* 1–3, *Ajia Bukkyō-shi, Nihon-hen* 3–5, ed. Nakamura Hajime et al. Diplomatic and cultural relations between Japan and China during the Kamakura period are described by Kawazoe Shōji, "Kamakura jidai no taigai kankei to bunbutsu no inyū," *Kōza Nihon rekishi 6,* pp. 41–83.

6. This periodization is generally accepted by Japanese scholars of Zen sectarian development. See, for instance, Imaeda Aishin, "Chūsei Bukkyō no tenkai," in *Nihon Bukkyō-shi,* 2, ed. Akamatsu Toshihide (Kyoto, 1967), pp. 153–221.

7. The history of Sōtō school development in medieval Japan is largely outside the scope of this study. As brief introductions, see Imaeda Aishin, "Sōtōshū no hatten," in *Shūkyō-shi* (Tokyo, 1966) pp. 212–230; and Takeuchi Michio, "Sōtō kyōdan no seiritsu," *Rekishi kyōiku* 10.6: 44–51 (June 1962). Additional references are provided in note 40 below and by Hirose Ryōkō in *Zen to chūsei bunka,* pp. 132–133.

8. *Gozan* monasteries and the *gozan* system are described below in Chapter Three. The words *"gozan"* and *"jissatsu"* are sometimes read *"gosan"* and *"jissetsu,"* as in the card catalogues in Komazawa University and in some dictionaries of Zen. To judge from the *Vocabulario da Lingua de Iapan,* the pronunciation heard by Iberian visitors in the sixteenth century was *"gosan."* Present-day Rinzai usage seems to be *gozan, jissatsu.* On early Daitokuji and its patrons, see Haga Kōshirō, *Daitokuji to chadō* (Kyoto, 1972); and Covell and Yamada, *Zen at Daitokuji* pp. 25–52.

9. Tamamura and Inoue, *Engakuji-shi,* pp. 138–151.

10. Yanagida Seizan, *Rinzai no kafū* (Tokyo, 1967), pp. 5–25. Chōgen played a central role in the medieval recovery of the Tōdaiji. Recently some Japanese scholars have raised doubts about his having visited China. See Kawazoe Shōji, "Kamakura jidai no taigai kankei to bunbutsu no inyū," p. 77, note 10. Shunjō definitely did visit China, from 1199–1211. While there, he studied the Vinaya and Zen. After his return to Japan, he revitalized the Sennyūji in Kyoto, where Tendai,

Shingon, Zen, and the Vinaya were all taught. For a recent collection of studies on aspects of Shunjō's career, see Ishida Mitsuyuki (Jūshin) ed., *Shunjō ritsushi* (Kyoto, 1972).

11. Reischauer, *Ennin's Diary*, pp. 44–45, 210; and the same author's *Ennin's Travels in T'ang China* (New York, 1955), pp. 173–174. See also Stanley Weinstein, "Imperial Patronage in the Formation of T'ang Buddhism."

12. Jacques Gernet, *Daily Life in China on the Eve of the Mongol Invasion* (London, 1962), pp. 212–214, provides a description of Hangchow as it might have been a half century before Dōgen's visit to China.

13. Tamamura Takeji, "Zenshū no hatten," in *Koza Nihon rekishi, Chūsei* 3 (Tokyo, 1963), pp. 281–302. Students of Chinese history and Chinese Buddhism may object that Chinese Buddhist monasteries rarely showed the clear-cut sectarian form implied here, that it is inaccurate to talk of "pure" Ch'an monasteries, and that we should rather think in terms of Buddhist monasteries in which there was a strong Ch'an component: a Ch'an master, meditation hall, etc. While this may describe the character of some Chinese monasteries of the day, we should bear in mind that the Five Mountains group all had "Ch'an monastery" as part of their official title, that most Japanese monks who went to China in this period studied under Ch'an masters, that all émigré monks who came to Japan in the late thirteenth or early fourteenth century described themselves as Ch'an masters, and that the codes they introduced were written for Ch'an communities.

14. Imaeda, *Chūsei Zenshū-shi no kenkyū*, pp. 141–146.

15. Differences between T'ang and Sung dynasty Zen are discussed in the works mentioned in note 4 above.

16. Imaeda, in *Kamakura Bukkyō, 2,* pp. 256–257; Takaaki Matsushita, *Ink Painting* (Tokyo, 1974), pp. 53–57; Rosenfield, "The Unity of the Three Creeds," pp. 205–225.

17. The vital role played by Ch'an monastic regulations (*ch'ing-kuei*) in the transmission process is discussed in Chapter Four.

18. Eisai, or more accurately Yōsai, was not firmly enshrined as the founder of Japanese Rinzai Zen until long after his death. According to the Zen monk Mujū Ichien (1226–1312), the compiler of the *Shasekishū*, a 10-volume compendium of Buddhist traditions, completed in 1283, Eisai observed Tendai, Shingon, and Ritsu teachings, as well as Zen, and encouraged his followers to practice the *nenbutsu*. Mujū stresses that Eisai was unable to reject the religious trends of his day, that he practiced Shingon overtly and Zen secretly, and that he predicted that within 50 years of his death the Zen school would flourish in Japan. See Watanabe Tsunaya, ed., *Shasekishū* (Tokyo, 1976), p. 453. Eisai

is given a more prominent position in the *Genkō shakusho* (Buddhist compilation of the Genkō era), compiled in 1322 by the Zen monk Kokan Shiren (1278–1346). Kuroita Katsumi, ed., *Genkō shakusho* in *Kokushi taikei*, (Tokyo, 1929–1966), 31, 42–46.

In addition to the above, this description of Eisai and his school makes use of Tsuji Zennosuke, *Nihon Bukkyō-shi, Chūsei*, II; Yanagida, *Rinzai no kafū*, pp. 26–88; the same author's commentary ("Eisai to *Kōzen gokokuron* no kadai,") to his modernized edition of the *Kōzen goko-kuron* included in Ichikawa Hakugen, Iriya Yoshitaka, and Yanagida Seizan, eds., *Chūsei Zenka no shisō* (Tokyo, 1972), pp. 439–486; Imaeda Aishin, "Eisai no shin Bukkyō undō," *Rekishi kyōiku* 14.9:65–72 (September 1966); and Tamamura Takeji, "Rinzaishū kyōdan no seiritsu," *Rekishi kyōiku* 10.6:37–43 (June 1962). Philip Yampolsky's introduction to *The Zen Master Hakuin* (New York, 1971), pp. 1–27, although brief, is excellent on Eisai, as on other aspects of Rinzai Zen development in Japan. An introduction to, and brief selection from, Eisai's writings will be found in *Sources of Japanese Tradition*, 1, 226–240.

19. The importance of the differences between the Enryakuji and Onjōji branches of Tendai in relation to the development of Zen is dealt with by Imaeda Aishin, "Eisai no shin Bukkyō undō," pp. 65–69.

20. On Kakua, see *Genkō shakusho*, p. 100; Tsuji, *Chūsei*, 2, 61–66; and Yanagida, *Rinzai no kafū*, p. 14.

21. *Genkō shakusho*, p. 100.

22. Tsuji, *Chūsei*, 2, 61–66; Imaeda, in *Kamakura Bukkyō*, 2, pp. 242–243; Yampolsky, *Hakuin*, p. 3.

23. Imaeda, "Eisai no shin Bukkyō undō," pp. 69–72.

24. *Sources of the Japanese Tradition*, 1, 237–240.

25. Tsuji, *Chūsei*, 2, 81–92; Tamamura, "Rinzaishū kyōdan no seiritsu," p. 38.

26. The fact that Eisai is mentioned some 30 times in the *Azuma kagami* (the official chronicle of the Kamakura *bakufu*) for the years between 1199 and 1215, the year of his death, is an indication of the warmth of the patronage extended him by Hōjō Masako and the Minamoto shoguns. In these entries, however, Eisai appears not as a Zen master engaging in debate or instructing his protégés in meditation but as the officiating priest at Buddhist memorial services and prayer meetings. He is described as a Ritsu Vinaya master. See, for instance, the entries of Kenkyū 10 (1199)/9/26 and Shōji 2(1200)/1/13, Kuroita Katsumi ed., *Azuma kagami, Kokushi taikei*, 32–33.

27. Although Ben'en Enni (Shōichi, or sometimes Shōitsu Kokushi) was a cardinal figure in the development of Sung Zen in Japan, he is generally neglected in comparison with Eisai and Dōgen, each of whom left a more

substantial corpus of written work. Biographical details can be found in the chronology compiled by the monk Enshin, *Shōichi kokushi nenpu, Dai-Nihon Bukkyō zensho*, 95, ed., Nanjō Bunyū (Tokyo, 1912), pp. 129–150; *Genkō shakusho*, pp. 109–119; Tsuji, *Chūsei*, 2, 98–124; Imaeda, *Kamakura Bukkyō*, 2, 164–74; and in Fontein and Hickman, *Zen Painting and Calligraphy*.

28. The architectural layout of Tōfukuji and other medieval Zen monasteries is discussed at length in Chapter Five. See also Fontein and Hickman, *Zen Painting and Calligraphy*, pp. 144–148, for a discussion of an early scroll painting of Tōfukuji attributed to Sesshū Tōyō (1430–1506).

29. Tsuji, *Chūsei*, 2, 116; Imaeda, in *Kamakura Bukkyō*, 2, 167; and Imaeda, "Sugyōroku to Kamakura shoki zenrin," in *Chūsei Zenshū-shi no kenkyū*, pp. 73–75.

30. Cited by Imaeda, in *Kamakura Bukkyō*, 2, 168.

31. Tsuji, *Chūsei*, 2, 118.

32. Imaeda, in *Kamakura Bukkyō*, 2, 168.

33. Tamamura Takeji, *Musō kokushi* (Kyoto, 1958), pp. 25–40.

34. Tsuji, *Chūsei*, 2, 92–98; Imaeda, in *Kamakura Bukkyō*, 2, 175–178; Yampolsky, *Hakuin*, p. 5.

35. Dōgen's career can be reconstructed in detail from his own writings and those of his followers. Of the numerous biographies available in Japanese, I have used Ōkubo Dōshū, *Dōgen Zenji-den no kenkyū* (Tokyo, 1966); Imaeda Aishin, *Dōgen to sono deshi* (Tokyo, 1972); and Takeuchi Michio, *Dōgen* (Tokyo, 1962). In English, see Dumoulin, *History of Zen Buddhism*, pp. 151–174, and Hee-Jin Kim's excellent study, *Dōgen Kigen—Mystical Realist* (Tucson, 1975).

36. Norman Waddell and Masao Abe, trans., "Dōgen's *Bendōwa*," *The Eastern Buddhist* 4.1: 148. (May 1971). See also Masao Abe, "Dōgen on Buddha Nature," *The Eastern Buddhist* 4.1:28–71 (1971).

37. Kagamishima, *Dōgen to sono monryū*, pp. 8–56, and Kim, *Dōgen Kigen*, pp. 34–37.

38. Waddell and Abe, "Dōgen's *Bendōwa*," p. 133 n. 37.

39. *Fukan zazengi* in Ōkubo, *Dōgen Zenji Zenshū*, 2, 3–4. See also Norman Waddell and Masao Abe, trans. "Dōgen's *Fukan zazengi* and *Shōbōgenzō zazengi*," *Eastern Buddhist* 6.2: 115–128. (October 1973).

40. The text of the *Gokoku shōbōgi* has been lost, and its content can now only be guessed at. There can be little doubt, however, that Dōgen attempted a spirited defense of his teaching. For a discussion of this point, see Imaeda, *Dōgen to sono deshi*, pp. 115–116.

41. *Shohō jissō* in Ōkubo, *Dōgen Zenji zenshū* 1, 370.

42. See *Shōbōgenzō, Jukai* in Ōkubo, *Dōgen Zenji zenshū* 1, 619.

43. The rapid provincial diffusion of the Sōtō school is described in Suzuki

Taizan, *Zenshū no chihō hatten* (Kyoto, 1942); the same author's "Sōtō Zen no gufu to sono gegosha," in *Kokumin seikatsu-shi kenkyū*, 4 ed., Itō Tasaburō (Tokyo, 1960), pp. 223–276; and his "Chihō jiin no seiritsu to tenkai." *Chihō-shi kenkyū* 14.4: 6–8 (August 1964); Matsuyama Zenshō, "Tōhoku chihō ni okeru Sōtōshū kyōdan seiritsu no tokushusei," *Nihon Bukkyō* 10: 38–54. (January 1961) and the same author's "Kinsei Tōhoku ni okeru shin Bukkyō no denpa to kyōdan keisei." in *Nihon shūkyō-shi kenkyū*, 9, ed., Kasahara Kazuo (Kyoto, 1967), pp. 179–203; Tamamuro Taijō, "Watakushi no Zenshū-kan," *Daihōrin* 30.1: 46–51. (January 1963); the same author's *Sōshiki Bukkyō* (Tokyo, 1964), pp. 233–236; and Yamamoto Seiki, "Kita jōshū ni okeru Sōtō Zen no denpa ni tsuite," in *Nihon ni okeru seiji to shūkyō*, ed., Kasahara Kazuo (Tokyo, 1974), pp. 55–82; as well as in the works mentioned in note 7 above.

2. CHINESE ÉMIGRÉ MONKS AND JAPANESE WARRIOR RULERS

1. Yasuda Motohisa, "Kamakura *bakufu*," in *Taikei Nihon-shi sōsho, Seiji-shi*, 1, ed., Fujiki Kunihiko and Inoue Mitsusada (Tokyo, 1965), pp. 284–293; and Amino Yoshihiko, *Mōko shūrai, Nihon no rekishi*, 10 (Tokyo, 1974), pp. 40–60.
2. Kawai, *Chūsei buke shakai*, p. 98; Washio Junkei, *Kamakura bushi to Zen* (Tokyo, 1935), p. 26.
3. See above, Chapter One.
4. Yasuda Motohisa, in *Hōjō Yoshitoki* (Tokyo, 1961), p. 264, assesses Yoshitoki's religious concerns at the point of death. Yasutoki's patronage and regulation of Buddhism form the subject of Chapter Six of Uwayokote Masataka's *Hōjō Yasutoki* (Tokyo, 1958), pp. 142–176. Yasutoki was a devoted patron of the Kegon-sect monk Myōe Shōnin (1173–1215). Yasutoki also patronized Eisai's disciple Gyōyū (1163–1241), but there is no indication that the regent practiced Zen with him. Gyōyū's principal function was to conduct religious ceremonies (p. 151).
5. Hōjō Tokiyori's patronage of Zen is discussed in Tsuji, *Chūsei*, 2, 125–156; Washio, *Kamakura bushi to Zen*, pp. 102–38; and Tamamura, *Engakuji-shi*, pp. 6–7. Tokiyori was broad-minded. Although there is no doubt of the sincerity of his interest in Zen, he was on reasonably amicable terms with the volatile Nichiren, patronized Eison (1201–1290), who revived the Japanese Ritsu sect, and attended esoteric Buddhist ceremonies. Ōno Tatsunosuke, *Nichiren* (Tokyo, 1958), pp. 58–153.

6. On the development of Kamakura under the Hōjō, see Ōyama Kyōhei, *Kamakura bakufu, Nihon no rekishi,* (Tokyo, 1974), 9, 361–370; Kamakura Shishi Hensan Iinkai, comp., *Kamakura shishi,* 1, *Sōsetsuhen* (Tokyo, 1959), 91–155; and Louis Frederic, *Daily Life in Japan in the Age of the Samurai* (New York, 1972), pp. 96–100.

7. From the *Azuma kagami* and *bakufu* regulations it is clear that the twelfth and thirteenth centuries were punctuated by monastic unrest and feuds involving warrior-monks from Enryakuji, Onjōji, Kōfukuji, and other powerful Buddhist monasteries. The *bakufu* issued frequent, seemingly unavailing prohibitions against the bearing of arms by monastery inhabitants. Pure Land *nenbutsu* devotees also contributed to social disorder. The *bakufu* issued prohibitions against the *nenbutsu* practice in 1200, 1207, 1222, 1224, 1227, and 1234. Hōjō Yasutoki issued prohibitions against *nenbutsu* followers in 1235. He was, however, more concerned to control the excesses of Shinran's followers than hostile to the basic teachings of Shinran himself. Uwayokote, *Hōjō Yasutoki,* p. 171. Of the leading popular preachers, Hōnen was banished to Shikoku at age 74; Shinran was exiled for taking a wife; and Nichiren was exiled twice, in 1260 and 1270, for his criticism of *bakufu* patronage of "heterodox" (i. e., all non-Lotus) sects. Harper H. Coates and Ryūgaku Ishizuka, trans., *Hōnen the Buddhist Saint* (Kyoto, 1925), pp. 550–608; Tamura Enchō, *Hōnen* (Tokyo, 1959), pp. 187–200; Akamatsu Toshihide, *Shinran* (Tokyo, 1961), pp. 101–133; and Ōno, *Nichiren,* pp. 58–153. See also Renondeau, "Moines Guerriers," pp. 221–245.

8. Kamakura *bakufu* patronage of the Kamakura Tsurugaoka Hachiman shrine is discussed in *Kamakura shishi,* 2, *shaji-hen,* pp. 12–32. The role of the Asō (Kyūshū) shrine in medieval society is examined by Sugimoto Hisao in *Chūsei no jinja to sharyō* (Tokyo, 1959). Warrior interest in Shintō beliefs is touched upon in Fujitani Toshio and Naoki Kōjirō, *Ise jingū* (Kyoto, 1960), pp. 80–100.

9. Fuji Naomoto, *Buke jidai no shakai to seishin* (Osaka, 1967), pp. 59–61.

10. Kyotsu Hori, "The Economic and Political Effects of the Mongol Wars," in *Medieval Japan,* pp. 186–187.

11. There is, to my knowledge, no detailed study of the Ch'an institution under the Mongols. These paragraphs are therefore speculative. The following have been referred to: Iwai Hirosato, "Gensho ni okeru teishitsu to Zensō no kankei ni tsuite," in *Nisshi Bukkyō-shi ronkō* (Tokyo, 1957), pp. 451–544; Ōyabu Masaya, "Genchō no shūkyō seisaku," *Rekishi kyōiku* 9.7: 36–42 (July 1961); Arthur Waley, trans., *The Travels of an Alchemist* (London, 1931), pp. 5–33; Ch'en, *Buddhism in China,* pp. 414–433; Paul Demieville, "La Situation religieuse en Chine

au temps de Marco Polo," in *Oriente Poliano* (Rome, 1957), pp. 193–228; John D. Langlois Jr., review of John W. Dardess, *Conquerors and Confucians, Journal of Asian Studies* 34.1: 218–220. (November 1974).

12. Ch'en, *Buddhism in China,* pp. 418–421.

13. Ibid., p. 420, n. 4; Ōyabu, "Genchō no shūkyō seisaku," pp. 37–39.

14. The *Ch'ih-hsiu Pai-chang Code* is included in *Dai-Nihon zoku zōkyō,* 2nd ed., vol. 16, fascicle 3.

15. The Ch'an monk Hai-yun, of the Lin-chi school, and his disciples served as religious and political advisors to the khans. See Ch'en, *Buddhism in China,* p. 415; and Iwai, "Gensho ni okeru teishitsu to Zensō," pp. 462–524.

16. Waddell and Abe, "Dōgen's *Bendōwa,*" p. 132.

17. The shifts of influence among the Sung and Yuan dynasty Ch'an schools in China are outlined by Tamamura Takeji in *Gozan bungaku* (Tokyo, 1955), pp. 39–40; and discussed in detail by Abe Chōichi, "Nansō kōki Zenshū no dōkō," *Bukkyō shigaku* 16.1: 20 (September 1972).

18. Tamamura, *Engakuji-shi,* p. 40, suggests that factional rivalries in Chinese Zen circles were imported into Japan, where they were a source of friction among émigré Chinese monks and, later, the Japanese Zen schools derived from them. He refers to the sporadic feuds between monks of Engakuji, belonging to the Wu-hsueh line, and Kenchōji monks, who belonged to the Lan-ch'i line.

19. Biographical details on Lan-ch'i are taken from *Genkō shakusho* vi; Tsuji, *Chūsei,* 2, 125–138; and Ogisu Jundō, *Nihon chūsei Zenshū-shi* (Tokyo, 1965), pp. 104–115.

20. Lan-ch'i's connection with Jōrakuji is dealt with in *Kamakura shishi,* 2, *Shaji-hen,* 413–418.

21. On the foundation and early history of Kenchōji, see Ōta Hirotarō, *Chūsei no kenchiku* (Tokyo, 1957), pp. 228–244; *Kamakura shishi, Shaji-hen,* pp. 268–308.

22. *Azuma kagami,* Kenchō 5 (1253)/11/25.

23. By 1323 the monk population of Kenchōji was at least 388. See below, Chapter Six.

24. "Kenchō hōgo kisoku," *Kamakura shishi, Shiryō-hen,* 3, No. 197.

25. Cited in Kawai, *Chūsei buke shakai,* p. 114.

26. Ibid., p. 115.

27. Nuki Tatsuto et al., *Kenchōji* (Kamakura, 1973), p. 18. The title *Kenchō Zenji* (Kenchō Zen Monastery) is also inscribed on the great bell belonging to the monastery, thought to have been cast in 1255. According to Tsuji, *Chūsei* 2, 130, the use of the phrase *Zenji* on this bell is the first recorded usage in Japan. The bestowal of the era name, Kenchō, was a mark of special favor. Enryakuji supporters protested

that their complex was the only one in Japan that should be honored with an era name, Enryaku, as part of its title.

28. Biographical details on Wu-an are taken from *Genkō shakusho* vi; Tsuji, *Chūsei* 2, 139-154; Ogisu, *Nihon chūsei Zenshū-shi*, pp. 131-135; Akamatsu, ed., *Nihon Bukkyō-shi*, 2, 163.

29. There does not seem to be any surviving documentary evidence for this anecdote.

30. Tamamura, *Engakuji-shi*, p. 22.

31. Akamatsu ed., *Nihon Bukkyō-shi*, 2, 162.

32. Tsuji, *Chūsei*, 2, 157; *Genkō shakusho* VI.

33. Although Tokimune is frequently given credit for the almost single-handed salvation of Japan from Mongol invasion, it is doubtful that he played such a central role. He was still in his teens when the first envoys came to Japan. He did not take part in the subsequent fighting but remained in Kamakura organizing prayers and ceremonies for the safety of the country. Crucial decisions were made by his leading advisors, including his father-in-law, Adachi Yasumori, and vassal, Taira Yoritsuna. See Amino, *Mōko shūrai*, pp. 136-223; and Kyotsu Hori, "The Mongol Invasions and the Kamakura *Bakufu*," (PhD dissertation, Columbia University, 1967), University Microfilms, pp. 119-147 and 217-233.

34. Cited by Imaeda, in *Kamakura Bukkyō*, 2, 189.

35. Musō Soseki, *Rinsen kakun;* see below, Chapter Four.

36. Tamamura, *Engakuji-shi*, pp. 8-26.

37. Ibid., pp. 28-31.

38. See below, Chapter Seven.

39. Tamamura, *Engakuji-shi*, p. 39.

40. Tsuji, *Chūsei*, 2, 178; Ogisu, *Nihon chūsei Zenshū-shi*, pp. 138-141.

41. Tamamura, *Musō kokushi*, p. 19.

42. Imaeda Aishin, "Sōtōshū Wanshi-ha no hatten to Asakura-shi," *Nihon Bukkyō* 21:1-14 (August 1965).

43. "Sūen (Hōjō Sadatoki) Zen'in seifu jōsho," (1294/1/-), *Kamakura shishi, Shiryō-hen* 2, 25-26.

44. "Sūen (Hōjō Sadatoki) Zen'in seifu jōsho," (1303/2/12), *Kamakura shishi, Shiryō-hen* 2, 35-36.

45. See below, Chapter Three.

46. H. Paul Varley, *Imperial Restoration in Medieval Japan* (New York, 1971), pp. 39-65; Yasuda Motohisa, "Hōjō Takatoki," in *Kamakura bakufu* (Tokyo, 1971), p. 309.

47. Tsuji, *Chūsei* 2, 189.

48. Ch'ing-cho's code, the *Taikan shingi*, is included in the *Taishō shinshū daizōkyō*, 81, 619-624. For a brief biography of Ch'ing-cho, see Sakurai

Kageo, *Nanzenji-shi* (Kyoto, 1940), pp. 153–158. Provincial warriors who patronized Ch'ing-cho included the Ogasawara, Ōtomo, Ashikaga, and Toki. Imaeda, in *Kamakura Bukkyō* 2, 209.

49. "Sūgan (Hōjō Takatoki) Engakuji seifu jōsho," (1327/10/1), *Kamakura shishi, Shiryō-hen* 2, 131–134.

50. "Hōjō Sadatoki jūsannenki kuyōki," *Kamakura shishi, shiryō-hen* 2, 76–128. Discussed in Tamamura, *Engakuji-shi*, pp. 80–83.

51. Kawai, *Chūsei buke shakai*, pp. 128–148; Kadokawa Gengi and Sugiyama Hiroshi eds., *Ai to mujō no bungaku, Nihon bungaku no rekishi* (Tokyo, 1967) 5, 226–261.

52. Matsushita, *Ink Painting*, p. 53; Ogisu, *Nihon chūsei Zenshū-shi*, pp. 182–190.

53. *Kamakura shishi, Shiryō-hen* 2, 200–212. On *karamono*, see Kawazoe, "Kamakura jidai no taigai kankei to bunbutsu no inyū," pp. 70–73; Varley, "Ashikaga Yoshimitsu and the World of Kitayama," pp. 191–192.

54. The Sung imperial ideal was a pervasive force in medieval Japanese politics. Its role in the Kenmu Restoration is emphasized by Satō Shin'ichi in *Nanbokuchō no dōran, Nihon no rekishi*, 9 (Tokyo, 1965), 70–101. Varley, in "Ashikaga Yoshimitsu and the World of Kitayama," p. 195, is sceptical about the impact of Neo-Confucian thought in elite circles in Japan during the early fourteenth century.

55. Takagi Yutaka, *Nichiren to sono montei* (Tokyo, 1965), pp. 69–72, 103.

56. *Taiheiki*, 6, "Akasaka kassen, Hitomi Honma no nukegake no koto," *Nihon Koten bungaku taikei* (Tokyo, 1973), 34, 199–208.

57. Imaeda, *Zenshū no rekishi*, p. 70, lists nearly 30 such patrons, most of whom were *shugo*. The leading secular patrons of Zen are also listed as donors in the record of the thirteenth anniversary ceremonies for Hōjō Sadatoki. See above, note 50. Patronage of Zen by the Kikuchi clan is discussed by Sugimoto Hisao, *Kikuchi-shi sandai* (Tokyo, 1966), pp. 213–219. For Akamatsu patronage, see Kōsaka Konomu, "*Akamatsu Enshin, Mitsusuke* (Tokyo, 1970), pp. 60–70.

58. Imaeda, in *Kamakura Bukkyō*, 2, 209.

59. This process is described by Kawai, *Chūsei buke shakai no kenkyū*, pp. 118–126; and by Fujioka Daisetsu, "Zenshū no chihō denpa to sono juyōsō ni tsuite," in *Nihon shūkyō-shi kenkyū*, ed., Kasahara Kazuo (Tokyo, 1967), 1, 116–118.

60. Kawai, *Chūsei buke shakai*, pp. 113–114.

61. On the growth of Hōjō house (*tokusō*) authority, see, for instance, Hori, "The Economic and Political Effects of the Mongol Wars," pp. 193–196.

62. Satō Shin'ichi, *Kamakura bakufu shugo seido no kenkyū* (Tokyo, 1971), pp. 243–248; and Hayashiya Tatsusaburō, "Chūsei-shi gaisetsu," *Kōza Nihon rekishi*, 5, *Chūsei* 1, 27.
63. Imaeda, in *Kamakura Bukkyō-shi*, 2, 209.
64. Takayanagi Mitsutoshi, *Ashikaga Takauji* (Tokyo, 1966), pp. 467–488.
65. Akamatsu ed., *Nihon Bukkyō-shi* 2, 489–495.
66. Imaeda Aishin, "Zen to kōshitsu," in *Kōza Zen,* 5, 170–181.
67. See below, Chapter Three.
68. Ichirō Ishida, "Zen Buddhism and Muromachi Art," *Journal of Asian Studies* 22.4: 417–430. (August 1963). Tamamura, *Musō kokushi,* pp. 121–148.
69. Fujioka, "Zenshū no chihō denpa," p. 118.
70. Iwahashi Koyata, *Hanazono tennō* (Tokyo, 1962), pp. 132–156; Imaeda, "Zen to kōshitsu," p. 175.
71. Imaeda, "Zen to kōshitsu," p. 177.
72. For a more detailed description of this expansion, see Imaeda Aishin et al., "Nihon Bukkyō no chiiki hatten," *Bukkyō shigaku* 9.3: 1–163; 9.4: 2–15, 58–162 (October 1961).
73. Tamamura, *Gozan Bungaku*, p. 45.

3. THE ARTICULATION OF THE GOZAN SYSTEM

1. For the background to this transition, see Varley, *Imperial Restoration*, pp. 66–94; and John W. Hall, *Government and Local Power in Japan 500–1700* (Princeton, 1966), pp. 191–208.
2. Tamamura, *Musō kokushi*, pp. 149–190; Tsuji, *Chūsei* 2, 80–98.
3. Tamamura, *Musō kokushi*, pp. 91–148. Tamamura suggests that Musō failed to win I-shan's sanction because of his attachment to the scriptural traditions of Buddhism. Although Musō frequently warned his disciples against trying to obtain *satori* by relying on passages from the scriptures or on the writings of Zen masters, his Zen teaching was, according to Professor Tamamura, a synthesis of Zen and the teaching schools (*kyōzen itchi*), incorporating the kinds of prayers and incantations that played such a vital role in Shingon Buddhism.
4. There is some doubt as to whether Daitokuji was made a full *gozan* monastery at this time. Go-Daigo certainly requested that it should be so honored. Some members of the *bakufu*, however, objected on the grounds that Daitokuji was a *tsuchien*, or closed monastery, and that it was still architecturally incomplete. Even if it was not accorded full *gozan* rank at this time, the important consideration from our point of view is that Go-Daigo had every intention of making it one of the leading monasteries in a Kyoto-centered *gozan* network. Tōfukuji monks

justified the privileged position of their monastery in the official system with the arguments that it was one of the oldest and grandest Zen foundations in Japan, and that it enjoyed the special favor of the imperial court and Kyoto aristocracy. These facts, they argued, were more important in *gozan* ranking than whether a monastery was a *tsuchien* or *jippō-satsu*. This problem is discussed by Akamatsu and Yampolsky "Muromachi Zen and the Gozan system," pp. 313–329. Musō's role in helping Engakuji, a Hōjō family temple, make the transition to drastically altered political circumstances is touched on in Tamamura, *Engakuji-shi*, p. 93.

5. Imaeda, "Zen to kōshitsu," pp. 172–175; Tsuji, *Chūsei*, 2, 1–28, 53.
6. Amino, *Mōko shūrai*, p. 418; Satō Kazuhiko, *Nanbokuchō nairan, Nihon no rekishi* 9 (Tokyo, 1974), 106; Nagahara Keiji, "Nanbokuchō nairan," *Kōza Nihon rekishi* 6, *Chūsei* 2, 65; and Tsuji, *Chūsei*, 3, 29–80, who analyses the attitudes of the major Buddhist institutions.
7. Matsumoto Shinhachirō, "Nanbokuchō no nairan," *Chūsei shakai no kenkyū* (Tokyo, 1956), p. 319.
8. Satō Shin'ichi, "Shugo ryōkoku-sei no tenkai," in Toyoda Takeshi, ed., *Chūsei shakai* (Tokyo, 1954), pp. 90–94.
9. Nagahara Keiji, *Nihon hōken seiritsu katei no kenkyū* (Tokyo, 1961).
10. Hall, *Japan: from Prehistory to Modern Times*, p. 103.
11. Varley, *Imperial Restoration*, p. 95, and *Japanese Culture*, p. 75.
12. Kuroda Toshio, "Chūsei no kokka to tennō," *Kōza Nihon rekishi* 6, *Chūsei*, 2, 294–297; Akamatsu Toshihide, "Muromachi *bakufu*," in *Taikei Nihon-shi sōsho, Seiji-shi*, 1, 312–329.
13. Kenneth A. Grossberg, "Central Government in Medieval Japan: The Politics of the Muromachi Bakufu," (PhD dissertation, Princeton University, 1977).
14. Satō, *Nanbokuchō no dōran*, pp. 98–101.
15. Usui Nobuyoshi, *Ashikaga Yoshimitsu* (Tokyo, 1960), p. 214. Usui states that Yoshimitsu (1358–1408) practiced Zen meditation assiduously while Gidō Shūshin (1325–1388) and Shun'oku Myōha (1311–1388) were alive. Thereafter, he turned increasingly to esoteric Buddhism. Tsuji, *Chūsei*, 3, 213–351, examines Yoshimitsu's and Yoshimochi's patronage of Zen. He concludes that neither had more than "a daimyō's cultural enthusiasm" for Zen. For a detailed study of Yoshimochi's patronage of Zen, see Tamamura Takeji, "Ashikaga Yoshimochi no Zenshū shinkō ni tsuite," *Zengaku kenkyū* 42: 20–43. (March 1951). Tamamura allows Yoshimochi a genuine spiritual commitment to Zen.
16. Haga Kōshirō, "Ashikaga Yoshimasa no shūkyō seikatsu to sekaikan," in *Higashiyama bunka no kenkyū* (Tokyo, 1945). In this essay, Haga

argues that the core of Yoshimasa's religious interest lay not in Zen but in Pure Land *nenbutsu* belief. On the building of the Higashiyama Sansō, see Kurokawa Tadanori, "Higashiyama sansō no zōei to sono haikei," in *Chūsei no kenryoku to minshū* (Osaka, 1970), pp. 236–258.

17. Gidō Shūshin, *Kūge nichiyo kufū ryakushū*, ed. Tsuji Zennusuke (Tokyo, 1939).

18. Zuikei Shūhō, *Ga'un nikkenroku batsuyū, Zoku shiseki shūran*, 3 (Kyoto, 1967), 307–508; also in *Dai-Nihon kokiroku*, Pt. 13. (Tokyo, 1961). Unsen Taikyoku, *Hekizan nichiroku, Zoku shiseki shūran* 3 (Kyoto, 1967), 508–574.

19. Tsuji, *Chūsei*, 4, 1–48.

20. See below, Chapter Seven.

21. Tsuji Zennosuke, "Ashikaga Takauji no shinkō," in *Shigaku zasshi* (September, 1916); Takayanagi, *Ashikaga Takauji*, pp. 467–470.

22. Akamatsu ed., *Nihon Bukkyō-shi*, 2, 489–495.

23. Tamamura Takeji, "Ashikaga Tadayoshi Zenshū shinkō no seikaku ni tsuite," *Bukkyō shigaku* 7.3: 1–22 (October 1958).

24. Satō Shin'ichi, "Muromachi *bakufu* kaizōki no kansei taikei," in Ishimoda Shō and Satō Shin'ichi, *Chūsei no hō to kokka*, (Tokyo, 1960), pp. 451–511.

25. Ibid., p. 486.

26. On the building of Tenryūji and the dispatch of the Tenryūji vessels, see Miura Shūkō, *Nihon-shi no kenkyū* (Tokyo, 1922), pp. 661–690; Tsuji, *Chūsei*, 3, 113–150; Ōta, *Chūsei no kenchiku*, pp. 305–330; and Satō Kazuhiko, *Nanbokuchō nairan*, pp. 142–145.

27. Imaeda Aishin, "Ashikaga Tadayoshi Tōjiji sōsetsu," *Chūsei Zenshū-shi no kenkyū*, 429–449.

28. This account of the Ankokuji and Rishōtō is based on Imaeda Aishin, "Ankokuji rishōtō no setsuritsu," *Chūsei Zenshū-shi no kenkyū*, pp. 77–138.

29. Ibid., p. 133.

30. For a detailed account of the articulation of the *gozan* system, see Imaeda Aishin, "Chūsei Zenrin no kanji kikō," *Chūsei Zenshū-shi no kenkyū*, pp. 139–268, on which this section is based.

31. Hayashiya Tatsusaburō et al., eds., *Kyōto no rekishi*, 3 (Kyoto, 1968), 116–118; Tsuji, *Chūsei*, 3, 228–336; and Imaeda Aishin, "Ashikaga Yoshimitsu no Shōkokuji sōken," in *Chūsei Zenshū-shi no kenkyū*, pp. 471–482.

32. See below, Chapter Six.

33. Imaeda, *Zenshū no rekishi*, pp. 105–108.

34. Ibid., p. 107.

35. Fujioka, "Zenshū no chihō denpa," pp. 124–125.

36. See above, Chapter Two.
37. Toyoda Takeshi, *Nihon shūkyō seido shi no kenkyū* (Tokyo, 1938), p. 13; Tamamura, *Engakuji-shi,* pp. 116-117; and Imaeda Aishin, "Zen-ritsu-gata to rokuon sōroku," in *Chūsei Zenshū-shi no kenkyū,* pp. 269-275.
38. On the *sōroku* office, see Tamamura, *Engakuji-shi,* pp. 117-118; and Imaeda, *Chūsei Zenshū-shi no kenkyū,* pp. 276-336. Although both scholars trace the origins of the *gozan sōroku* to the Chinese *seng-lu* of the Ming dynasty, they provide no information on the actual authority of the Chinese institution.
39. Shiba Yoshimasa's patronage of Shun'oku Myōha is discussed in detail by Imaeda Aishin in "Shiba Yoshimasa no Zenrin ni taisuru taido." in *Chūsei Zenshū-shi no kenkyū,* pp. 450-470.
40. Ogawa Makoto, *Hosokawa Yoriyuki* (Tokyo, 1972), pp. 119-135, 243-273; Satō Kazuhiko, *Nanbokuchō no nairan,* pp. 325-330.
41. Satō Shin'ichi and Ikeuchi Yoshisuke, *Chūsei hōsei shiryōshū, Muro-machi bakufu hō* (Tokyo, 1957), 2, 41-42.
42. Satō Kazuhiko, *Nanbokuchō nairan,* p. 329; Sakurai, *Nanzenji-shi,* pp. 201-206; Tsuji, *Chūsei,* 3, 295-336; and Imaeda, "Shiba Yoshimasa," pp. 461-465. The Nanzenji Gate incident is also discussed by Imatani Akira, *Sengoku-ki no Muromachi bakufu,* pp. 63-69.
43. Imaeda, "Zenritsugata to rokuon sōroku," pp. 357-366.
44. Tamamura Takeji, "Inryōken oyobi inryōshoku-kō," *Rekishi chiri* 75.4: 51-67; 5: 48-67; and 6: 53-72 (1940).
45. For details of Kobayakawa family patronage of the Zen monk Gūchū Shūkyū (1323-1409), see Fujioka, "Zenshū no chihō denpa," pp. 118-122; Kikuchi family patronage of Zen is discussed by Sugimoto, *Kikuchi-shi sandai,* pp. 129-133 and 213-219. For Imagawa Ryōshun's interests in Zen and Neo-Confucianism, see Kawazoe Shōji, *Imagawa Ryōshun* (Tokyo, 1964), pp. 49-52.
46. Sasaki Ginya, *Muromachi bakufu, Nihon no rekishi,* 13 (Tokyo, 1975), pp. 128-136; *Kyōto no rekishi,* 3, 123-124.
47. Hall, *Japan: from Prehistory to Modern Times,* p. 112.
48. *Kyōto no rekishi,* 3, 124-126.
49. For a more detailed discussion of the economic decline of the *gozan,* see below, Chapter Seven.
50. On the rising influence of Daitokuji, see *Kyōto no rekishi,* 3, 126-131; and Imaeda Aishin, "Muromachi jidai ni okeru Zenshū no hatten," in *Muromachi Bukkyō, Ajia Bukkyō-shi,* ed., Nakamura Hajime (Tokyo, 1972), pp. 63-74.
51. On the early history of Myōshinji, see Amakuki Sessan, *Myōshinji roppyakunen-shi* (Tokyo, 1935), pp. 44-205; Tamamura Takeji, "Shoki Myōshinji-shi no ni san giten," *Nihon Bukkyō-shi,* 3, 1957.

52. *Kyōto no rekishi*, pp. 132–133.
53. Imaeda, *Zenshū no rekishi*, p. 209.

4. THE ZEN MONASTIC LIFE AND RULE

1. James H. Sanford, "Ikkyū Sōjun: A Zen Monk of Fifteenth Century Japan" (PhD dissertation, Harvard University, 1972). Ikkyū was a vitriolic critic of formalization.
2. Cooper, *They Came to Japan*, pp. 321, 328. Most Iberian visitors to Japan in the sixteenth century expressed at least grudging respect for Zen monks as individuals and the Zen sect as an organization. Alessandro Valignano (1539–1606), the Jesuit Visitor General for the Orient, admired the organization of the Zen sect so much that he partially modeled the Jesuit mission along the same lines in order to make it a more effective force in Japanese society. See also, George Elison, *Deus Destroyed* (Cambridge, Mass., 1973), pp. 62, 79. Western visitors were clearly impressed by the surviving form of the institution. Ikkyū lamented that the form was empty, that for most monks the Zen monastic life had lost its meaning.
3. *Taishō shinshū daizōkyo*, 50, 770–771.
4. Ibid., 51, 250–251. The "Ch'an-men-knei-shih" is appended to the biography of Tai-chang in the *Ching-te ch'uan-teng-lu*.
5. Kondō Ryōichi, "Hyakujo shingi no seiritsu to sono genkai," pp. 19–49.
6. Shiina Hiroo, "Shotō Zensha no ritsu'in kyojū ni tsuite," pp. 770–772.
7. Yanagida, "Chūgoku Zenshū-shi," p. 28.
8. *Zoku zōkyō*, 2, 16, 3.
9. Ibid., 2, 16, 5. Here I use the annotated Japanese edition of the code prepared by Kagamishima, Satō, and Kosaka, *Yakuchū Zen'on shingi*.
10. Kondō, "Hyakujō shingi no seiritsu to sono genkei," pp. 21–30.
11. Ibid., pp. 22–23.
12. The following extracts from the "Ch'an-men kuei-shih" are translated from *Daizōkyō*, 51, 250.
13. The "Ch'an-men kuei-shih" does not name all 10 offices. Those mentioned by name are the rice steward, vegetable steward, and registrar. Although it is possible to build up a sketchy impression of the early Ch'an monastic bureaucracy from T'ang dynasty Ch'an writings, the first coherent picture is provided in the *Ch'an-yuan Code* (1103).
14. *Yakuchū Zen'on shingi*.
15. *Zoku zōkyō*, 2, 17, 1.
16. *Yakuchū Zen'on shingi*, p. 79.
17. Ibid.
18. *Zoku zōkyō*, 2, 16, 3., section 2, *"nien-sung."*

19. *Yakuchū Zen'on shingi*, p. 115.
20. Ibid., pp. 167–175 on the "*hua-chu.*"
21. Dōgen's early universalism is implied in the title of the first work he wrote after returning from China: *Fukan zazengi*, (Principles for the universal promotion of *zazen*), in Ōkubo Dōshu, ed., *Dōzen Zenji zenshū*, 2, (Tokyo, 1970), 3–4.
22. "Shukke" (Leaving the world), *Shōbō genzō* bk. 75, in Ōkubo, *Dōgen Zenji zenshū* (Tokyo, 1960), 1, 597–599. For a further discussion of Dōgen's attitude to monastic practice, see Kim, *Dōgen kigen: Mystical Realist*, pp. 228–308.
23. Imaeda, "Shingi no denrai to rufu," pp. 67–71.
24. Eisai's emphasis on the precepts is discussed by Yanagida in *Chūsei Zenka no shisō*, pp. 439–480.
25. *Kōzen gokokuron*, Yanagida, *Chūsei Zenka no shisō*, p. 11.
26. Ibid., pp. 80–86.
27. Ōkubo, *Dōgen Zenji Zenshū*, 2, 295–367.
28. See, for instance, the "Tenzo kyōkun," ibid., pp. 295–303.
29. Kagamishima Genryū, *Dōgen Zenji no inyō kyōten goroku no kenkyū* (Tokyo, 1965), pp. 181–192.
30. Imaeda, "Shingi no denrai to rufu," p. 61.
31. Ibid., pp. 61–62.
32. The following description of Musō and Rinsenji is based on Tamamura, *Musō Kokushi*, pp. 253–269.
33. The development and character of warrior *kakun* are discussed by Carl T. Steenstrup in *Hōjō Shigetoki (1198–1261) and his Role in the History of Political and Ethical Ideas in Japan*, (London, 1979). For a detailed study of one important sixteenth-century warrior house law, see James Kanda, "Japanese Feudal Society in the Sixteenth Century as Seen Through the *Jinkaishū* and other Legal Codes" (PhD dissertation, Harvard University, 1974).
34. Yanagida, *Rinzai no kafū*, p. 126.
35. The following translation is based on the *kanbun* and modernized Japanese texts included in *Kokuyaku Zenshū sōsho*, (Tokyo, 1920), 5, 210–222 and 107–113 (*kanbun*).
36. It was originally intended that the monk Gen'o Hongen should be the *kaisan*. His untimely death led Go-Daigo to confer the title of founder on Musō.
37. One of the ceremonial duties of the monk accompanying the new abbot was to strike a board with a wooden mallet at the beginning and end of the lectures given during the installation ceremony.
38. Zen monastic buildings are described in Chapter Five.
39. The Zen monastic bureaucracy is discussed in Chapter Six.

40. The *ryōgen* was the monk responsible for the supervision of the reading room (*shuryō*) where monks studied and relaxed between meditation sessions.

41. The *jinfu* organized the emptying and cleaning of the latrines.

42. The *shōsō jisha* kept the monks' hall in order, tidied up monks' sandals, bowls, bedding, etc., and served tea between meditation sessions.

43. The *Bonmōkyō (Fan-wang-ching,* Sutra of the Brahma's net), explains the 10 major and 48 supplementary regulations for Mahayana *bodhisattva* aspirants. J. J. M. deGroot, trans., *Le Code du Mahayana en Chine* (Amsterdam, 1893), p. 71.

44. The place of *shami* and *kasshiki* in the Zen monastery, and the problems they could cause, are discussed in Chapter Six. *Kasshiki* were boys aged from about 7 to 14. *Shami* were youths who had taken the novice's robe, been tonsured, and taken the 10 vows of the novice. Musō's concerns here are that *shami* and *kasshiki* especially were often treated indulgently by the monks. They contributed little to the community but had to be fed and clothed. They were also a cause of distraction and a potential source of sexual rivalry.

45. What Musō seems to be saying here is that ritual should not be separated from the regular round of established monastic observances; that there is no justification for the introduction of novelties.

46. In the colder months, Zen monks took a full bath once every 5 days, in hot weather a daily splash.

47. The mid-year festival of the dead.

48. Jōshū Jūshin, the T'ang dynasty Ch'an master Chao-chou Ts'ung-shen, a protagonist of many Zen anecdotes.

49. Literally "striking the board *zazen*." The sound of the board warned the monks to gather and begin meditation. For a description of the use of the board in the meditation hall of a twentieth-century Chinese monastery, see Holmes Welch, *The Practice of Chinese Buddhism* (Cambridge, Mass., 1967), pp. 47–74.

50. The prayers (*kitō*) that Musō objects to here were those accompanied by elaborate esoteric ritual. The problem, from a Zen point of view, was that time given to such liturgical activities reduced the time that could be spent in meditation or debate. It encouraged reliance on external assistance towards enlightenment, and there was the added danger that such practices would bind the monastery too closely to the secular patrons who sponsored the ceremonies. The *Huan-chu-an Code* (1317) stipulated that chanting of prayers should be limited to twice daily, morning and evening. In the *Muchū mondō*, Musō points out that, originally in Zen monasteries, they prayed only once a day. In time, a second session was added, and in Japanese Zen monasteries the Mongol crisis led

to the introduction of a third session:

When Kenchōji was founded, there was no mid-day prayer, but at the time of the Mongol invasions they started reading the *Kannon-kyō* (a sutra considered particularly effective in the face of calamities) during the day. This became customary, and there are now prayers three times a day. This is certainly not the aim of the Zen school, but, because the practice has been in effect for a long time, abbots of later generations have not put a stop to it. There are a number of monks who feel it is useless to do *zazen* in this degenerate age, and reducing prayers would be of little or no benefit to them. Furthermore, it would disappoint the wishes of patrons. Zen temples should not neglect the thrice-daily prayer. The intention is simply for peace in the world and the reassurance of patrons. *Muchū mondō*, Part 1, Section 15, Satō Taishun, ed. (Tokyo, 1934), p. 55.

While Musō accepts the retention of the existing practice he goes on to say that any further extension would inevitably cut into time that could be more profitably employed in *zazen*, and add nothing to the efficacy of prayers that are already being said.

51. The Buddha, the Dharma, and the Sangha.
52. To the Buddha, to rulers, to parents, and to benefactors.
53. The sentient world of desire, the world of form, and the formless world.
54. The *bodhisattva* is the Mahayanist, who, fired by compasssion, in addition to working for his own enlightenment and salvation (*jirigyō*), strives to assist others (*ritagyō*). The *śrāvaka* monk, or Hinayanist "hearer," confines his energies to the less ambitious but still demanding aim of saving himself by pursuing the Four Noble Truths and studying the Dharma. Musō is reminding his monks that they are at once *bodhisattva* and *śrāvaka*; that, while the *bodhisattva* ideal of assisting others is lofty and admirable, it also carries with it the potential for slackness and sybaritic antinomianism. Only when the *śrāvaka* has really mastered himself can he assume the world.
55. The codes in question are:

(1) "Hōjō Sadatoki Zen'in seifu jōsho" (Hōjō Sadatoki's regulations for Zen monasteries, 1294). *Kamakura shishi, Shiryō-hen* 2, pp. 25–26.

(2) "Sūen (Hōjō Sadatoki) Engakuji seifu jōsho" (Hōjō Sadatoki's regulations for Engakuji, 1303). *Kamakura shishi, Shiryō-hen* 2, pp. 35–36.

(3) "Sūgan (Hōjō Takatoki) Engakuji seifu jōsho" (Hōjō Takatoki's regulations for Engakuji, 1327). *Kamakura shishi, Shiryō-hen* 2, pp. 131–134.

(4) Musō Soseki's *Rinsen kakun*, 1339.

(5) "Ashikaga Tadayoshi Engakuji kishiki jōsho" (Ashikaga Tadayoshi's

regulations for Engakuji, 1340). *Kamakura shishi Shiryō-hen* 2, pp. 170-172.

(6) "Ashikaga Tadayoshi's Engakuji tsuika jōsho" Ashikaga Tadayoshi's supplementary regulations for Engakuji, 1342). *Kamakura shishi, Shiryō-hen 2*, pp. 175-176.

(7) "Kamakura gosho (Motouji) Zensatsu kishiki jōsho" (Ashikaga Motouji's regulations for Zen monasteries, 1354). *Kamakura shishi, Shiryō-hen* 2, pp. 190-193, and *Chūsei seiji shakai shisō 1* (Tokyo, 1972), pp. 162-168, p. 446.

(8) "Muromachi shogunke (Yoshimitsu) Zen'in hōshiki jōsho" (Muromachi shogunate regulations for Zen monasteries, 1381). *Kamakura shishi, Shiryō-hen 2*, pp. 292-294.

5. THE MONASTERY AND ITS SUB-TEMPLES

1. Taga, *Eisai*, p. 77.
2. See, for instance, "Senmen" (washing the face) and "Senjō" (ablutions), sections 50 and 54 of *Shōbō genzō*. Terada Tōru and Mizuno Yaoko, eds., *Dōgen*, (Tokyo, 1972) 2, 93-108, 132-142. The various sections of the *Eiheiji shingi* also illustrate Dōgen's interest in the practical details of monastic life and architecture. Ōkubo, *Dōgen Zenji zenshū*, 2, 295-367.
3. Yokoyama Hideya, *Zen'en bunka no kanshō* (Tokyo, 1973), pp. 47-48. I have relied heavily on the works of Professors Yokoyama, Kawakami, Sekiguchi, Iida, and Ōta in writing this chapter. Their studies are the starting points for anybody wishing to understand the physical framework of medieval Zen monastic life. On the development of traditional Japanese architecture in general the following books are helpful: Ōta Hirotarō, *Nihon kenchiku-shi josetsu* (Tokyo, 1947); Kondō Yutaka, *Koji saiken* (Tokyo, 1967); Itō Nobuo, *Kokenchiku no mikata* (Tokyo, 1967). For the background of Zen monastic architecture in China see: Sekino Tei, *Shina no kenchiku to geijitsu* (Tokyo, 1938); Iida Sugaki, *Chūgoku kenchiku no Nihon kenchiku ni oyobaseru eikyō* (Tokyo, 1953); Takeshima Takuichi, *Eizō hōshiki no kenkyū 1-3* (Tokyo, 1972). Zen monastic architecture in medieval Japan is discussed in: Ōta Hirotarō, *Chūsei no kenchiku*; Yokoyama Hideya, *Zen no kenchiku* (Tokyo, 1967); Kawakami Mitsugu, *Zen'in no kenchiku* (Kyoto, 1967); Ōta Hirotarō, Matsushita Ryūshō, and Tanaka Seidai, eds. *Zendera to sekitei, Genshoku Nihon no bijutsu*, 10 (Tokyo, 1967); Itō Nobuo, *Zenshū kenchiku, Nihon no bijutsu*, 126 (Tokyo, 1975). For detailed analyses of Kamakura Zen monasteries and their buildings, see Sekiguchi Kinya, *Kamakura no chūsei kenchiku* (Kanagawa Ken Kyōiku Iinkai, 1967) and the same author's studies of monastery buildings in *Kenchiku gakkai kenkyū hōkoku*, 1968.

4. Ibid.

5. These *gakuji* are also attributed to the famous layman calligrapher Chang Chi-chih (1186-1226); Fontein and Hickman, *Zen Painting and Calligraphy*, pp. 24-28. See also the catalogue, "Sōgen ga to Zen'in gakuji," of the exhibition of Zen painting and calligraphy held at the Kyoto National Museum, August-September, 1973.

6. Imaeda, in Akamatsu, ed., *Kamakura Bukkyō*, 2, 165.

7. Yokoyama, *Zen'en bunka*, pp. 39-42.

8. For a more complete analysis of the *Gozan jissatsu-zu*, on which the above is based, see Yokoyama Hideya, *Zen no kenchiku*, pp. 46-66. For illustrations of the whole Daijōji *Gozan jissatsu-zu*, see *Zengaku daijiten* 3, 10-32.

9. Yokoyama, *Zen no kenchiku*, p. 61.

10. A large-scale version of this is included in Ōta Hirotarō et al., *Zendera to sekitei*, p. 177. Unfortunately this illustration omits the measurements which seem to be included in the surviving original. See, Nuki et al., *Kenchōji*, p. 15; and Ōta, *Chūsei no kenchiku*, p. 237.

11. Nuki et al., *Kenchōji*, p. 16.

12. For an illustration, see *Kamakura shishi, shaji-hen*, facing page 382.

13. An illustration of the Sanshōji ground plan will be found in Ōta, *Chūsei no kenchiku*, p. 106.

14. Yokoyama, *Zen no kenchiku*, p. i.

15. Fontein and Hickman, *Zen Painting and Calligraphy*, pp. 144-148.

16. Ōta et al., *Zendera to sekitei*, pp. 138-142. Ōta Hirotarō, Tamamura Takeji, and others have recently suggested that the Engakuji Reliquary, which is famed as one of the oldest surviving examples of *karayō* (Chinese Zen style) architecture in Japan, is not the original Engakuji building, but was moved from Taiheiji, a local Zen nunnery, at a later, uncertain, date. See, Ōta, *Zendera to sekitei*, p. 165; and Tamamura Takeji, "Bunkenjō yori mitaru Engakuji shariden" *Nihon zenshū-shi ronshū* 1, 695-748.

17. Ōta et al., *Zendera to sekitei*, p. 155.

18. Ibid., pp. 179-181.

19. Ibid., p. 30.

20. Ibid., pp. 150-151.

21. Tamamura Takeji, "Gozan sōrin no tatchū ni tsuite," *Rekishi chiri* 76. 5, 6: 44-58, 33-64. (November and December 1940). *Tatchū* architecture is discussed in detail in Kawakami Mitsugu, *Zen'in no kenchiku*.

22. Yokoyama, *Zen no kenchiku*, p. 281.

23. Yokoyama, *Zen'en bunka*, p. 200; Ōta, *Chūsei kenchiku*, p. 107; Ōta et al., *Zendera to sekitei*, pp. 176-178, 214-235.

24. Ōta et al., *Zendera to sekitei*, pp. 95-99.

25. On Musō as a garden designer, see Kawase Kazuma, *Zen to teien* (Tokyo, 1968).

26. See, for instance, the *Kenchōji sashizu*.
27. On the seven-hall layout, see Yokoyama, *Zen no kenchiku*, pp. 67–71, on which the following section is based, and from which the diagrams are taken.
28. Yokoyama, *Zen no kenchiku*, p. 281.
29. For illustrations of surviving *sanmon*, see Ōta et al., *Zendera to sekitei*, pp. 24, 75; and for a detailed discussion, Yokoyama, *Zen no kenchiku*, pp. 122–134.
30. Yanagida ed., *Kōzen gokokuron*, in *Chūsei zenka no shisō*, pp. 80–81.
31. Yokoyama, *Zen no kenchiku*, 136–145.
32. Ibid., pp. 145–148.
33. Nuki et al., *Kenchōji*, pp. 25–26.
34. For a discussion of these tablets, see Yokoyama, *Zen'en bunka*, pp. 83–86; for an illustration, see the same author's *Zen no kenchiku*, p. 281.
35. Ōkubo, *Dōgen Zenji zenshū*, 2, 400.
36. Yokoyama, *Zen no kenchiku*, pp. 148–153.
37. Ibid., p. 281; Ōta et al., *Zendera to sekitei*, p. 177.
38. Ōta, *Chūsei no kenchiku*, p. 207.
39. Ōta et al., *Zendera to sekitei*, p. 116. Sennyūji is now a Shingon temple. In the Kamakura period Ritsu and Zen practices were also observed there.
40. On the *hōjō*, see Yokoyama, *Zen no kenchiku*, pp. 153–162.
41. *Daizōkyō*, 51, 250.
42. Yokoyama, *Zen no kenchiku*, p. 281.
43. Ōta, *Chūsei no kenchiku*, p. 106.
44. Yokayama, *Zen'en bunka*, pp. 95–103.
45. Yokoyama, *Zen no kenchiku*, pp. 211–227.
46. Ibid., p. 314.
47. Ibid., p. 373.
48. Ōta et al., *Zendera to sekitei*, p. 179.
49. See, for instance, "Senjō" (Ablutions), in Terada, *Dōgen*, 2, 132–142.
50. Yokoyama, *Zen no kenchiku*, pp. 211–219.
51. Ibid., p. 373.
52. For a detailed description and illustrations of a number of Zen monks' halls, see Yokoyama, *Zen no kenchiku*, pp. 174–190, 299–307.
53. See above, Chapter Four.
54. Kagamishima et al., *Yakuchū Zen'on shingi*, pp. 255–257.
55. Ibid., pp. 37–38.
56. For illustrations, see Yokoyama, *Zen no kenchiku*, pp. 300, ii.
57. Ibid., p. ii.
58. Cited in Yokoyama, *Zen no kenchiku*, p. 177.
59. Ibid.

60. Yokoyama, *Zen no kenchiku*, pp. 191–200.
61. For illustration, see Yokoyama, *Zen no kenchiku*, p. 308.
62. Dōgen, "Jūundō-shiki," in Ōkubo, *Dōgen Zenji zenshū*, 2, 305.
63. "Eiheiji shuryō shinki," in Ōkubo, *Dōgen Zenji zenshū*, 2, 363.
64. This building is described by Yokoyama, *Zen no kenchiku*, pp. 201–209.
65. Dōgen, "Tenzo kyōkun," in Ōkubo, *Dōgen Zenji zenshū*, 2, 295.

6. THE COMMUNITY

1. "Engakuji nenjū jiyōmai chūshinjō" and "Engakuji beisen nōgechō" (1283/9/27), documents nos. 13 and 14 in *Kamakura shishi, Shiryō-hen*, 2 (*Engakuji monjo*). Hereafter cited as *EGM*.
2. In modern equivalents, 1 *shō* equals 1.8 liters. Until some degree of standardization was introduced by Hideyoshi, medieval measures varied widely between 0.6 and 0.9 of the modern *shō*. Even within a single monastery and its scattered domains, several different measures might be in use for different purposes. It is unclear what measure was used in allocating rice at Engakuji at this time, but it was almost certainly smaller than the modern *shō*. If the widely used Kyoto *masu* was employed, the equivalent would be 0.96 of the modern measure. The problem of medieval measures is discussed in detail by Hōgetsu Keigo, *Chūsei ryōsei-shi no kenkyū* (Tokyo, 1961).
3. "Engakuji nenjū jiyōmai chūshinjō."
4. Tamamura, *Engakuji-shi*, p. 72.
5. "Sūen (Hōjō Sadatoki) Engakuji seifu jōsho," (1303/2/12), art. 1, *EGM*, No. 37.
6. "Hōjō Sadatoki jūsannen kuyōki," *EGM*, No. 69.
7. "Sūgan (Hōjō Takatoki) Engakuji seifu jōsho" (1327/10/1), art. 5, *EGM*, No. 75.
8. Tamamura, *Engakuji-shi*, p. 93.
9. Imaeda, *Chūsei Zenshū-shi no kenkyū*, p. 220.
10. "Ashikaga Tadayoshi Engakuji kishiki jōsho" (1340/11/-), art. 2, *EGM*, No. 127.
11. "Engakuji hyōjōshū rensho kishiki jōsho," (1364/1/28), art. 3, *EGM*, No. 175.
12. "Musō Soseki sanjūsannenki butsuji ketsuge," *Kamakura shishi Shiryō-hen*, 3, No. 27.
13. *Kamakura shishi, Sōsetsu-hen*, 1, 386.
14. Tamamura, *Engakuji-shi*, pp. 179–315.
15. "Hōjō Sadatoki jūsannenki kuyōki," *EGM*, No. 69.
16. Ibid.

17. Takahashi Ryūzō, "Rinzaishū kanji no seido," parts 1 and 2, *Kokushi-gaku*, 23 and 24: 9–43 and 13–30 (May and October 1935).

18. Hiraizumi, *Chūsei ni okeru shaji to shakai*, p. 49, states that Tōfukuji had a population of nearly 700 monks, in spite of repeated *bakufu* efforts to hold the number down to 350.

19. Imaeda, *Chūsei Zenshū-shi no kenkyū*, pp. 165–180.

20. *EGM*, No. 75.

21. Imaeda, *Chūsei Zenshū-shi no kenkyū*, p. 180.

22. Kawasaki and Kasahara, eds., *Shūkyō-shi*, p. 219.

23. Imaeda, *Zenshū no rekishi*, pp. 188–209; and above, Chapter Three, note 52.

24. Ibid., pp. 151–187; and Chapter One, note 40.

25. See, for instance, the excerpts from the "Ch'an-men kuei-shih," translated in Chapter Four.

26. Matsushita, *Ink Painting*, pp. 70–74.

27. On the problems associated with the appointment and reappointment of abbots in medieval Zen monasteries, see Takahashi, "Rinzaishū kanji no seido," part 1, pp. 24–38; Sakurai, *Nanzenji-shi*, pp. 257–262; and Imaeda Aishin, "Chūsei Zenrin ni okeru jūji seido no shomondai," *Chūsei Zenshū-shi no kenkyū*, pp. 397–407.

28. I have found no instances of Zen monasteries being designated *monzeki*. When shogun Yoshimitsu wished to find sinecure positions for his numerous male and female progeny he placed them in *monzeki* temples, but none of these were Zen temples. See *Kyōto no rekishi*, 3, 52–53; and Hall and Mass, *Medieval Japan*, p. 28.

29. It is assumed in Japanese writing on the history of Zen that this rule was, in fact, strictly observed in Chinese public monasteries and that the breach was made in Japan. Imaeda, "Chūsei Zenrin no kanji kikō," p. 154. I have not seen any thorough examination of the office of abbot in continental Ch'an monasteries. It is possible that the distinction between China and Japan here was less clear-cut than is generally assumed.

30. "Closed" monasteries were known as *tsuchien*, "open" monasteries as *jippōsatsu*.

31. The various kinds of certificates of appointment are discussed in greater detail in Takahashi, "Rinzaishū kanji no seido," part 1, pp. 24–31; Sakurai, *Nanzenji-shi*, pp. 343–359; and Imaeda Aishin, "Kumon to kansen," *Chūsei Zenshū-shi no kenkyū*, pp. 408–428.

32. See, for instance, the *Rinsen kakun*, Chapter Four, above. For the form of the ceremony in Northern Sung dynasty Ch'an monasteries as stipulated by the *Ch'an-yuan Code*, see *Yakuchū Zen'on shingi*, pp. 255–256.

33. "Muromachi shōgunke Zen'in hōshiki" (1381/12/28), art. 3, *EGM*, No. 256.

34. Takahashi, "Rinzaishū kanji no seido," part 1, p. 25.

35. Imaeda, "Kumon to kansen," pp. 411–412.
36. Takahashi, "Rinzaishū kanji no seido," part 1, pp. 26–28; and Imaeda, "Kumon to kansen," pp. 408–414.
37. Takahashi, "Rinzaishū kanji no seido," part 1, pp. 27–28.
38. On this problem, see Tsuji, *Chūsei,* 5, 340.
39. The financial importance of the *gozan* to the *bakufu* is discussed in Imaeda, "Kumon to kansen," pp. 415–427.
40. The development of Ch'an bureaucratic structure can be traced through the "Ch'an-men kuei-shih" regulations, *Ch'an-yuan Code, Eiheiji chiji Code* and the *Ch'ih-hsiu Pai-chang Code.* The *Zenrin shōkisen* is also helpful, and secondary discussions will be found in Tamamura Takeji, "Gozan no sōshoku," *Engaku,* No. 11; Imaeda Aishin, "Chūsei Zensō no seikatsu," *Kokubungaku kaishaku to kanshō* 31, 12: 215–223 (December 1966); Imaeda Aishin, "Chūsei Zenrin kikō no seiritsu to tenkai," in *Chūsei Zenshū-shi no kenkyū,* pp. 77–428. The Ch'an bureaucracy as it survived in twentieth-century Chinese monasteries is described in Holmes Welch, *The Practice of Chinese Buddhism,* pp. 3–46.
41. Elison, *Deus Destroyed,* pp. 62, 79.
42. "Sūen (Hōjō Sadatoki) Engakuji seifu jōsho" (1303/2/12), art. 5, *EGM,* No. 37.
43. Dōgen, "Tenzo kyōkun," in Ōkubo, *Dōgen Zenji zenshū,* 2.
44. Satō, "Hokusō sōrin no keizai seikatsu," pp. 14–20.
45. See Chapter Seven.
46. Fujioka Daisetsu, "Zen'in nai ni okeru tōhanshū ni tsuite," *Nihon rekishi* 145: 19–28 (July 1960).
47. Satō, "Hokusō sōrin no keizai seikatsu."
48. Takahashi, "Rinzaishū kanji no seido," part 2, pp. 13–15; and Tamamura, *Engakuji-shi,* p. 121.
49. Although these categories of servant and worker are mentioned frequently in Zen monastic documents, there is no study delimiting their various functions or analyzing their social background.
50. For a brief comparison with the social structure of a major Tendai monastery, see Kageyama, *Hieizan,* Chapter 10, pp. 99–103.
51. Takahashi, "Rinzaishū kanji no seido," part 1, pp. 38–43.
52. Ibid.
53. Donald Keene, *Nō: the Classical Theatre of Japan* (Tokyo, 1966), p. 181.
54. See Chapter Four, above.

7. THE ZEN MONASTIC ECONOMY

1. Jacques Gernet, *Les Aspects Economiques du Bouddhisme dans la Société Chinoise du Ve au Xe Siècle* (Saigon, 1956); Denis C. Twitchett, "The Monasteries and China's Economy in Medieval Times"; Denis C.

Twitchett, "Monastic Estates in T'ang China," *Asia Major* (New Series) 5: 123–146 (1956); Lien-sheng Yang, "Buddhist Monasteries and Four Money-Raising Institutions in Chinese History," *Harvard Journal of Asiatic Studies* 13:174–191 (1950); Kenneth Ch'en, "The Economic Background of the Hui-ch'ang Suppression of Buddhism," *Harvard Journal of Asiatic Studies* 19:67–105 (1956); Kenneth Ch'en, *Buddhism in China*, pp. 261–273; and Kenneth Ch'en, *The Chinese Transformation of Buddhism*, pp. 261–178.

2. Kagamishima, "Hyakujō koshingi henka katei," p. 8.

3. Ui Hakuju, *Zenshū-shi kenkyū* (Tokyo, 1939), pp. 81–90; Nakamura Hajime, "Zen ni okeru seisan to kinrō no mondai," *Zen bunka* 2:27–35 (September 1955).

4. Shiina Hiroo, "Higashiyama hōmon keisei no kaikei," *Komazawa shūkyō-gaku kenkyū*, No. 12.

5. Kondō Ryōichi, "Tōdai Zenshū no keizai kiban," Nihon Bukkyō Gakkai, ed., *Bukkyō to seiji-keizai* (Kyoto, 1972), pp. 137–151.

6. Satō Tatsugen, "Hokusō sōrin no keizai seikatsu," pp. 14–28.

7. Kagamishima et. al., *Yakuchū Zen'on shingi*, pp. 142–149.

8. Ibid. p. 149.

9. Ibid. pp. 167–175.

10. Ibid. pp. 141–142.

11. Cited by Fujioka Daisetsu, "Gozan kyōdan no hatten ni kansuru ichi kōsatsu," *Bukkyō shigaku* 6·2:57 (March 1957).

12. *Kamakura shishi, Shiryō-hen 2 (Engakuji monjo)*, cited hereafter as *EGM*, Sakurai Kageo and Fujii Manabu eds., *Nanzenji monjo*, Vols., 1 and 2 (Kyoto, 1972-), cited as *NZM*; Tokyo Daigaku Shiryō Hensanjo, ed., *Daitokuji monjo*, Vols., 1–10 (Tokyo, 1943-), cited as *DTM*. Secondary studies of the landholdings of these three monasteries include: Tamamura Takeji and Inoue Zenjō, *Engakuji-shi*; Nuki Tatsuto, "Enga-kuji-ryō ni tsuite," *Tōyō daigaku kiyō* 11:17–29 (1957); Sakurai Kageo, *Nanzenji-shi*; Takenuki Genshō, "Rinka ni okeru kyōdan keiei ni tsuite," *Bukkyō shigaku* 15·2:105–143; Nishioka Toranosuke, "Shugo daimyō ryōka no kiryō shōen," in Takamura Shōhei and Komatsu Hōkyō, eds., *Hōkensei to shihonsei* (Tōkyō, 1956), pp. 73–119.

13. Kuroda Toshio, "Chūsei jisha seiryoku-ron," pp. 180–295.

14. The map, "Owari no kuni Tomita shō ezu," is included in Nishioka Toranosuke, ed., *Nihon shōen ezu shūsei* (Tokyo, 1976), 1, 98. A larger reproduction of the same map, with a commentary by Takeuchi Rizō, will be found as a supplement to *Kanagawa kenshi: Shiryō-hen 2, kodai-chūsei*. Tomita-no-shō has been the subject of a number of studies. These include: Abe Takeshi, "Engakuji-ryō Owari no kuni Tomita-no-shō," *Chūsei Nihon shōen-shi no kenkyū* (Tokyo, 1967), pp. 186–195;

Ōyama Kyōhei, "Owari no kuni Tomita-no-*shō* ni tsuite," *Ōikonomika* 1.1:110–133 (April 1964); Sasaki Ginya, *Chūsei shōhin ryūtsū-shi no kenkyū,* pp. 224–227; and Tsukamoto Manabu and Arai Kikuo, *Aichiken no rekishi* (Tokyo, 1972), pp. 89–96.

15. *EGM,* No. 6 (1283/3/25).
16. *EGM,* No. 8.
17. *EGM,* Nos. 7, 8, 60.
18. Figures for income are based on *EGM,* No. 14 (1283/9/22). The same document gives a figure for rice outlay of 1,374.7 *koku,* a rice surplus of 195.1 *koku,* a cash expenditure of 1,745 *kanmon* and a cash deficit of 169.746 *kanmon.* The figure for total cash income actually given in the document is 1,575.451 *kanmon.* Figures for rice and cash outlay, respectively, are based on *EGM,* No. 13 (1283/9/27) and *EGM,* No. 18 (1284/9/-). Document No. 13 gives no details of cash expenditure for 1283. Document No. 18 gives the following figures for rice outlay in 1284: designated total—1,369.8 *koku*; surplus—200 *koku*; total—1,569.8 *koku.* It does not, however, provide an itemized breakdown of rice allocation. At prevailing exchange rates, 1 *koku* (about 5 bushels) of rice was equivalent to about 1 *kanmon* in cash.
19. *EGM,* No. 74.
20. For detailed information on other Engakuji holdings, see the articles cited in note 14 above.
21. *EGM,* No. 23.
22. *EGM,* No. 60 (1295/10/3).
23. *EGM,* Nos. 28–31.
24. *EGM,* Nos. 60, 32.
25. *EGM,* No. 69 (p. 78).
26. *EGM,* No. 40.
27. *EGM,* No. 66.
28. *EGM,* No. 66.
29. *EGM,* No. 67.
30. *EGM,* Nos. 168 (p. 220), 80 (pp. 137–138).
31. *EGM,* No. 168 (p. 214).
32. *EGM,* Nos. 83, 85, 86, 91, 92.
33. *EGM,* No. 80.
34. *EGM,* No. 102.
35. *EGM,* No. 107.
36. *EGM,* No. 168 (p. 225).
37. *EGM,* Nos. 161, 163, 164, 165, 231, 232.
38. *EGM,* No. 213.
39. *EGM,* No. 223.
40. *EGM,* Nos. 249, 319, 320, 337.

41. *EGM*, Nos. 214, 267, 268, 269, 270, 271, 290, 291, 292.

42. *EGM*, Nos. 224, 321.

43. *EGM*, No. 248.

44. *EGM*, Nos. 117, 118, 120, 122.

45. *EGM*, No. 111.

46. *EGM*, Nos. 156, 157, 158, 182, 203, 211; *EGM*, No. 167 (pp. 201 and 204); *EGM*, No. 297.

47. *EGM*, No. 307.

48. *EGM*, Nos. 86, 99.

49. *EGM*, Nos. 103, 104, 105, 106.

50. *EGM*, Nos. 113, 114, 115.

51. *EGM*, No. 124.

52. *EGM*, No. 297.

53. *EGM*, Nos. 168 (p. 223), 133.

54. *EGM*, No. 167 (p. 203).

55. *EGM*, No. 185.

56. *EGM*, Nos. 283, 284, 286.

57. *EGM*, No. 296.

58. *EGM*, No. 333.

59. *EGM*, Nos. 360, 361, 362.

60. *EGM*, No. 391.

61. *EGM*, Nos. 478, 393.

62. Nuki, "Engakuji-ryō ni tsuite," p. 29.

63. The standard history of Nanzenji is the excellent study by Sakurai Kageo, *Nanzenji-shi*, of which the first volume deals with Nanzenji in the medieval period and the second volume, *Zoku Nanzenji-shi*, traces the fortunes of the monastery through the Tokugawa period and the Meiji Restoration. Documents relating to the history of Nanzenji, *Nanzenji monjo*, are being published in a three-volume edition edited by Sakurai Kageo and Fujii Manabu. Volume 1 covers the period up to 1466; Volume 2 includes documents for the period 1467-1622.

64. *NZM 1*, Nos. 2, 3, 4, 125 (p. 188).

65. *NZM 1*, Nos. 15, 16; 20-27, etc.

66. *NZM 1*, No. 33.

67. *NZM 1*, Nos. 39, 89, 125 (p. 197).

68. *NZM 1*, No. 12 (pp. 87, 92, 94, 96).

69. *NZM 1*, No. 93 (p. 164).

70. *NZM 1*, No. 189.

71. Sakurai, *Nanzenji-shi*, p. 292.

72. Imatani Akira, *Sengoku-ki no Muromachi bakufu* (Tokyo, 1975), pp. 17, 30-33. For *gozan* exemption from debt moratoria (*tokuseirei*), see *Muromachi bakufu tsuika-hō*, article 223, in Satō Shin'ichi and Ikeuchi Yoshisuke, eds., *Chūsei hōsei shiryōshū 2, Muromachi bakufu-hō* (Tokyo,

1957), p. 80; and Kasamatsu Yasushi "Muromachi bakufu-hō" in Ishii, Kasamatsu et. al., eds., *Chūsei seiji shakai shisō 1* (Tokyo, 1972) p. 174.

73. Kikei Shinzui et. al., *Inryōken nichiroku*, cited hereafter as *IKN*, Chōroku 2 (1457)/2/27; and *NZM*, Nos. 200, 201, 202.
74. *NZM 1*, No. 139.
75. *Kyoto no rekishi 3*, p. 125.
76. Sakurai, *Nanzenji-shi*, p. 369.
77. *NZM 2*, No 225; and Sakurai, *Nanzenji-shi*, p. 369.
78. *IKN*, Chōkyō 2 (1488)/6/24.
79. *NZM 2*, No. 257; Sakurai, *Nanzenji-shi*, p. 372.
80. *NZM 2*, No. 272; Sakurai, *Nanzenji-shi*, p. 372.
81. The recovery of Nanzenji, and the other *gozan* monasteries, under the patronage of Hideyoshi and Ieyasu is described in Sakurai, *Zoku Nanzenji-shi*, pp. 1–103; and in *Kyoto no rekishi 4*, pp. 179–188.
82. *NZM 2*, No. 303.
83. *NZM 2*, Nos. 378, 384.
84. Sakurai, *Zoku Nanzenji-shi*, pp. 75–103; and *Kyoto no rekishi 4*, p. 180.
85. Studies of the economic history of Daitokuji in this period include: Takenuki Genshō, "Rinka ni okeru kyōdan keiei ni tsuite," *Bukkyō shigaku* 15.2:225–263; and Sasaki Ginya, *Chūsei shōhin ryūtsū-shi no kenkyū*, pp. 195–250. Nishioka Toranosuke has made several detailed studies of Takaie-no-*shō* in Kii province. Printed documentary materials relating to the landholdings of Daitokuji are included in the 10 volumes of the *Daitokuji monjo*.
86. *DTM 1*, No. 124.
87. *DTM 1*, No. 25.
88. Imatani, *Sengoku-ki no muromachi bakufu*, p. 54.
89. Patronage of Daitokuji by Sakai merchants and *sengoku daimyō* is detailed in *Ajia Bukkyō-shi, Nihon-hen 6, Muromachi Bukkyō*, pp. 73–74.
90. Further details on these and other Daitokuji *tatchū* will be found in Kawakami Mitsugu, *Zen'in no kenchiku*, pp. 127–265.
91. Kuwata Tadachika, *Toyotomi Hideyoshi kenkyū*, pp. 341–358.
92. Sasaki Ginya, *Chūsei shōhin ryūtsū-shi no kenkyū*, pp. 201–236.
93. Fujioka, "Gozan kyōdan no hatten," p. 58.
94. Imatani, *Sengoku-ki no Muromachi bakufu*, p. 55.
95. Sakurai, *Nanzenji-shi*, p. 248.
96. Fujioka, "Gozan kyōdan no hatten," p. 58.
97. The role of the *nassho* in medieval Zen monasteries is examined briefly by Takenuki Genshō, "Zenshū kyōdan un'ei to *nassho*," *Indogaku Bukkyōgaku kenkyū* 23.2:908–911 (March 1975).
98. Tettō Gikō, *Daitokuji hattō*, art. 8. Cited in Takenuki, "Rinka ni okeru kyōdan keiei," p. 109.

99. Fujioka, "Gozan kyōdan no hatten," p. 60; and Sakurai, *Nanzenji-shi*, p. 250.

100. Kudō Keiichi, "Shōensei no tenkai," *Kōza Nihon rekishi 5, Chūsei 1* (Tokyo, 1975), p. 284.

101. *IKN*, Chōkyō 3 (1489)/6/3. Cited in Sakurai, *Nanzenji-shi*, p. 250.

102. Fujioka, "Gozan kyōdan no hatten," p. 61.

103. Fujioka, "Gozan kyōdan no hatten," p. 62; and Sakurai, *Nanzenji-shi*, p. 251.

104. This gift-giving is detailed in Imatani, *Sengoku-ki no Muromachi bakufu*, pp. 35–45.

105. Fujioka, "Zen'in nai ni okeru tōhan-shū ni tsuite," pp. 19–28.

106. Imatani, *Sengoku-ki no Muromachi bakufu*, p. 29.

107. Medieval *shidōsen*-based moneylending is discussed by Fujioka, "Gozan kyōdan no hatten," p. 62; and by Hōgetsu Keigo, "Chūseio shidōsen ni tsuite," in Ichishi Shigeki Sensei Kiju Kinen-kai ed., *Ichishi Shigeki hakushi kiju kinen ronshū* (Nagano, 1971), pp. 25–45.

108. *DTM 1*, No. 219.

109. Nagahara Keiji et al., *Chūsei-shi handobukku*, pp. 480–481.

110. Sakurai, *Nanzenji-shi*, pp. 25–54.

111. For an introduction to the problem of *kajisshi*, see *Chūsei-shi handobukku*, p. 111.

112. *Kyoto no rekishi 4*, p. 180.

113. Nothing has been said in this chapter about the economic organization of the Sōtō school monasteries in the medieval period. They deserve a full-scale study in their own right.

Bibliography

Abe Chōichi 阿部肇一 . "Sōdai Zenshū shakai no haaku ni tsuite" 宋代禅宗社会の把握について (Zen society in the Sung dynasty), *Rekishi kyōiku* 9.8:85–92 (August 1961).

—— "Nansō kōki Zenshū no dōkō" 南宋後期禅宗の動向 (Trends in Late Southern Sung Zen Buddhism), *Bukkyō shigaku* 16.1:1–20 (September 1972).

Abe, Masao. "Dōgen on Buddha Nature," *The Eastern Buddhist* 4.1:28–71 (1971).

Abe Takeshi 阿部猛 *Chūsei Nihon shōen-shi no kenkyū* 中世日本荘園史の研究 (Studies in the history of *shōen* in medieval Japan), Tokyo, Shinseisha, 1967.

Aizawa Ekai 相沢恵海 *Zengaku yōkan* 禅学要鑑 (Essentials of Zen Buddhist studies). Tokyo, Segawa Shobō, 1908.

Akamatsu Toshihide 赤松俊秀 . *Shinran* 親鸞 (Shinran). Tokyo Yoshikawa Kōbunkan, 1961.

—— "Muromachi bakufu" 室町幕府 (The Muromachi *bakufu*), *Taikei Nihon-shi sōsho* 大系日本史叢書 , *Seiji-shi*, 1 政治史 . Tokyo, Yamakawa Shuppansha, 1966.

——, ed. *Nihon Bukkyō-shi* 日本仏教史 . Kyoto, Hōzōkan, 1967.

——, and Philip B. Yampolsky. "Muromachi Zen and the Gozan System," in Hall and Toyoda, eds., *Japan in the Muromachi Age*. University of California Press, 1977.

Amakuki Sessan 天岫接三 . *Myōshinji roppyakunen-shi* 妙心寺六百年史 (Myōshinji: six hundred years of history). Tokyo, 1935.

Amino Yoshihiko 網野善彦 . *Mōko shūrai* 蒙古襲来 (The Mongol invasions), *Nihon no rekishi*, 10 日本の歴史 . Tokyo, Shōgakkan, 1974.

Andō Fumihide 安藤文英 . *Eihei daishingi tsūkai* 永平大清規 通解 (Commentary on the pure regulations for Eiheiji). Tokyo, Kōmeisha, 1969.

Anesaki, Masaharu. *History of Japanese Religion.* Tokyo, Tuttle, 1963.

Araki Kengo 荒木見悟 . *Bukkyō to Jukyō* 仏教と儒教 *Buddhism and Confucianism.* Kyoto, Heirakuji Shoten, 1963.

—— "Zen"禪 , in *Chūgoku bunka sōsho,* 6 中国文化叢書 *Shūkyō* 宗教 . Ed., Kubo Tokutada 窪徳忠 and Nishi Junzō 西順藏 . Tokyo, Taishūkan, 1968.

Arnesen, Peter Judd. *The Medieval Japanese Daimyo.* New Haven, Yale University Press, 1979.

Asakawa Kan'ichi. "The Life of a Monastic Shō in Medieval Japan," *Land and Society in Medieval Japan.* Tokyo, Japan Society for the Promotion of Science, 1965.

Azuma kagami 吾妻鏡 (The mirror of the East), in Kuroita Katsumi 黒板勝美 , ed., *Shintei zōho kokushi taikei* 新訂増補国史大系 , vols. 32 and 33. Tokyo, Yoshikawa Kōbunkan, 1933.

Baishōron 梅松論 (Plum and pine theses), in Hanawa Hokiichi 塙保己一 comp., *Gunsho ruijū* 群書類従 , vol. 20. Tokyo, Taiyōsha, 1929.

Ben'en Enni. See Enni Ben'en

"Ch'an-men kuei-shih" ("Zenmon kishiki") 禪門規式 ("The Zen Gate Regulations"), included in *Ch'ing-te ch'uan-teng-lu (Keitoku den-tōroku)* 景德傳燈錄 , Takakusu Junjirō 高楠順次郎 ed., *Taishō shinshū daizōkyō,* 51, 250. Tokyo, Taishō Issaikyō Kankōkai, 1928.

Ch'en, Kenneth. "The Economic Background of the Hui-ch'ang Suppression of Buddhism," *Harvard Journal of Asiatic Studies* 19:67–105 (1956).

—— *Buddhism in China: A Historical Survey.* Princeton, Princeton University Press, 1964.

——*The Chinese Transformation of Buddhism.* Princeton, Princeton University Press, 1973.

Ch'ing-cho Cheng-ch'eng 清拙正澄 . *Taikan shingi* 大鑑清規 (The great mirror regulations), *Taishō shinshū daizōkyō,* 81, 619.

Chung-feng Ming-pen 中峰明本 . *Huan-chu-an ch'ing-kuei (Gen-jūan shingi)* 幻住庵清規 (Regulations for the Huan-chu-an).

Dai-Nihon zoku zōkyō 大日本続蔵経 . 2-16-5. Ed. Nakano Tatsue 中野達慧, . Kyoto, Zōkyō Shoin, 1905-1912.

Coates, Harper H., and Ryūgaku Ishizuka, trans., *Hōnen the Buddhist Saint.* Kyoto, Chion'in, 1925.

Collcutt, Martin. "Gozan Literature: The Practice of Zen and the Pursuit of Poetry," *Monumenta Nipponica* 33.2:201-205 (1979).

Cooper, Michael. *They Came to Japan.* Berkeley, University of California Press, 1965.

Covell, Jon Carter and Sōbin Yamada. *Zen at Daitokuji.* Tokyo, Kōdansha International, 1974.

Davis, David L. "*Ikki* in Late Medieval Japan," in Hall and Mass eds., *Medieval Japan: Essays in Institutional History.* New Haven, Yale University Press, 1974.

de Bary, William Theodore, Yoshito Hakeda, and Philip Yampolsky, eds. *The Buddhist Tradition.* New York, Modern Library, 1969.

Demieville, Paul. "La Situation religieuse en Chine au temps de Marco Polo," in *Oriente Poliano.* Rome, Istituto Italiano per il Medio ed Estremo Oriente, 1957.

Dōgen Kigen 道元希元 . *Fukan zazengi* 普勧坐禅儀 (Principles for the universal promotion of *zazen*), in Ōkubo Dōshū 大久保 道舟 , ed., *Dōgen Zenji zenshū* 道元禅師全集 , 2. Tokyo, Chikuma Shobō, 1970.

Dumoulin, Heinrich. *A History of Zen Buddhism.* Translated from the German by Paul Peachey. New York, Pantheon Books, 1963. Boston, Beacon Press, 1963.

Egashira Tsuneharu 江頭恒治 . *Kōyasan shōen no kenkyū* 高野山 荘園の研究 (A study of the *shōen* belonging to Mt. Kōya). Tokyo, Yūhikaku, 1938.

Eisai. See Myōan Eisai.

Elison, George. *Deus Destroyed: The Image of Christianity in Early Modern Japan.* Harvard East Asian Series. Cambridge, Harvard University Press, 1973.

Enni Ben'en 円爾弁円 . *Shōichi Kokushi goroku* 聖一国師 語録 (Records of Shōichi Kokushi). *Kokuyaku Zenshū sōsho* 国訳禅宗叢書 , Vol 10. Tokyo, Kokuyaku Zenshū Sōsho Kankōkai, 1920.

Enshin Tetsugyū 円心鉄牛 . *Shōichi Kokushi nenpu* 聖一国師 年譜 (Chronology of Shōichi Kokushi), *Dai-Nihon Bukkyō Zensho* 大日本仏教全書 , Vol. 95. Ed. Nanjō Bunyū 南條文碓 Tokyo, Bussho Kankōkai, 1912.

Foard, James H. "Ippen Shōnin and Popular Buddhism in Kamakura Japan." PhD dissertation, Stanford University, 1977.

Fontein, Jan, and Money L. Hickman. *Zen Painting and Calligraphy*. Boston, Museum of Fine Arts, 1970.

Frederic, Louis. *Daily Life in Japan in the Age of the Samurai*. New York: Praeger, 1972.

Fuji Naomoto 藤直幹 . *Buke jidai no shakai to seishin* 武家時代 の社会と精神 (The society and spirit of the warrior age). Osaka, Sōgensha, 1967.

Fujiki Hisashi 藤木久志 . *Sengoku shakai-shi ron* 戦国社会史 論 (Essays in the social history of the Sengoku period). Tokyo, Tokyo Daigaku Shuppankai, 1974.

Fujiki Kunihiko 藤木邦彦 and Inoue Mitsusada 井上光貞 *Taikei Nihon-shi sōsho, Seiji-shi 1* 大系日本史叢書, 政治史 1 (Papers on Japanese History, Vol. I, Politics). Tokyo, Yama-kawa Shuppansha 1965.

Fujioka Daisetsu 藤岡大拙 . "Gozan kyōdan no hatten ni kansuru ichi kōsatsu" 五山教団の発展に関する一考察 (The development of the *gozan* schools of Zen) *Bukkyō shigaku* 6.2:47–66 (March 1957).

—— "Zen'in nai ni okeru tōhanshū ni tsuite" 禅院内に於ける 東班衆について (The eastern ranks in Zen monasteries), *Nihon rekishi* 145:19–28 (July 1960).

—— "Zenshū no chihō denpa to sono juyōsō ni tsuite" 禅宗の地方伝播 とその受容層について (The provincial diffusion of the Zen schools and their local patrons), in *Nihon shūkyō-shi kenkyū, 1* 日本宗教史研究 , *Soshiki to dendō* 組織と伝道 . Ed., Kasahara Kazuo 笠原一男 . Tokyo, Hōzōkan, 1967.

Fujitani Toshio 藤谷俊雄 and Naoki Kōjirō 直木孝次郎. *Ise jingū* 伊勢神宮 (The Ise shrine). Kyoto, San'ichi Shobō, 1960.

Furuta Shōkin 古田紹欽 *Rinzai-roku no shisō* 臨済録の思想 (The thought in the Rinzai-roku). Tokyo, Shunjūsha, 1967.

Gernet, Jacques. *Les Aspects Economiques du Bouddhisme dans la Société Chinoise du Ve au Xe Siècle*. Saigon, 1956.

—— *Daily Life in China on the Eve of the Mongol Invasion.* London, Allen and Unwin, 1962.

Gidō Shūshin 義堂周信 . *Kūge nichiyō kufū ryakushū* 空華 日用工夫略集 (Chronicles of the empty flower). Ed. Tsuji Zennosuke 辻善之助 . Tokyo, Taiyōsha, 1939.

Greenblatt, Kristin Yü. "Yun-ch'i Chu-hung, The Career of a Ming Buddhist Monk." PhD dissertation, Columbia University, 1973.

Groot, J. J. M. de, trans. *Le Code du Mahayana en Chine.* Amsterdam, J. Müller, 1893.

Grossberg, Kenneth A. "Central Government in Medieval Japan: The Politics of the Muromachi Bakufu." PhD dissertation, Princeton University, 1977.

Haga Kōshirō 芳賀幸四郎 . "Ashikaga Yoshimasa no shūkyō seikatsu to sekaikan" 足利義政の宗教生活と世界 観 (The religious life and world view of Ashikaga Yoshimasa), in *Higashiyama bunka no kenkyū* 東山文化の研究 . Tokyo, Kawade Shobō, 1945.

—— *Chūsei Zenrin no gakumon oyobi bungaku ni kansuru kenkyū* 中世禅林 の学問及び文学に関する研究 (Scholarship and literature in the medieval Zen monasteries). Tokyo, Nihon Gakujutsu Shinkōkai, 1956.

—— *Daitokuji to chadō* 大徳寺と茶道 (Daitokuji and the way of tea). Kyoto, Tankōsha, 1972.

Hall, John Whitney. *Government and Local Power in Japan 500–1700, A Study based on Bizen Province.* Princeton, Princeton University Press, 1966.

—— *Japan: From Prehistory to Modern Times.* New York, Dell, 1970.

Hall, John W., and Jeffrey P. Mass, eds. *Medieval Japan: Essays in Institutional History.* New Haven, Yale University Press, 1974.

Hall, John W., and Toyoda Takeshi, eds. *Japan in the Muromachi Age.* University of California Press, 1977.

Hayashiya Tatsusaburō 林屋辰三郎 . "Chūsei-shi gaisetsu" 中世史概説 (A survey of medieval history), in *Kōza Nihon rekishi*, 5 講座日本歴史 , *Chūsei* 1. Tokyo, Iwanami Shoten, 1962.

——, et al., eds. *Kyōto no rekishi*, 3 京都の歴史 (A history of Kyoto), Kyoto, Gakugei Shorin, 1968.

—— "Kyoto in the Muromachi Age," in Hall and Toyoda, eds. *Japan in the Muromachi Age.* University of California Press, 1977.

Hioki Shōichi 日置昌一 . *Nihon sōhei kenkyū* 日本僧兵研究 (A study of monk-soldiers in Japan). Tokyo, Kokusho Kankōkai, 1972.

Hiraizumi Kiyoshi 平泉澄 . *Chūsei ni okeru shaji to shakai to no kankei* 中世に於ける社寺と社会との関係 (The relationship between shrines and temples in medieval society). Tokyo, Shibundō, 1934.

Hiraoka Jōkai 平岡定海 . "Sōhei ni tsuite" 僧兵について (On the monk-soldiers), in Hōgetsu Keigo Sensei Kanreki Kinenkai, eds., *Nihon shakai keizai-shi kenkyū, kodai chūsei hen* 日本社会経済史研究古代中世編 Tokyo, Yoshikawa Kōbunkan, 1967.

Hirata Toshiharu 平田俊春 . *Sōhei to bushi* 僧兵と武士 (Monk-soldiers and warriors). Tokyo, Nihon Kyōbunsha, 1965.

Hirose Ryōkō 広瀬良弘 . "Tokushū kankei bunken kaisetsu" 特集関係文献解説 (Critical bibliography for the special edition devoted to Zen and medieval Japanese culture), *Zen to chūsei bunka, Rekishi kōron* 10:130–136 (October 1977).

Hōgetsu Keigo 寶月圭吾 . *Chūsei ryōsei-shi no kenkyū* 中世量制史の研究 (A study of medieval weights and measures). Tokyo, Yoshikawa Kōbunkan, 1961.

Hōgetsu Keigo Sensei Kanreki Kinenkai 寶月圭吾先生還暦記念会 ed. *Nihon shakai keizai-shi kenkyū, kodai chūsei hen* 日本社会経済史研究古代中世編 (Essays in Japanese social and economic history, ancient and medieval periods). Tokyo, Yoshikawa Kōbunkan, 1967.

Hori, Kyotsu. "The Mongol Invasions and the Kamakura *Bakufu*." PhD dissertation, Columbia University, 1967. University Microfilms, pp. 119–147, 217–233.

Hurvitz, Leon. *Chih-i* (538–597), *Mélanges Chinois et Bouddhiques 12*. Bruxelles: L'Institut Belge des Hautes Études Chinoises, 1962.

Ichishi Shigeki Sensei Kiju Kinen-kai 一志茂樹先生喜寿記念会 , eds. *Ichishi Shigeki hakushi kiju kinen ronshū* 一志茂樹博士喜寿記念論集 (Essays in honor of the seventy-seventh birthday of Professor Ichishi Shigeki). Nagano, 1971.

Iida Sugaki 飯田須賀斯 . *Chūgoku kenchiku no Nihon kenchiku ni oyobaseru eikyō* 中国建築の日本建築に及ぼせる影響 (The impact of Chinese architecture on Japanese architecture). Tokyo, Sagami Shoten, 1953.

Imaeda Aishin 今枝愛真 et al. "Nihon Bukkyō no chiiki hatten"

日本仏教の地域発展 (The regional dispersion of Japanese Buddhism), *Bukkyō shigaku* 9.3:1–163; 9.4:2–15, 58–162 (October 1961).

—— *Zenshū no rekishi* 禅宗の歴史 (A history of the Zen schools). Tokyo, Shibundō, 1962.

—— "Zenshū—sengoku jidai chūshin ni" 禅宗—戦国時代中心に (The Zen schools in the Sengoku period) *Rekishi kyōiku* 10.8:9–17 (1962).

—— "Sōtōshū Wanshi-ha no hatten to Asakura-shi" 曹洞宗宏智派の発展と朝倉氏 (The development of the Wanshi branch of the Sōtō school and the Asakura family) *Nihon Bukkyō* 21:1–130 (August 1965).

—— *Japanese Zen.* Tokyo, International Society for Educational Information, 1965.

—— "Sōtōshū no hatten" 曹洞宗の発展 (The development of the Sōtō school) in Kawasaki and Kasahara, eds., *Shūkyō-shi* 宗教史. Tokyo, Yamakawa Shuppansha, 1966.

—— "Chūsei Zensō no seikatsu 中世禅僧の生活 (The life of the medieval Zen monk) *Kokubungaku: kaishaku to kanshō* 31.12:215–223 (December 1966).

—— "Eisai no shin Bukkyō undō" 栄西の新仏教運動 (Eisai's Buddhist reform movement), *Rekishi kyōiku* 14–9:65–72 (September 1966).

—— "Chūsei Bukkyō no tenkai" 中世仏教の展開 (The development of medieval Buddhism), in Akamatsu Toshihide, ed., *Nihon Bukkyō-shi*, 2 日本仏教史. Kyoto, Hōzōkan, 1967.

—— "Zen to kōshitsu" 禅と皇室 (Zen and the imperial house), in Nishitani Keiji, et. al. eds., *Kōza Zen*, 5 講座禅. Tokyo, Chikuma Shobō, 1968.

—— *Chūsei Zenshū-shi no kenkyū* 中世禅宗史の研究 (Studies in the history of the medieval Zen schools). Tokyo, Tokyo Daigaku Shuppankai, 1970.

—— "Muromachi jidai ni okeru Zenshū no hatten" 室町時代に於ける禅宗の発展 (The development of the Zen schools in the Muromachi period), in Nakamura Hajime 中村元, et. al., eds., *Ajia Bukkyō-shi, Nihon-hen, 6, Muromachi Bukkyō* アジア仏教史, 日本編, 6 室町仏教. Tokyo, Kōsei Shuppansha, 1972.

—— *Dōgen to sono deshi* 道元とその弟子 (Dōgen and his disciples). Tokyo, Mainichi Shinbunsha, 1972.

Imatani, Akira 今谷明 . *Sengoku-ki no Muromachi bakufu* 戦国期の室町幕府 (The Muromachi *bakufu* in the Sengoku period). Tokyo, Kadokawa Shoten, 1975.

Inoue Toshio 井上鋭夫 . *Ikkō ikki no kenkyū* 一向一揆の研究 (A study of the Ikkō uprisings). Tokyo, Yoshikawa Kōbunkan, 1968.

Ishida, Ichirō. "Zen Buddhism and Muromachi Art," *Journal of Asian Studies* 22.4:417–430 (August 1963).

Ishida Mitsuyuki (Jūshi) 石田充之 , ed. *Shunjō ritsushi* 俊芿律師 (Shunjō, the Ritsu Master). Kyoto, Hōzōkan, 1972.

Ishii Susumu 石井進 . *Nihon chūsei kokka-shi no kenkyū* 日本中世国家史の研究 (A study of the medieval Japanese state). Tokyo, Iwanami Shoten, 1970.

——, Ishimoda Shō 石母田正 , Kasamatsu Hiroshi 笠松宏至 . Katsumata Shizuo 勝俣鎮夫 , and Satō Shin'ichi 佐藤進一 , eds. *Chūsei seiji shakai shisō 1* 中世政治社会思想 (Medieval political and social thought). Tokyo, Iwanami Shoten, 1972.

Iwahashi Koyata 岩橋小弥太 *Hanazono tennō* 花園天皇 (Emperor Hanazono). Tokyo, Yoshikawa Kōbunkan, 1962.

Iwai Hirosato 岩井大慧 . *Nisshi Bukkyō-shi ronkō* 日支仏教史論攷 (Essays in the history of Chinese and Japanese Buddhism). Tokyo, Tōyō Bunko, 1957.

Itō Nobuo 伊藤延男 . *Kokenchiku no mikata* 古建築の見方 (The appreciation of ancient architecture). Tokyo, Daiichi Hōki, 1967.

——. *Zenshū kenchiku* 禅宗建築 (Zen architecture). Tokyo, Shibundō, 1975.

Kadokawa Gengi 角川源義 and Sugiyama Hiroshi 杉山博 , eds. *Nihon bungaku no rekishi, 5* 日本文学の歴史 (A history of Japanese literature). Tokyo, Kadokawa Shoten, 1967.

Kagamishima Genryū 鏡島元隆 . *Dōgen Zenji to sono monryū* 道元禅師とその門流 (The Zen-master Dōgen and his followers). Tokyo, Seishin Shobō, 1961.

—— *Dōgen Zenji no inyō kyōten goroku no kenkyū* 道元禅師の引用教典・語録の研究 (A study of the sermons of Zen-master Dōgen and the citations used in his writings). Tokyo, Mokujisha, 1965.

—— "Hyakujō koshingi henka katei no ichi kōsatsu" 百丈古清規変化過程の一考察 (Thoughts on the process of development of Pai-chang's pure regulations), *Komazawa daigaku bungakubu kenkyū kiyō*

駒沢大学文学部研究紀要 , No. 25 (March 1967).

——, Satō Tatsugen 佐藤達玄 , and Kosaka Kiyū 小坂機融 , eds. *Yakuchū Zen'on shingi* 訳註禅苑清規 (Annotated edition of the Ch'an-yuan Code). Tokyo, Sōtōshū Shūmuchō, 1972.

Kageyama Haruki 影山春樹 . *Hieizan* 比叡山 (Mount Hiei). Tokyo, Kadokawa Shoten, 1975.

Kamakura Shishi Hensan Iinkai 鎌倉市史編纂委員会 . *Engakuji monjo* 円覚寺文書 (Documents relating to Engakuji), in *Kamakura shishi* 鎌倉市史 , *Shiryō-hen* 2. Tokyo, Yoshikawa Kōbunkan, 1958.

—— *Kamakura shishi* 鎌倉市史 (A history of the city of Kamakura). 6 vols. Tokyo, Yoshikawa Kōbunkan, 1956–1959.

Kamei Katsuichirō 亀井勝一郎 . "Muromachi geijutsu to minshū no kokoro" 室町芸術と民衆の心 (Muromachi arts and the popular spirit). *Nihonjin no seishin-shi kenkyū* 日本人の精神史研究 . Tokyo, Bungeishunjū, 1966.

Kanagawa-ken Kenshi Henshūshitsu 神奈川県県史編集室 , ed. *Kanagawa kenshi* 神奈川県史 (History of Kanagawa-ken) Shiryō-hen 2. Kanagawa-ken, 1973–.

Kanai Tokuyuki 金井徳幸 . "Sōdai shakai ni okeru jiin to jūjisei no mondai" 宋代社会に於ける寺院と住持制の問題 (Problems of temples and abbacies in Sung dynasty society), *Rekishi kyōiku* 10.8:52–58 (August 1962).

Kanaoka Shūyū 金岡秀友 , ed. *Bukkyō shūha jiten* 仏教宗派辞典 (A dictionary of schools of Buddhism). Tokyo, Tōkyōdō Shuppan, 1974.

Kanda, James. "Japanese Feudal Society in the Sixteenth Century as Seen Through the *Jinkaishū* and Other Legal Codes." PhD dissertation, Harvard University, 1974.

Kasahara Kazuo 笠原一男 . *Ikkō ikki no kenkyū* 一向一揆の研究 (Studies in the Ikkō uprisings). Tokyo, Yamakawa Shuppansha, 1954.

—— *Nihon shūkyō-shi kenkyū nyūmon* 日本宗教史研究入門 (An introductory guide to the study of the history of Japanese religion). Tokyo, Hyōronsha, 1971.

—— *Nihon ni okeru seiji to shūkyō* 日本における政治と宗教 (Politics and religion in Japan). Tokyo, Yoshikawa Kōbunkan, 1974.

Katsuno Ryūshin 勝野隆信 . *Sōhei* 僧兵 (Monk-soldiers). Tokyo, Shibundō, 1956.

Kawai Masaharu 河合正治 . *Chūsei buke shakai no kenkyū* 中世武家社会の研究 (Studies in medieval warrior society). Tokyo, Yoshikawa Kōbunkan, 1973.

Kawakami Mitsugu 川上貢　. *Zen'in no kenchiku* 禅院の建築 (Zen monastic architecture). Kyoto, Kawara Shoten, 1967.

Kawasaki Yōsuke 川崎庸之　and Kasahara Kazuo 笠原一男, eds. *Taikei Nihon-shi sōsho,* 18, Shūkyō-shi 大系日本史叢書, 18, 宗教史 Tokyo, Yamakawa Shuppansha, 1966.

Kawase Kazuma 川瀬一馬　. *Zen to teien* 禅と庭園　(Zen and gardens). Tokyo, Kodansha, 1968.

Kawazoe Shōji 川添昭二　. *Imagawa Ryōshun* 今川了俊　(The warrior Imagawa Ryōshun). Tokyo, Yoshikawa Kōbunkan, 1964.

—— "Kamakura jidai no taigai kankei to bunbutsu no inyū" 鎌倉時代の対外関係と文物の移入 (Foreign relations and the importation of cultural objects during the Kamakura period), in *Kōza Nihon rekishi* 6. Tokyo, Iwanami Shoten, 1975.

Keene, Donald. *Nō: The Classical Theatre of Japan.* Tokyo, Kōdansha International, 1966.

Keijo Shūrin 景徐周麟　, et. al. *Rokuon nichiroku* 鹿苑日録 (The diary of the Rokuon'in). Ed. Tsuji Zennosuke. 辻善之助. Tokyo, Taiyōsha, 1935–1938.

Kikei Shinzui 季瓊真蘂　, et. al. *Inryōken nichiroku* 蔭涼軒日録 (The diary of the Inryōken). Ed. Tamamura Takeji 玉村竹二 and Katsuno Ryūshin 勝野隆信. Tokyo, Shiseki Kankōkai, 1954.

Kim, Hee-Jin. *Dōgen Kigen—Mystical Realist.* Tucson, The University of Arizona Press, 1975.

Kitabatake Chikafusa 北畠親房　. *Jinnō shōtōki* 神皇正統記 (The record of the legitimate line of the divine sovereigns). *Nihon koten bungaku taikei* 日本古典文学大系　, 87. Ed. Iwasa Masashi 岩佐正　. Tokyo, Iwanami Shoten, 1965.

Kitagawa, Joseph M. *Religion in Japanese History.* New York, Columbia University Press, 1966.

Kokan Shiren 虎関師錬　*Genkō shakusho* 元亨釈書　(Buddhist chronicles of the Genkō period). *Shintei zōho kokushi taikei* 新訂増補国史大系　, 31. Ed. Kuroita Katsumi 黒坂勝美. Tokyo, Yoshikawa Kōbunkan, 1930.

Kondō Ryōichi 近藤良一　. "Hyakujō shingi to Zen'on shingi" 百丈清規と禅苑清規　(Pai-chang's pure regulations and the Ch'an-yuan pure regulations), *Indogaku Bukkyōgaku kenkyū* 17.2:328–330 (1969).

—— "Hyakujō shingi no seiritsu to sono genkei" 百丈清規の成立とその原型 (The composition of the Pai-chang pure regulations and their original form)," *Hokkaidō Komazawa Daigaku kenkyū kiyō* 3:19–48.

—— "Tōdai Zenshū no keizai kiban" 唐代禅宗の経済基盤 (The economic basis of T'ang dynasty Zen), in *Bukkyō to seiji-keizai* 仏教と政治経済. Comp. Nihon Bukkyō Gakkai. Kyoto, Heirakuji Shoten, 1972.

Kondō Yutaka 近藤豊 . *Koji saiken* 古寺細見 (Old temples revisited). Tokyo, Rajiosha, 1967.

Kōsaka, Konomu 高坂好 . *Akamatsu Enshin, Mitsusuke* 赤松円心・満祐 . Tokyo, Yoshikawa Kōbunkan, 1970.

Kudō Keiichi 工藤敬一 . "Shōensei no tenkai" 荘園制の展開 (The development of the *shōen* system). *Kōza Nihon rekishi* 5, *Chūsei* 1. Tokyo, Iwanami Shoten, 1975.

Kuroda Toshio 黒田俊雄 . "Chūsei no kokka to tennō" 中世の国家と天皇 (State and emperor in medieval Japan), in *Kōza Nihon rekishi* 6, *Chūsei* 2. Tokyo, Iwanami Shoten, 1963.

—— *Mōko shūrai* 蒙古襲来 (The Mongol invasions). *Nihon no rekishi* 8 日本の歴史 . Tokyo, Chūō Kōron-sha, 1965.

—— "Chūsei jisha seiryoku ron" 中世寺社勢力論 (On the power of medieval temples and shrines"), in *Kōza Nihon rekishi* 6, *Chūsei* 2. Tokyo, Iwanami Shoten, 1975.

—— "Enrayakuji shūto to Sasaki-shi" 延暦寺衆徒と佐々木氏 (Enryakuji monks and the Sasaki family), in *Nihon chūsei no kokka to shūkyō* 日本中世の国家と宗教 . Tokyo, Iwanami Shoten, 1975.

Kurokawa Tadanori 黒川忠範 . "Higashiyama sansō no zōei to sono haikei" 東山山荘の造営とその背景 (The background to the building of the Higashiyama Pavilion), in *Chūsei no kenryoku to minshū* 中世の権力と民衆 . Ōsaka, Sōgensha, 1970.

Kuwata Tadachika 桑田忠親 . *Toyotomi Hideyoshi kenkyū* 豊臣秀吉研究 (A study of Toyotomi Hideyoshi). Tokyo, Kadokawa Shoten, 1975.

Kyoto Kokuritsu Hakubutsukan 京都国立博物館 . "Sōgen-ga to Zen'in gakuji" 宋元画と禅院額字 (Sung and Yuan paintings and calligraphic plaques used in Zen monasteries). Exhibition Catalogue. Kyoto Kokuritsu Hakubutsukan, 1973.

Lancaster, Lewis and Whalen Lai, eds. *The Early History of Ch'an in China and Tibet*. The Berkeley Buddhist Studies Series. Forthcoming.

Langlois, John D., Jr. Review of John W. Dardess, *Conquerors and Confucians: Aspects of Political Change in Late Yuan China, Journal of Asian Studies* 34.1:218–220 (November 1974).

Mangen Shiban 卍元師蛮 . *Enpō dentōroku* 延宝伝燈録 (The Enpō period transmission of the lamp). *Dai-Nihon Bukkyō Zensho*, vols. 69 and 70 大日本仏教全書

Mass, Jeffrey P. *Warrior Government in Early Medieval Japan*. New Haven, Yale University Press, 1974.

Matsumoto Shinhachirō 松本新八郎 . "Nanbokuchō no nairan" 南北朝の内乱 (The warfare between the Northern and Southern courts), in *Chūsei shakai no kenkyū* 中世社会の研究 Tokyo, Tokyo Daigaku Shuppankai, 1956.

Matsushita, Takaaki. *Ink Painting*. Tokyo, Weatherhill, 1974.

Matsuyama Zenshō 松山善昭 . "Tōhoku chihō ni okeru Sōtōshū kyōdan seiritsu no tokushusei" 東北地方における 曹洞宗教団成立の特殊性 (Characteristics of the development of the Sōtō school in the northeastern region of Japan), *Nihon Bukkyō* 10:38–54 (January 1961).

—— "Kinsei Tōhoku ni okeru shin Bukkyō no denpa to kyōdan keisei" 近世東北における新仏教の伝播と教団形成 (The diffusion of "new" Buddhism and sect formation in northeastern Japan during the early modern period), in *Nihon shūkyō-shi kenkyū*, 9 日本宗教史研究 . Ed., Kasahara Kazuo, Kyoto, Hōzōkan, 1967.

McCullough, Helen Craig, trans. *The Taiheiki: A Chronicle of Medieval Japan*. New York, Columbia University Press, 1959.

Minegishi Sumio 峰岸純夫 . "Ikkō ikki" 一向一揆 (The Ikkō uprisings), in *Kōza Nihon rekishi* 8, *Chūsei* 4. Tokyo, Iwanami Shoten, 1976.

Miura Shūkō 三浦周行 . *Nihon-shi no kenkyū* 日本史の研究 (Studies in Japanese history). Tokyo, Iwanami Shoten, 1922.

Miyasaka Yūshō 宮坂宥勝 . *Kōyasan-shi* 高野山史 (A history of Mt. Kōya). Tokyo, Kōyasan Bunka Kenkyūkai, 1962.

Mizuno Kōgen 水野弘元 and Hirata Takashi 平田高士 . *Dōgen: Rinzai Zenkashū* 道元：臨済禅家集 (Selected works of Dōgen and Rinzai Zen masters). Tokyo, Tamagawa Daigaku Shuppan-bu, 1972

Mochizuki Shinjō 望月信成 , et al. *Butsuzō (zoku-hen)* 仏像

続編 (Buddhist statues). Tokyo, Nihon Hōsō Shuppan Kyōkai, 1965.

Mori Katsumi 森克巳 . *Nissō bōeki no kenkyū* 日宋貿易の 研究 (Studies in Japanese-Sung trading relations). Tokyo, Kokuritsu Shoin, 1948.

Mujaku Dōchū 無著道忠 . *Zenrin shōkisen* 禅林象器箋 (A compilation of terms used in Zen monasteries). Kyoto, Kaiyō Shoin, 1909.

Mujū Ichien 無住一円 . *Shasekishū* 沙石集 (Collection of sand and pebbles). *Nihon koten bungaku taikei* 日本古典文学大系 vol. 85. Ed. Watanabe Tsunaya 渡邊綱也 . Tokyo, Iwanami Shoten, 1976.

Musō Soseki 夢窓疎石 . *Muchū mondō* 夢中問答 (Discussions in dreams), in *Zengaku taikei* 禅学大系 , *Soroku-bu* 祖録部 , Vol. 4. Tokyo, Ikkatsusha, 1912. Also, *Muchū mondōshū*, Ed. Satō Taishun 佐藤泰舜 . Tokyo, Iwanami Shoten, 1934.

—— *Rinsen kakun* 臨川家訓 (The Rinsenji House Code). *Kokuyaku Zenshū sōsho*. Vol. 5. 国訳禅宗叢書 . Tokyo, Kokuyaku Zenshū Sōsho Kankōkai, 1920.

—— *Musō Kokushi goroku* 夢窓国師語録 (The record of Musō Kokushi). *Kokuyaku Zenshū sōsho*. Vol. 5.

Myōan Eisai (Yōsai) 明庵栄西 . "Shukke taikō" 出家大綱 (Basic provisions for entry to the monastic life). In Kinomiya Yasuhiko 木宮泰彦 , *Eisai Zenji* 栄西禅師 (The Zen master Eisai). Tokyo, Hinoeuma Shuppansha, 1916.

—— "Kōzen gokokuron" 興禅護国論 (Promulgation of Zen as a defense of the nation). In Furuta Shōkin, *Nihon no Zen goroku Eisai*. And in Ichikawa Hakugen 市川白弦 , Iriya Yoshitaka 入矢義高 , and Yanagida Seizan 柳田聖山 eds. *Chūsei Zenka no shisō* 中世 禅家の思想. (The thought of medieval Japanese Zen masters). Tokyo, Iwanami Shoten, 1972.

—— "Kissa yōjōki" 喫茶養生記 (Enhancement of life through the drinking of tea). In Furuta Shōkin, *Nihon no Zen goroku 1, Eisai* 日本の 禅語録 1, 栄西 (The records of Japanese Zen masters 1, Eisai). Tokyo, Kōdansha, 1977.

Nagahara Keiji 永原慶二 . *Minamoto Yoritomo* 源頼朝 (The warrior Minamoto Yoritomo). Tokyo, Iwanami Shoten, 1958.

—— *Nihon hōken seiritsu katei no kenkyū* 日本封建成立過程 の研究 (Studies in the formation of Japanese feudalism). Tokyo, Iwanami Shoten, 1961.

—— "Nanbokuchō nairan" 南北朝内乱   (The civil wars between the Northern and Southern courts), in *Kōza Nihon rekishi* 6, *Chūsei* 2. Tokyo, Iwanami Shoten, 1963.

——, et. al., eds. *Chūsei-shi handobukku* 中世史ハンドブック   (A handbook for medieval historical studies). Tokyo, Kondō Shuppansha, 1973.

—— "Shōensei kaitai katei ni okeru nanbokuchō nairanki no ichi" 荘園制解体過程に於ける南北朝内乱期の位置 (The place of the Northern and Southern court civil war period in the process of *shōen* dissolution), in *Nihon chūsei shakai kōzō no kenkyū*. Tokyo, Iwanami Shoten, 1976.

Nakamura Hajime 中村元   . "Zen ni okeru seisan to kinrō no mondai" 禅に於ける生産と勤労の問題   (The problem of labor and production in Zen), *Zen bunka* 2:27–35 (September 1955).

—— *Muromachi Bukkyō* 室町仏教 (Muromachi Buddhism), in *Ajia Bukkyō-shi–Nihon hen*, 6. Tokyo, Kōsei Shuppansha, 1972.

——, et. al, eds. *Kamakura Bukkyō*, 1–3 鎌倉仏教 (Kamakura Buddhism), in *Ajia Bukkyō-shi–Nihon hen*, vols. 3–6 アジア仏教史 日本編 . Tokyo, Kōsei Shuppansha, 1972 .

Nakazawa Benjirō 中沢弁次郎   . *Nihon beika hendō-shi* 日本米価変動史 (A history of the fluctuations in Japanese rice prices). Tokyo, Meibundō, 1933.

Nanzenji monjo 南禅寺文書   (Documents relating to Nanzenji). Compiled by Sakurai Kageo 櫻井景雄   and Fujii Manabu 藤井学 . 3 vols. Kyoto, Nanzenji, 1972.

Nishimura, Eshin. *Unsui: A Diary of Zen Monastic Life.* Ed. Bardwell L. Smith. Honolulu, University of Hawaii Press, 1973.

Nishioka Toranosuke 西岡虎之助   . "Daitokuji-ryō Kii no kuni Takaie-no-shō" 大徳寺領紀伊国高家荘   (Daitokuji's Takaie-no-shō in Kii province), *Rekishigaku kenkyū* 6.9:2–21 (1936).

—— "Chūsei ni okeru ichi shōen no shōchō" 中世に於ける一荘園の消長 (The vicissitudes of a medieval *shōen*), in Nishioka, *Shōen-shi no kenkyū* 荘園史の研究   , vol. 1. Tokyo, Iwanami Shoten, 1953.

——, ed. *Nihon shōen ezu shūsei* 日本荘園絵図集成   , 1. (Collection of maps of Japanese *shōen*). Tokyo, Tōkyōdō Shuppan, 1976.

—— "Shugo daimyō ryōka no jiryō shōen" 守護大名領下の寺領荘園   (Temple-held *shōen* within the *shugo daimyō* domain), in *Hōkensei to shihonsei* 封建制と資本制   . Tokyo, Yūhikaku, 1956.

Nishitani Keiji 西谷啓治 , et. al. *Kōza Zen* 講座禅 (Essays on Zen). 7 vols. Tokyo, Chikuma Shobō, 1968.

Nukariya, Kaiten. *The Religion of the Samurai*. London, Luzac, 1913.

Nuki Tatsuto 貫達人 . "Engakuji-ryō ni tsuite" 円覚寺領について (On Engakuji domains), in *Tōyō daigaku kiyō* 11:17–29 (1957).

——, et. al. *Kenchōji* 建長寺 (The monastery of Kenchōji). Kamakura, Daihonzan Kenchōji, 1973.

Ogawa Makoto 小川信 . *Hosokawa Yoriyuki* 細川頼之 (The warrior Hosokawa Yoriyuki). Tokyo, Yoshikawa Kōbunkan, 1972.

Ogisu Jundō 荻須純道 . *Nihon chūsei Zenshū-shi* 日本中世禅宗史 (A history of medieval Japanese Zen). Tokyo, Mokujisha, 1965.

Ōishi Shinzaburō 大石慎三郎 , et. al. *Nihon keizai-shi ron* 日本経済史論 (Essays in Japanese economic history). Tokyo, Ochanomizu Shobō, 1967.

Ōkubo Dōshū 大久保道舟 . *Dōgen Zenji-den no kenkyū* 道元禅師伝の研究 (A study of Dōgen's biography). Tokyo, Chikuma Shobō, 1966.

Ōkura Seishin Bunka Kenkyūjo 大倉精神文化研究所 *Nihon shisō-shi bunken gedai* 日本思想史文献解題 (Explanatory bibliography of materials relating to Japanese intellectual history). Tokyo, Kadokawa Shoten, 1965.

Ōno Tatsunosuke 大野達之助 . *Nichiren* 日蓮 (Nichiren). Tokyo, Yoshikawa Kōbunkan, 1958.

Ōta Hirotarō 太田博太郎 *Chūsei no kenchiku* 中世の建築 (Medieval Japanese architecture). Tokyo, Shōkokusha, 1957.

——, Matsushita Ryūshō (Takaaki) 松下隆章 , and Tanaka Seidai 田中正大 , eds. *Zendera to sekitei* 禅寺と石庭 (Zen temples and stone gardens). *Genshoku Nihon no bijutsu*, 10 原色日本の美術 . Tokyo, Shōgakkan, 1967.

—— *Nihon kenchiku-shi josetsu* 日本建築史序説 . Tokyo, Shōkokusha, 1947.

Ōyabu Masaya 大薮正哉 . "Genchō no shūkyō seisaku" 元朝の宗教政策 (The religious policies of the Yuan dynasty), *Rekishi kyōiku* 9.7:36–42 (July 1961).

Ōyama Kyōhei 大山喬平 . "Owari no kuni Tomita-no-shō ni tsuite" 尾張の国富田の荘について (A study of Tomita-no-*shō* in Owari province), *Ōikonomika* 1.1:110–133 (April 1964).

—— *Kamakura bakufu* 鎌倉幕府 (The Kamakura *bakufu*), *Nihon no rekishi*, 9. Tokyo, Shōgakkan, 1974.

Prip-Møller, Johannes. *Chinese Buddhist Monasteries*. London, Oxford University Press, 1937.

Reischauer, Edwin O., trans. *Ennin's Diary: The Record of a Pilgrimage to China in Search of the Law*. New York, The Ronald Press, 1955.
—— *Ennin's Travels in T'ang China*. New York, The Ronald Press, 1955.
Reinan Shūjo 嶺南秀恕. *Nihon tōjō rentōroku* 日本洞上聯燈録 (Records of Japanese Sōtō school monks). *Dai-Nihon Bukkyō Zensho*, vol. 71

Renondeau, G. "Histoire des Moines Guerriers du Japon," *Bibliothèque de l'Institute des Hautes Études Chinoises, Mélanges* 9:159–344 (1957).

Rosenfield, John M. "The Unity of the Three Creeds: A Theme in Japanese Ink Painting of the Fifteenth Century." In Hall and Toyoda eds. *Japan in the Muromachi Age*. University of California Press, 1977.

Ryūkoku Daigaku Bukkyōgaku Kenkyūshitsu 龍谷大学仏教学研究室 ,ed. *Bukkyōgaku kankei zasshi ronbun bunrui mokuroku* 仏教学関係雑誌·論文分類目録 (A classified catalogue of journal articles relating to the study of Buddhism). Kyoto, Nagata Bunshōdō, 1971.

Sakugen Shūryō 策彦周良 .*Boshi nyūminki* 戊子入明記 (Chronicles of a voyage to Ming China). *Zoku shiseki shūran*, 1 続史籍集覧.

Sakurai Kageo (Keiyū) 櫻井景雄 . *Nanzenji-shi* 南禅寺史 (A history of Nanzenji). Kyoto, Daihonzan Nanzenji, 1940.

Sanford, James H. "Ikkyū Sōjun: A Zen Monk of Fifteenth Century Japan." PhD dissertation, Harvard University, 1972.

Sasaki Ginya 佐々木銀彌. *Chūsei shōhin ryūtsū-shi no kenkyū* 中世商品流通史の研究 (Studies in medieval commodity circulation). Tokyo, Hōsei Daigaku Shuppan-kyoku, 1972.

—— *Muromachi bakufu* 室町幕府 (The Muromachi *bakufu*), *Nihon no rekishi*, 13. Tokyo, Shōgakkan, 1975.

Satō, Elizabeth. "The Early Development of the *Shōen*," in Hall and Mass, eds., *Medieval Japan: Essays in Institutional History*. New Haven, Yale University Press, 1974.

Satō Kazuhiko 佐藤和彦 . *Nanbokuchō nairan* 南北朝内乱 (The civil wars between the Northern and Southern courts). *Nihon no rekishi*, 9. Tokyo, Shōgakkan, 1974.

Satō Shin'ichi 佐藤進一 . "Shugo ryōkoku-sei no tenkai" 守護領国制の展開 (The development of the *shugo* domain system), in Toyoda Takeshi 豊田武 , ed., *Chūsei shakai* 中世 社会. Tokyo, Asakura Shoten, 1954.

—— "Muromachi bakufu kaisōki no kansei taikei" 室町幕府開創期 の官制大系 (The administrative structure of the early Muromachi *bakufu*), in Ishimoda Shō 石母田正 and Satō Shin'ichi, eds., *Chūsei no hō to kokka* 中世の法と国家 . Tokyo, Tokyo Daigaku Shuppankai, 1960.

—— et al. *Kōza Nihon rekishi, Chūsei* 3. Tokyo, Iwanami Shoten, 1963.

—— *Nanbokuchō no dōran* 南北朝の動乱 (The disturbances between the Northern and Southern courts), *Nihon no rekishi*, 9. Tokyo, Chūō Kōronsha, 1965.

—— *Kamakura bakufu shugo seido no kenkyū* 鎌倉幕府守護制度 の研究 (The *shugo* system of the Kamakura *bakufu*). Tokyo, Tokyo Daigaku Shuppankai, 1971.

—— and Ikeuchi Yoshisuke 池内義資 , comps. *Chūsei hōsei shiryōshū* 中世法制資料集 (Collection of documents relating to medieval legal institutions). 2 vols. Tokyo, Iwanami Shoten, 1957.

SatōTatsugen 佐藤達玄 . "Hokusō sōrin no keizai seikatsu" 北宋叢林の経済生活 (The economic life of Ch'an monasteries in the Northern Sung dynasty), *Komazawa daigaku Bukkyōgakubu kiyō* 25:14–28 (1967).

Sekiguchi Kinya 関口欣也 . *Kamakura no chūsei kenchiku* 鎌倉 の中世建築 (The architecture of medieval Kamakura). Kanagawa-ken, Kyōiku Iinkai, 1967.

Sekiguchi Shindai 関口真大 . *Daruma no kenkyū* 達磨の研究 (A study of Bodhidharma). Tokyo, Iwanami Shoten, 1967.

—— *Tendai shikan no kenkyū* 天台止観の研究 (A study of Tendai Buddhist Shikan meditation). Tokyo, Iwanami Shoten, 1969.

Sekino Tei 関野貞 . *Shina no kenchiku to geijutsu* 支那の建築 と芸術 (Chinese architecture and arts). Tokyo, Iwanami Shoten, 1938.

Shiina Hiroo 椎名宏雄 . "Shotō Zensha no ritsu'in kyojū ni tsuite" 初唐禅者の律院居住について (On the residence of early

T'ang dynasty Ch'an devotees in Lü School monasteries), *Indogaku Bukkyōgaku kenkyū* 17.2:325–327 (1969).

—— "Higashiyama hōmon keisei no haikei" 東山法門形成の背景 (The background to the formation of the community at Tung-shan), *Komazawa shūkyōgaku kenkyū,* no. 12.

Shimizu, Yoshiaki, and Carolyn Wheelwright, eds. *Japanese Ink Paintings from American Collections: The Muromachi Period.* Princeton, The Art Museum, Princeton University, 1976.

Shinchi Kakushin 心地覚心. *Hottō kokushi zazengi* 法澄国師坐禅儀 (Hottō Kokushi's instructions for *zazen*). *Dai-Nihon Bukkyō Zensho,* vol. 96

Shingyō Norikazu 新行紀一. *Ikkō ikki no kiso kōzō* 一向一揆の基礎構造 (The basic structure of the Ikkō uprisings). Tokyo, Yoshikawa Kōbunkan, 1975.

Shun'oku Myōha 春屋妙葩. *Musō Kokushi nenpu* 夢窓・国師年譜 (A chronology for the life of Musō Kokushi). Kyoto, Tenryūji, c. 1700.

Solomon, Michael. "Rennyo and the Rise of Honganji in Muromachi Japan." PhD dissertation, Columbia University, 1972.

Steenstrup, Carl T. *Hōjō Shigetoki (1198–1261) and his Role in the History of Political and Ethical Ideas in Japan.* London, Curzon Press, 1979.

Sugimoto Hisao 杉本尚雄. *Chūsei no jinja to sharyō* 中世の神社と社領 (Medieval shrines and shrine domain). Tokyo, Yoshikawa Kōbunkan, 1959.

—— *Kikuchi-shi sandai* 菊池氏三代 (Three generations of the Kikuchi family). Tokyo, Yoshikawa Kōbunkan, 1966.

Suzuki, Daisetsu Teitarō. *The Training of the Zen Buddhist Monk.* Kyoto, Eastern Buddhist Society, 1934.

—— *Zen and Japanese Culture.* New York, Pantheon, 1959.

Suzuki Taisan 鈴木泰山. *Zenshū no chihō hatten* 禅宗の地方発展 (The provincial diffusion of the Zen schools). Kyoto, Unebi Shobō, 1942.

—— "Sōtō Zen no gufu to sono gegosha" 曹洞禅の弘布とその外護者 (The diffusion of Sōtō Zen and its patrons), in Itō Tasaburō 伊東多三郎, ed., *Kokumin seikatsu-shi kenkyū* 国民生活史研究. 5 vols. Tokyo, Yoshikawa Kōbunkan, 1957–1962.

—— "Chihō jiin no seiritsu to tenkai" 地方寺院の成立と展開 (The establishment and growth of provincial monasteries), *Chihō-shi kenkyū* 14.4:6–8 (August 1964).

Tachibana, Kōsen. "The Codes of Chōsokabe Motochika and the Economy of Buddhist Temples in His Day," *Indogaku Bukkyōgaku kenkyū* 21.1:470 (December 1972).

Taga Munehaya 多賀宗隼 . *Eisai* 栄西 (The monk Eisai). Tokyo, Yoshikawa Kōbunkan, 1965.

Taiheiki 太平記 (Chronicle of great peace). *Nihon koten bungaku taikei* 日本古典文学大系 , vols. 34–36. Ed. Gotō Tanji 後藤丹治 and Kamada Kisaburō 釜田喜三郎 . Tokyo, Iwanami Shoten, 1973.

Takagi Yutaka 高木豊 . *Nichiren to sono montei* 日連とその門弟 (Nichiren and his followers). Tokyo, Kōbundō, 1965.

Takahashi Ryūzō 高橋隆三 . "Rinzaishū kanji no seido" 臨済宗官寺の制度 (The system of official Zen monasteries in the Rinzai Zen school), *Kokushigaku* 23:9–43; 24:13–30 (May and October 1935).

Takayanagi Mitsutoshi 高柳光寿 . *Ashikaga Takauji* 足利尊氏 (The warrior Ashikaga Takauji). Tokyo, Shunjūsha, 1966.

Takenuki Genshō 竹貫元勝 . "Rinka ni okeru kyōdan keiei ni tsuite" 林下における教団経営について (Sectarian organization in the Rinka group of Zen monasteries), *Bukkyō shigaku* 15.2:105–143 (July 1971).

—— "Zenshū kyōdan un'ei to nassho" 禅宗教団運営と納所 (The nassho office and the management of the Zen school), *Indogaku Bukkyōgaku kenkyū* 23.2:908–911 (March 1975).

Takeshima Takuichi 竹島卓一 . *Eizō hōshiki no kenkyū* 1–3 営造法式の研究 (A study of the Ying-tsao Fa-shih manual of architecture). Tokyo, Chūkō Bijutsu, 1972.

Takeuchi Michio 竹内道雄 . "Sōtō kyōdan no seiritsu" 曹洞教団の成立 (The formation of the Sōtō school of Zen), *Rekishi kyōiku* 10.6:44–51 (June 1962).

—— *Dōgen* 道元 (Dōgen). Tokyo, Yoshitawa Kōbunkan, 1962.

Takeuchi Rizō 竹内理三 . *Jiryō shōen no kenkyū* 寺領荘園の研究 (Studies of Temple *shōen*). Kyoto, Unebi Shobō, 1942.

—— *Nihon jōdai jiin keizai-shi no kenkyū* 日本上代寺院経済史の研究 (The economic history of ancient Japanese temples). Tokyo, Ōokayama Shoten, 1934.

Tamamura Takeji 玉村竹二 . "Inryōken oyobi inryōshoku-kō" 蔭凉軒及び蔭凉職考 (Thoughts on the Inryōken and the Inryō office), *Rekishi chiri* 75.4:51–67; 5:48–67; 6:53–72 (1940). Also included in Tamamura, *Nihon Zenshū-shi ronshū* 1, pp. 103–196.

—— "Gozan sōrin no tatchū ni tsuite" 五山叢林の塔頭に
ついて (On the sub-temples of the *gozan* monasteries), *Rekishi chiri* 76, nos.
5 and 6 (1940). Also included in Tamamura, *Nihon Zenshū-shi ronshū* 1,
pp. 197–243.

—— "Ashikaga Yoshimochi no Zenshū shinkō ni tsuite" 足利義持の
禅宗信仰について (Ashikaga Yoshimochi's devotion to Zen),
Zengaku kenkyū 42:20–43 (March 1951).

—— *Gozan bungaku* 五山文学 (The literature of the Five Mountains).
Tokyo, Shibundō, 1955.

—— *Musō Kokushi* 夢窓国師 (Musō, the national master). Kyoto,
Heirakuji Shoten, 1958.

—— "Ashikaga Tadayoshi Zenshū shinkō no seikaku ni tsuite" 足利直義
禅宗信仰の性格について (The character of Ashikaga
Tadayoshi's devotion to Zen), *Bukkyō shigaku* 7.3:1–22 (October 1958).

—— "Rinzaishū kyōdan no seiritsu" 臨済宗教団の成立 (The
establishment of the Rinzai school organization), *Rekishi kyōiku* 10.6:37–
43 (June 1962).

—— "Gozan sōrin no jippō jūji seido ni tsuite" 五山叢林の十方
住持制度について (The system of open appointment of abbots
in *gozan* Zen monasteries), *Nihon Zenshū-shi ronshū* 1, 249–279.

—— and Inoue Zenjō 井上禅定, *Engakuji-shi* 円覚寺史 (A
history of Engakuji). Tokyo, Shunjūsha, 1964.

—— "Zenshū no hatten" 禅宗の発展 (The growth of the Zen
schools), in *Kōza Nihon rekishi, Chūsei* 3. Tokyo, Iwanami Shoten, 1963.

—— "Zen" 禅 (Zen), in *Chūgoku bunka sōsho* 10 中国文化叢書
Nihon bunka to Chūgoku 日本文化と中国. Ed. Bitō Masahide
尾藤正英. Tokyo, Taishūkan, 1968.

—— *Nihon Zenshū-shi ronshū* 日本禅宗史論集 (Essays on the
history of Zen in Japan). Tokyo, Shibunkaku, 1976.

Tamamuro Fumio 圭室文雄. "Bakuhan ryōshu no shūkyō tōsei"
幕藩領主の宗教統制 (The control of religion under the
Bakuhan system), in Tamamuro Fumio and Miyata Noboru, *Shomin shinkō
no gensō*. Tokyo, Mainichi Shinbunsha, 1977.

—— *Shinbutsu bunri* 神仏分離 (The separation of Shintō and Buddhism).
Tokyo, Kyōikusha, 1977.

Tamamuro Taijō 圭室諦成. "Watakushi no Zenshū-kan" 私の
禅宗観 (My view of Zen Buddhism), *Daihōrin* 30.1:46–51 (January
1963).

—— *Sōshiki Bukkyō* 葬式仏教 (Buddhism and funeral practices). Tokyo, Daihōrinkaku, 1964.

Tamura Enchō 田村円澄 . *Hōnen* 法然 (The monk Hōnen). Tokyo, Yoshikawa Kōbunkan, 1959.

Te-hui 德輝 . *Ch'ih-hsiu Pai-chang ch'ing-kuei* (*Chokushū hyakujō shingi*) 勅集百丈清規 (Imperial compilation of the pure regulations of Pai-chang). *Dai-Nihon zoku zōkyō* 2-16-3 大日本続蔵経

Terada Tōru 寺田透 and Mizuno Yaoko 水野弥穂子 , eds. *Dōgen* 道元 (Dōgen). 2 vols. Tokyo, Iwanami Shoten, 1972.

Thompson, Laurence G. *Studies in Chinese Religion: A Comprehensive and Classified Bibliography of Publications in English, French, and German Through 1970.* California, Dickenson Publishing Company, 1976.

Tōfukuji-shi 東福寺誌・ (Chronicles of Tōfukuji). Ed. Shiraishi Hōryū 白石芳盈 . Kyoto, Daihonzan Tōfukuji, 1930.

Tokyo Daigaku Shiryō Hensanjo 東京大学史料編纂所 comp. *Daitokuji monjo* 大德寺文書 (Documents relating to Daitokuji). *Dai-Nihon komonjo, Iewake* 17. 10 vols. Tokyo, Tokyo Daigaku Shuppankai, 1971.

—— *Tōjukuji monjo* 東福寺文書 (Documents relating to Tōfukuji). *Dai-Nihon komonjo*, Iewake 20. 大日本古文書家わけ 3 vols. Tokyo, 1959.

Toyoda Takeshi 豊田武 . *Nihon shūkyō seido shi no kenkyū* 日本宗教制度史の研究 (A history of religious organization in Japan). Tokyo, Kōseikaku, 1938.

—— "Genkō tōbaku no shoseiryoku ni tsuite" 元弘討幕の諸勢力について (The various forces involved in the overthrow of the Kamakura *bakufu*), *Bunka* 31.1:61–90 (July 1967).

——, ed. *Kōyasan-ryō shōen no shihai to kōzō* 高野山領荘圓の支配と構造 (The control and structure of *shōen* belonging to Mt. Kōya). Tokyo, Gannandō, 1977.

—— (Zōtei) *Chūsei Nihon shōgyō-shi no kenkyū* (増訂)中世日本商業史の研究 (A history of commercial activity in medieval Japan). Tokyo, Iwanami Shoten, 1957.

—— and Hiroshi Sugiyama. "The Growth of Commerce and the Trades." In Hall and Toyoda, eds., *Japan in the Muromachi Age.* University of California Press, 1977.

Tsan-ning 贊寧 , et. al. *Sung kao-seng-chuan* (Sōkōsōden) 宋高僧傳 (The Sung edition of the biographies of eminent monks). *Taishō shinshū daizōkyō*, vol. 50.

Tse-shan I-hsien 澤山弌咸 . *Ch'an-lin pei-yung ch'ing-kuei* (*Zenrin biyō shingi*) 禪林備用清規 (Pure regulations for Ch'an monasteries). *Dai-Nihon zoku-zōkyō* 2-17-1.

Tsuji Zennosuke 辻善之助 . "Ashikaga Takauji no shinkō" 足利尊氏の信仰 (Ashikaga Takauji's religious interests), *Shigaku zasshi*, September 1916.

—— *Nihon Bukkyō-shi* 日本仏教史 (A history of Japanese Buddhism). 10 vols. Tokyo, Iwanami Shoten, 1944–1970.

Tsukamoto Manabu 塚本学 and Arai Kikuo 新井喜久夫 *Aichi-ken no rekishi* 愛知県の歴史 (A history of Aichi prefecture). Tokyo, Yamakawa Shuppansha, 1972.

Tsung-tse 宗賾 , comp. *Ch'an-yuan ch'ing-kuei* (*Zen'on shingi*) 禪苑清規 (Pure regulations for Ch'an monasteries). *Dai-Nihon zoku zōkyō*, 2-16-5. See also, *Yakuchū zen'on shingi* 訳註禅苑清規 . Ed. Kagamishima Genryū 鏡島元隆 , et. al. Tokyo, Sōtōshū Shūmuchō, 1972.

Tsunoda, Ryūsaku, Wm. Theodore de Bary, and Donald Keene, comps. *Sources of Japanese Tradition*, 1. New York, Columbia University Press, 1964.

Twitchett, Denis C. "Monastic Estates in T'ang China." *Asia Major*. New Series 5:123–146 (1956).

—— "The Monasteries and China's Economy in Medieval Times," *Bulletin of the School of Oriental and African Studies* 19.3:526–549 (1957).

Ui Hakuju 宇井伯壽 . *Zenshū-shi kenkyū* 禪宗史研究 (Studies in the history of Zen). Tokyo, Iwanami Shoten, 1939.

—— *Dai-ni Zenshū-shi kenkyū* 第二禪宗史研究 (Further studies in the history of Zen). Tokyo, Iwanami Shoten, 1942.

—— *Bukkyō shisō kenkyū* 仏教思想研究 (Studies in Buddhist thought). Tokyo, Iwanami Shoten, 1942.

Umeda Yoshihiko 梅田義彦 . *Nihon shūkyō seido shi* 日本宗教制度史 (A history of religious organization in Japan). Kyoto, Hyakkaen, 1962.

Unsen Taikyoku 雲泉大極 . *Hekizan nichiroku* 碧山日録 (The azure mountain records). In Kondō Heijō 近藤瓶城 ed. *Zoku shiseki shūran* 3. Kyoto, Rinsen Shoten, 1967.

Ury, Marian. *Poems of the Five Mountains: An Introduction to the Literature of the Zen Monasteries*. Tokyo, Mushinsha, 1977.

Usui Nobuyoshi 臼井信吉 . *Ashikaga Yoshimitsu* 足利義満

(The shogun Ashikaga Yoshimitsu). Tokyo, Yoshikawa Kōbunkan, 1960.

Uwayokote Masataka 上横手雅敬 . *Hōjō Yasutoki* 北条泰時 (The regent Hōjō Yasutoki). Tokyo, Yoshikawa Kōbunkan, 1958.

Van de Wetering, Janwillem. *The Empty Mirror.* Boston, Houghton Mifflin, 1976.

Varley, H. Paul. *The Ōnin War.* New York, Columbia University Press, 1967.

—— *Imperial Restoration in Medieval Japan.* New York, Columbia University Press, 1971.

—— *Japanese Culture.* New York, Praeger, 1973.

—— "Ashikaga Yoshimitsu and the World of Kitayama: Social Change and Shogunal Patronage in Early Muromachi Japan," in Hall and Toyoda, eds., *Japan in the Muromachi Age.* University of California Press, 1977.

Vessie, Patricia A. *Zen Buddhism: A Bibliography of Books and Articles in English 1892-1975.* Ann Arbor, University Microfilms International, 1976.

Waddell, Norman and Masao Abe, trans. "Dōgen's *Bendōwa*," *The Eastern Buddhist* 4.1:148 (May 1971).

——, trans. "Dōgen's *Fukan zazengi* and *Shōbōgenzō zazengi*," *The Eastern Buddhist* 6.2:115-128 (October 1973).

Wakita Haruko 脇田晴子 . *Nihon chūsei shōgyō hattatsu-shi no ken-kyū* 日本中世商業発達史の研究 (Studies in the development of Japanese medieval commerce). Tokyo, Ochanomizu Shobō, 1969.

—— "Towards a Wider Perspective on Medieval Commerce," *Journal of Japanese Studies* 1.2:321-345 (Spring 1975).

Wakita Osamu 脇田修 . "Jinaimachi no kōzō to tenkai," 寺内町の構造と展開 (The structure and transformation of temple towns), *Shirin* 41.1:1-24 (1958).

Waley, Arthur, trans. *The Travels of an Alchemist.* London, Routledge, 1931.

Washio Junkei 鷲尾順敬 . *Kamakura bushi to Zen* 鎌倉武士と禅 (Kamakura warriors and Zen). Tokyo, Nihon Gakujutsu Fukyūkai, 1935.

Wei-mien 惟勉 , comp. *Chiao-ting ch'ing-kuei* (*Kōjō shingi*) 校定清規 (Wei-mien's pure regulations), *Dai-Nihon zoku zōkyō*, 2-17-1. 大日本続蔵経 .

Weinstein, Stanley. "Rennyo and the Shinshū Revival," in Hall and Toyoda, eds., *Japan in the Muromachi Age.* University of California Press, 1977.

—— "Imperial Patronage in the Formation of T'ang Buddhism," in Arthur F. Wright and Dennis Twitchett eds., *Perspectives on the T'ang*. New Haven, Yale University Press, 1973.

Welch, Holmes. *The Practice of Chinese Buddhism*. Cambridge, Harvard University Press, 1967.

Wu-liang Tsung-shou 無量宗壽, comp. *Ju-chung jih-yung ch'ing-kuei* (*Nyusshū nichiyō shingi*) 入衆日用清規 (Introductory regulations for daily life in the Ch'an community). *Dai-Nihon zoku zōkyō*, 2-16-5. Also in *Kokuyaku Zenshū sōsho*, series 2, vol. 5.

Yamamoto Seiki 山本世紀. "Kita jōshū ni okeru Sōtō Zen no denpa ni tsuite" 北上州における曹洞禅の伝播について (The diffusion of Sōtō Zen in northern Kōzuke province), in Kasahara Kazuo, ed., *Nihon ni okeru seiji to shūkyō* 日本における政治と宗教. Tokyo, Yoshikawa Kōbunkan, 1974.

Yamamura, Kōzō. "The Development of the *Za* in Medieval Japan," *Business History Review* 47.4:438–465 (Winter 1973).

Yampolsky, Philip. *The Platform Sutra of the Sixth Patriarch*. New York, Columbia University Press, 1967.

—— *The Zen Master Hakuin*. New York, Columbia University Press, 1971.

—— and Toshihide Akamatsu. "Muromachi Zen and the Gozan System," in Hall and Toyoda, eds., *Japan in the Muromachi Age*. University of California Press, 1977.

Yanagida Seizan 柳田聖山. *Rinzai no kafū* 臨済の家風 (The style of Rinzai Zen). Tokyo, Chikuma Shobō, 1967.

—— *Shoki zenshū-shi shisho no kenkyū* 初期禅宗史史書の研究 (Studies in the early historical materials relating to the history of the Ch'an School). Kyoto, Hōzōkan, 1967.

—— "Chūgoku Zenshū-shi" 中国禅宗史 (A history of the Ch'an Schools in China), in Nishitani Keiji et al., eds., *Kōza Zen* 3. Tokyo, Chikuma Shobō, 1968.

—— *Daruma no goroku* 達磨の語録 (The records of Bodhidharma). *Zen no goroku* 1. Tokyo, Chikuma Shobō, 1969.

—— "Eisai to *Kōzen gokokuron* no kadai" 栄西と『興禅護国論』の課題 (Eisai and the Agenda of the *Kōzen Gokokuron*), in Ichikawa Hakugen 市川白弦, Iriya Yoshitaka 入矢義高, and Yanagida Seizan, eds., *Chūsei Zenka no shisō*. 中世禅家の思想 Tokyo, Iwanami Shoten, 1972.

—— and Umehara Takeshi 梅原武 . *Mu no tankyū* 無 の 探 求 (The search for emptiness). *Bukkyō no shisō* 7 仏教 の 思 想 . Tokyo, Kadokawa Shoten, 1969.

Yang, Lien-sheng. "Buddhist Monasteries and Four Money-Raising Institutions in Chinese History," *Harvard Journal of Asiatic Studies* 13:174–191 (1950).

Yasuda Motohisa 安田元久 . *Hōjō Yoshitoki* 北条義時 (The regent Hōjō Yoshitoki). Tokyo, Yoshikawa Kōbunkan, 1961.

——, ed. *Shōen* 荘園 (*Shōen*). Tokyo, Kondō Shuppansha, 1977.

—— "Kamakura *bakufu*" 鎌倉幕府 (The Kamakura *bakufu*), in Fujimoto Kunihiko 藤本邦彦 and Inoue Mitsusada 井上光貞 , eds., *Taikei Nihon-shi sōsho, Seiji-shi* 1. Tokyo, Yamakawa Shuppansha, 1965.

—— *Kamakura bakufu* 鎌倉幕府 (The Kamakura *bakufu*). Tokyo, Shin Jinbutsu Ōraisha, 1971.

Yokoyama Hideya 横山秀武 . *Zen no kenchiku* 禅 の 建 築 (Zen monastic architecture). Tokyo, Shōkokusha, 1967.

—— *Zen'en bunka no kanshō* 禅苑文化 の 鑑賞 (The appreciation of Zen culture). Tokyo, Sankibō Busshorin, 1973.

Zengaku Daijiten Hensansho 禅学大辞典編纂所 . *Zengaku daijiten* 1–3 禅学大辞典 (A dictionary of Zen studies). Tokyo, Taishūkan, 1978.

Zuikei Shūhō 瑞溪周鳳 . *Ga'un nikkenroku batsuyū* 臥雲日件録 抜尤 (The diary of Zuikei Shūhō). *Zoku shiseki shūran*, 3. Kyoto, Rinsen Shoten, 1967. Also in Tokyo Daigaku Shiryō Hensanjo ed., 東京 大学史料編纂所 . *Dai-Nihon Kokiroku* 大日本古記録 . Pt. 13. Tokyo, Iwanami Shoten, 1961.

Zürcher, Erik. *The Buddhist Conquest of China*. Leiden, E. J. Brill, 1959.

Glossary

A-yü-wang shan 阿育王山

A-yü-wang-shan kuang li ch'an ssu
阿育王山廣利禪寺

Adachi Yasumori 足達泰盛

Aeba Ujitada 饗庭氏直

Agara *mura* 阿賀良村

Ahiru-no-*shō* 畔蒜莊

Aizen Myōō 愛染明王

Akamatsu Norisuke
赤松則祐

Amida 阿彌陀

andō 行堂

andogata 安堵方

andojō 安堵狀

anja 行者

anjadō 行者堂

Ankokuji 安國寺

Asano 淺野

Ashikaga Mochiuji 足利持氏

Ashikaga Motouji
足利基氏

Ashikaga Nariuji
足利成氏

Ashikaga Sadauji
足利貞氏

Ashikaga Tadayoshi
足利直義

Ashikaga Takauji
足利尊氏

Ashikaga Yoshiakira
足利義詮

Ashikaga Yoshihisa
足利義尚

Ashikaga Yoshimasa
足利義政

Ashikaga Yoshimitsu
足利義滿

Ashikaga Yoshimochi
足利義持

Ashikaga Yoshinori
足利義教
Asō 麻生
ateokonaijō 充行状
Atsuta Jingū 熱田神宮
Awa 阿波
Awaji 淡路
Awajiya Jugen 淡路屋壽源
azana 字
azukari-dokoro 預所
Azuma kagami 吾妻鏡

Baishōron 梅松論
bakufu 幕府
Bendōhō 辨道法
Bendōwa 辨道話
Bingo 備後
Bitchū 備中
Biwako 琵琶湖
Bizen 備前
bodaiji 菩提寺
bon 盆
Bonmōkyō 梵網經
Bonten 梵天
bōryō 望寮
Boshi nyūminki
戊子入明記
bugyō 奉行
bugyōnin 奉行人
buke 武家
Bukkoku Zenji 佛國禪師

Bukkyō 佛敎
Bungo 豊後
buninjō 補任状
Buppō daimeiroku
佛法大明錄
Buppō shugyō 佛法修行
bushi 武士
busshō 佛聖
butsuden 佛殿
Butsunichi'an kōmotsu
    mokuroku
佛日庵公物目錄
Buzen 豊前
byakutsui 白槌

cha yoriai 茶寄合
chajin 茶人
Ch'an 禪
Ch'an-lin pei-yung ch'ing-kuei
禪林備用清規
"Ch'an-men kuei-shih"
禪門規式
Ch'an-tien 禪典
Ch'an-yuan ch'ing-kuei
禪苑清規
Ch'ang-an 長安
Chang Chi-chih 張即之
Ch'ang-mi 常密
Chao-chou Ts'ung-shen
趙州從諗
Chen-chou 鎭州

Ch'en-hsu 陳詡

Ch'en Meng-jung 陳孟榮

chia-ch'a 甲刹

Chiao-ting ch'ing-kuei
校定清規

chiden 知殿

chieh-tu-shih 節度使

chien-ssu 監司

chien-yuan 監院

Ch'ien-fu-ssu 千福寺

chigyō 知行

Chih-i 智顗

chih-k'o 知客

chih-shih 知事

chih-sui 直歲

chih-yü 知浴

Ch'ih-hsiu Pai-chang ch'ing-kuei
勅修百丈清規

chiji 知事

"Chiji shingi" 知事清規

Chikuzen 筑前

Chin-shan-ssu 金山寺

Ching-shan 徑山

Ching-shan hsing shen wan shou
  ch'an ssu
徑山興聖萬壽禪寺

Ch'ing-t'ang Chueh-yuan
鏡堂覺圓

Ching-te ch'uan-teng-lu
景德傳燈錄

Ch'ing-cho Cheng-ch'eng
清拙正澄

ch'ing-i 請益

ch'ing-kuei 清規

chinsō 頂相

Chion'in 知恩院

chiyoku 知浴

chō 町

Chōfukuji 長福寺

Chōgen 重源

Chōkōdō 長講堂

Chokushū hyakujō shingi
勅修百丈清規

Chōrakuji 長樂寺

chōrō 長老

chōshu 頭主

Chu Hsi 朱熹

Chu-hsien Fan-hsien
竺仙梵僊

Ch'u 楚

Ch'üan-ku 全古

chuang 莊

chuang-chu 莊主

chūbun 中分

Chūhō Chūshō 仲方中正

Chung-ch'üan 仲詮

Chung-feng Ming-pen 中峯明本

chūsei 中世

Daidenhō'in 大傳法院

Daigoji 醍醐寺

Daigon Shuri Bosatsu
大權修理菩薩

Daijōkan 太政官

Daijōji 大乘寺

Daikaku-ha 大覺派

Daikakuji 大覺寺

Daikakuji-*tō* 大覺寺統

daikan 代官

Daikatsu Ryōshin 大暍了心

daikyakuden 大客殿

Daikyū Shōnen 大休正念

daimyō 大名

Dainichibō Nōnin
大日房能忍

Dainichikyō 大日經

daisan 大参

Daisen'in 大仙院

Daisenji 大山寺

Daishōji 大聖寺

daitetsudō 大徹堂

Daitō Kokushi 大燈國師

Daitokuji 大德寺

Daitokuji hatto 大德寺法度

"Daitokuji jiyō gegyō
    sadamebumi"
大德寺寺用下行定文

Daizōkyō 大藏經

Daruma (Bodhidharma) 達磨

dengaku 田樂

Dewa 出羽

dojidan 土地壇

dojidō 土地堂

Dōgen Kigen 道元希元

Dōkō 道杲

Dōsen 道璿

Dōshō 道昭

dosō 土倉

dōsu 堂主

Echigo 越後

Echizen 越前

Eichō 榮朝

Eihei shingi 永平清規

Eiheiji 永平寺

Eiheiji garanzu 永平寺伽藍圖

"Eiheiji shuryō shinki"
永平寺衆寮箴規

Eikōji 永光寺

Eisai (Yōsai). See Myōan Eisai

Eison 叡尊

Engakuji 圓覺寺

Engakuji keidai ezu
圓覺寺境内繪圖

"Engakuji seifu jōsho"
圓覽寺制符條書

enjudō 延壽堂

Enni Ben'en 圓爾辨圓

Ennin 圓仁

Enpō dentōroku
延寶傳燈錄

Enpukuji 圓福寺

Enryakuji 延曆寺

Enshin 袁晉

Enshin Tetsugyū 圓心鐵牛

Entairyaku 圓太暦
Etchū 越中

Fa-chen 法眞
Fa-chi 法寂
Fa-hsiang 法相
fa-t'ang 法堂
Fa-tuan 法端
Fan-wang-ching 梵網經
fang-chang 方丈
Fo-fa ta-ming-lu
佛法大明錄
fo-tien 佛殿
fu-liao 副寮
fu-ssu 副寺
Fudō Myōō 不動明王
fugin 諷經
Fukan zazengi
普勸坐禪儀
Fukui 福井
fukuryō 副寮
Fumon (Mukan Gengo) 普門
Fumonji 普門寺
Funatsu 船津
Fuse Shōchin 布施昌椿
fusetsu 普說
"Fushuku hanpō"
赴粥飯法
fūsu 副寺
fusuma 襖

gaidō 外堂

gakuji 額字
Gakuonji 樂音寺
Gakuzō 覺藏
Ganshō 願性
Ga'un nikkenroku
臥雲日件錄
Gazan Jōseki 峨山韶碩
gekan 下間
Genjūan shingi 幻住庵清規
Genjū-ha 幻住派
genkan 玄關
Genkō shakusho
元亨釋書
Gen'ō Hongen 元翁本元
Genpo Reisan 玄圃靈三
geten 外典
Getsugai Chōja 月蓋長者
Getsuō Chikyō 月翁智鏡
Gidō Shūshin 義堂周信
Gikū 義空
gō 鄉
Go-Daigo *tennō*
後醍醐天皇
Go-Fukakusa *tennō*
後深草天皇
Go-Fushimi *tennō*
後伏見天皇
Go-Murakami *tennō*
後村上天皇
Go-Saga *tennō* 後嵯峨天皇
Go-Toba *tennō*
後鳥羽天皇

Go-Tsuchimikado *tennō* 後土御門天皇

Go-Uda *tennō* 後宇多天皇

godō 後堂

godō shuso 後堂首座

Gohō Myōō 護法明王

goka (kōka) 後架

gokenin 御家人

Gokoku shōbōgi 護國正法義

Gokurakuji 極樂寺

goroku 語錄

gosaie 後齋會

gōso 強訴

Gottan Funei 兀庵普寧

gozan (gosan) 五山

gozan bungaku 五山文學

Gozan jissatsu zu 五山十刹圖

gozanban 五山版

gōzoku 豪族

Guchū Shūkyū 愚中周及

gyakuhan zazen 擊板坐禪

gyōji 行事

Gyōyū 行勇

Hai-yun 海雲

Hakudō Bon'i 柏堂梵意

Hakuin Ekaku 白隱慧鶴

Hakusan 白山

han (monastic) 班

han (territorial) 藩

Hanazono *tennō* 花園天皇

Hangchow 杭州

hanzei 半濟

Harima 播磨

Hatakeyama Yoshitsuna 畠山義綱

Hatano Yoshishige 波多野義重

Hatsukura-no-*shō* 初倉莊

hattō 法堂

Hayashi *mura* 林村

Heian 平安

Heijō-kyō 平城京

Hekizan nichiroku 碧山日錄

Hida 飛驒

Hie Taisha 日吉大社

Hieizan 比叡山

Higashiyama 東山

Higashiyama Sansō 東山山莊

hijiri 聖

hikan 被官

hikitsukegata 引付方

Hino Arinori 日野有敎

hinpotsu 秉拂

Hitachi 常陸

Hizen 肥前

ho 保

ho-shih 喝食

Hoan-ha 破庵派

hobetsu-sen 帆別錢

Hōdōji 寶幢寺

hōgo 法語

hōjō 方丈

hōjō anja 方丈行者

Hōjō Masako 北條政子

Hōjō Sadatoki 北條貞時

Hōjō Takatoki 北條高時

Hōjō Tokimune 北條時宗

Hōjō Tokiyori 北條時賴

Hōjō Yasutoki 北條泰時

Hōjō Yoshitoki 北條義時

Hokke 法華

Hōnen 法然

Honganji 本願寺

honke 本家

honke shiki 本家職

honrai no menboku
本来の面目

honzon 本尊

Hori 堀

Hōrinji 寶林寺

Hōsenji 法泉寺

Hosokawa Katsumoto
細川勝元

Hosokawa Mochiyuki
細川持之

Hosokawa Takakuni
細川高國

Hosokawa Yoriyuki
細川賴之

Hossō 法相

Hottō Kokushi 法燈國師

Hottō Kokushi zazengi
法燈國師坐禪儀

hou-t'ang shou-tso
後堂首座

hōza 法座

Hōzan hennen ryakuki
寶山編年略記

Hsi-ch'an-yuan 西禪院

hsi-t'ang 西堂

hsi-ts'ang 西藏

hsiao-ts'an 小參

hsieh-yuan-chu 廨院主

hsing-che 行者

Hsing-ch'üan 行全

Hsing-t'ang-hsien 行唐懸

Hsu-an Huai-ch'ang
虛菴懷敞

hsuan-ming 宣明

hua-chu 化主

Hua-yen 華嚴

Huan-chu-an 幻住庵

Huan-chu-an ch'ing-kuei
幻住庵清規

Huang-lung p'ai 黃龍派

Hui-neng 惠能

Hui-shen 惠深

Hui-tsung 徽宗

Hui-yun 惠雲

Hung-chien 弘鑒

Hung-chih Cheng-chueh
宏智正覺

Hung-jen 弘忍

Hupei 湖北

Hyōgo 兵庫

hyōjōshū 評定眾

Hyūga 日向

I-k'ung 義空

I-shan I-ning 一山一寧

I *shuso* 緯首座

ibu jisha (ehatsu-jisha)
衣鉢侍者

ichien fuyu 一圓不輸

Ichijō Kanera 一條兼良

Idaten 韋駄天

Iga 伊賀

Iio Sadayuki 飯尾貞行

ikai 遺誡

Ikai gojō 遺誡五條

Ikedera-no-*shō* 池寺莊

ikki 一揆

Ikkō-*ikki* 一向一揆

Ikkōshū 一向宗

Ikkyū Sōjun 一休宗純

Imagawa Norikuni 今川範國

Imagawa Ryōshun 今川了俊

Imamiyasha 今宮社

Imamura Fukumanji 今村福滿寺

imina 諱

inari kumon 展成公文

inka 印可

inō 維那

Inryōken 蔭涼軒

Inryōken nichiroku
蔭涼軒日錄

inryōshoku 蔭涼職

Ippen 一遍

Ise 伊勢

Ise Jingū 伊勢神官

Ishida 石田

Ishikawa 石川

Ishin Sūden 以心崇傳

Issan Ichinei 一山一寧

Iwashimizu Hachiman *bugyō*
石清水八幡奉行

Iwashimizu Hachimangū
石清水八幡官

Izumi 和泉

Izumo 出雲

jago 謝語

jie 侍衣

jijō 侍狀

jika 侍客

jika gyōji 寺家行事

jikidō 食堂

jikō 侍香

Jikusen Bonsen 竺仙梵僊

Jimyō'in 持明院

jinaimachi 寺内町

Jingoji 神護寺

jinjū 浄頭

Jinnō shōtōki
神皇正統記

jippō jūji 十方住持

jippō satsu 十方刹

jirigyō 自利行

jiryō 寺領

jisha 侍者

jishi 地子

Jishū 時宗

jissatsu (jissetsu) 十刹

jitō 地頭

jitō shiki 地頭職

jitō ukesho 地頭請所

jiyaku 侍藥

Jizō 地藏

Jōchiji 淨智寺

Jōdo 淨土

jōdō 上堂

Jōdo shinshū 淨土眞宗

Jōdoji 淨土寺

jōei shikimoku 貞永式目

Jōen 淨圓

jōgakuji 定額寺

jōkan 上間

Jōmyōji 淨妙寺

Jōrakuji 常樂寺

Josetsu 如拙

Jōshū Jūshin 趙州從諗

Jōzan Sozen 定山祖禪

Ju-chung jih-yung ch'ing-kuei
入衆日用清規

ju-shih 入室

juen 入院

Jufukuji 壽福寺

jūji 住持

jukai 授戒

jukkyō 十境

Jukō'in 聚光院

jūshū yōdōki 十宗要道記

"Jūundōshiki" 十雲堂職

Kaga 加賀

Kai 甲斐

kairitsu 戒律

kaisan 開山

kaisandō 開山堂

Kaji-no-shō 加地莊

kajishi 加地子

kajishi myōshu shiki
加地子名主職

Kakua 覺阿

Kamakura 鎌倉

Kameyama jōkō 龜山上皇

Kameyama gō 龜山鄉

kami 神

Kamikatsura-no-shō 上桂莊

kamikaze 神風

kan 貫

Kanazawa 金澤

kanbun 漢文

Kangiten 歡喜天

kan'in 監院

kanji 漢字

kanmon 貫文

Kannon 觀音

kannondō 觀音堂

Kannon-kyō 觀音經

kanrei 管領

kansen 官錢

kansu 監寺

Kantō bugyō 關東奉行

Kanzan Egen 關山慧玄

kaō 花押

karaburo 空風呂

karamono 唐物

karayō 唐樣

Kasama-ho 笠間保

kasho 過書

kasshiki (katsujiki) 喝食

Kasuga Jinja 春日神社

kata 掛塔

Katsurayama Kagetomo
  (Ganshō)
  葛山景倫（顧生）

kawaya 廁

Kazusa 上總

Kegon 華嚴

Kegon-kyō 華嚴經

Keichin 惠鎮

Keijo Shūrin 景徐周麟

Keitoku dentōroku
  景德傳燈錄

Keizan shingi 瑩山清規

Keizan Jōkin 瑩山紹瑾

ken 間

Kenchō kōkoku Zenji
  建長興國禪寺

Kenchōji 建長寺

Kenchōji kishiki
  建長寺規式

Kenchōji sashizu
  建長寺指圖

Kenmu no shinsei
  建武の新政

Kenmu shikimoku
  建武式目

Kenninji 建仁寺

Kenshun 賢俊

kesa (kaṣāya) 袈裟

Kian Soen 規庵祖圓

Kichizan Minchō 吉山明兆

Kii 紀伊

Kikei Shinzui 季瓊眞藥

Kikkawa 吉川

Kikuchi 菊池

kikyūryō 耆舊寮

Kinai 畿內

kinhin 經行

kinsei 禁制

Kira 吉良

Kissa yōjōki 喫茶養生記

Kitatamamura gō
  北多摩村鄉

Kitayama 北山

kitō 祈禱

kitōsō 祈禱僧

kōan 公案

Kobayakawa 小早川

kōdō 講堂

Kōfukuji 興福寺

Koga Michimune
久我通宗

Kōgakuji 廣覺寺

Kōgimon'in 廣義門院

Kōgon *tennō* 光嚴天皇

Kōhō Kennichi 高峰顯日

Kōjō shingi 校定清規

Kokan Shiren 虎關師錬

Kokawadera 粉河寺

Kōkokuji 興國寺

koku 石

Kokubu 國分

Kokubunji 國分寺

kokuga 國衙

kokujin 國人

Kokuseiji 國清寺

kokushi 國師

kokushi 國司

Kōmyō *tennō* 光明天皇

Kōmyōin shinki
光明院箴規

Konchi'in 金地院

kondō 金堂

Kongōbuji 金剛峰寺

Konoe 近衛

Kō no Moronao 高師直

Kosa *gō* 小佐鄉

Kosaka-no-*shō* 小坂莊

kōsatsu (kassatsu, kōsetsu) 甲刹

Kosen Ingen 古先印元

Kōshōji 興聖寺

Kōya-hijiri 高野聖

Kōyasan 高野山

Kōzanji 高山寺

Kōzen gokokuron
興禪護國論

Kōzuke 上野

Kuan-yin 觀音

kudokunari 功德成

k'u-ssu 庫司

k'u-t'ou 庫頭

kuge 公家

Kuge nichiyō kufū ryakushū
空華日用工夫略集

kuin 庫院

kujō *(kōjō)* 公帖

Kujō Michiie 九條道家

Kujō Noriie 九條敎家

Kūkoku Meiō 空谷明應

Kumedadera 久米田寺

kumon 公文

kūmon 空門

kung-an 公案

kura 倉

kuri 庫裡

Kuro Genzaemon Morishige
玄源左衛門盛繁

Kuroda 黑田

Kusuba *sekisho* 楠葉關所

kyakuden 客殿

kyō 經

kyōchi 境致

kyōgen 狂言

kyōzen itchi 敎禪一致

kyōzō 經藏

Lan-ch'i Tao-lung
蘭溪道隆

li 里

liao-chu 寮主

liao-shou-tso 寮首座

liao-tso 寮作

Lin-chi I-hsuan 臨濟義玄

Ling-yin-ssu 靈隱山

Lü 律

Maeda 前田

Maejima 前島

Mandokoro 政所

Mangen Shiban 卍元師蠻

Manjuji 萬壽寺

Mannenzan 萬年山

Manpukuji 萬福寺

mappō 末法

masu 枡

matsuji 末寺

mensō 免僧

Miidera 三井寺

Mikawa 三河

Mimasaka 美作

Min *tsūbun* 珉都聞

Minamoto Sanetomo 源實朝

Minamoto Yoriie 源賴家

Minamoto Yoritomo 源賴朝

Minchō 明兆

mindō 明堂

Ming-chi Ch'u-chün
明極楚俊

Ming-chou 明兆

Minki Soshun 明極楚俊

Mino 美濃

mirokudō 彌勒堂

Mito 水戸

Mitsunari *gō* 三成鄉

Mitsunari-no-*shō* 三成莊

Miura 三浦

Miyoshi Nagayoshi
三好長慶

Mizoguchi 溝口

Mōko shurai 蒙古襲來

mon 文

monchūjo 問注所

mondō 問答

Monju 文珠

Monkan 文觀

monzeki 門跡

monzenmachi 門前町

Mōri 毛利

Mori-no-shō 杜莊

Morinaga *shinnō*
護良親王

mou 畝

Mu Ch'i 牧谿

Muchū mondō 夢中問答

Mugaku Sogen 無學祖元

Muin Genkai 無隱元晦

Mujaku Dōchū 無著道忠

mujō sanmai 無諍三昧

Mujū Ichien 無住一圓

Mukan Gengo (Fumon)
無關玄悟 (普門)

Mumon Ekai 無門慧開

Mumonkan 無門關

Munakata Jinja 宗像神社

Munakata-no-shō 宗像莊

munebetsu-sen 棟別錢

Murata Jukō 村田珠光

Muromachi 室町

musamon 無作門

Musashi 武藏

Musō Soseki (Kokushi)
夢窻疎石

musōmon 無相門

Mutsu 陸奧

Myōan Eisai (Yōsai)
明庵榮西

Myōe Shōnin 明惠上人

Myōkakuji 妙覺寺

Myōkō Sōei 明江宗叡

Myōkōji 妙光寺

Myōshinji 妙心寺

myōshu shiki 名主職

Nagashima 長島

naidō 內堂

Nan-fang-huo-te 南方火德

Nan-shan ching tz'u pao en
   kuang hsiao ch'an ssu
南山淨慈報恩光孝禪寺

Nanpo Jōmyō 南浦紹明

Nanto *bugyō* 南都奉行

Nanzenji 南禪寺

Nara 奈良

nassho 納所

Negoroji 根來寺

Negorosan 根來山

nehan 涅槃

nehandōri 涅槃堂裏

nenbutsu 念佛

nengu 年貢

nenpu 年譜

Nichiren 日蓮

nien-sung 念誦

Niimi-no-shō 新見莊

Nijō Yoshizane 二條良實

Niki Yoshinao 仁木義直

ninku 人工

Ninnaji 仁和寺

ninriki 人力

Ninshō 忍性

Nippō Sōshun 日峰宗舜

Nippon tōjō rentōroku
日本洞上聯燈錄

nisshitsu sanzen 入室參禪

Nitta Yoshisada 新田義貞

nō 能

Nōnin 能忍

Noto 能登

Nyoi'an 如意庵

Ōbaku 黃檗

Ōbaku shingi 黃檗清規

Oda Nobunaga 織田信長

Ogasawara Sadamune
小笠原貞宗

Oki 隱岐

Ōmi 近江

Ōnin 應仁

Onjōji 圓城寺

onshōgata 恩賞方

Ōryū-ha 黃龍派

Ōsaka 大阪

Ōshio-no-*shō* 大鹽莊

oshō 和尚

Ōtabumi 大田文

Ōtaka Shigenari 大高重成

Ōtomo Sadachika
大友貞親

Ōtomo Sadamune 大友貞宗

Ōtomo Sōrin 大友宗麟

Ōtomo Ujiyasu 大友氏泰

Ōtsu 大津

Ōuchi Yoshihiro 大內義弘

Owa Shirōzaemon
尾和四郎左衛門

Owari 尾張

Oyake-no-*shō* 小宅莊

Pai-chang 百丈

Pai-chang ch'ing-kuei
百丈清規

Pei-shan 北山

Pei-shan ch'ing te ling yin ch'an
ssu
北山景德靈隱禪寺

Pei-yung ch'ing-kuei
備用清規

Pi-shan ssu 碧山寺

Po'an p'ai 破菴派

P'u-chi 普寂

p'u-ch'ing 普清

P'u-sa ying-lo-ching
菩薩瓔珞經

p'u-shuo 普說

raima 禮間

rakandō 羅漢堂

Rankei Dōryū 蘭溪道隆

Reinan Shūjo 嶺南秀恕

renga 連歌

rengashi 連歌師

ri 理

rinji 綸旨

rinka (ringe) 林下

Rinsen kakun 臨川家訓

Rinsenji 臨川寺

Rinzai 臨濟

Rinzai Gigen 臨濟義玄

Rishōtō 利生塔

ritagyō 利他行

Ritsu 律

Rokuhara *tandai* 六波羅探題

Rokuō'in 鹿王院

Rokuon nichiroku 鹿苑日錄

Rokuon *sōroku* 鹿苑僧錄

Rokuon'in 鹿苑院

rōshi 老師

ryōgen 寮元

ryōke 領家

ryōsaku 寮作

ryōshu 領主

ryōshu 寮主

ryō-shuso 寮首座

Ryūgen'in 龍源院

Ryūgin'an 龍吟庵

Ryūshōji 龍翔寺

sadō (chadō) 茶堂

Sado 佐渡

Saga Arashiyama 嵯峨嵐山

Saga *tennō* 嵯峨天皇

Sagami 相模

Saichō 最澄

Saihōji ("Moss Temple," Kokedera 苔寺) 西芳寺

Saihōji ikun 西芳寺遺訓

saikyojō 裁許状

Saiokuken Sōchō 柴屋軒宗長

Saishōkō'in 最勝光院

Saitō Ritei-ni 齋藤利貞尼

Sakai 堺

Sakamoto 坂本

sakaya 酒屋

sake 酒

Sakugen Shūryō 策彦周良

samu 作務

samurai dokoro 侍所

Sane'in 三會院

Sane'in ikai 三會院遺誡

sangedatsu mon 三解脱門

Sangen'in 三玄院

sankyō itchi 三教一致

sanmon 三門 (山門)

Sanmon bugyō 山門奉行

Sano 佐野

Sanpō'in 三寶院

Sanshōji garanzu 三聖寺伽藍圖

sanzen 參禪

Sara 娑羅

sarugaku 猿樂

Sasaki Sadashige
佐々木貞重

Sasaki Sadatsuna
佐々木貞綱

Sasaki Takauji
佐々木高氏

Sasaki Ujiyori
佐々木氏頼

Sasaki-no-shō 佐々木荘

satori 悟

Sei *tsūbun* 盛都聞

seidō 西堂

Seido'in jōjō kishiki
誓度院條々規式

seihan 西班

seihanshū 西班衆

seijin 西淨

Seikenji 清見寺

Seisetsu Shōchō
清拙正澄

seizō 西藏

seji 世事

sekisho 關所

sekkai 說戒

Sekkō Sōshin 雪江宗深

Sen no Rikyū 千利休

senbutsujō 選佛場

sendanrin 栴檀林

sen'e 洗衣

seng-lu 僧錄

seng-t'ang 僧堂

sengoku daimyō 戰國大名

senjō 洗淨

senjudō 千手堂

"senmen" 洗面

senmon dōjō 專門道場

Sennyūji 泉涌寺

Senyōmon'in 宣陽門院

Sera Shinnō 世良親王

sesshin 接心

Sesshū Tōyō 雪舟等揚

Sesson Yūbai 雪村友梅

Setsudō Sōboku 拙堂宗朴

Settsu 攝津

Shaka Nyorai 釋迦如来

shami 沙彌

shang-t'ang 上堂

shang-tso 上座

shariden 舍利殿

sharyō 社領

Shasekishū 沙石集

Shen-hsiu 神秀

Shen-hui 神會

sheng-seng 聖僧

Shiba Takatsune 斯波高經

Shiba Yoshimasa 斯波義將

shichidō garan 七堂伽藍

shidōsen 祠堂錢

shih-ch'a 十刹

shih-che 侍者

shih-fang chu-ch'ih 十方住持

Shih-shih 誓實

Shihi-no-*shō* 志比莊

Shihon 至本

shiji no zazen 四時の坐禪

shika 知客

shikan 止觀

shikan taza 只管打座

shiki 職

shikken 執權

Shima 志摩

shimobe 下部

Shimōsa 下總

Shinano 信濃

Shinchi (Muhon) Kakushin
心地 (無本) 覺心

shinden-zukuri
寢殿造

shindō 寢堂

shingi 清規

Shingonshū 眞言宗

Shinjo-*gō* 新所鄉

Shinju'an 眞珠庵

shinka jisha 請客侍者

shinnyo hokkai 眞如法界

Shinnyoji 眞如寺

Shinoki-no-*shō* 篠木莊

Shinran 親鸞

Shinshō Shōnin 眞盛上人

Shintō 神道

shin'yo 神輿

shishi 獅子

shissui 直歲

shitaji chūbun 下地中分

shitomido 蔀戶

shō 莊

shō 升

Shōbai'in 松梅院

Shōbō genzō 正法眼藏

Shōden'an hatto
正傳菴法度

shōdō 照堂

shōeki 請益

shōen 莊園

Shōfukuji 承福寺

Shōgaku-ni 正覺尼

Shōgen'in 松源院

Shōgen-ha 松源派

Shōgo'in 聖護院

shōgun 將軍

shohō jissō 諸法實相

Shōichi Kokushi 聖一國師

shoin-zukuri 書院造

shōji 承仕

shojō jisha 書狀侍者

shoki 書記

shōkō jisha 燒香侍者

Shōkokuji 相國寺

Shōni 少弍

Shōren'in 青蓮院

shōrō 鐘樓

shōsan 小參

shōshin 照心

shōsō 聖僧

shōsō jisha 聖僧侍者
shōsōdō 聖僧堂
shōsu 莊主
shou-tso 首座
shozan 諸山
"Shozan juen kinsei jōjō"
諸山入院禁制條々
shu-chi 書記
Shudatsu chōja 須達長者
shugo 守護
shugo daimyō 守護大名
Shūhō Myōchō 宗峰妙超
shukkan 出官
shukke 出家
Shukke taikō 出家大綱
shumidan 須彌壇
Shunjō 俊芿
Shunjōbō Chōgen
俊乗坊重源
Shun'oku Myōha
春屋妙葩
shuryō 衆寮
"Shuryō shingi"
衆寮清規
shuso 首座
Shuzenji 修禪寺
shuzōshi 修造司
Sō tsūbun 湊都聞
sōbō 僧房
sōdō 僧堂
sōhei 僧兵

Sōjiji 總持寺
Sōkan 宗觀
Sōken'in 總見院
sokushin jōbutsu 即身成佛
sōmon 總門
sōrin 叢林
Sōrin Zenmon 宗隣禪門
sōroku 僧錄
soshidan 祖師壇
soshidō 祖師堂
sōshobun 總處分
Sōtō 曹洞
Ssu 寺
ssu-chu 寺主
Sūen 崇演
Sūgan 崇鑑
Sugawara 菅原
Sugyōroku 宗鏡錄
Sūjuji 崇壽寺
Sukō tennō 崇光天皇
Sung 宋
Sung kao-seng-chuan
宋高僧傳
Sung Lien 宋濂
Sung-wen-hsien-kung-ch'üan-chi
宋文憲公全集
Sung-yuan p'ai
松源派

Suō 周防
Suruga 駿河

Ta-hsiu Cheng-nien 大休正念

Ta-hui 大慧

ta-ts'an 大參

Tachikawa-ryū 立川流

Tai-pai-shan t'ien t'ung ching te ch'an ssu 太白山天童景德禪寺

"Taidai kohō" 對大己法

taigi meibun 大義名分

Taiheiji 太平寺

Taiheiki 太平記

Taikan shingi 大鑑清規

Taikeiji 大慶寺

taimitsu 台密

Taira Kiyomori 平清盛

Taira Yoritsuna 平賴綱

Tajima 但馬

Takaie-no-shō 高家莊

Takakura tennō 高倉天皇

Takeda 武田

takuhatsu 托鉢

tan 反

Tan-hsia 丹霞

tan-liao 單寮

T'an-yu 曇幽

Tanba 丹波

tandai 探題

T'ang 唐

tansen 段錢

Tao-an 道安

Tao-hsuan 道璿

tatami 疊

tatchū 塔頭

Te-hui 德輝

Te-shan Hsuan-chien 德山宣鑑

Tendai 天台

Tendō Nyojō 天童如淨

tenjin 點心

tenka sōroku 天下僧錄

Tenryūji 天龍寺

Tenryūji-bune 天龍寺船

Tenryūji kinen kōryaku 天龍寺記念考略

Ten'yo Seikei 天與清啓

tenzo 典座

"Tenzo kyōkun" 典座教訓

Tettō Gikō 徹翁義亨

Tettsū Gikai 徹通義介

tien-tso 典座

t'ien-ching 天井

T'ien-jan Ch'an-shih 天然禪師

T'ien-t'ai 天台

Tien-t'ai-shan 天台山

T'ien-t'ung Ju-ching 天童如淨

T'ien-t'ung-shan 天童山

T'ien-t'ung-ssu 天童寺

to 斗

Tō tsubun 當都聞

tōchigyō 當知行

Tōdaiji 東大寺

tōdō 東堂

Tōfukuji 東福寺

Tōfukuji jōjōgoto 東福寺條々事

Tōfukuji-shi 東福寺誌

Tōgan Ean 東嚴慧安

Tōgudō 東求堂

tōhan 東班

tōhanshū 東班衆

Tōji 東寺

Tōji *bugyō* 東寺奉行

Tōji'in 等持院

Tōjiji 等持寺

Tōkeiji 東慶寺

Toki 土岐

Tōkōji 東光寺

tokubun 得分

Tokugawa Hidetada
德川秀忠

Tokugawa Iemitsu
德川家光

Tokugawa Ieyasu
德川家康

Tokuhashi *gō* 得橋鄉

tokusei 德政

tokuseirei 德政令

tokusō 得宗

Tokuzenji 德禪寺

Tokuzenji hatto
德禪寺法度

Tomita-no-*shō* 富田莊

Tomiyoshi-no-*shō* 富吉莊

Tōmyō Enichi 東明惠日

Tōmyōji 東妙寺

tōnin 頭人

Tosa 土佐

Tōshōdaiji 唐招提寺

Tōshōji 東勝寺

tōsu 東司

Totoku Shinnō 都督親王

Tōtōmi 遠江

t'ou chu 頭主

tōyaku jisha 湯藥侍者

Toyotomi Hideyoshi
豐臣秀吉

Tōzenji 東漸寺

tōzō 東藏

Tsan-ning 贊寧

Tse-shan I-hsien 澤山弌咸

tsūbun 都聞

tsuchi ikki (do-ikki) 土一揆

tsuchien 度弟院

Tsung-ching-lu 宗鏡錄

Tsung-tse 宗賾

Ts'ung-shih 從實

tsuridono 釣殿

Tsurugaoka Hachimangu
鶴岡八幡宮

tsūsu 都寺

tu-liao 獨寮

tu-ssu 都寺

tu-wei-no 都維那

Tung-ming Hui-jih 東明惠日

Tung-shan 東山

tung-ssu 都寺

tung-ts'ang 東藏

Udono *sekisho* 鵜殿關所

Uesugi Zenshū 上杉禪秀

Uji 宇治

ujidera 氏寺

undō 雲堂

Unganji 雲巖寺

unpan 雲版

Unsen Taikyoku 雲泉大極

Uragami Zenmon 浦上禪門

Ususama Myōō
烏芻沙摩明王

usuya 臼屋

waka 和歌

Wakasa 若狹

Wan-nien-ssu 萬年寺

Wang Hsuan-ts'e 王玄策

wang-liao 望寮

Wanshi-ha 宏智派

Wanshi Shōgaku 宏智正覺

wayo 和與

Wei-mien 惟勉

wei-no 維那

Wu-an P'u-ning 兀庵普寧

Wu-chun Shih-fan
無準師範

Wu-feng 五峯

Wu-hsueh Tsy-yuan
無學祖元

Wu-liang Tsung-shou
無量宗壽

Wu-men Hui-k'ai 無門慧開

Wu-ming Hui-hsing
無明慧性

Wu-t'ai-shan 五臺山

Wu Tse-t'ien 武則天

yakubuku-mai 役夫工米

Yakuchū Zen'on shingi
譯註禪苑清規

yakunin 役人

Yamaguchi 山口

Yamamoto-no-*shō* 山本莊

Yamana Tokiuji 山名時氏

Yamanouchi-no-*shō* 山內莊

Yamanoue 山上

Yamashiro 山城

Yamato 大和

Yang-ch'i p'ai 楊岐派

Yano Betsumyō 矢野別名

Yano-no-*shō* 矢野莊

Yodo *sekisho* 淀關所

Yōgi-ha 楊岐派

Yokoyama Gonnokami
　Yoshiharu 横山權頭吉春

yokushitsu 浴室

Yōsai. See Myōan Eisai

Yoshino 吉野

Yōsō Sōi 養叟宗頤

Yōtoku'in 養德院

Yuasa Sōken 湯淺宗顯

Yuge-no-*shō* 弓削莊

yūgen 幽玄

Yun-men Wen-yen
雲門文偃

Yura-no-*shō* 由良莊

za 座

zakumon 坐公文

zasshō 雜掌

zasso ketsudansho
雜訴決斷所

zasu 座主

zazen 坐禪

Zeami 世阿彌

Zekkai Chūshin 絕海中津

Zen 禪

Zen daiku 禪大工

Zendō 禪堂

Zendō shuso 禪堂首座

Zenji 禪寺

Zenkaku 禪客

Zenkōji 禪興寺

zenkon 善根

Zenkyo'an 禪居庵

"Zenmon kishiki"
禪門規式

Zen'on shingi 禪苑清規

Zenpukuji 禪福寺

Zenrin biyō shingi
禪林備用清規

Zenrin shōkisen
禪林象器箋

Zenrinji 禪林寺

Zenritsu bugyō 禪律奉行

Zenritsugata 禪律方

Zenritsugata tōnin
禪律方頭人

Zenzai Dōji 善財童子

zōeiryō 造營料

zōsu 藏主

Zuikei Shūhō 瑞溪周鳳

"Zuiryūzan Taihei Kōkoku
Nanzen Zenji" 瑞龍山太平興
國南禪寺

Zuisenji 瑞泉寺

Index

A-yü-wang-shan, xviii, 36, 206; as a model for Japanese monasteries, 177

Abbot (*jūji* or *chōrō*), 228-236; duties of, 77, 143, 154, 164, 170, 196, 211, 232; *bakufu* regulations on, 88, 167, 168-169, 231; installment of, 155-156, 169, 189, 194, 208, 227, 232-233; as the Buddha, 195; *bodhisattva* vows of, 228; appointment of, 228-231, 233; in China (*shang-tso*), 236; training of, 244; income of, 269, 270

Abbots' halls (*fang-chang; hōjō*), 35, 124 180, 181, 189, 197-201, 215; functions of, 126, 143, 197-199, 201; ground plans of, 179, 199-200; architectural style of, 200

Absentee guarantor (*honke*), 255

Accountant (*chih-sui*), 236

Acolyte (*jisha*), 169, 227, 228, 229, 237, 243-245; monks' hall (*shōsō jisha*), 157; appointment fees for, 236; kinds of, 239, 243; training of, 243; income of, 270

Agents (*azukari-dokoro*), 255

Aizen Myōō, 49

Akamatsu Norisuke (1314–1371), 118, 121

Akamatsu Toshihide, 96

Altar platform (*shumidan*): tablets for, 191-192

Analects, 79

Amida, 27, 31, 80-81, 145; hall of, 99. *See also* Pure Land

Andogata (Commissioner for Confirming Rights to Land), 104

Andojō (certificates of confirmation of land rights), 103

Ankokuji (Temples for Peace in the Realm), 101, 103, 106-109, 110, 113, 114, 294

Appointment, certificates of (*zakumon* or *inari kumon*), 233; selling of, 234, 235

Architecture, styles of, 200

Arhats, 189-190, 196

Arhat hall (*rakandō*), 190

Arnesen, Peter, 15

Artisans (*ninku*), 245

Ashikaga family, 18; patronage of Zen by, xvi, 29-30, 81, 84, 91, 98-102, 180, 222, 253, 254, 258, 260, 293; and Zen culture, 80, 102; and *gozan* system, 91, 98-102, 109, 287, 288; and Go-Daigo, 95-96, 104-105; Zen practice of, 98-99; and conflict with Enryakuji, 105-106, 287; temple of, 106; proliferation of *shozan* under, 115; protection of *gozan* by, 124; regulation of *gozan* by, 165-170, 246; ties with Nanzenji, 263

Ashikaga Mochiuji (1398-1439), 262

Ashikaga Motouji (1340-1367), regulation of *gozan* by, 165

Ashikaga Sadauji (c. 1274-1333), 81

Ashikaga Tadayoshi (1306-1352), 13, 84, 95, 98, 259; and Musō Soseki, 102, 107; and division of power with Takau-ji, 103; household government of, 104, 118; trade mission organized by, 105; building under, 107; expansion of military power by, 108-109; assassination of, 109; *gozan* system under, 110, 260,

Harvard East Asian Monographs

46. W. P. J. Hall, *A Bibliographical Guide to Japanese Research on the Chinese Economy, 1958–1970*

47. Jack J. Gerson, *Horatio Nelson Lay and Sino-British Relations, 1854–1864*

48. Paul Richard Bohr, *Famine and the Missionary: Timothy Richard as Relief Administrator and Advocate of National Reform*

49. Endymion Wilkinson, *The History of Imperial China: A Research Guide*

50. Britten Dean, *China and Great Britain: The Diplomacy of Commercial Relations, 1860–1864*

51. Ellsworth C. Carlson, *The Foochow Missionaries, 1847–1880*

52. Yeh-chien Wang, *An Estimate of the Land-Tax Collection in China, 1753 and 1908*

53. Richard M. Pfeffer, *Understanding Business Contracts in China, 1949–1963*

54. Han-sheng Chuan and Richard Kraus, *Mid-Ch'ing Rice Markets and Trade: An Essay in Price History*

55. Ranbir Vohra, *Lao She and the Chinese Revolution*

56. Liang-lin Hsiao, *China's Foreign Trade Statistics, 1864–1949*

57. Lee-hsia Hsu Ting, *Government Control of the Press in Modern China, 1900–1949*

58. Edward W. Wagner, *The Literati Purges: Political Conflict in Early Yi Korea*

59. Joungwon A. Kim, *Divided Korea: The Politics of Development, 1945–1972*

60. Noriko Kamachi, John K. Fairbank, and Chūzō Ichiko, *Japanese Studies of Modern China Since 1953: A Bibliographical Guide to Historical and Social-Science Research on the Nineteenth and Twentieth Centuries, Supplementary Volume for 1953–1969*

61. Donald A. Gibbs and Yun-chen Li, *A Bibliography of Studies and Translations of Modern Chinese Literature, 1918–1942*

62. Robert H. Silin, *Leadership and Values: The Organization of Large-Scale Taiwanese Enterprises*

63. David Pong, *A Critical Guide to the Kwangtung Provincial Archives Deposited at the Public Record Office of London*

64. Fred W. Drake, *China Charts the World: Hsu Chi-yü and His Geography of 1848*

65. William A. Brown and Urgunge Onon, translators and annotators, *History of the Mongolian People's Republic*

66. Edward L. Farmer, *Early Ming Government: The Evolution of Dual Capitals*

67. Ralph C. Croizier, *Koxinga and Chinese Nationalism: History, Myth, and the Hero*

68. William J. Tyler, tr., *The Psychological World of Natsume Sōseki*, by Doi Takeo

69. Eric Widmer, *The Russian Ecclesiastical Mission in Peking during the Eighteenth Century*

70. Charlton M. Lewis, *Prologue to the Chinese Revolution: The Transformation of Ideas and Institutions in Hunan Province, 1891–1907*

71. Preston Torbert, *The Ch'ing Imperial Household Department: A Study of its Organization and Principal Functions, 1662–1796*

72. Paul A. Cohen and John E. Schrecker, eds., *Reform in Nineteenth-Century China*

73. Jon Sigurdson, *Rural Industrialism in China*

74. Kang Chao, *The Development of Cotton Textile Production in China*

75. Valentin Rabe, *The Home Base of American China Missions, 1880–1920*

76. Sarasin Viraphol, *Tribute and Profit: Sino-Siamese Trade, 1652–1853*

77. Ch'i-ch'ing Hsiao, *The Military Establishment of the Yuan Dynasty*

78. Meishi Tsai, *Contemporary Chinese Novels and Short Stories, 1949–1974: An Annotated Bibliography*

79. Wellington K. K. Chan, *Merchants, Mandarins and Modern Enterprise in Late Ch'ing China*

80. Endymion Wilkinson, *Landlord and Labor in Late Imperial China: Case Studies from Shandong by Jing Su and Luo Lun*

81. Barry Keenan, *The Dewey Experiment in China: Educational Reform and Political Power in the Early Republic*

82. George A. Hayden, *Crime and Punishment in Medieval Chinese Drama: Three Judge Pao Plays*

83. Sang-Chul Suh, *Growth and Structural Changes in the Korean Economy, 1910–1940*

84. J. W. Dower, *Empire and Aftermath: Yoshida Shigeru and the Japanese Experience, 1878–1954*

85. Martin Collcutt, *Five Mountains: The Rinzai Zen Monastic Institution in Medieval Japan*

86. Kwang Suk Kim and Michael Roemer, *Growth and Structural Transformation*

87. Anne O. Krueger, *The Developmental Role of the Foreign Sector and Aid*

88. Edwin S. Mills and Byung-Nak Song, *Urbanization and Urban Problems*

89. Sung Hwan Ban, Pal Yong Moon, and Dwight H. Perkins, *Rural Development*

90. Noel F. McGinn, Donald R. Snodgrass, Yung Bong Kim, Shin-Bok Kim, and Quee-Young Kim, *Education and Development in Korea*

91. Leroy P. Jones and Il SaKong, *Government, Business, and Entrepreneurship in Economic Development: The Korean Case*

92. Edward S. Mason, Dwight H. Perkins, Kwang Suk Kim, David C. Cole, Mahn Je Kim, et al., *The Economic and Social Modernization of the Republic of Korea*

93. Robert Repetto, Tai Hwan Kwon, Son-Ung Kim, Dae Young Kim, John E. Sloboda, and Peter J. Donaldson, *Economic Development, Population Policy, and Demographic Transition in the Republic of Korea*

94. Parks M. Coble, Jr., *The Shanghai Capitalists and the Nationalist Government, 1927–1937*

95. Noriko Kamachi, *Reform in China: Huang Tsun-hsien and the Japanese Model*

96. Richard Wich, *Sino-Soviet Crisis Politics: A Study of Political Change and Communication*

97. Lillian M. Li, *China's Silk Trade: Traditional Industry in the Modern World, 1842–1937*

98. R. David Arkush, *Fei Xiaotong and Sociology in Revolutionary China*

99. Kenneth Alan Grossberg, *Japan's Renaissance: The Politics of the Muromachi Bakufu*

100. James Reeve Pusey, *China and Charles Darwin*

101. Hoyt Cleveland Tillman, *Utilitarian Confucianism: Ch'en Liang's Challenge to Chu Hsi*

102. Thomas A. Stanley, *Ōsugi Sakae, Anarchist in Taishō Japan: The Creativity of the Ego*

103. Jonathan K. Ocko, *Bureaucratic Reform in Provincial China: Ting Jih-ch'ang in Restoration Kiangsu, 1867–1870*

104. James Reed, *The Missionary Mind and American East Asia Policy, 1911–1915*

105. Neil L. Waters, *Japan's Local Pragmatists: The Transition from Bakumatsu to Meiji in the Kawasaki Region*

106. David C. Cole and Yung Chul Park, *Financial Development in Korea, 1945–1978*

107. Roy Bahl, Chuk Kyo Kim, and Chong Kee Park, *Public Finances during the Korean Modernization Process*

108. William D. Wray, *Mitsubishi and the N.Y.K., 1870–1914: Business Strategy in the Japanese Shipping Industry*

109. Ralph William Huenemann, *The Dragon and the Iron Horse: The Economics of Railroads in China, 1876–1937*

110. Benjamin A. Elman, *From Philosophy to Philology: Intellectual and Social Aspects of Change in Late Imperial China*

111. Jane Kate Leonard, *Wei Yuan and China's Rediscovery of the Maritime World*

112. Luke S. K. Kwong, *A Mosaic of the Hundred Days: Personalities, Politics, and Ideas of 1898*

113. John E. Wills, Jr., *Embassies and Illusions: Dutch and Portuguese Envoys to K'ang-hsi, 1666–1687*

114. Joshua A. Fogel, *Politics and Sinology: The Case of Naitō Konan (1866–1934)*

115. Jeffrey C. Kinkley, ed., *After Mao: Chinese Literature and Society, 1978–1981*

116. C. Andrew Gerstle, *Circles of Fantasy: Convention in the Plays of Chikamatsu*

117. Andrew Gordon, *The Evolution of Labor Relations in Japan: Heavy Industry, 1853–1955*

118. Daniel K. Gardner, *Chu Hsi and the* Ta Hsueh: *Neo-Confucian Reflection on the Confucian Canon*

119. Christine Guth Kanda, *Shinzō: Hachiman Imagery and its Development*

120. Robert Borgen, *Sugawara no Michizane and the Early Heian Court*

121. Chang-tai Hung, *Going to the People: Chinese Intellectual and Folk Literature, 1918–1937*

122. Michael A. Cusumano, *The Japanese Automobile Industry: Technology and Management at Nissan and Toyota*

123. Richard von Glahn, *The Country of Streams and Grottoes: Expansion, Settlement, and the Civilizing of the Sichuan Frontier in Song Times*

124. Steven D. Carter, *The Road to Komatsubara: A Classical Reading of the Renga Hyakuin*

125. Katherine F. Bruner, John K. Fairbank, and Richard T. Smith, *Entering China's Service: Robert Hart's Journals, 1854–1863*

126. Bob Tadashi Wakabayashi, *Anti-Foreignism and Western Learning in Early-Modern Japan: The New Theses of 1825*

127. Atsuko Hirai, *Individualism and Socialism: The Life and Thought of Kawai Eijirō (1891–1944)*

128. Ellen Widmer, *The Margins of Utopia:* Shui-hu hou-chuan *and the Literature of Ming Loyalism*

129. R. Kent Guy, *The Emperor's Four Treasuries: Scholars and the State in the Late Ch'ien-lung Era*

130. Peter C. Perdue, *Exhausting the Earth: State and Peasant in Hunan, 1500–1850*

131. Susan Chan Egan, *A Latterday Confucian: Reminiscences of William Hung (1893–1980)*

132. James T. C. Liu, *China Turning Inward: Intellectual-Political Changes in the Early Twelfth Century*

133. Paul A. Cohen, *Between Tradition and Modernity: Wang T'ao and Reform in Late Ch'ing China*

134. Kate Wildman Nakai, *Shogunal Politics: Arai Hakuseki and the Premises of Tokugawa Rule*

135. Parks M. Coble, *Facing Japan: Chinese Politics and Japanese Imperialism, 1931–1937*

136. Jon L. Saari, *Legacies of Childhood: Growing Up Chinese in a Time of Crisis, 1890–1920*

137. Susan Downing Videen, *Tales of Heichū*